Future Electricity Technologies and Systems

Where will our electricity come from in the future, and how will we use it? The United Kingdom is aiming for a 60 per cent reduction of 1990 carbon dioxide emission levels by 2050, yet the electricity industry and patterns of electricity use must change radically if this is to be achieved. This authoritative overview analyses a range of possible scenarios for the future of electricity in the United Kingdom. Specialists in various renewable electricity technologies demonstrate the potential that each has to play a significant role. Other routes to a low-carbon electricity system are also considered, including nuclear power, improved power electronics, a wider use of superconducting technology, and microgeneration systems including combined heat and power. The book concludes by examining opportunities for demand-side improvements in architecture, industry and transport. Each chapter is written by a technical expert in a manner accessible to readers interested in energy technology, policy and economics.

TOORAJ JAMASB is a Senior Research Associate at the Faculty of Economics, University of Cambridge.

WILLIAM J. NUTTALL is Course Director and Senior Lecturer at the Judge Business School, University of Cambridge. His post is shared with Cambridge University Engineering Department.

MICHAEL G. POLLITT is a Senior Lecturer in Business Economics at the Judge Business School, University of Cambridge. He is also Fellow and Director of Studies in Economics and Management at Sidney Sussex College, Cambridge.

University of Cambridge
Department of Applied Economics
Occasional Papers 67
Future Electricity Technologies and Systems

Future Electricity Technologies and Systems

edited by

Tooraj Jamasb, William J. Nuttall and
Michael G. Pollitt

CAMBRIDGE
UNIVERSITY PRESS

CAMBRIDGE UNIVERSITY PRESS
Cambridge, New York, Melbourne, Madrid, Cape Town, Singapore, São Paulo, Delhi

Cambridge University Press
The Edinburgh Building, Cambridge CB2 8RU, UK

Published in the United States of America by Cambridge University Press, New York

www.cambridge.org
Information on this title: www.cambridge.org/9780521860499

© Faculty of Economics, University of Cambridge 2006

First published 2006

A catalogue record for this publication is available from the British Library

ISBN 978-0-521-86049-9 hardback

Transferred to digital printing 2009

Contents

Figures

Tables

List of contributors

GEHAN AMARATUNGA 1966 Professor of Engineering and Head of the Electronics, Power and Energy Conversion Group in the Engineering Department at the University of Cambridge.

GRAHAM AULT Senior Research Fellow in Electronic and Electrical Engineering in the Institute for Energy and Environment at Strathclyde University.

RONNIE BELMANS Full Professor and Head of ELECTA (Electrical energy and computer architecture), Department of Electrical Engineering at the Katholieke Universiteit Leuven, Belgium.

ANDREAS BIERMANN Formerly Senior Policy Analyst at the Energy Savings Trust. Currently at the International Energy Agency, Paris.

TONY BRIDGWATER Professor of Chemical Engineering and Head of the Bio-Energy Research Group at Aston University, Birmingham.

ARCHIE M. CAMPBELL Director of the Interdisciplinary Research Centre in Superconductivity at the University of Cambridge. Professor of Electromagnetism in the Engineering Department at the University of Cambridge.

HANNAH DEVINE-WRIGHT Research Fellow in Environmental Psychology at the Institute of Energy and Sustainable Development, De Montfort University, Leicester.

PATRICK DEVINE-WRIGHT Senior Research Fellow in Environmental Psychology at the Institute of Energy and Sustainable Development, De Montfort University, Leicester.

PETER P. EDWARDS Professor and Head of Inorganic Chemistry at the University of Oxford. Coordinator of the Engineering and Physical Sciences Research Council (EPSRC) UK Sustainable Hydrogen Consortium.

WOLFGANG EICHHAMMER Deputy Head of the Department of Energy Technology and Energy Policy at the Fraunhofer Institute for Systems and Innovation Research, Karlsruhe, Germany.

IAN ELDERS Senior Research Fellow in Electronic and Electrical Engineering in the Institute for Energy and Environment at Strathclyde University.

CHRISTINA GALITSKY Senior Research Associate in the Energy Analysis Department of the Environmental Energy Technologies Division at Lawrence Berkeley National Laboratory, California.

STUART GALLOWAY Senior Research Fellow in Electronic and Electrical Engineering in the Institute for Energy and Environment at Strathclyde University.

TIM C. GREEN Professor of Power Engineering and Deputy Head of the Control and Power Research Group at Imperial College, University of London.

MALCOLM C. GRIMSTON Honorary Visiting Senior Research Fellow at the Centre for Environmental Technology at Imperial College, University of London.

CARLOS A. HERNÁNDEZ ARÁMBURO Lecturer in the Control and Power Research Group at Imperial College, University of London.

TOORAJ JAMASB Senior Research Associate in the Faculty of Economics at the University of Cambridge.

SIMON R. JOHNSON Research Fellow in the Inorganic Chemistry Laboratory at the University of Oxford.

MARTIN OWEN JONES Senior Research Fellow and Director of Research in the Edwards Research Group at the Inorganic Chemistry Laboratory at the University of Oxford. Honorary Research Fellow in Materials at the University of Birmingham.

JONATHAN KÖHLER Senior Research Associate in the Faculty of Economics at the University of Cambridge. Manager of Tyndall Centre research theme 'Integrating Frameworks'.

VLADIMIR L. KUZNETSOV Research Fellow in the Inorganic Chemistry Laboratory at the University of Oxford. Operations Secretary for the Engineering and Physical Sciences Research Council UK Sustainable Hydrogen Consortium.

EFTERPI LAMPADITOU Research Associate in the Imperial College Centre for Energy Policy and Technology at Imperial College, University of London.

MATTHEW LEACH Head of Decentralised Generation in the Imperial College Centre for Energy Policy and Technology (ICEPT) at Imperial College, University of London.

MATTHEW T. J. LODGE Research Fellow in the Inorganic Chemistry Laboratory at the University of Oxford.

JIM MCDONALD Professor and Head of Department of Electronic and Electrical Engineering in the Institute for Energy and the Environment at Strathclyde University.

POUL ERIK MORTHORST Senior Research Specialist in the Systems Analysis Department at the Risø National Laboratory, Roskilde, Denmark.

ASIM MUMTAZ Research Associate in the Department of Engineering at the University of Cambridge. Founder of Enecsys.

WILLIAM J. NUTTALL Director of the M.Phil. in Technology Policy and Senior Lecturer in Technology Policy at Cambridge University, a post shared between the Judge Business School and the Department of Engineering.

MICHAEL G. POLLITT Acting Executive Director ESRC Electricity Policy Research Group and University Senior Lecturer in Business Economics at the Judge Business School, University of Cambridge.

LYNN PRICE Deputy Group Leader of the International Energy Studies Group in the Energy Analysis Department of the Environmental Energy Technologies Division at the Lawrence Berkeley National Laboratory, California.

NILS A. RØKKE Vice-President, Gas Technology, at SINTEF, the Gas Technology Center, NTNU-SINTEF (the Norwegian University of Science and Technology, and the Foundation for Scientific and Industrial Research at the Norwegian Institute of Technology), Trondheim.

ALAN RUDDELL Senior Research Engineer in the Energy Research Unit at the Council for the Central Laboratory, of the Research Councils (CCLRC) at the Rutherford Appleton Laboratory, Didcot, United Kingdom.

TOM THORPE Head of Global Project Development at Energetech, Randiwick, Australia.

PIETER VERMEYEN Research Assistant at ELECTA, Department of Electrical Engineering at the Katholieke Universiteit Leuven, Belgium.

ROBIN WALLACE Leader of the Institute for Energy Systems at the University of Edinburgh. Leader of 'Future Sources of Energy' Theme at the UK Energy Research Centre, London.

ERNST WORRELL Staff scientist at the Environmental Energy Technologies Division of Lawrence Berkeley National Laboratory, California. Currently Manager Energy Efficiency at Ecofys, Utrecht, the Netherlands.

Foreword

Electrical power has become a 'hot topic' – and a complex one. Ever-rising demands for the conveniences that electricity provides, and growing awareness of the varied environmental impacts associated with electricity generation, give rise to a tension that has historically been expressed through battles over particular technologies (such as nuclear power), and managed primarily through 'end-of-pipe' fixes (such as the removal and disposal of sulphur emissions from coal power stations). Continuing growth in the scale of electricity demands and the emergence of climate change as the dominant environmental threat make such technology- and issue-specific approaches no longer adequate: the debate now needs to encompass the whole portfolio of options, and more fundamental issues about the structure of the electricity system and the balance between supply and demand.

Competing beliefs about the potential for, merits of and drawbacks to different electricity-related technologies remain fundamental in this debate. This book aims to provide an authoritative overview of the main technologies that could help to shape the future of electricity systems in the United Kingdom and globally, and to set these in the context of an overall view of the British electricity system and scenarios for its future possibilities. We do not pretend, or intend, that the book provides a blueprint for a 'best' approach to electricity; rather, its aim is to lay out the fact base and analysis of options upon which a serious public debate can be grounded, and upon which future analytic work should build.

The book is a first published product of the *SuperGen – Future Networks* programme of the United Kingdom's Engineering and Physical Sciences Research Council. The Future Networks consortium combines eight research centres in the United Kingdom, and is tasked with providing an integrated understanding of the possibilities for the United Kingdom's future electricity system in the context of the UK Energy White Paper's objectives, which include the aim of achieving a 60 per cent national reduction in CO_2 emissions by 2050. Other consortia under the overall SuperGen programme address specific technologies in more depth, and several of the chapters in this book draw directly on their expertise.

We have not confined the contributions to national boundaries or to generation technologies only. Where appropriate expertise was not readily available nationally, the editors have sought contributions from overseas to ensure the chapters are at the leading edge of research: thus, for example, the contributions from Denmark, the home of the modern wind energy industry, and Norway, which operated the first CO_2 gas-stream-capture and sequestration facility. Another key feature of the book, which sets it apart from many previous books on electricity, is the determination of the editors to ensure a balanced coverage of technologies covering generation, systems and demand; hence the inclusion also of chapters from Germany, at the forefront of research into low-energy buildings; from Belgium, with cutting-edge insights into the future of rail and public transport; and from the Lawrence Berkeley Laboratories in the United States, a world-leading centre of expertise on industrial energy efficiency. We are indebted to the authors of these and all the other chapters, who have freely given their time and energy to crafting their chapters and responding to review comments.

The book is a result of collaboration between two of the 'work packages' within the SuperGen Future Networks consortium: the 'System Evolution and Incentives' work package, which is charged with analysing the possible evolution of the power system from its present state, and the 'Outreach' work package, which carries the responsibility for liaison with other SuperGen consortia. Its origins lie in a workshop convened jointly between these work packages at the outset of the SuperGen programme, held in Cambridge in November 2003. Most of the chapters have their origins in the write-up of the papers presented to that workshop, to which additional chapters have been added to increase the overall coverage, and all the chapters have been through an extensive process of development and blind peer review coordinated by the editors.

The editors – Tooraj Jamasb, William J. Nuttall and Michael G. Pollitt – themselves represent an interdisciplinary collaboration central to taking forward this extensive task and bringing it to fruition. On behalf of the SuperGen programme we are grateful to them, and to all the authors of the individual chapters for responding to repeated queries and review comments. Finally, of course, we are indebted to EPSRC, for the vision of the SuperGen programme and the financial support that has made this whole project possible.

MICHAEL GRUBB
Coordinator,
SuperGen Networks work package on System Evolution and Incentives

JANUS BIALEK
Coordinator,
SuperGen Networks work package on Outreach

Acknowledgements

The editors are very grateful to a large number of individuals without whom this book would not have been possible. We acknowledge the help and support of the UK Research Councils and the SuperGen community, especially all those who supported the November 2003 workshop at which most of the papers in the book were initially presented. We also acknowledge the support of the Cambridge–MIT Institute Electricity Project (now the ESRC Electricity Policy Research Group), out of which our cross-disciplinary interest in this subject arose. Between them, these two projects have given us valuable access to a wide range of individuals concerned about the future of the electricity system and its place in meeting carbon emissions reduction targets.

We particularly wish to thank Michael Grubb, the leader of the Super-Gen initiative at the Faculty of Economics in Cambridge, for his constant support and advice. A special mention must be made of Lucy Butler, research assistant at the Cambridge Faculty of Economics, who has managed the entire process since the early days with quite exceptional skill, organisation, patience and good humour throughout: this book project would have been impossible without her. We are also grateful to Beth Morgan, Sean Holly of the Faculty and Chris Harrison and Lynn Dunlop at Cambridge University Press for their work in approving and preparing the book for publication. And, last but not least, we extend our heartfelt thanks to all the authors and the many anonymous referees for each chapter. They have ensured the quality of the substance of the book by their sustained support for the enterprise.

TOORAJ JAMASB
WILLIAM J. NUTTALL
MICHAEL G. POLLITT

Abbreviations

AAGR	average annual growth rate
ABWR	advanced boiling water reactor
AC	alternating current
ADS	accelerator-driven system
AGR	advanced gas-cooled reactor
AMSC	American superconductor
AP600 / AP1000	advanced passive reactors
APF	active power filter
ASD	adjustable-speed drive
ASME	Amercian Society of Mechanical Engineers
ASU	air separation unit
ATR	auto-thermal reformer
AWS	Archimedes Wave Swing
AZEP	advanced zero-emission power plant
BCS Theory	Bardeen, Cooper and Schrieffer's 1957 theory for conventional superconductivity
BEAMA	British Electrotechnical and Allied Manufacturers' Association
BEV	battery-powered electric vehicle
BN-600	Russian fast reactor
BNFL	British Nuclear Fuels Plc
BSCCO	bismuth strontium calcium copper oxide
BTG	Biomass Technology Group BV
BWEA	British Wind Energy Association
BWR	boiling water reactor
c€/kWh	euro cents per kilowatt-hour
CADDET	Centre for the Analysis and Dissemination of Demonstrated Energy Technologies
CAES	compressed air energy storage
CANDU	Canadian deuterium uranium reactor
CANMET	CANMET Energy Technology Centre

CAS	compressed air storage
CCGT	combined-cycle gas turbine
CCP	carbon capture project
c.e.f.	charge energy factor
CFB	circulating fluidised bed
CHP	combined heat and power
c/KWh	cents per Kilowatt-hour
CLC	chemical looping combustion
CNRS Nancy	Centre de Recherche en Informatique de Nancy
cP	centipoise, unit of viscosity
CRES	Center for Renewable Energy Sources
CS-HVDC	current-source high-voltage DC
cSt	centistoke, unit of kinematic viscosity
CV	conventional
DC	direct current
DEFRA	Department of Environment, Food and Rural Affairs
DFIG	doubly fed induction generator
DG	distributed generation
DGCG	Distribution Generation Coordinating Group
DIY	do it yourself
DNO	distribution network operator
DOE	Department of Energy, United States
D-SMES	distribution superconducting magnetic energy storage
DSSC	dye-sensitised solar cell
DTI	Department of Trade and Industry, United Kingdom
DVR	dynamic voltage restorer
ECCP	European Climate Change Programme
ECPM	electronically commutated permanent magnet
ECEEE	European Council for an Energy-Efficient Economy
ED	electrodialysis
EGR	enhanced gas recovery
EIA	Energy Information Administration
EJ	exajoule
EMC	electromagnetic compatibility
EMEC	European Marine Energy Centre
EOR	enhanced oil recovery
EPI	Energy Products of Idaho
EPR	European pressurized water reactor
EPRI	Electric Power Research Institute
EPSRC	Engineering and Physical Sciences Research Council
ESI	electricity supply industry

ESRC	Economic and Social Research Council
EST	Energy Saving Trust
EU	European Union
EWEA	European Wind Energy Association
f.h.r.	fuel heat rate
FACTS	flexible AC transmission system
FC	fuel cell
FCEV	fuel-cell electric vehicle
FCV	fuel-cell vehicle
GHG	greenhouse gas
FR	fast reactor
GIF	Generation IV International Forum
GJ	gigajoule
GJth	gigajoule thermal
GSP	grid supply point
Gt	gigatonne (one billion tonnes)
GTO	gate turn-off
GTRI	Georgia Technical Research Institute
GW	gigawatt
GWP	gigawatt peak
HEV	hybrid electric vehicle
HHV	higher heating value
hp	horsepower
HRSG	heat recovery steam generator
HTGR	high-temperature gas-cooled reactor
HTS	high-temperature superconducting
HVAC	heating, ventilation and air conditioning
HVDC	high-voltage direct current
Hz	hertz
IAEA	International Atomic Energy Agency
ICE	internal combustion engine or Inter City Express, Germany
ICT	information and communication technologies
IEA	International Energy Agency
IEEE	Institute of Electrical and Electronics Engineers
IGBT	insulated gate bipolar transistor
IGCC	integrated gasification combined cycle
INPRO	International Project on Innovative Nuclear Reactors and Fuel Cycles
IPCC	Intergovernmental Panel on Climate Change
IRCC	integrated reforming combined cycle
IT	information technologies

ITP	Industrial Technologies Program, United States
JAERI	Japan Atomic Energy Research Institute
JASE	Society of Automotive Engineers of Japan
kAm	kiloamp metre
KARA	KARA Energy Systems BV
km/h	kilometres per hour
kW	kilowatt
kWe	kilowatt electric
kWh	kilowatt-hour
kWth	kilowatt thermal
LCD	liquid crystal display
LED	light-emitting diode
LHV	lower heating value
LNG	liquefied natural gas
LPG	liquefied petroleum gas
LRTA	Light Rail Transit Association
LTS	low-temperature superconducting
LV	low voltage
LWR	light water reactor
MC-ASD	magnetically coupled adjustable-speed drive
MCFC	molten carbonate fuel cell
MCM	mixed conducting membrane
MEA	monoethanol amine
MF	microfiltration
MHV	medium heating value
MJ	megajoule
MOP	meter operator
MOSFET	metal oxide field-effect transitor
MOx	mixed oxide fuel
MPPT	maximum-power point tracking
m/s	metres per second
Mtoe	million tonnes of oil equivalent
MV	medium voltage
MVAr	megavolt-ampere reactive
MW	megawatt
MWe	megawatt electric
MWth	megawatt thermal
NaREC	New and Renewable Energy Centre
NEA	Nuclear Energy Agency
NEPD	National Energy Policy Development group, United States
NF	nanofiltration

NMTWG	New Metering Technology Working Group
NFFO3	Non-Fossil Fuel Obligation 3
NOVEM	Netherlands Organization for Energy and the Environment
NREL	National Renewable Energy Laboratory
NTNU	Norwegian University of Science and Techonology
O&M	operations and maintenance
OCGT	open-cycle gas turbine
odt	over-dry tonne
OECD	Organisation for Economic Co-operation and Development
OST	Office of Science and Technology (United States)
OWC	oscillating water column
P&T	partitioning and transmutation
PAFC	phosphoric acid fuel cell
PBMR	pebble bed modular reactor
PCU	power-conditioning unit
P/E	power/energy (ratio of rated power to energy capacity)
PEM	polymer electrolyte membrane
PEMFC	proton exchange membrane fuel cell
p/kWh	pence per kilowatt-hour
PM	permanent magnet
POST	Parliamentary Office of Science and Technology (United Kingdom)
PV	photovoltaic
PWR	pressurised water reactor
PyNe	Pyrolytic Network, Aston University
R&D	research and development
R,D&C	research, development and commercialisation
RES-E	electricity from renewable energy sources
RO	reverse osmosis
rpm	revolution per minute
SCADA	supervisory control and data acquisition
SHEC	Sustainable Hydrogen Energy Consortium
SHS	solar home system
SINTEF	Foundation for Scientific and Industrial Research at the Norwegian Institute of Technology
SMES	superconducting magnetic energy storage
SMWG	Smart Metering Working Group
SOFC	solid oxide fuel cell
SR	switched reluctance
SRES	*Special Report on Emissions Scenarios*

Statcom	static compensator
Statcon	static condenser
STIG	steam-injected gas turbine
SVC	static VAr compensator
T	tesla, unit of magnetic flux density
T&D	transmission and distribution
T$_c$	superconducting critical temperature
TDP	technical development pathway
TGV	Train à Grande Vitesse, France
TSO	transmission system operator
TV	television
TWh	terawatt-hour (1,000 GWh, 10^9 kWh)
t/y	tonnes per year
UF	ultrafiltration
UIRR	International Union of Combined Road-Rail Transport Comparies
UPFC	unified power flow controller
UPQC	unified power quality controller
UPS	uninterruptible power supply
VAR	volt-ampere reactive
VFD	variable-frequency drive
VS-HVDC	voltage-source high-voltage DC
VVER	Russian pressurised water reactor
W	watt, unit of power
W/W	by weight
WAMS	wide-area measurement system
Wh	watt-hour, unit of energy
WNA	World Nuclear Association
WP	written pole
wt	weight
YBCO	yttrium barium copper oxide
ZENG	zero-emission natural gas

Fraction	Prefix	Symbol	Multiple	Prefix	Symbol
10^{-3}	milli	m	10^3	kilo	k
10^{-6}	micro	μ	10^6	mega	M
10^{-9}	nano	n	10^9	giga	G
10^{-12}	pico	p	10^{12}	tera	T
10^{-15}	femto	f	10^{15}	peta	P
10^{-18}	atto	a	10^{18}	exa	E

1 New electricity technologies for a sustainable future

Tooraj Jamasb, William J. Nuttall and Michael G. Pollitt

1.1 Introduction

One technological innovation more than any other accelerated the development of civilisation in the twentieth century – electricity. The first awakening of the electricity industry occurred in the latter half of the nineteenth century with the competing systems of George Westinghouse and Thomas Edison. Following the invention of the incandescent light bulb in 1879 electricity developed rapidly, until, by the end of the twentieth century, not only had power networks spanned most of the planet but also whole new industrial sectors in computing, communications and entertainment had emerged as a direct consequence of developments in electricity.

In these early years of the twenty-first century electricity is once again poised to permit fundamental shifts in the nature of our civilisation. We face a future in which concerns for our global environment, for social welfare and for stable market economics are all linked to the future development of electricity systems. Will electricity remain a reliable, large-scale centralised technology dominated by supply-side concerns? Or will it in future decentralise and move to a distributed model with far greater consideration given to end use? This book explores the potential for various electricity technologies to contribute to economic, social and environmental sustainability. As noted in Michael Grubb and Janus Bialek's foreword this book arises from a UK government initiative, and UK policy towards climate change forms the contextual background for the presentations in the book. In 2003 in the United Kingdom a government Energy White Paper produced by the Department of Trade and Industry (DTI, 2003) set out ambitious long-term aspirations for carbon reduction by 2050. This position and its consequences for the development of an electricity system in a country that has led the world in market-based electricity reforms is bound to be of interest both in the United Kingdom and internationally.

1.2   Electricity and carbon

With the significant exceptions of nuclear power and large-scale hydroelectricity the electricity system of the twentieth century relied upon the combustion of fossil fuels – initially coal and oil, and now increasingly natural gas. The Brundtland Commission's definition of sustainability requires that a sustainable electricity system must be able to meet current needs without compromising the ability of future generations to meet their own needs (World Commission on Environment and Development, 1987). As such, electricity systems based upon the depletion of finite fossil fuel reserves are fundamentally unsustainable. Sustainability is far more than an environmental concern, and in recent years attention has focused on three central pillars of social, environmental and economic sustainability – or, more colloquially, the three Ps of people, planet and profits.

The above formulation of sustainability allows for weaknesses in one of the three areas to be compensated for by measures elsewhere. For instance, environmental damage might be mitigated via active remediation funded from the profits of the activity. Much of the electricity industry has, however, relied upon the even weaker paradigm of 'deplete and innovate'. That is, a belief that natural resources should be depleted without any concern for future resource availability because, as primary fuels become scarce, technological innovation will be spurred, and via such technology-led innovations the necessary societal shifts will occur. The shift from whale and seal oil to mineral oil in the nineteenth century might be regarded as a good example of such thinking.

While the lack of sustainability arising from resource depletion, the operation of liberalised electricity markets ensuring socially sustainable electricity services and the safety of the industry are all important concerns, this book is dominated by one aspect of sustainability in particular: the stability of the global climate. The editors of this book are not climate scientists and it is not the purpose of this book to review the scientific literature concerning anthropogenic greenhouse gas emissions (GHGs) and their effects on global climate. Rather, we take on trust the advice of the majority of scientific opinion that such effects are occurring and that they are dangerous. These concerns more than any other shape the discussion of a sustainable future for electricity in the chapters that follow.

While some economies, such as that of the United Kingdom, have shown that economic growth can be achieved concomitant with decreased energy intensity, the global picture is far from encouraging. Across a swath of developed countries, economic growth and, in

Table 1.1 *World total final consumption (Mtoe)*

	1971	2002	2010	2030	2002–2030[a]
Coal	617	502	516	526	0.2
Oil	1,893	3,041	3,610	5,005	1.8
Gas	604	1,150	1,336	1,758	1.5
Electricity	377	1,139	1,436	2,263	2.5
Heat	68	237	254	294	0.8
Biomass and Waste	641	999	1,101	1,290	0.9
Other Renewables	0	8	13	41	6.2
Total	4,200	7,057	8,267	11,176	1.6

Note:
[a] Average annual percentage rate of growth.

Source: IEA (2004a, p. 68).

Table 1.2 *Share of electricity in energy demand by sector (%)*

	OECD		Transition economies		Developing countries	
	2002	2030	2002	2030	2002	2030
Total final consumption	20	22	13	15	12	20
Industry	25	27	18	22	17	25
Residential	32	38	11	14	8	20
Services	48	57	24	25	31	47

Source: IEA (2004a, p. 193).

particular, the growing share of the service sector and new applications have contributed to a growth in demand for electric energy. In developing countries, economic growth and population growth have combined with increased access to service – while an estimated 1.7 billion of their population are yet to be connected – to ensure a higher rate of increase in demand for electricity. Between 2002 and 2030 the worldwide final consumption of electricity is expected to grow at 2.5 per cent per annum (higher than other energy sources), while the relative share of electricity in total final energy consumption will increase from 16 to 20 per cent (see table 1.1). In the same period the share of electricity in total energy demand for major sectors of the economy in OECD, transition and developing countries is expected to increase (table 1.2).

Conventional technologies for the production, conversion and consumption of energy account for a significant share of the environmental

Table 1.3 *Energy-related CO_2 emissions (million tonnes)*

	OECD		Transition economics		Developing countries		World	
	2002	2030	2002	2030	2002	2030	2002	2030
Power Sector	4,793	6,191	1,270	1,639	3,354	8,941	9,417	16,771
Industry	1,723	1,949	400	618	1,954	3,000	4,076	5,576
Transport	3,384	4,856	285	531	1,245	3,353	4,914	8,739
Residential and Services	1,801	1 950	378	538	1,068	1,930	3,248	4,417
Other[a]	745	888	111	176	605	1,142	1,924	2 720
Total	12,446	15,833	2,444	3,501	8,226	18,365	23,579	38,214

Note:
[a] Includes international marine bunkers (for world totals only) and other transformation and non-energy use.

impacts from pollutants and climate change. While electricity is essentially a clean energy source at consumption, a variety of environmental impacts are associated with its generation. 'By 2030, the power sector could account for almost 45% of global energy-related CO_2 emissions. Carbon-dioxide emissions from power stations in developing countries will treble from 2002 to 2030. In 2030, coal plants in developing countries will produce more CO_2 than the entire power sector in the OECD in that year' (IEA, 2004a). As table 1.3 shows, by 2030 global CO_2 emissions levels are forecast to increase to 38 billion tonnes – that is, a 62 per cent increase in relation to 2002. 50 per cent of this increase is expected to take place in the electricity sector.

Worldwide, investments in electricity between 2001 and 2030 have been projected at approximately \$9,481 billion, a substantial amount by most measures (figure 1.1). However, this is still equivalent to only about 1 per cent of world GDP. Nearly one-half of these investments will be in generation facilities, and the other half in transmission and distribution networks. In addition to signifying future growth in demand for electricity, this represents significant capital and natural resource requirements, as well as environmental impacts if the current pattern of supply and demand persists. Research and development in new and emerging technologies can offer significant improvements in all the above areas, through technical progress and improved cost-effectiveness. However, despite their considerable potential for improvement, the current level of energy R&D

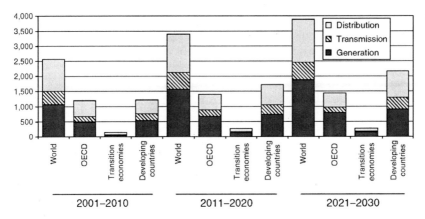

Figure 1.1. Worldwide investments in electricity, 2001–2030 ($ billion 2000).
Source: IEA (2003).

spending constitutes only a fraction of future capital needs. In other words, the potential economic, environmental and social returns from energy R&D investments are very substantial indeed.

1.3   Electricity and renewables

The above analysis of the significance of electricity suggests the importance of the introduction of renewable electricity generation if serious reductions in the total amount of CO_2 produced are going to be made. The potential for a large contribution is high, because the current contribution of renewables is modest and declining. The share of renewables in electricity generation fell from 24.1 per cent to 15.1 per cent between 1970 and 2001 in IEA countries (IEA, 2004b) This was primarily due to the dominance of hydro in total renewable generation (86% of all renewables) and the rapid growth of electricity demand since 1970.

With this in mind, the European Union has set a target of 21 per cent renewables by 2010, against 15.2 per cent in 2001, which comprises a range of varying national targets (see European Commission, 2004). There are a range of subsidy and support mechanisms for renewable energy sources in place in the Union, although these are not yet harmonised across member countries. However, it may be argued that, to the extent that conventional energy sources also receive subsidies and support, the effectiveness of subsidies and support mechanisms for renewable energy sources and their competitiveness may be reduced. In 2001 the total amount of energy subsidies in the EU-15 was estimated at about

€29 billion, of which about €5 billion were earmarked for renewable sources (EEA, 2004). This is while a significant amount of harmful environmental impact has been attributed to subsidies to conventional energy sources (OECD, 2003).

Among the most ambitious of these national targets is that of the United Kingdom, which has a target of 10 per cent by 2010, against 2.4 per cent in 2003. The EU targets are enshrined in the 2001 Directive (2001/77) on the Promotion of Electricity from Renewable Energy Sources (known as the 'RES-E' Directive). These targets for electricity from renewables are in the context of the European Union overall Kyoto commitment to an 8 per cent reduction in 1990 CO_2 emission levels by 2010.

In addition, the United Kingdom has an aspiration to a 20 per cent renewables contribution to electricity generation by 2020. It also has a national goal of a 60 per cent reduction in 1990 CO_2 emission levels by 2050. This 2050 target is not associated with electricity specifically but, given the fact that electricity is expected to make a disproportionately large contribution to cutting total CO_2 emission levels in both 2010 and 2020, it is safe to assume that the government's 2050 target implies at least a 60 per cent renewables contribution to electricity generation by that date.

The United Kingdom's National Audit Office (2005) recently reviewed the government's expenditure in supporting renewable electricity generation and the likelihood of it meeting its targets. The 2010 target is assessed as challenging, with a strong possibility that the government will only reach a 7.5 per cent renewables level by then. This is in spite of the current policy of requiring suppliers to purchase increasing amounts of green certificates up to the amount of the target of 10 per cent by 2010. In 2003–4 renewables accounted for 2.4 per cent of electricity generation, significantly lower than the obligation level of 4.3 per cent. The policy comes at a price, with the expected total cost of renewables support being £700 million per annum between 2003 and 2006, of which two-thirds is paid by consumers through the renewables obligation. The cost to consumers is expected to be equivalent to a 5.7 per cent increase in the price of electricity by 2010.

The National Audit Office (2005) concluded that the roll-out of renewables faced several major difficulties. These were difficulties in gaining planning permission for new generation sites, timely grid reinforcement, low market electricity prices, uncertainty that the renewables obligation scheme will continue into the longer term and the need for additional funding for new technologies.

In 2003 38 per cent of the United Kingdom's carbon dioxide emissions were from energy industries, 21 per cent from road transport,

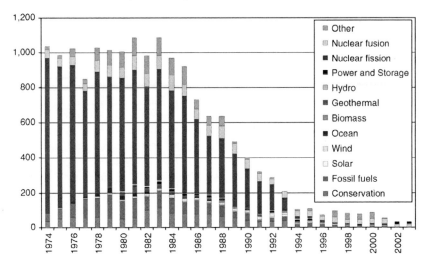

Figure 1.2. UK government energy R&D expenditure ($ million 2003 prices and exchange rates).
Source: IEA, Energy R&D Database.

18 per cent from other industries and 15 per cent from residential fossil fuel use (DEFRA, 2005). Since 1990 energy industry emissions have reduced by 10 per cent and other industrial emissions by 11 per cent, while residential emissions have increased by 11 per cent and road transport emissions by 8 per cent.

Although UK government targets for renewables generation sources are challenging, the government's support for renewables R&D is modest at present. UK government R&D is shown in figure 1.2. Liberalisation in the early 1990s was accompanied by a precipitate decline in total R&D expenditure. R&D expenditure on renewables has always been relatively small, and although it has picked up recently it remains below the levels of the 1970s. It remains to be seen whether market support mechanisms can deliver the innovation and the penetration of new technologies that the government might like.

1.4   Purpose and structure of the book

The electricity supply system has a pivotal role to play in ensuring the environmental and social sustainability of future economic and energy systems due to the size of its current contribution to emissions of greenhouse gases. A key factor in achieving a sustainable electricity system is technological progress at all levels, from generation through to end use. The promise of technological progress allows us to envisage electricity systems for the future that are radically different from today's conventional systems. The systems' main characteristics have, since the inception of the industry, and the triumph of George Westinghouse's alternating current approach, remained largely unchanged. At the same time, in no other sector has there been such a wide range of emerging and prospective technologies promising to transform nearly every aspect of the organisation and operation of industry and commerce. As a result, it is important to survey the new electricity technologies and to assess how these may shape the future of our electricity system.

This book is intended as a broad overview of the issues and progress path of new electricity technologies, and as an accessible resource to academics, decision-makers and others with an interest in the future of electricity systems. It allows all the authors to make their own claims for the technologies they discuss. As editors we do not offer an economic assessment of these claims, nor have we sought to limit their enthusiasms, as this would be inappropriate for a book with a primary focus that is technological and visionary. Some implicit costs are contained in the analysis of chapter 2, but the purpose of this chapter is similarly visionary, aiming to provide a set of plausible futures in order to stimulate discussion rather than supply a costed statement of likely futures.

Collectively, the chapters in this book present a holistic vision of the future. Written by leading experts in their respective technology areas, they review the state of the art of these key areas in an accessible manner and offer insights as to how these may evolve to shape the future of the industry. New technologies are expected to transform nearly all aspects and stages of the electricity system, from how electricity is generated, transported through networks, stored for later use and, finally, consumed. The organisation of the book broadly follows the structure and hierarchy of activities in the electricity system.

As part of the book we have included an opening chapter (chapter 2) outlining some scenarios for the future development of the electricity system in the United Kingdom that illustrate the place of each of the technologies we discuss in the book.

Chapter 2 is important in postulating the role and significance of the particular technologies that we examine. It is also significant in outlining different possible futures for the UK electricity sector and indicating something of the range of possibilities that exist. In line with the long-term objectives of the UK government to reduce carbon emissions by 60 per cent by 2050, the electricity sector is examined at that date. Six scenarios are outlined. To contrast two of the results we examine the *Business as Usual* scenario and the *Green Plus* scenario.

Under *Business as Usual*, economic growth is the same as recently, technological change is evolutionary, environmental attitudes are similar to now and the market remains liberalised. The result is that, in 2050, of total capacity 30 per cent is renewables and 50 per cent is conventional large plant generation. There is significant use of advanced control of the grid, strategic energy storage and asset management. Under *Green Plus* the market remains liberalised and economic growth remains similar, but technological change is revolutionary (more rapid) and attitudes to protecting the environment from GHGs become much more strongly positive. The result is that 80 per cent of electricity is generated from renewables and zero in large conventional power stations. Interconnectors and offshore transmission are very important, sophisticated network control is utilised and there is significant use of storage, micro-grids and demand-side management. Other scenarios lie between these extremes. Under the *Green Plus* scenario wind provides 40 –45 per cent of total energy, photovoltaic generation 3–5 per cent, biomass 25 per cent, wave 5–10 per cent. Micro-renewables account for 20 per cent of electricity production. There is no role for nuclear or carbon capture. However, significant use is made of superconductivity in high-voltage transmission links, advanced power electronics, energy storage, efficient end-use technologies and electric transport. Hydrogen is used in transport, but is produced from conventional sources.

The subsequent chapters on electricity technologies cover electricity production from a number of new technologies and improved conventional sources. Here, technical progress has been made on a number of fronts. Although the exact role of individual technologies is unclear, it is plausible to assume that renewable and other sustainable options will be available and these will account for a larger share of electricity generation. Many of these are likely to be smaller in scale than current conventional technologies. Furthermore, the intermittent nature of their production patterns will pose challenges for the electricity system and for end users. The intermittency of some generation technologies will not necessarily lead to poor reliability for consumers. Rather, a coevolution of patterns in generation, transmission, distribution and end use is expected, so that all consumers will receive the electricity-based services they require at the times of their choosing and at affordable prices.

The technologies are presented in four parts.

Part I examines the most promising new renewable technologies. We include wind (chapter 3) in this as being new and exclude hydro as being old and limited in its future scope. We also review the prospects for solar energy (chapter 4), biomass (chapter 5) and wave energy (chapter 6).

All four of these technologies feature prominently in the *Green Plus* scenario noted above.

Part II reviews the key technologies that could serve to deliver carbon benefits from existing thermal technologies. We begin by looking at how conventional fossil fuel technologies might reduce their carbon emissions by employing carbon capture (chapter 7). We go on to examine how the future of nuclear power might develop (chapter 8) and how a trend towards miniaturisation might facilitate the use of efficient embedded generation technologies at the household level (chapter 9).

Part III looks at technologies that support the wider use of renewable energy by facilitating its conversion to more usable forms or by improving the reliability and accessibility of remotely produced renewable energy. Thus we examine the use of superconductors to facilitate electrical loss reduction in transmission systems (chapter 10) and advances in power electronics to accommodate frequency and voltage disturbances created by renewables (chapter 11). We also look at the prospects for the use of hydrogen energy as a carrier for renewable electrical energy for use throughout the day and in transport (chapter 12). We conclude by looking at how new storage technologies, such as using compressed air, can facilitate the connection of intermittent renewables (chapter 13).

Part IV examines the role of technology in reducing the demand for energy by using electrical energy more efficiently. In this part we survey possible technological advances in buildings (chapter 14) and industry (chapter 15) that would reduce demand, and the use of electrical transportation to facilitate the use of clean electricity and reduce overall GHG production (chapter 16). We also review the scope for the use of smart meters that facilitate greater efficiency in the domestic demand for electricity (chapter 17).

The electricity system of the future is likely to be more flexible and responsive than that in operation today. One has only to look at the evolution of telephony in the last thirty years, from a situation of expensive, centralised monopoly providers using fixed infrastructures to the world of today, with diversity of quality, far wider flexibility of use, far greater availability of services and a real move to competitive markets. We appear to be in the early stages of a similar revolution in the electricity system.

1.5   Technology chapter summaries

The different chapters in this book review the state of the art and the potential impact of a range of new electricity technologies. The chapters cover various generation and end-use technologies, as well as storage and power technologies that will enable more active transport networks and will allow the supply and demand sides to interact in new and innovative ways. These chapters may be summarised.

Part I: Renewable Generation Technologies
Chapter 3. Wind power

As the current renewable generation technology of choice, wind is a good place to start this part of the book. In this chapter Morthorst reports on the very rapid growth of wind power in recent years. The economics of the technology are dominated by capital costs, and this implies a significant sensitivity to the discount rates adopted. A detailed breakdown of the cost structure of a 1MW wind turbine is presented. The recent trend in the sector is reported to be a move towards larger turbines with improved cost-effectiveness over previous plans. The roles of wind speed and wind resource intermittency are discussed in the context of wind power technologies and the economics of this form of electricity generation. The chapter stresses the recent emphasis on offshore wind farms, with anticipated power costs for a 3MW offshore turbine predicted to be 4.2 c€/kWh. This will be somewhat higher than the equivalent cost for onshore wind power production of 2.4–3.0 c€/kWh. In such circumstances it is argued that onshore wind power will certainly be economically competitive with natural-gas-fuelled electricity and that offshore wind power systems will be not too far behind.

Chapter 4. Solar energy: photovoltaic electricity generation

Mumtaz and Amaratunga open their chapter with a history of solar electricity and semiconductor photovoltaic technology. A text box describes the scientific fundamentals of photovoltaic technology and describes the voltage/current trade-offs to be made in deploying such technologies. The chapter discusses the main ways of fabricating photovoltaic cells and points to recent attempts to reduce the relatively high costs of production. One technology, amorphous silicon-based photovoltaic, has the great benefit of being available in physically flexible (bendable) sheets. A key drawback of the technology, however, is its lower operating lifetime. The chapter emphasises both off-grid and on-grid applications of solar power. The former market is well developed, and, while the back-up batteries associated with off-grid applications are expensive, an off-grid set-up is frequently significantly less expensive than the costly alternative of providing access to national grid infrastructures. For remote, unmanned, off-grid applications it is important to remember the costs of regular maintenance and cleaning for the efficient operation of these systems. On-grid applications, however, face a tougher economic climate. Despite this, costs have fallen substantially and are now far lower than generally perceived. Key to the economics of on-grid solar power are capital costs, maintenance, reliability and system lifetimes. Solar panels are, however, unique among major electricity generation technologies, as they can be genuinely distributed close to the points of electricity use. They are particularly well matched to urban installation. In that context, the chapter discusses the relationship between solar panels and prestige architectural materials. Once the full costs of building construction, office use and energy demands are factored together, solar power can appear very attractive. The chapter concludes with some forward-looking comments regarding possible technology innovations for both solar panel design and their end use.

Chapter 5.   Biomass

Bridgwater reviews bioenergy technologies. Bioenergy is a renewable source utilising crops, and agricultural and forestry woods. In addition to being a source of electricity generation, biomass is the only renewable source that produces solid, gaseous and liquid fuels for transport and other uses. The technology has the potential to be a part of sustainable future energy systems and comprises a range of approaches. These can broadly be grouped into biological conversion, physical conversion and thermal conversion. This chapter focuses on thermal conversion processes. The main thermal processes reviewed here are combustion, gasification and pyrolysis. Gasification offers the highest efficiencies among these technologies.

The overall power efficiencies of combustion technologies are between 15 per cent and 35 per cent. There are already examples of commercially successful operation of the technology. Emissions and ash handling remain technical issues in need of further progress. For gasification technologies, the power efficiencies are between 35 per cent and 50 per cent. Some of the gasification technologies exhibit both technological strength and market attractiveness. There is, however, limited operating experience with these technologies. Moreover, the technology faces high cost and non-technical barriers and requires integration in a biomass energy system. Pyrolysis technology is based on thermal decomposition in the absence of oxygen, and much research is focused on fast pyrolysis for liquids production. Here also there are cost and non-technical barriers to overcome. Thermal bioenergy sources are likely to come mostly from small-scale plants and will thus need to compete with other sources at smaller scales. A combination of high-value chemicals and low-value fuels can improve the economics of bioenergy technologies.

Chapter 6.   Wave energy

In their chapter Thorpe and Wallace discuss the considerable potential for the generation of electricity from wave energy in certain coastal and offshore locations. A particularly favourable location is off the northern coast of Scotland. The maximum exploitable resource is estimated at around 31 TWh in the United Kingdom (or around 7 per cent of present demand). There currently exist working prototypes for the exploitation of onshore wave power using oscillating water column technology. A variety of offshore technologies are being explored. These offer the prospect of bigger and less unsightly facilities, but have proved more technically challenging. Some of both types have performed successfully for a number of years at a single site. However, they remain vulnerable to catastrophic damage during storms and currently suffer from very high capital costs relative to their energy capture. Interest in the technology is increasing, especially in the United Kingdom, where government funding is currently among the most generous. The chapter highlights three constraints to further development in the United Kingdom: the legacy of the failure of an earlier government-supported push in the 1970s, the cost of connection to the electricity grid (which can be up to 50 per cent of the capital cost of new projects) and the difficulty of obtaining planning permission.

Part II: New Technologies for Thermal Generation
Chapter 7.   Carbon capture

Moving on to the part addressing existing thermal technologies, Røkke examines the prospects for carbon capture. Some of the options to reduce the amount of man-made CO_2 emissions are the more efficient use of energy and the use of low-carbon fuels. Many of the necessary improvements will be made possible via technological innovation. However, to the extent that fossil-fuel-based generation technologies will continue to be used, carbon sequestration technologies can play a significant part in the reduction or even utilisation of CO_2 emissions from electricity generation. A range of technologies, including pre-combustion, post-combustion and oxy-fuel solutions, exist. The CO_2 will then be transported and deposited in reservoirs, or alternatively, injected in oil reservoirs in enhanced oil recovery operations. The carbon capture is the stage in the chain of activities where further technical progress and cost reduction is needed through R&D and demonstration efforts.

Chapter 8.   Nuclear energy

Grimston begins this chapter with an exploration of the barriers to a regrowth of nuclear power in Western countries. He highlights four difficulties to be overcome: a low level of research and development, a shortage of skilled workers, poor public perceptions, and difficulties surrounding the management of radioactive wastes. The chapter provides a description of the fundamentals of nuclear fission and of nuclear power production. The problems of nuclear power are particularly associated with the worsening economics of nuclear projects in the years after the Three Mile

Island accident in the United States in 1979 and the Chernobyl disaster in the Ukraine in 1986. Nuclear power is characterised as a power technology with high capital costs and strong incentives towards economies of scale. Grimston counters the views of many commentators when he points out that nuclear power is not one technology but many. As such, it is unhelpful to talk about nuclear power as being 'mature' given that many potential nuclear power technologies are at present underdeveloped. He describes successive generations of nuclear power generation and discusses in some detail future Generation IV technologies and the technologies favoured by the US-led Generation IV International Forum.

Chapter 9.   Microgeneration

For most of the period after the Second World War there was a tendency to increasing scale in power generation. In this chapter Biermann points out how this tendency was reversed in the 1990s with the emergence of combined-cycle gas turbine technology, which could be operated at a much smaller scale than pre-existing coal-fired plants. Now much smaller scales are being commercialised that are capable of being installed at the point of electricity consumption, all the way down to the household. This chapter discusses the emerging technologies: micro-CHP plants down to 1kW and renewable microgenerators such as the photovoltaic solar cell (solar PV). Many of these technologies are being developed privately, with the exception of solar PV and fuel cells, and offer considerable market potential. For example, the market for household micro-CHP is the market for boilers. These are replaced at 5 per cent to 6 per cent per annum in the United Kingdom. A 1.2kW Stirling micro-CHP unit can produce heat and an annual average of around 2,400kWh of electricity, mostly at periods of peak system consumption. Currently the purchasing cost (before installation) of these units is about twice as expensive as a conventional boiler, and this is the major barrier to their adoption. However, if these units were used to replace 30 per cent of conventional boilers, they could produce a quarter of domestic electricity demand and significantly reduce distribution and transmission system losses. The significance of this is that responsibility for generation dispatch will shift significantly from large-scale power plants to small-scale units, fundamentally changing how the system will need to be operated. In particular, network investment will be required to install much more flexible switchgear and transformers at the local distribution level.

Part III: Electricity Conversion and Storage

Chapter 10.   Superconductors in the electrical power industry

Moving on to supporting conversion and transmission technologies, Campbell starts his chapter with a history of the discovery and development of superconductivity. Recent decades have seen a move towards Type II alloy materials in the 1960s, the discovery of High T_C superconductivity in 1987 and, most recently, the promise of magnesium diboride conductors. The main applications of superconductors to a sustainable energy future are listed as being in: motors and generators, energy storage, fault current limiters, power cables and levitated trains. In many cases the main challenges are twofold: better materials and more efficient cooling. Superconductors are reported to be a low-hazard technology and an environmentally benign contributor to improvements in electricity transmission, distribution and end use. It seems likely that applications of these relatively high-cost and sophisticated technologies will be specific and selective, rather than ubiquitous and pervasive in the electricity sector as a whole. The main barrier to wider deployment is argued to be the economic disadvantage of these efficient technologies in an artificially inexpensive fossil-fuel-based electricity system.

Chapter 11.   Power electronics

For Green and Hernández Arámburo the main promises of power electronics technologies are the better flexibility and controllability of power systems. While power electronics is a mature technology that has proved useful in other areas, from mobile phones to rail transport, its potential benefits for power systems are underutilised.

The technological basis of power electronics is semiconductor devices able to switch large currents and voltages. Potential benefits of power electronics are in low and high power ratings in generation, supply-side, demand-side and network control. Power electronics can facilitate the use of new forms of generation sources and provide network reinforcement features not offered by traditional technologies. More specifically, important application areas for power electronics technologies are: (i) frequency and voltage transformation for connecting renewable sources to networks; (ii) the reduction of voltage disturbance caused by generators in local distribution networks; (iii) improvements in stability and voltage tolerance from new power sources; and (iv) limiting the negative impacts of intermittent sources on the quality of supply.

The main challenges facing power electronics are high costs, high energy losses, and increases in system complexity resulting from the extensive integration of such devices. Moreover, realisation of some of the potential benefits of power electronics is contingent upon changes in design and practice aspects of power systems need to be altered.

Chapter 12.   Sustainable hydrogen energy

As Edwards and his co-authors point out in this chapter, the vision of a hydrogen-powered economy is one that many, including the European Commission, continue to take seriously. The value of hydrogen is that it can store and transport energy produced from intermittent sources (such as wind). Thus it can be used to provide electricity for use at different times and it can be used to power vehicles, thus facilitating the use of renewable electricity in road transport. However, the barriers to the widespread use of hydrogen are significant. In vehicles hydrogen is 2.5 times heavier than petrol per unit of energy and it takes up four to nine times more volume. It is also expensive and difficult to store safely. Another significant issue is the distribution of hydrogen. Petrol has an established distribution system; investing in the hydrogen distribution pipe network would be very costly, while the extra bulk of hydrogen would make tanker distribution significantly more expensive than for petrol. However, the potential of hydrogen remains high, with an estimated global demand for fuel cell products (in portable, stationary and transportation power applications) reaching $46 billion by 2011. The authors conclude by suggesting that the viability of the hydrogen economy depends on political will, first to make hydrogen competitive in the near term and then to support a prolonged period of coexistence with fossil fuels until these run out.

Chapter 13.   Electrical energy storage

Ruddell reviews electrical energy storage technologies. A fundamental problem with electrical energy is that it is very expensive to store once it has been produced. Large-scale pumped storage hydro is the only widely used way of converting and storing electricity, and the expansion possibilities for this are limited. Electrical energy storage is an issue because of the uneven pattern of demand, which means that the electricity system costs can be reduced if electricity can be produced at periods of low demand and stored electrical energy released at periods of high demand. Renewable electricity sources tend to be intermittent and difficult to synchronise with the demand, imposing additional system costs in the absence of storage. This chapter investigates the state of storage technologies that could facilitate the increased use of renewables. It examines electrochemical storage (batteries and flow cells), electromechanical storage (pumped hydro, compressed air and flywheels) and electrical storage (superconducting magnetic energy storage and supercapacitors). All these technologies are challenging to make cost-effective, and some, such as battery technologies, have additional negative environmental impacts. Several have technical problems associated with the limited number of cycles of charging and discharging that they can be subjected to before failing. The most promising new technology is compressed air storage, which can store electricity for up to two hours and offer power capacities of up to 3GW but requires suitable underground sites (such as redundant mines) for the storage of the compressed air.

Part IV: End-Use Technologies and Patterns of Future Demand
Chapter 14.   Buildings

Turning to demand-reduction technologies, Eichhammer assesses the prospects for more energy-efficient buildings. In the buildings sector, two long-term visions outline prospects of radical changes not only in the way buildings consume electricity but also in the way they interact with the supply side of the system. In the *Integrated World* buildings are integrated into active networks, which connect and coordinate a variety of new and conventional generation sources to buildings, which also function as distributed supply sources. Advancements in a variety of components and networking technologies will be needed for realising these networks. Moreover, new technologies can help in managing supplies from intermittent renewable sources and reduce the transaction costs of integrating small-scale units in electricity systems. In the *Component World* vision the energy efficiency potential of buildings will reduce demand for energy to levels where interconnection to wider electricity systems will become uneconomic. In this world, technical progress in the components and materials used in appliances and in building shells can yield considerable energy savings and transform the conventional mode of supplying energy to buildings from centralised systems to self-sufficient and decentralised systems. Even further into the future, new technologies may transform building and vehicles into a major source of energy supplies to electricity systems.

Chapter 15.   Industrial end-use technologies

Price, Galitsky and Worrell present the main aspects of the industrial end use of electricity. Industry accounts for about 40 per cent of global commercial energy, through a variety of applications. As the authors describe, an array of new technologies are on the horizon, with the promise of improved efficiency in electricity end use. Technological progress is expected at the level of small, medium and large generation units for different industrial applications and scales. The chapter focuses on three main categories of electricity-efficient technologies: efficiency-improving technologies, efficient fuel switching to electricity, and the industrial co-generation of heat and power. Motor systems account for over a half of the industrial consumption of electricity. Here new types of motors, system designs that match generation and end use, and controls can contribute to the more efficient use of electricity. New membrane technologies for use in a variety of separation processes will facilitate efficient fuel switching to electricity in different industries. Industrial self-generation based on new gasification or advanced co-generation technologies can reduce the demand for electricity. Other new technologies, such as fuel cells, are also likely to become commercially available and widen the range of technological options for industrial applications.

Chapter 16.   Transport

Vermeyen and Belmans point out that the transport sector is the most rapidly growing source of GHG emissions. However, electrically supplied transport modes may facilitate the substitution of cleanly produced electricity for fossil fuels. This chapter discusses the prospects for electric vehicles – both road and rail – in Europe. Electric vehicles require sophisticated frequency control to allow them to use power from the grid, while regenerative braking allows them to improve their energy efficiency substantially by supplying power while moving downhill or braking. Electric passenger trains using magnetic levitation technology can travel at up to 500km/h while offering reasonable energy efficiency due to the reduced friction. There exists greater potential for the use of intermodal transport using electric freight trains to carry conventional fossil fuel trucks. The chapter also looks at battery-powered, hybrid and fuel-cell electric road vehicles. In the near term the hybrid vehicle (where the combustion engine drives the generator, which powers the vehicle) offers substantial energy efficiency advantages without requiring any external infrastructure investment. The authors conclude with a review of an IEA study that suggests that CO_2 emissions in 2020 from road and rail transport in Western Europe could be reduced substantially by measures (such as fiscal incentives and better labelling) to encourage the deployment of electric vehicles. The impact on system electricity demand of such policies would be positive but negligible.

Chapter 17.   Smart metering

Devine-Wright and Devine-Wright discuss the prospects for electricity demand reduction by the use of 'smart' meters. Traditional household electricity meters are only capable of recording the cumulative amount of electricity consumed by a household and have to be manually read *in situ*. 'Smart' meters are capable of a two-way electronic information flow, between the supplier and the household. This information flow can be frequent, multi-format, accurate, real-time and high-quality. These meters offer the prospect of allowing the price and quantity of electricity consumed to be varied remotely in real time, subject to the terms of a contract that offers an incentive to the householder to defer or reduce consumption at times of high system demand. They would also facilitate the roll-out of household microgeneration. It has been estimated that more flexible household supply contracts, facilitated by smart meters, could reduce total electricity consumption in the United Kingdom by 2 per cent. Smart meters that can do this already exist, and some are already cost-effective. Italy has installed 30 million smart household meters since 2000. Based on interviews with industry participants, the chapter highlights the need to provide incentives for the adoption of smart metering in the United Kingdom; it suggests that, under the current system, neither distribution network companies nor electricity supply companies have a strong incentive to encourage consumers to install a smart meter.

1.6   Common and contextual factors affecting new technologies

As we noted in the above overview, the new energy technologies exhibit different characteristics, such as cost level, scale, underlying technologies, stage of development and maturity, and diffusion. The future development of these technologies may depend not only on their own merits and distinct characteristics. In the long run, a number of factors exogenous to technology characteristics can be influential in the level of R&D efforts and the promotion of new energy technologies. These issues are explored further in chapter 2. However, given their importance, we highlight them up-front.

- **New technologies and electricity market liberalisation**
  It is conceivable that much, if not most, future technical progress in sustainable energy is likely to take place in market-oriented operating environments. The 1990s witnessed the emergence of electricity sector reforms in many countries across the world. The main objective of the reforms has been to improve the operational and investment efficiency of the sector through restructuring, competition, regulatory reform and privatisation. The reforms have taken place against the backdrop of a wider paradigm shift from state ownership and the centralised management of infrastructure industries to market-oriented structures, independent regulatory oversight and private ownership structures (OECD, 2003). Indeed, the main driving forces and mechanisms of liberalisation reform have had little to do with technical progress, and the promotion of new energy technologies has been on the sidelines (see, e.g., Russell and Bunting, 2002). However, it is the case that the coincidental innovation of the combined-cycle gas turbine plant (the low-cost technology of choice in the electricity sector) facilitated competitive entry into liberalised electricity markets (Newbery, 2000). Technology-push and market-pull policies and instruments to promote new technologies can be regarded as corrective measures and interventions in liberalised sectors in order to correct for market failures.

- **Energy R&D and technology policies**

  It is conceivable that, in time, the current cost band within which the new technologies lie will gradually become narrower. Within this context, the role of technology and market support policies, to the extent that these are not technology-neutral, will be more important and will increase. Most power technologies have enjoyed significant government support (either directly or through non-competitively awarded contracts) at some point during their life cycle. This is even true of CCGTs, which were born out of the heavily subsidised and protected aerospace industry. Government support for renewables has been increasing across the IEA countries in recent years and seems set to increase further (IEA, 2004b).

- **Fossil fuel prices and security of supply**

  The cost of electricity from conventional thermal technologies is dependent on the price of fossil fuels. The cost difference of electricity production from conventional relative to new technologies is, therefore, influenced by long-term trends in fossil fuel markets. Small and medium-sized CCGTs have been instrumental in the development of liberalised electricity markets. The price of natural gas is closely linked to the price of crude oil in European markets. It is conceivable that economies of scale and technological progress in the medium term will lower the cost of transporting liquefied natural gas. A move to increased LNG trading will result in a larger and more competitive international market for natural gas that is more correlated with the volatile oil market. To the extent that such market integration reduces prices, it will make renewables less attractive. However, to the extent that it makes gas and oil prices move together, it will increase the value of renewables within a portfolio of electricity generation (Awerbuch, 2003). A sustained increase in the price of fossil fuels combined with uncertainty over these supplies will lead to an increase in R&D efforts and the adoption of new energy technologies (such as we have seen in the period 2004–6). The new technologies with a cost advantage and an option value will attract more support.

- **Macroeconomic factors**

  Generally, a high-growth economic environment can lead to higher spending on, and the promotion of, new technologies. The new energy technologies tend to be more capital-intensive than conventional energy technologies. Although cost reductions may reduce the capital intensity of these technologies, they are likely to retain this characteristic for the foreseeable future. The price of capital will therefore be a crucial factor affecting the cost, development and competitiveness of new technologies. High interest rates will push up the cost of new energy technologies disproportionately relative to conventional technologies. In an economic environment with sustained high interest levels, the cost of investments in capital-intensive technologies and the promotional subsidies to support them will increase. Moreover, if the competitiveness of capital-intensive technologies diminishes it can result in less R&D spending in these technologies. The 1970s can be viewed as a period of low real interest rates, while the most recent years may be characterised as a period of relatively high real interest rates. The extent to which high energy prices cause structural changes in the economy or affect national competitiveness will be important in either encouraging such investment (if oil and gas prices are high) or discouraging such investment in renewables (if their relative cost is seen to be high).

- **Public acceptance**
  In the coming years a range of issues, such as environmental and climate change concerns, security of supply and the performance of liberalised markets, are likely to engage public opinion and interest groups in energy and technology policy. The public's perception of these issues can lead to demands for limiting certain conventional sources of electricity and/or promoting new and emerging technologies. Public acceptance is instrumental in the adoption and success of policies with regard to new energy technologies. So long as new technologies cannot compete directly with conventional sources, public acceptance will play an important role in maintaining market support mechanisms and policies favouring new technologies. Ultimately, the large-scale deployment of renewable energy sources through market instruments and institutional frameworks will depend largely on the extent to which expressions of public support translate into support for the development of actual projects (Wolsink, 2000).

1.7   Concluding observations

In closing, we make a number of observations based on the various chapters.

First, the technologies we include are not comprehensive. We do not discuss nuclear fusion, tidal or geothermal technologies, for instance. This is because the technologies we do consider are those that are likely to reach maturity in the next three decades and that are capable of making a contribution on a large scale.

Second, conventional technologies such as coal and nuclear fission are likely to be significant for some time to come. This makes support for 'clean' conventional technologies (carbon capture and new forms of nuclear) potentially attractive.

Third, renewables pose significant environmental and siting problems of their own. These relate to the difficulty of obtaining suitable sites with appropriate levels of local support for the generation, storage and transmission technologies. Careful siting is required, as well as innovation in minimising the visual impact.

Fourth, technology does offer the prospect of lower demand for energy, via reduced system losses and industrial, commercial and residential demand. This is clearly significant in reducing requirements for new generation capacity. It may be that support for this aspect of carbon reduction may be very cost-effective in the short term.

Fifth, there is widespread agreement that almost all the new technologies that we discuss are still reliant on government funding support mechanisms. For some the required outlay will initially be modest, as they are still at the fundamental design stage (such as tidal). However, for some of the technologies that are close to maturity (such as wind) the subsidies are financially very significant, due to the large amount of installed capacity.

Sixth, renewables require a range of support policies. These include a favourable price for renewable electricity generation but also the direct subsidy of particular technologies at early stages of development. In the United Kingdom technology-neutral price support mechanisms have been less effective than policies in other countries in encouraging either the quantity or diversity of renewable generation.

Seventh, none of our authors suggest that their technology is the only one that should be used to address the carbon reduction targets set for the electricity sector. It is clear from the range of potential technology options and their associated limitations (e.g. in terms of maximum potential capacity) and risks that the encouragement of a diversity of technological approaches is desirable.

In closing, it is important to note that any view of the future can only 'look through a glass darkly'. Technological change cannot be anticipated clearly. This is particularly true in the area of climate change. New information about the future effects of climate change and the possibly severe nature of the effects themselves may impact substantially on the technologies we discuss. Events may also provide impetus to even newer technologies before 2050.

1.8   References

Awerbuch, S. (2003). Determining the real cost: why renewable power is more cost-competitive than previously believed, *Renewable Energy World*, 6(2): 53–61.

DEFRA (2005). *e-Digest of Environmental Statistics*, March, London: Department of Environment, Food and Rural Affairs.

DTI (2003). *Our Energy Future: Creating a Low-Carbon Economy*, Energy White Paper no. 68, Cm5761, London: Department of Trade and Industry, available from http://www.dti.gov.uk/energy/white paper/our energy furture. pdf.

EEA (2004). *Energy Subsidies in the European Union: A Brief Overview*, Technical Report 1/2004, Copenhagen: European Environment Agency.

European Commission (2004). *Electricity from Renewable Energy Sources*, Brussels: European Commission, Directorate-General for Energy and Transport.

IEA (2003). *World Energy Investment Outlook 2003*, Paris: International Energy Agency.

(2004a). *World Energy Outlook 2004*, Paris: International Energy Agency.

(2004b). *Renewable Energy: Market and Policy Trends in IEA Countries*, Paris: International Energy Agency.

National Audit Office (2005). *Renewable Energy*, HC 210 Session 2004–2005, 11 February, London: National Audit Office.

Newbery, D. M. G. (2000). *Privatization, Restructuring, and Regulation of Network Utilities*, Cambridge, MA: MIT Press.

OECD (2003). *Environmentally Harmful Subsidies: Policy Issues and Challenges*, Paris: Organisation for Economic Co-operation and Development.

Russell, S., and A. Bunting (2002). Privatisation, electricity markets and renewable energy technologies, in A. Jamison and H. Rohracher (eds.), *Technology Studies and Sustainable Development*, Munich and Vienna: Profil Verlag, 407–33.

Wolsink, M. (2000). Wind power and the NIMBY-myth: institutional capacity and the limited significance of public support, *Renewable Energy*, 21(1): 49–64.

World Commission on Environment and Development (1987). *Our Common Future*, Oxford: Oxford University Press.

2 Electricity network scenarios for the United Kingdom in 2050

Ian Elders, Graham Ault, Stuart Galloway, Jim McDonald, Jonathan Köhler, Matthew Leach and Efterpi Lampaditou

2.1 Introduction

This chapter attempts to illustrate how the technologies described elsewhere in this book may be deployed in combination with one another, with other new and developing technologies and with existing technologies in the electricity network of 2050. This task is accomplished through the development of a small number of 'high-level' future network scenarios, encompassing different economic and technological possibilities that may arise.

The following chapters in this book discuss a number of technologies that are likely to be important to the development of the electricity network in the United Kingdom over the coming decades. In Part I, four renewable generation technologies – wind, solar photovoltaic, biomass and wave energy – are presented. Of these, wind is already gaining a foothold in the British generation mix, with a great deal more capacity in development or planning. Biomass is established in a relatively unsophisticated form, while solar photovoltaic generation currently has a very small level of application. Wave energy is also at an early stage of development, with a number of prototype devices under test. In all these generation technologies significant research and development is in progress, aimed at helping them to reach their full potential.

In Part II, a number of technologies relevant to more conventional non-renewable generation are presented. The capture and storage of CO_2 would permit fossil-fuelled generators to continue to contribute to the electricity supply without the release of large volumes of greenhouse gases into the atmosphere. In chapter 8, issues relating to nuclear generation are discussed, together with new technological prospects that might improve its attractiveness and mitigate some of the current barriers to its development in the United Kingdom. Microgeneration has the potential to bring about significant change in the electricity industry, through the proliferation of very small generators, including micro-renewables and domestic-scale combined heat and power systems. Such micro-CHP systems are beginning to see application in this country, and, as discussed in chapter 9, there is scope for very considerable expansion of this market.

Beyond generation, there are considerable advances in prospect in the conversion and transmission technologies which are covered in Part III. Superconductor technology has developed in its capability and its economics in recent years and is beginning to see application in power systems, as discussed in chapter 10. Power electronics has become increasingly common in many roles related to power systems, from DC interconnectors and large reactive compensation equipment to newer applications such as network integration of small renewable generators. As discussed in chapter 11, power electronics has the potential to play a variety of important roles in future power systems. Hydrogen has the potential to be a sustainable climate-neutral energy carrier, replacing hydrocarbon-based fuels. Chapter 12 outlines the developments in the production, storage and use of hydrogen that are in prospect, together with challenges to, and strategies for, its widespread adoption. Hydrogen is also a possible medium for the storage of energy in the electricity system – an activity that may become considerably more important in the future. As discussed in chapter 13, a number of technologies are in development, or are already being applied, which are expected to be suited to the various time and power requirements of future energy storage applications.

Finally, energy use technologies are discussed in Part IV. Chapter 14 presents two future directions of development in energy demand in buildings, considering both significant further progress in energy efficiency, and a much closer integration and coordination of energy demand and diverse and distributed generation. In chapter 15, future prospects for the consumption of electricity by industry are surveyed. The chapter discusses three important areas of technological development affecting industrial energy consumption. Transport is another major energy area of energy use, to which electricity has the potential to contribute in the form of electrified railways and electric and hybrid road vehicles. Chapter 16 surveys technological developments and applications in these areas. Chapter 17 discusses the prospects for the application of more advanced, or 'smart', electricity meters in the domestic market, and presents alternative customer–supplier relationships that might evolve as a result of their deployment.

The scenarios presented in this chapter have been developed by the authors as part of the SuperGen Future Networks Technologies research effort, which brings together a consortium of researchers from a number of academic institutions to consider the application, and effects of the application, of new and emerging technologies to power systems in the first half of the twenty-first century. The scenarios are intended to permit the analysis of network performance (including economic, technical and environmental measures) under a variety of future circumstances.

Six scenarios have been developed and are presented here, each considering a set of technical, economic, environmental and regulatory possibilities that are felt by the authors to be plausible and achievable. The selection of a relatively small number of scenarios is intended to permit their analysis in reasonable detail, together with consideration of variations to each scenario so as to determine the influence and importance of individual technologies and external factors. It also permits a relatively detailed presentation in the context of this chapter.

The limited number of scenarios also imposes a restriction, in that very radical scenarios and unexpected 'wild-card' technologies can be accommodated only at the expense of other, more plausible, possibilities. Such developments are inherently difficult to model and analyse as a result of their very unpredictability, although the influence of such technologies might be estimated to an extent by considering their effects, such as significant changes in demand, reductions in energy costs, reductions in emissions from large generators, or great increases in small-scale energy storage, for example. Such analysis might be incorporated into the study of variations around the six 'core' scenarios discussed here. Furthermore, the relatively slow pace at which change generally proceeds in the electricity industry, as discussed below, means that very radical scenarios are much more unlikely to arise than those presented here. Thus, while such scenarios might present very large challenges to the electricity industry, the risk presented is offset by their low likelihood. Overall, then, it is the belief of the authors that the benefits of omitting these more radical scenarios and unexpected technologies from our discussion here outweigh the disadvantages.

While the selection of 2050 as a target date for the scenarios may appear to some to be a long way into the future, the electricity supply industry operates under very high expectations of reliability in its product. This gives rise to a tendency towards technological conservatism and the incremental development of existing technologies in preference to the rapid deployment of revolutionary new ideas. Furthermore, plant lifetimes in the industry are generally long in comparison to other industries – fifty years or more for some types of equipment – and it is likely that existing technologies will survive in strength for a number of decades. These effects mean that the pace of technological change in electricity networks will tend to be relatively slow; therefore, 2050 was selected as a suitable date by which significant and wide-ranging changes in the British electricity network might have come to fruition.

In this chapter, the process by which the six scenarios were developed is described, and the key characteristics that are used to delineate possible 'future worlds' are tabulated. The set of six 'high-level' scenarios, focusing on the year 2050, of possible future circumstances in which electricity networks will be required to operate is summarised.

Each of the scenarios is then described in more detail, and a description of the network that might be developed by 2050 under the scenario is given. Each of these illustrations discusses how the factors inherent in the scenario influence network development, and assess the extent to which the technologies forming the subject of later chapters are applied.

2.2   Scenario generation methodology

The process by which the scenarios discussed in this chapter were generated is summarised in figure 2.1.

The starting point in the process is the identification for detailed consideration of four key activities facilitated by electricity networks.

- Energy use.
- Electricity generation.
- Energy transportation.
- Markets and regulation.

Reference material, which is listed at the end of the chapter, presenting opinions, forecasts and analyses relating to these areas over the coming fifty years, was collated and reviewed by those of the authors with particular expertise in each area. Key sources included:

- Department of Trade and Industry modelling and projections of future energy demand;
- DTI-supported analysis of future generation mixes;
- surveys of potential future developments in network technology;
- industry forecasts of future development in specific technology areas; and
- material on energy use, electricity generation and network technology presented at the workshop summarised by this book.

Information from these sources about key factors likely to influence the future development of electricity networks was summarised, and possible ranges of variation in these factors were proposed for study. Specific technologies that might be included in the scenarios were identified,

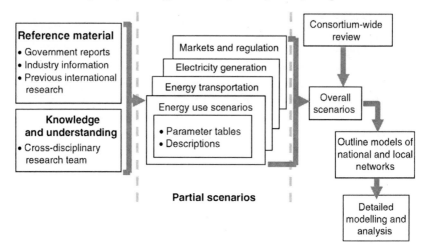

Figure 2.1. Scenario identification process.

together with conditions under which they might see more or less extensive deployment in a scenario. This information was used to generate small sets of five or six possible future partial scenarios focused on each of the four key areas individually. These partial scenarios were thus based on future combinations of electricity demand, generation and network technology mixes resulting from previously published predictions and forecasts from a variety of sources. In addition to narrative descriptions of these partial scenarios, tables of key parameters covered by the scenarios were generated. As described below, the partial scenarios for each individual area then formed the basis of the 'overall' high-level scenarios described in this chapter, which combine key features of the environment in which networks might operate.

The key inputs to the process of generating the overall scenarios are as follows.

- Narrative descriptions of proposed partial scenarios covering each of the four areas individually: energy use; electricity generation; energy transportation; and markets and regulation.
- Tables of principal scenario parameters and corresponding qualitative ranges of values.
- Opinions and experience from other work packages within the Super-Gen Future Networks Technologies consortium.

Using this information, the following process was undertaken to understand better the relationship between the scenarios, and to identify drivers for overall scenarios.

1. The scenario drivers from the parameter tables were compared in order to identify common and related themes across the partial scenarios.
2. The scenario descriptions for each area were reviewed to identify further related issues in the scenarios.
3. From the scenario descriptions, the qualitative values of each relevant parameter were identified and tabulated.
4. Partial scenarios were tabulated according to the values given to related parameter groups identified at stage 2.
5. Partial scenarios were retabulated to identify the degree of mutual similarity between pairs of scenarios.
6. Key factors and qualitative ranges were proposed to differentiate overall scenarios.
7. Potential overall scenarios were identified.
8. Using their descriptions, individual partial scenarios were tabulated against potential overall scenarios to evaluate their narrative coverage and identify potential redundancy.
9. The resulting descriptions of the potential scenarios were presented and discussed at a workshop attended by researchers from across the SuperGen consortium, at which opinions on the technological, economic, regulatory and social aspects of the scenarios were canvassed.
10. The results of these discussions were used to refine the range of important factors and to make corresponding revisions to the overall scenarios.

The overall scenarios were then used, together with additional technical background material, to generate a corresponding set of descriptions, or outline models, of the electricity network that might develop by 2050 under each scenario. These 'network visions' consider the effects of the generation mix envisioned by each scenario, together with important issues such as the range of transmission and distribution technologies likely to have been developed and applied, and the effects of public environmental concern on network development.

In the future, as shown in figure 2.1, the scenarios and network descriptions presented in this chapter will form the basis of a set of detailed quantitative models of various aspects of the British electricity system. These models will be analysed to determine the outcomes of each scenario in respect of metrics such as the cost of operating the network, CO_2 and other emissions, and the reliability of electricity supply, as well as the influence on these outcomes of the important uncertainties addressed by each scenario.

2.3   Principal factors in scenario development

As a result of the analysis described above, the following key parameters on the overall scenarios are proposed.

Economic growth

This parameter influences factors including increases in energy demand and levels of investment finance. In these scenarios, the following range of values is considered:

- low growth, whereby economic growth is significantly less than recent levels; and
- high growth, in which economic growth is somewhat higher than current levels.

Technological growth

The technological growth parameter governs the appearance and application of new technology to electric power networks. The following range of possibilities is considered:

- revolutionary development, in which radical new technologies are developed and applied widely; and
- evolutionary development, in which technological advance is restricted to the application and gradual improvement of current and currently foreseen technologies.

Environmental attitudes

The strength or weakness of the prevailing environmental attitude determines factors including emissions constraints and incentives and the acceptability of the power network. In these scenarios, the following range of possibilities is considered:

- weak environmental attitudes whereby concern reduces in comparison to the current UK atmosphere to a situation similar to that current in the United States; and
- strong environmental attitudes, whereby popular and governmental concern for the environment strengthen significantly with respect to the current situation.

Political and regulatory attitudes

This parameter concerns the attitudes of government and society in general to the management and development of energy industries

Table 2.1 *Names and key parameters of UK electricity industry scenarios*

Scenario name	Economic growth	Technological growth	Environmental attitudes	Political and regulatory environment
Strong Optimism	More than recently	Revolutionary	Stronger	Liberalised
Business as Usual	Same as recently	Evolutionary	As at present	Liberalised
Economic Downturn	Less than recently	Evolutionary	Weaker	Liberalised
Green Plus	Same as recently	Revolutionary	Much stronger	Liberalised
Technological Restriction	More than recently	Evolutionary	Stronger	Liberalised
Central Direction	Same as recently	Evolutionary	Stronger	Interventionist

in general, including energy use, transportation and electricity generation. Two possibilities are considered:

- liberal attitudes, in which the current preference for relatively light regulation, together with a market-driven approach, continues; and
- an interventionist approach, in which a centrally directed model of management and development is adopted, with greater and more prescriptive government involvement.

Some other scenario-based work, such as that of the UK government's Foresight Energy Futures Task Force, has presented scenarios graphically as quadrants within a 'scenario space'. While early iterations of the scenarios described in this chapter made use of such a representation, further reflection and wider discussion with members of the SuperGen research consortium suggested that, in this case, the approach tended to encourage the consideration of technically uninteresting and mutually similar scenarios, while failing to represent adequately the diversity of issues of interest. Instead, a process of formal presentation, review and criticism of draft scenarios by the consortium has been adopted, in order to assure the relevance and diversity of the final scenarios presented here.

2.4   Scenarios of the UK electricity industry in 2050

The parameters described above were combined to yield the six overall scenarios summarised in table 2.1 They are described in more detail in the subsequent sections. These scenarios capture a range of possible future paths for development of conditions in which energy networks exist.

These scenarios are described in the following sections, together with the corresponding electricity network that might develop by 2050.

2.5   Future energy technologies

In addition to the technologies discussed in the following chapters a number of other existing, developing and future technologies were reviewed that might either form part of power systems in the years leading up to 2050 or influence their development. As part of this process, the authors consulted a number of general and more technology-specific reviews and road maps that have been published in technical journals and by government and industry bodies. These sources are included in the references.

As a result of this review, and from the discussion presented in the various chapters of this book, a set of important technologies and types of devices were identified as being relevant to the six electricity network scenarios. Some technologies are of general interest throughout the set of scenarios, but in differing roles dependent on the particular circumstances. For example, power electronics play a prominent role in all the scenarios, but in applications such as interconnectors, flexible alternating current transmission systems, energy storage and microgeneration dependent on the conditions prevailing in the scenario.

Conversely, some technologies feature only in some scenarios, or have some of their possible applications ruled out of all scenarios on technical or economic grounds. For example, while DC network technology is applied to transmission systems in some scenarios, DC distribution is considered to be impractical, since it would either require the wholesale replacement of appliances or the mass installation of household DC–AC converters as individual local networks are converted. The ability of ageing distribution cables to support DC distribution might also be questionable.

In order to illustrate how new and existing technologies are applied in each scenario, a graphical illustration is provided for each which shows the broad geographical locations within Great Britain in which large-scale generation and network technologies are applied, and identifies smaller-scale technologies that are applied in rural and urban networks. In these diagrams, generation and network technologies are represented using the symbols shown below.

⊕ Local rural network
⊛ Local urban network
⊷ Interconnector

⟟ Overhead
  AC transmission

⟟ Overhead
  DC transmission
⊙ Undersea
  DC transmission
▣ Underground
  AC transmission
▭ Underground
  DC transmission

⟟ Offshore wind
⟟ Onshore wind
⊸ CCGT

⟟ CCGT with
  carbon
  sequestration
◆ Coal generation

⟟ Coal with carbon
  sequestration
○ Nuclear

⟋ Wave generation

⟨ Tidal generation
⊸ Biomass
⊙ Photovoltaic
  generation

⋔ CHP

⟋ FACTS

⟋ Microgrid

⫿ Energy storage

⟋ Demand-side
  control

2.6   Strong Optimism

2.6.1   *Scenario background*

This scenario takes as its central theme a future in which there is
sustained strong economic growth. Over the period to 2050 the overall
effect is of growth in excess of recent rates. At the same time, there is a
significant increase in the interest in, and importance attached to, power
generation, transmission and distribution technologies. This results in
considerable investment in R&D in these technologies, so that new and
improved kinds of equipment, and methods of operation and management, are rapidly brought to market and applied. These advances are
broadly spread over a wide range of fields related to energy systems and
bring benefits in cost, reliability and environmental performance.

A sharpening of current levels of environmental consciousness takes
place in this scenario, continuing current trends towards greater popular
awareness of these issues. The availability of more capable, newly developed devices permits the replacement or reinforcement of existing
equipment in less intrusive form. Additionally, there is significant undergrounding of electricity circuits, supported by the deployment of network and control technologies, such as DC transmission. Environmental
concerns, together with increasing prices of fossil fuels (notably natural
gas), also help to increase the adoption of existing and new efficiency
measures, such as low-energy buildings and consumer devices. Carbon
trading is extended to industry and individual buildings, including the
domestic sector.

The current liberalised and market-based approach to regulation and the implementation of government objectives remains in place. However, increases in the share of generation accounted for by renewable technologies, together with improved system control capabilities resulting from technological development, will lead to an increase in the sophistication of market mechanisms to balance the needs and capabilities of a variety of electricity producers and consumers. In addition, standard contractual and technical agreements are developed to streamline the connection of domestic and office CHP and for microgrids, including such aspects as metering, protection and control requirements, automated demand-side energy management systems and automated building energy systems.

The success of the United Kingdom's system of markets and regulation leads to similar arrangements becoming widespread in Europe. Ultimately, this results in the development of complementary and integrated energy markets at a European scale. Thus there is increased cross-border trading of energy, with correspondingly increased demand for energy transportation between countries, leading to a significant increase in both gas and electricity interconnector capacity between Britain and mainland Europe.

Complementing the development of energy-related markets at a European scale, locally focused markets in energy and existing and novel energy services (such as the provision of power quality and energy storage devices, and the trading of network capacity) become widespread. These markets serve to focus the development of local networks and small-scale generation resources on local needs. Therefore, there will be two types of electricity market in the United Kingdom: a sector of many microgrids for small-scale demand – homes and offices; and a national, countrywide, market. Large-scale wind, marine, biomass and large 'conventional' plants will participate directly in the UK market, as will larger-scale consumers. Increased interconnector capacity will permit extensive trading between the national market and international markets. Mechanisms are introduced to permit the aggregation of small generators (which would otherwise participate in local markets) in order to allow them to trade in the nationwide market.

The increased range of technologies in use, particularly in the form of renewable and/or small-scale generation, results in a wider variety of ownership than today. The vertical integration of companies deploying mature technologies tends to develop, with an increasing movement of these organisations into energy services products. Smaller-scale independent companies will develop, focusing on new markets and technologies such as automated control systems and IT. As these technologies mature and become more widely deployed, their suppliers may become consolidated into larger organisations.

2.6.2   2050 electricity network

In this scenario, strong economic growth leads to a corresponding increase in the demand for energy services as people become more affluent and able to afford new and improved energy-consuming devices as they are developed. Equipment such as air-conditioning becomes more popular and railway electrification is extended. The resulting increase in demand is offset to a degree by the application of existing and new efficiency measures, but the overall demand for electricity grows at a relatively strong average rate of 1.25 per cent annually to approximately 600TWh/year by 2050 (from approximately 345 TWh in 2003), within current geographical patterns. Variability in electricity demand is reduced, as a result of a significant deployment of energy storage systems and demand-side control at a small scale, the technology of which develops rapidly in the period to 2050. Peak demand is approximately 80GW (from approximately 60GW in 2003).

Renewable generation accounts for around 50 per cent of total generation, of which half is made up of offshore wind. Figure 2.2 illustrates the location of these renewable generators and other features likely to be important in the *Strong Optimism* scenario. Offshore wind generation is principally located around Scotland (with important concentrations in the Moray Firth), in the Irish Sea and off East Anglia. The size of individual developments will increase, being generally in the hundreds of MWs, as will individual turbine size, with machines of 20MW being typical. Relatively remote wind farms will be developed, with some in international waters. Onshore wind development is restricted by growing concern over its environmental impact, which prevents larger and more cost-effective turbines from being deployed; most onshore wind will be located in Scotland.

Biomass makes up the second largest renewable energy source. In urban areas, this will be in the form of waste-fuelled developments, often allied to district heating schemes in new building projects (promoted through planning regulations and the development of energy service providers) to form relatively large CHP systems. In rural areas, gasification-based biomass generation, fuelled by energy crops, will predominate; the size of these plants will be restricted by the costs of transporting biomass and the increasing efficiency of relatively small biomass power plants. There will also be a significant presence of small-scale combustion-based biomass generators. Marine – i.e. wave and

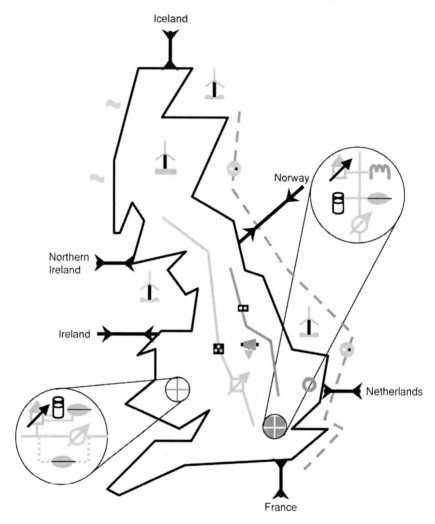

Figure 2.2. *Strong Optimism* scenario: electricity network in 2050.

small-scale tidal – generation will be located along the west coast of Scotland and in the Western Isles.

Large central generation stations will account for 10 to 20 per cent of generation. These will be a mixture of gas-fired CCGT systems, which may include liquid oxygen feedstock units, participating in carbon sequestration schemes, and new-technology nuclear power stations located adjacent to existing nuclear generation sites. Both of these generation technologies are likely to be mainly located in the South; the precise mix will be determined by economic factors, although increases in fossil fuel prices are likely to make some level of new nuclear construction attractive. The remainder of generation capacity, totalling approximately 40 per cent, will be composed of CHP systems, as discussed below. The overall effect of this change in generation technologies will be that the proportion of generation in the Midlands and South reduces somewhat as large central generating stations are replaced by increases in renewable energy in the North.

As shown in figure 2.2, interconnectors are constructed to a variety of countries with varying generation profiles. Existing interconnectors to France and Northern Ireland are increased in capacity when major refurbishment or replacement is required. The varying generation and demand profiles of the countries and systems linked by these interconnectors mean that there is likely to be 'through traffic' in the transmission system, as energy from renewable-rich countries such as Iceland and Norway is transported to mainland Europe via the southern interconnectors. It should be noted that the interconnectors to Ireland will provide an additional north–south transmission path.

The overall result of these developments will be an increased demand for electricity transmission, particularly along the north–south axis. At the same time, there will be significant undergrounding of the transmission network, particularly in environmentally sensitive areas, resulting in considerable change to its operational characteristics. Superconductors will be deployed in situations in which it is critical to maximise capacity within a confined space, such as in cities and at river crossings. In order to secure increased capacity from the transmission network, a number of technologies will be applied. Advanced control systems, allied to power electronic-based FACTS systems, will be widely deployed. In addition, energy storage systems will be used to provide 'rapid-response' capabilities to support the power system during a disturbance event. Such facilities will be closely integrated with advanced network control and protection systems.

Additionally, notwithstanding the reduced variability of electricity demand, large-scale energy storage systems at strategic locations will provide 'peak-smoothing' capabilities, enabling bulk energy transport to take place in a more controlled manner. These systems are likely to be based on advanced electrochemical technology, although other technologies may be adopted where local conditions are favourable.

Some transmission facilities will be replaced by HVDC circuits when undergrounding is undertaken. These are likely to be strategic north–south transmission paths in which the undergrounding of AC circuits cannot provide the required transmission capacity. Superconducting DC cables are likely to be applied in order to minimise losses.

Demand for electricity transmission and available capacity will move closer together. At the same time, the British and European electricity and transmission markets are likely to become more closely connected, and novel mechanisms may be necessary to allocate peak capacity between demands for domestic north–south transmission and through flows from Iceland and Scandinavia to mainland Europe. Under such circumstances, it is possible that new facilities (such as coastal DC transmission) could be developed by investors to support these flows.

As noted previously, local networks will see a considerable penetration of small-scale generation. Small CHP installations, mainly installed and managed by energy services organisations, will account for 30 to 40 per cent of total generation, with strong penetration of the domestic market. By 2050 the majority of such systems will be based on fuel cell technology with integrated conversion of natural gas, but there will be a significant base of older CHP installations, including turbine and Stirling Engine systems. In remote rural areas, biomass-based CHP systems will be popular. There will be a mixture of combustion and integrated gasification technologies, depending on the particular requirements of the application and the date at which the equipment is installed. In rural communities, community-scale biomass CHP will be developed, based on gasification technology. Photovoltaic generation will be deployed to a limited extent, often integrated into new buildings, but its contribution to the overall generation total will be small.

This increase in small-scale generation will promote the adoption of microgrids in both urban and rural settings, to the extent that their application is very widespread. Power electronic devices similar in concept to FACTS devices will manage the interface between the microgrid and the regional power network. However, as noted below, interaction and cooperation with devices connected to the microgrid will be important and will be facilitated through the medium of wireless communication technology, which will be very widely available. Larger embedded generators – for example, rural biomass systems – may be connected on one or other side of this boundary, depending on local conditions.

Energy storage systems will be widely deployed within microgrids. In rural areas, local or building-focused storage systems will be strongly applied. In urban areas, these will be supplemented by larger-scale systems installed to address the needs of the energy services market place.

As noted above, interaction among the generation, storage and energy-consuming devices within microgrids will be important in maintaining local system conditions and in managing the interaction of the microgrid

Table 2.2 *Technology application in the* Strong Optimism *scenario*

Chapter	Technology	Scope of application
3	Wind generation	Very strong development, of which the vast bulk is offshore. Total wind generation capacity is 50–60GW, supplying 25 per cent of electricity demand.
4	Photovoltaic generation	Integrated into many new buildings, deeply embedded in distribution networks. Generation capacity is around 5GW, generating 1–2 per cent of electrical energy.
5	Biomass electricity generation	Strong application of large- and small-scale plants and CHP. Total generation capacity is around 10–15GW, generating 15 per cent of electricity.
6	Wave generation	Large application in relatively small developments. Including tidal generation, capacity is approximately 15GW, accounting for 10 per cent of electrical energy.
7	CO_2 capture	Applied to about 10GW of new CCGT. Significant role in hydrogen production.
8	Nuclear generation	Nuclear capacity is 8–10GW of new technology generation, generating 10–15 per cent of electricity.
9	Microgeneration	Strong fuel cell deployment. Total capacity is 30–35GW, producing 35 per cent of electricity.
10	Superconductivity	Some network application in constrained locations and onshore HVDC and storage.
11	Power electronics	Very extensive application in a variety of roles.
12	Hydrogen	Strong use in transport and as domestic/industrial fuel. Mainly produced from fossil sources.
13	Energy storage	Considerable application at all sizes and timescales. A variety of technologies are in use.
14	End-use technologies	Deployment of efficiency measures allied to strong deployment of small distributed generation closely integrated with local networks.
15	Industrial electricity use	Strong adoption of new technologies to increase efficiency and profitability. Significant integration of electricity generation into production processes, using combustion and advanced fuel cells.
16	Transport	Increased use of electricity for rail transport; road transport mainly hydrogen-fuelled hybrid vehicles.
17	Smart metering	Strong application, supported by universally available communications infrastructure. Advanced metering capabilities integrated into demand/generation/storage management systems.

with the regional power system. This will be achieved through the large-scale adoption of integrated intelligent control of demand, generation and energy storage. Initially adopted for large industrial and commercial developments, building-scale systems will propagate to progressively smaller applications, so that by 2050 there is significant adoption of such technology at a domestic scale. Such systems will permit wide participation in both conventional and novel markets, and will permit significant development of demand-side control schemes. The coordination of generation, storage and energy consumption across the microgrid will be facilitated by the development of novel local markets. The widespread use of metering systems with capabilities such as time-of-use pricing, automated demand control (often integrated into household or building energy management systems) and automated meter reading will help to facilitate these developments.

A large-scale transition to hydrogen fuel for road vehicles will lead to the development of fixed hydrogen infrastructure in urban areas. In other areas hydrogen will be distributed by road or rail. Much of the hydrogen will be produced from fossil fuels (with carbon sequestration), but some will be imported, and a small proportion will be produced by electrolysis; hydrogen-based energy storage systems will also interact with the distribution system.

2.6.3   Scenario summary

The *Strong Optimism* scenario represents a case in which strong economic growth is supported by the availability and application of advanced electricity generation, transport and use technologies. A mix of generation technologies is deployed, although there is an increased focus on renewables; other network technologies are developed and deployed to improve environmental outcomes, the quality of service and cost-effectiveness. The influence in 2050 of each of the technologies described in the various chapters is summarised in table 2.2. For each of the generation technologies mentioned, the table gives the expected installed generation capacity, and the proportion of annual electrical energy demand supplied by that technology.

2.7   Business as Usual

2.7.1   Scenario background

This scenario represents a continuation of current trends. Economic growth continues, on average, at recent rates. As a result, there is an increase in the demand for energy services as people become more affluent and business expands. This trend is countered by the application of energy efficiency – for example, in the form of better appliances and machines or improved insulation – largely on economic grounds, particularly in the light of increased natural gas prices, but with some environmental motivation.

Technological development in the energy sector continues at much the same rate as at present, and tends to result in the evolution of existing technologies, and the application of those currently under development, rather than to revolutionary changes in the technology applied to energy systems. Thus, new kinds of power system equipment and generators tend to be recognisably similar to systems that are currently in use or in close prospect for application.

The level of environmental consciousness in this scenario generally remains constant at its current point, or sharpens slightly, but does not impose significant additional restrictions. Resistance to increases in the visual and environmental impact of electricity networks remains relatively strong. Gaining approval for the construction of new transmission infrastructure remains costly and time-consuming, and there is pressure for the undergrounding of existing circuits in specific environmentally sensitive areas as refurbishment or replacement becomes necessary. However, there is no pressure for generalised removal or undergrounding. Furthermore, there is less concern over the smaller structures used by distribution systems.

The government remains supportive of current liberalised, market-based approaches to regulation. However, the perceived success of these structures in the current environment means that they are relatively slow to adapt to the needs and opportunities of very small-scale generation, restricting their initial competitiveness. Ultimately, however, increased competitiveness through gradual technological improvement influences the adoption of favourable regulatory and market mechanisms. An important development in this regard will be the emergence of energy service providers, optimising light, power and – ultimately – heat provision from national energy markets, a portfolio of renewable and large generators, and – as the technology develops – on-site microgeneration.

The liberalisation of energy markets and industries continues across Europe. However, although some new electricity and gas interconnectors are constructed, limited transfer capacity means that UK participation in these markets is limited. Thus, although UK markets become more closely aligned to those of mainland Europe, integration is far from complete. There is, however, strong development in integrated cross-European markets for emissions trading.

A centralised market remains the principal method of electricity trading in the United Kingdom. The market design is gradually optimised to allow the participation of a considerable volume of wind and CHP generation and to take account of their implications for generation and load profiles. Energy service providers participate in half-hourly or shorter-term markets on behalf of groups of customers; some small-scale and domestic customers participate directly, taking advantage of domestic energy storage systems. Limited incentives for renewables are available in the early years of this scenario, in line with environmental attitudes, but interest in these tends to slacken as network-imposed constraints on the development of renewables are approached. Carbon trading applies mainly to industrial and large commercial users and takes place in a pan-European market; the price of carbon will be relatively low.

Ownership patterns continue largely as at present, with a variety of individual companies with limited vertical integration. There is some decentralisation of the management of local networks, although they are likely to remain closely coupled to the electricity network at large. The development of microgrids is likely to be restricted to specific industrial or commercial settings, with a large amount of embedded generation under common control.

2.7.2   2050 electricity network

In this scenario, economic growth brings about an increase in demand for energy services as people become more affluent and business activity increases. The increasing cost of natural gas leads to a small amount of fuel switching as electricity becomes more attractive in some applications. However, some of this growth is offset by energy efficiency measures. Demand for electricity grows at an annual average rate of around 1 per cent, reaching to approximately 540TWh/year in 2050. This demand remains distributed within current geographical patterns. The variability of demand reduces somewhat as a result of increased participation in demand-side control schemes, but as this is far from universal, peak load continues to grow and at around 80GW remains significantly above the average load.

Renewable technologies account for around 30 per cent of generation. Figure 2.3 illustrates the location of these renewable generators and other features likely to be important in the *Business as Usual* scenario. Of this renewable generation, just under a half is found in offshore wind developments, located in the Irish Sea and off East Anglia and north-east Scotland, using machines in the 10 to 20MW range. There is some additional onshore wind capacity, located in Scotland and the South-West, but this is limited by the greater efficiency offered by the larger turbines acceptable in offshore developments, which preferentially absorb the capacity of the network to accommodate intermittent generation. Onshore wind is restricted to 2 or 3 per cent of total generation.

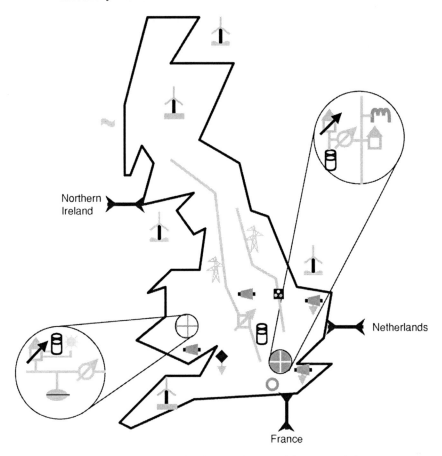

Figure 2.3. *Business as Usual* scenario: electricity network in 2050.

A further 10 to 15 per cent of total generation is in the form of biomass-fuelled systems, mainly in the form of gasifiers coupled to combined-cycle turbines. Biomass generators are generally relatively small in scale and are often embedded within local networks. The remaining 3 to 5 per cent of total generation from renewable sources is made up of marine generation on the west coast of Scotland and a small amount of photovoltaic generation integrated into new buildings.

Large central generation will account for around 50 per cent of total generation. Large CCGT developments will predominate, with their location being driven by a combination of transmission constraint avoidance and the availability of existing sites for redevelopment. However, increases in the cost of natural gas will make the construction of a small number of advanced coal-fired stations attractive where a supply of suitable fuel can be secured. With a significant concentration of renewable generation in the North in Scotland, it is likely that the majority of these new generators will be located in the Midlands and the South. Between a quarter and a half of new CCGT units will be equipped for carbon capture; to counter environmental objections, new coal generators will exploit this technology. Coastal sites with easy access to undersea storage facilities are most likely to participate in carbon sequestration. The construction of new nuclear generation is relatively unlikely, but economic conditions may favour the construction of one or two new stations of the next evolutionary design. As noted below, some low-cost generation capacity at strategic locations, in the form of OCGT units, may be necessary to relieve transmission constraints under high load conditions. The remaining 20 per cent of generation will be made up of small CHP systems.

Existing interconnectors will be renewed and refurbished as necessary, and will benefit from increases in capacity as a result of technological improvements. New interconnector construction will be confined to a second relatively short link to mainland Europe of similar capacity to existing facilities. Energy transfer between Great Britain and Europe will be dependent on relative energy prices, and thus on the availability of renewable resources. However, since interconnector capacity will amount to less than 10 per cent of domestic generation, its influence is likely to be limited.

The demand for bulk electricity transmission will increase as a result of demand growth. The increased proportion of electricity generated from intermittent renewable sources means that flow patterns in the transmission network are less predictable beyond the short term. As there is little construction of new transmission facilities, the need arises to increase the effective capacity of existing facilities while increasing the overall flexibility of the system – a situation complicated by the undergrounding of specific environmentally sensitive sections of many transmission circuits. These objectives are met through the deployment of advanced and highly interconnected control systems, together with power-electronics-based FACTS-like devices. Additionally, strategic energy storage systems using electrolytic or compressed air technology and strategically located generation will be used to alleviate pressure on the transmission system at times of peak demand. Superconducting technology may be used in particular locations where space for transmission system capacity is at a premium.

As mentioned above, there will be a large increase in generation connected to local electricity networks. Most CHP systems will be small-scale units of existing technology (e.g. microturbines or Stirling Engines) fuelled by natural gas; a small proportion of more recently installed systems will use fuel cell technology, mainly using on-site natural gas reformers. This growth will be driven by the emergence of energy service providers. In rural areas, biomass will be an important generation technology. In remote areas, biomass-fuelled CHP will be widely deployed, while larger-scale systems mainly fuelled by waste will be deployed in more populous areas.

Demand and control pressures on relatively lightly constructed rural networks with significant embedded renewable generation may lead to the adoption of microgrid technology in such areas. Interaction with the regional network in such situations will remain relatively strong, with the likelihood of strong net imports of energy. Domestic generation, including small biomass and photovoltaic technologies, together with larger-scale network-connected generation and demand-side control capacity, will be controlled through local market mechanisms. Energy storage in such networks is likely to be restricted to domestic-scale systems designed to insulate individual consumers from short-term price spikes in the energy market. These systems will be based on flywheel or battery technology.

In urban settings, the application of microgrid technology will be restricted to 'power parks' – new developments in which energy service providers are responsible for providing heat and electricity to industrial and commercial customers, although some residential and mixed-use power parks may develop. In such networks, there will be deployment of relatively large CHP systems linked to district heating, and community-scale energy storage systems serving the entire microgrid. Participation in demand-side control schemes will be facilitated by building management systems furnished by the energy service provider, which will include more advanced metering capabilities permitting variable pricing for energy and services such as demand-side response. Outside these power parks, urban networks will experience a strong increase in the deployment of small-scale single-building CHP systems, but will otherwise see little change.

In this scenario, demands placed on electricity networks will tend to increase. There will therefore be a strong focus on the development and deployment of asset management and condition-monitoring systems in order to derive maximum reliability and value from the installed asset base while minimising the overall cost of operating the system.

Table 2.3 *Technology application in the* Business as Usual *scenario*

Chapter	Technology	Scope of application
3	Wind generation	Strong development. 20–25GW of offshore capacity and around 5GW onshore, generating 12–15 per cent of electrical energy.
4	Photovoltaic generation	Integrated into some new buildings, deeply embedded in distribution networks. Total generating capacity is around 4GW, producing around 1 per cent of electricity.
5	Biomass electricity generation	Strong application of mainly smaller-scale plants and CHP. Total capacity is around 10GW, supplying 10–15 per cent of electrical energy demand.
6	Wave generation	Some application in relatively small developments. Total marine generation capacity, including tidal generation, is 6–7GW, of which wave accounts for three-quarters. 3–5 per cent of electricity demand is supplied from marine generation.
7	CO_2 capture	Applied to a proportion of new CCGT and coal generators; 10–20GW plant capacity is equipped. Adopted for hydrogen production.
8	Nuclear generation	One or two new stations using developments of existing technology, giving a total capacity of 2–4GW, supplying 5–10 per cent of electricity demand.
9	Microgeneration	Strong deployment, mainly using existing technology; total installed capacity of around 15GW, accounting for 20 per cent of electrical energy production.
10	Superconductivity	Applied in a few specific, constrained locations.
11	Power electronics	Very extensive application in a variety of roles, including transmission control systems. Distributed generation is an important application.
12	Hydrogen	Little interaction with electricity network; main use is in transport. Almost entirely produced from fossil sources.
13	Energy storage	Main application is at domestic level, with a few large strategic installations.
14	End-use technologies	Microgeneration mainly operates in isolation; a few integrated 'power park' developments combining control of demand, generation and heating.
15	Industrial electricity use	Replacement of existing equipment with more efficient and flexible plant on economic grounds or at life expiry. Increased employment of cogeneration, particularly at large and medium scales using turbine plant. Some small-scale using turbines and reciprocating engines.
16	Transport	Road transport mainly hydrogen-fuelled hybrid vehicles; little additional railway electrification.
17	Smart metering	Mainly applied though energy service providers, and in association with small-scale energy storage and generation; most users retain traditional meters.

2.7.3   Scenario summary

The *Business as Usual* scenario represents a case in which current economic and technical trends continue largely without change. Conventional generation remains the most important source of electricity, but with a considerably increased contribution from renewables and small-scale plant; other network technologies are developed and deployed to improve the reliability and cost-effectiveness of supply while delivering some environmental benefits. The influence in 2050 of each of the technologies described in the various chapters is summarised in table 2.3. For each of the generation technologies mentioned, the table gives the expected installed generation capacity, and the proportion of annual electrical energy demand supplied by that technology.

2.8   Economic Downturn

2.8.1   Scenario background

The principal factor driving this scenario is a significant reduction in economic growth from recent rates, as a result of factors such as fuel price shocks or global recession. As a result of these events, people generally have less money to spend on additional devices and appliances. Thus the growth in demand for electricity occasioned by such purchases is reduced in comparison to other scenarios. Similarly, the growth of business, commerce and industry is slower than in other scenarios, limiting the energy demands of these sectors. There is considerable interest in the conservation of energy on economic grounds; energy efficiency becomes a strong selling point for replacement appliances when it can be achieved at modest cost.

Limited funding is available for R&D activities, and spending on these activities reduces and becomes focused on relatively short-term goals. Technological advance in energy systems is mainly confined to the evolution of existing technologies and is focused on increasing the cost-effectiveness of energy supply. Economic concerns tend to divert awareness from environmental issues, and environmental consciousness thus becomes less strong than at present. Energy efficiency is motivated largely by economic drivers; although there is considerable interest in more efficient buildings that incur lower energy costs, moves in this direction are limited by relatively short-term cost pressures and a reduced rate of turnover in the building stock.

Similarly, restrictions on the availability of finance mean that investment is largely limited to the like-for-like replacement of life-expired assets, together with limited network extension to connect new generation, unless economic benefits can be realised from the deployment of more capable plant.

Notwithstanding the economic difficulties, the government remains generally committed to liberalised, market-based regulation in the United Kingdom, in the belief that this will promote more efficient and cost-effective energy supply than a more interventionist policy. Market structures are directed towards the promotion of cost reduction and efficiency in energy supply. Some financial assistance from the government towards the implementation of such measures is forthcoming when overall benefits can be secured. The liberalisation of European energy markets continues, although the pace of reform tends to slacken as economic pressures become more evident. In any case, lack of interconnector capacity and uncertainty over the economics of new interconnectors between Britain and mainland Europe continue to restrict the capability to transfer electricity. As a result, there is little opportunity for UK participation in European electricity markets. New interconnector capacity is focused on the import of natural gas. There is, however, strong interest in the convergence of technical standards between energy industries in the United Kingdom and the rest of Europe, in the hope of realising economies in the manufacture and purchase of equipment. Nonetheless, the economic climate is difficult for manufacturers of power system apparatus.

Market structures are therefore likely to remain similar to those currently planned for implementation. Carbon trading will be adopted under the current EU system; however, its scope is not likely to expand beyond generators and large energy-intensive industrial concerns. Wider economic and political considerations will keep emission allocations large, and prices correspondingly low. With the focus being placed on encouraging the most economic generation technologies, incentives for renewable generation will be allowed to expire; future regulatory incentives will promote greater efficiency.

Economically motivated consolidation is likely to be the principal driver of ownership patterns, as the amalgamation of existing companies into large, possibly vertically integrated companies takes place. As a result, a few big combined generation and supply companies will dominate the market.

2.8.2   2050 electricity network

In this scenario, the relatively low rate of economic growth restricts the increase in demand for energy services. People tend to postpone the purchase of new devices and appliances, and new models tend to emphasise efficiency rather than performance. The adoption of capital-intensive energy efficiency measures, such as the replacement of the building stock with more efficient designs, is limited by restrictions on the availability of finance. However, smaller-scale efficiency measures, such as improved appliance design, better insulation and the progressive improvement and adoption of building control systems, is sufficient to lead to electricity consumption either remaining constant or declining at an annual average rate of up to 0.5 per cent, falling to approximately 275TWh/year by 2050. The geographical pattern of demand is largely unchanged. There is no adoption of domestic-scale energy storage, for economic and technological reasons, and the lack of demand growth means that there is no incentive to promote the adoption of demand-side control in other than particular local circumstances. The variability of electricity demand is therefore largely unchanged in comparison to today, and peak demand is approximately 45GW.

In this scenario, renewable generation is divided roughly equally between onshore wind and biomass technologies, and accounts for between 10 per cent and 20 per cent of generation. Figure 2.4 illustrates the location of these renewable generators and other features likely to be important in the *Economic Downturn* scenario. The renewable generation capacity is largely made up of smaller-scale developments of a few tens of megawatts connected to either local or regional power networks dependent on the size of the generation scheme, although older onshore wind farms will be larger, ranging up to 500MW. Onshore wind generation is principally located in Scotland and Wales and makes use of turbines typically in the 2–5MW range on the grounds of environmental impact.

Energy-crop-fuelled biomass generators using a mixture of gasification and combustion technologies are distributed in many rural areas, with important concentrations in Scotland, Wales and the North of England. Marine and photovoltaic technologies do not develop to the point at which their application becomes economically attractive.

Large central plants account for around 75 per cent of generation. CCGT is the dominant technology, although a number of new coal-fired power stations will be built in order to provide an element of fuel diversity and to reduce the potential impact of gas price fluctuations. There is little or no uptake of carbon capture and sequestration technology. New large generators make use of existing power station sites in order to reuse existing transmission network connections. CCGT generation is preferentially located at sites with convenient connections to the national gas transmission network and to gas import facilities, while new coal-fired plants are located close to ports to permit the use of imported coal. No

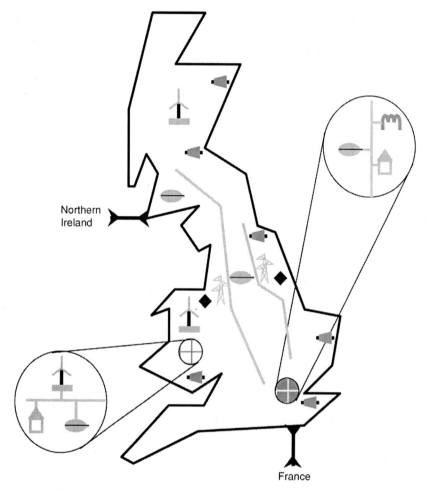

Figure 2.4. *Economic Downturn* scenario: electricity network in 2050.

new nuclear plants will be constructed: nuclear generation will have been eliminated by 2050 under this scenario. Small-scale CHP, mainly in industrial and commercial settings, will account for the remaining 5 per cent to 10 per cent of generation.

Existing interconnectors are life-extended, with refurbishment and renewal as necessary. This results in modest increases in capacity as a result of technological development, but no new interconnectors are constructed. Given the likely fuel price issues resulting from a strongly fossil-fuelled generation mix, it is likely that the UK–France intercon-nector will act mainly as an energy import route, and will also offset fuel security concerns to an extent. Depending on generation development in Northern Ireland and the Republic of Ireland, the Scotland–Northern Ireland interconnector is likely to facilitate energy exchanges to balance the availability of intermittent renewable resources in Great Britain and Ireland.

The development of small-scale embedded generation is driven largely by pressure for cost savings. In addition to embedded renewable sources discussed above, CHP developments will account for between 5 per cent and 10 per cent of total generation. Industrial and commercial sites will be the dominant users of such systems; domestic-scale generation will be largely driven by security of supply concerns and will thus be something of a niche market, confined to more remote areas. CHP technology will remain focused on small turbines or Stirling Engines fuelled by natural gas.

No new energy storage facilities are deployed. The development of large-scale systems is frustrated by the combination of a lack of suitable sites for traditional technologies, such as pumped storage, and the high capital costs of such developments. The deployment of smaller-scale systems is pre-vented by their high initial costs and the lack of perceived need. These factors serve to restrict the amount of intermittent renewable generation that can be accommodated by the network while minimising the amount of reserve generation capacity used.

The relatively modest penetration of small-scale generation and the fact that demand-side control schemes remain scarce mean that there is little pressure for the adoption of microgrid technology. Local power networks remain largely passive systems. Any installation of remote control and monitoring equipment is driven by cost-saving and asset management needs rather than the need for improved control of the network.

The slow pace of technological development means that hydrogen is not widely adopted as a fuel or an energy storage medium. Road trans-port continues to make use of petrol and diesel fuels, with the adoption of hydrogen being frustrated by the high cost and technical difficulty of storing sufficient fuel to achieve an acceptable range. There is very limited application to short-range vehicles (such as delivery vans), where a supply of hydrogen is available from other industrial activities. There is some adoption of hybrid vehicle technology on efficiency grounds; how-ever, these vehicles are entirely fossil fuelled; there is no adoption of battery charging from the electricity network.

The overall result of these trends is that the technical demands placed on transmission and distribution systems can, in general, be met by the power network of today. However, economic constraints mean that there

Table 2.4 *Technology application in the* Economic Downturn *scenario*

Chapter	Technology	Scope of application
3	Wind generation	Limited onshore application (total installed capacity is approximately 10GW) in relatively small developments. 5–10 per cent of electrical energy is generated from wind sources.
4	Photovoltaic generation	Minimal application.
5	Biomass electricity generation	Application mainly in small-scale plants. Total generating capacity is around 5GW, supplying 5–10 per cent of electricity demand.
6	Wave generation	Not economically attractive.
7	CO_2 capture	Application to one or two CCGT plants, if used at all.
8	Nuclear generation	No nuclear generation.
9	Microgeneration	Application of microturbines and Stirling engines in industrial settings. Total installed capacity is around 5 GW, accounting for 5–10 per cent of electricity produced.
10	Superconductivity	No applications in electricity networks.
11	Power electronics	Main applications are in new or replacement compensation and control systems, in refurbished interconnectors and in microgeneration.
12	Hydrogen	Limited use in specific vehicle applications.
13	Energy storage	No additional deployment of energy storage systems.
14	End-use technologies	Strong emphasis on efficiency and reduction in energy use, at reasonable cost.
15	Industrial electricity use	High-efficiency technologies adopted for new facilities and replacement of life-expired plant when capital cost differential allows a short payback period. Cogeneration integrated into construction of many new facilities on economic grounds; capital cost pressures favour use of turbines and reciprocating engines.
16	Transport	Transport remains largely based on fossil fuel sources.
17	Smart metering	Little application; refurbishment and reuse of electromechanical meters continues strongly. Some application of simple remote-readable meters in new developments on cost-saving grounds.

is a strong focus on the life extension of existing plant items to avoid the need for expenditure on renewal or replacement. When such a course of action becomes impractical, life-expired assets are likely to be replaced on a least-cost like-for-like basis. However, when cost savings could be achieved through rationalisation of the network, it is likely to be undertaken at this point of asset replacement. There may be modest investment in extending the remote control of local distribution networks in order to save on the operational expenses associated with manual operation.

The power network of 2050 under this scenario is likely to be very similar to that of today in its structure, technology mix and operational approach. The most important issue of concern to network operators will be the reliability of ageing plant. There will be considerable deployment of asset management and condition-monitoring technology, as well as research into the behaviour and characteristics of such plant, in order to manage this issue and prevent significant degradation of the quality of supply to customers without incurring unnecessary expense on maintenance or plant replacement. When replacement of an asset becomes necessary, the least-cost modern equivalent capable of performing the task will usually be selected, unless another course of action will yield cost savings in the short to medium term.

2.8.3   Scenario summary

The *Economic Downturn* scenario represents a case in which the effects of adverse economic events are dominant. Investment for research and development is relatively scarce and as a result renewable technologies develop to only a limited degree. Investment in the electricity network is generally minimised except where relatively rapid economic benefits can be realised. The influence in 2050 of each of the technologies described in the various chapters is summarised in table 2.4. For each of the generation technologies mentioned, the table gives the expected installed generation capacity, and the proportion of annual electrical energy demand supplied by that technology.

2.9   Green Plus

2.9.1   Scenario background

This scenario envisages a future in which environmental concerns relating to all aspects of electricity generation, transport and consumption become significantly stronger than today. Factors underlying this sharpening of attitudes include increasingly manifest effects of climate change on this country. Significantly increased constraints on energy use and on the generation and transport of electricity arise as a result of these environmental concerns. In particular, a disproportionate share of ambitious CO_2 emission reduction targets falls upon the electricity industry which is felt to be well placed to contribute to these goals.

Overall, the effect on the economy of this change in environmental attitude is largely neutral, as 'environmentally responsible' technologies become a significant area of national expertise and output. Technological growth in energy systems is strong, and focuses on improving environmental performance. Economic growth continues at recent rates over the period of this scenario. As a result, there is continued growth in the demand for energy services, offset by strong investment in energy efficiency measures which are supported by government incentives and regulations.

An important effect of the increased level of environmental concern is a strong increase in resistance to the impact of electricity networks. The construction of new transmission facilities is essentially impossible and there is strong pressure for the undergrounding or outright removal of existing circuits. New and refurbished distribution circuits are invariably undergrounded. Alternatives to oil-filled distribution equipment are sought in order to avoid an increasing regulatory burden aimed at the prevention of environmental contamination.

Local networks tend to become more diverse in this scenario, resulting in an increasing trend towards the local management and, possibly, ownership of networks. The development of microgrids is influenced by the need for local networks to exchange energy with the electricity system at large in response to local surfeits or shortfalls in generation. The scale of the adoption of local energy storage devices and the effectiveness of the local balancing of generation and load will determine the extent of such energy exchanges and trading.

In general, a liberalised and market-oriented approach to regulation is seen as successful, and is broadly retained. The government uses a combination of direct regulation and market-based mechanisms (analogous to the current carbon trading system) to provide incentives for significantly increased environmental responsibility on the part of energy users and generators and transporters of electricity.

There is widespread liberalisation of energy industries across Europe. Energy is increasingly traded on a European as well as national scale. This process is facilitated by increased interconnection capacity between European energy systems, including the development of a strategic European hydrogen network. These changes permit the development of markets in novel commodities, such as various forms of renewable energy, in which the United Kingdom is able to participate strongly. Markets also develop in various forms of environmentally focused permissions, such as emissions permits. This latter group of markets is promoted by the imposition of increasingly stringent limits on emissions.

The centralised national electricity market declines in importance, and is supplemented by a set of regional markets, and European markets. Market structures are optimised for decentralised generation and control and the large-scale deployment of both continuous sources and intermittent sources that are predictable over a range of timescales. Emissions trading (primarily in CO_2) becomes highly prevalent, extending to households and individuals, with a very high carbon price. Standard contractual agreements for domestic and office CHP and microgrids will be introduced, including such aspects as metering, automated demand-side energy management systems and automated building energy systems.

Ownership will be decentralised into many specialist companies in a variety of areas, including energy services; energy and emissions trading; system control and optimisation; and local system operation.

2.9.2   2050 electricity network

In this scenario, the strong application of efficiency measures reduces the demand for energy services. However, electricity use increases moderately by 2050, as the initial deployment of fossil-fuelled CHP systems on the grounds of efficiency gives way to the use of electrically driven heat pumps to meet a large proportion of the space and water heating requirements from carbon-free energy sources. The overall result is that electricity consumption increases on average by up to 0.25 per cent annually until 2050, giving an annual electricity demand of approximately 390TWh. The variability of electricity demand is strongly reduced in comparison with the present situation, as a result of the strong deployment of demand-side control and increased domestic-scale generation. Peak load is thus reduced to around 50GW.

Renewable energy accounts for around 80 per cent of generation in this scenario. Figure 2.5 illustrates the location of these renewable generators and other features likely to be important in the *Green Plus* scenario. Offshore wind is the significant renewable source, accounting for almost a half of this total, with major concentrations of generation in the Irish Sea, around south-east England, including East Anglia and the Thames Estuary, and off the Scottish coast. Large developments of several hundred MW are common, typically using turbines of 30 to 40MW. The rapid early adoption of onshore wind generation leads to development in more remote rural areas, including northern and southern Scotland, central Wales and south-west England. However, this development is subsequently restricted by concern over the environmental impact of onshore wind. Thus, most developments are relatively small, at no more than 200MW, and use turbines no larger than the 5 to 10MW range. By 2050 onshore wind accounts for 5 per cent to 10 per cent of total generation. At this point, any new

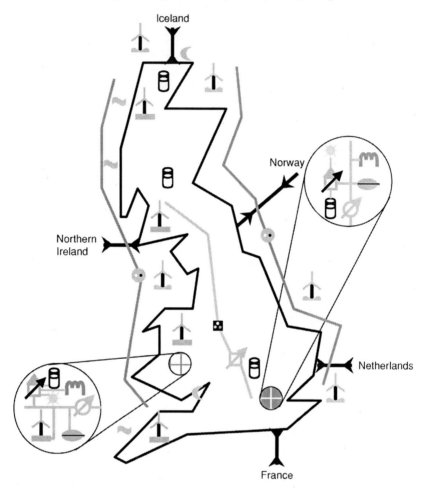

Figure 2.5. *Green Plus* scenario: electricity network in 2050.

onshore wind developments will be small-scale community-focused schemes deeply embedded within local distribution networks.

Biomass, largely in the form of combustion turbines fed by gasification accounts for the second largest share of generation, at around 25 per cent. There is a strong increase in the cultivation of energy crops to support the needs of biomass generation. In order to minimise the requirement for the transportation of raw biomass, power plants tend to be relatively small, and will connect to local or regional power networks rather than to the national transmission system.

Marine energy sources account for a further 5 per cent to 10 per cent of generation. Wave energy is exploited on the west coast of Scotland, in the Western Isles and in south-west England, with tidal generation being sited in the Bristol Channel and the Pentland Firth. In both these cases large numbers of small generators are preferred to a few intrusive, high-capacity devices.

Small-scale systems will account for 5 per cent of generation from renewable sources, in the form of technologies such as photovoltaics and small hydro, with capacity measured in kW. These will be connected either to local distribution networks or integrated at the customer level. The other 20 per cent of generation will be supplied by CHP systems.

Interconnector capacity to mainland Europe will be increased through reinforcement of the existing link and the construction of new capacity. In addition, new interconnectors will be constructed to Iceland and Norway, both rich in renewable resources. In the regulatory environment outlined above, the ability to exploit cheap, reliable and plentiful renewable resources will make the construction of these interconnectors attractive to investors; a contribution from government or EU sources in recognition of the environmental benefits of such a scheme is also possible. The scale of energy transfers across these interconnectors will be dependent on the day-to-day availability of intermittent renewable resources and stored energy reserves across the European energy market. It is therefore likely that these flows will exhibit some volatility. Since significant 'through traffic' between Iceland and Scandinavia across these interconnectors is likely, energy flows in this country's transmission network may be similarly volatile.

The overall effect of these developments will be a strong increase in the demand for electricity transmission from remote renewable sources to urban load centres and to and from interconnector landfall points. As noted above, it will become more difficult to predict energy flows in the electricity system more than three or four hours ahead. At the same time, resistance to the environmental impact of the overhead transmission network will lead to pressure for the removal or undergrounding of much of the network. To address these conflicting needs, high-capacity DC transmission circuits will be constructed off the east and west coast of Great Britain, connected at strategic points to the onshore transmission network and to interconnector terminal points. DC connections may also be projected inland to major load centres using superconducting technology. These new facilities will take on much of the north–south transmission role of the existing network, resulting in the rationalisation of its capacity and the undergrounding of much of the remaining system, which will fulfil the role of the onward transport of electricity from a small number of DC terminal points to load centres.

Given the modest load growth, and environmentally driven pressure for reductions in transmission assets, there will be a requirement to maximise the use of onshore transmission capacity. These needs will be addressed through the deployment of advanced control systems in conjunction with advanced power electronic devices. Superconductors will be used to provide increased capacity over more conventional systems where space is at a premium, such as in cities. Environmental objections to oil-filled and SF_6-based plant will see conventional transformers and switchgear replaced by power electronic devices incorporating one or both of these roles, together with the provision of fast-acting compensation linked to fast-acting energy storage systems. These developments will be paralleled by developments in sub-station technology that reduce the environmental impact of the power system while improving capacity and reliability.

Strategic large-scale energy storage systems will be located close to concentrations of generation and near major load centres in order to smooth the flow of electricity over the transmission system. At times of high transmission utilisation, energy will be accumulated close to generation and released from storage systems at load centres. The balance will be restored through additional transfers at 'quiet' times. Furthermore, energy storage will increasingly be integrated with remote intermittent generation such as wave, wind and tidal developments, in order to optimise the utilisation of the grid connection and to enable more effective participation in energy markets. A variety of energy storage technologies will be used. Flow cells are likely to feature prominently, although, where there is ready access to a hydrogen transport network, large fuel cell installations are likely to be used instead. Smaller, more cost-sensitive installations, such as those associated with individual renewable energy developments, may use batteries or flywheels. One or two strategic pumped storage facilities may be constructed in remote areas.

As noted previously, small-scale CHP systems, embedded in local networks, will account for 20 per cent of total generation. Most of these generators are likely to use fuel cell technology consuming hydrogen. Most hydrogen consumed in the United Kingdom will be produced by large-scale natural gas reformation with carbon capture. There will also be significant hydrogen imports, and some will be electrically produced at times of low demand for electricity, often in conjunction with energy storage systems. Biomass and 'dual-fuel' CHP will be developed at a 'community scale' in some rural areas, while small biomass CHP will be applied in remote parts of the country. Small gas turbine technology is likely to be used in these latter two applications. In urban areas, waste-fuelled generation may contribute to district heating schemes. As noted previously, significant quantities of small-scale renewable generation, such as photovoltaics, and small wind and hydro generators will be integrated into local networks, amounting to as much as 5 per cent of generation.

There will be widespread deployment of advanced building control systems, integrating control of demand, energy storage and generation systems for new buildings. By 2050 integrated building management systems will have been fitted to the majority of older buildings as well. These systems will optimise the environmental outcomes of energy use, and provide information to customers about, for example, the current availability of renewably generated electricity to help in making decisions about electricity consumption. Integration of all forms of energy consumption within these systems will permit participation in household-scale emissions trading schemes.

Many new buildings will be designed to accommodate small renewable generators such as photovoltaics and small wind turbines within their structure. Some retrofitting of such generators to existing buildings will also take place. Small-scale energy storage systems will also be integrated with buildings, sometimes forming part of fuel-cell-based CHP systems. Participation in demand-side control schemes will take place on a very large scale.

All these developments will lead to the widespread deployment of microgrid technologies. Power electronic systems will control the interfaces between the microgrid and the regional electricity system and between individual generators, customers and the microgrid. The operation of the microgrid will be facilitated by a novel set of localised markets, which will be designed to optimise the use of available generation and storage resources as well as the capacity of the microgrid and its grid connection. Interaction between microgrids and the regional and national electricity systems will be governed by a further set of markets. Microgrid operators may opt to invest in medium-scale energy storage systems in order to serve better the needs of their customers, or to improve their position in regional markets.

2.9.3   Scenario summary

The *Green Plus* scenario represents a case in which environmental concerns are paramount. Renewable generation technologies are strongly deployed; other technologies are adopted in order to permit this technological shift

Table 2.5 *Technology application in the* Green Plus *scenario*

Chapter	Technology	Scope of application
3	Wind generation	Very strong: largest single generation source. Total installed capacity is around 60GW, with the great majority offshore. 45–50 per cent of electricity is generated from wind.
4	Photovoltaic generation	Significant small-scale application, deeply embedded in distribution networks. Total capacity is around 10GW, producing 3–5 per cent of electricity.
5	Biomass electricity generation	Strong application of small-scale plants and CHP: total capacity is around 15GW, producing 25 per cent of energy.
6	Wave generation	Large application in relatively small developments With tidal generation, total marine capacity is 10–15GW, accounting for 5–10 per cent of electrical energy output.
7	CO_2 capture	No application in electricity generation. Significant role in hydrogen production.
8	Nuclear generation	No nuclear generation.
9	Microgeneration	Strong fuel cell deployment – total installed capacity around 10GW; micro-renewables are also important. Microgeneration supplies about 20 per cent of electrical energy consumption.
10	Superconductivity	Application in constrained locations and onshore HVDC.
11	Power electronics	Very extensive application in a variety of roles.
12	Hydrogen	Strong use in transport and as domestic/industrial fuel. Mainly produced from fossil sources.
13	Energy storage	Significant application in large-scale storage systems and integrated with renewable generation; interaction likely with hydrogen system.
14	End-use technologies	Strong emphasis on efficiency and reduction in energy use, with some deployment of small distributed generation.
15	Industrial electricity use	Widespread adoption of advanced technologies to improve energy efficiency. Some fuel switching takes place to take advantage of renewably generated electricity and avoid carbon trading costs. Cogeneration, including the use of waste heat and waste products from industrial processes, is integrated into the design of all new plants using turbine and advanced fuel cell technologies.
16	Transport	Increased use of electricity for rail transport; road transport mainly hydrogen-fuelled hybrid vehicles.
17	Smart metering	Strong application promotes awareness of the environmental consequences of electricity consumption and permits optimisation of electricity use to minimise emissions; commonly integrated into building control systems, but 'stand-alone' smart meters also exist.

while minimising the impact of the electricity network on the environment. The influence in 2050 of each of the technologies described in the various chapters is summarised in table 2.5. For each of the generation technologies mentioned, the table gives the expected installed generation capacity, and the proportion of annual electrical energy demand supplied by that technology.

2.10   Technological Restriction

2.10.1   Scenario background

This scenario shares with the *Strong Optimism* scenario a sustained level of strong economic growth above recent rates. However, in this scenario there is much less importance attached by investors, researchers and technologists to the creation and development of power generation, transmission, distribution and end-use technologies. Research funding and effort is instead channelled preferentially into other areas of innovation, such as biotechnology or advanced computing and communications technology, where greater opportunities for innovation and returns on invested effort and money are perceived. Technological advance in energy systems is therefore mainly confined to the evolution of existing technologies and the deployment of those currently in development.

Environmental consciousness strengthens somewhat in comparison to current levels, but not to the extent of the *Green Plus* scenario. As a result, resistance to the environmental impact of electricity networks continues to increase, so that the construction of new transmission facilities becomes virtually impossible, and there is significant pressure for the undergrounding of existing circuits at all levels of the network.

Strong economic growth leads to a corresponding increase in the demand for energy services, as people can afford to purchase new devices, and their performance expectations improve. The air-conditioning of domestic properties becomes more common. This effect is offset to a degree by the increased application of energy efficiency measures, including improved building design, the effect of which is supported by the relatively high turnover of building stock, which the economy can support. The adoption of energy efficiency is motivated by a combination of economic and environmental factors.

The current liberalised regulatory arrangements remain in force, with the government committed to market-based approaches. However, as the difficulties and costs imposed by rising electricity demand and increased renewable generation become clear, modifications are progressively made to the regulatory regime to encourage greater installation of small-scale generation and participation in demand-side control schemes. Liberalisation of electricity markets across Europe continues. However, technological constraints mean that electricity interconnectors remain costly and development is thus limited, with more focus being placed on gas importation. UK participation in European electricity markets is therefore restricted. There is strong development of European markets for emissions trading. Trading of CO_2 extends to industrial and commercial users, with a moderate to high price for carbon.

As with the *Strong Optimism* scenario, there will be two main levels of electricity market that will develop in the United Kingdom. The first level will consist of a series of local markets, corresponding to microgrids and local networks, with participation by small-scale demand and generation. In addition to local energy markets, markets in energy services at the local level are likely to develop. To encourage the adoption of small-scale generation and efficient use of the network, these markets may be encouraged by regulators to offer novel services, such as portfolio management of domestic-scale generation or real-time trading of network capacity entitlements. These local markets will underpin a single national market, in which large-scale wind, marine, biomass and 'conventional' plants will participate, as will larger-scale consumers and the limited interconnector capacity. Much of the back-up generation capacity to support intermittent renewable sources is provided by participants in this market, although market mechanisms to encourage the use of small-scale generation and CHP for this purpose are progressively developed. Market structures develop to support a high level of renewables, but little storage.

Existing ownership patterns are likely to remain unchanged in relation to networks and large generators, but are likely to be paralleled by the development of energy service companies operating in the domestic/small energy demand market. Local ownership of microgrids and small-scale generation is likely to increase.

Small-scale CHP generation does not show strong development at the outset as a result of high initial costs. However, constraints on the electricity network as a result of rising demand and renewable penetration become increasingly costly to satisfy, and, as it becomes clear that environmental aspirations cannot be satisfied through renewables due to disappointing technological progress, increasing incentives for the adoption of small-scale generation and demand-side controls are put in place. CHP remains natural-gas-fired, with limited development of fuel cell or hydrogen systems. The management of local networks therefore becomes appreciably more complex, with a trend towards more localised management and, in some cases, ownership of these networks. Local networks with strong concentrations of embedded generation and demand-side control will become increasingly autonomous and may become able to operate largely in isolation from the electricity network at large.

2.10.2   2050 electricity network

Strong economic growth in this scenario leads to an increase in business and industrial activity. As described above, new and more capable devices are purchased, and people tend to be able to afford to use more energy to increase the comfort of their daily lives, leading to a corresponding increase in the demand for energy services. These factors are offset to a degree by the increased application of energy efficiency measures, motivated by a combination of economic and environmental factors, so that demand for electricity grows at an annual average rate of about 1.5 per cent, within current geographic patterns, to reach some 680TWh/year in 2050. Increased participation in demand-side control schemes tends to divert electricity use away from peak times so that the variability of demand tends to reduce somewhat, but growth in the peak load value continues, remaining significantly above the average load by 2050 at approximately 100GW.

Renewable generation accounts for approximately 40 per cent of generation. Figure 2.6 illustrates the location of these renewable generators and other features likely to be important in the *Technological Restriction* scenario. Onshore wind takes the largest share of renewable generation at around 20 per cent of the total. Individual wind farms of up to 1,000MW are developed, although turbine sizes are restricted to around 15MW on the grounds of technological capability and environmental impact. Offshore wind will remain restricted to relatively shallow-water sites, usually close to land, and will thus be restricted by environmental impact concerns to a few sites. Its economic potential is restricted as turbine sizes reach a plateau. In general, the deployment of intermittent renewable generation, such as wind, is restricted by concerns over the extent to which the transmission network can accommodate it. The risk of significant output constraints being placed upon new development weakens the economic case for their construction.

Biomass is the other major renewable energy source, with between 15 per cent and 20 per cent of total generation, mainly in the form of large combustion-based plants in rural areas. Some small, community-focused biomass generation will also be developed. The market penetration of biomass generation is restricted by the difficulty of producing and

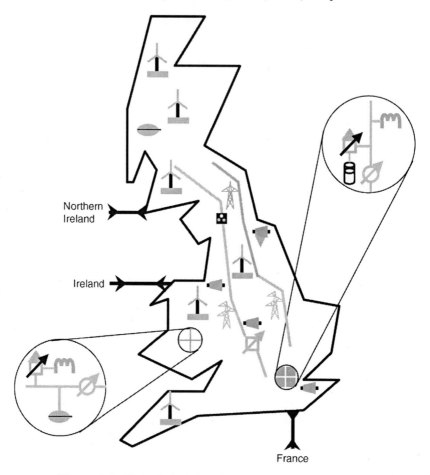

Figure 2.6. *Technological Restriction* scenario: electricity network in 2050.

transporting biomass to the generation plant. Other renewable energy sources will account for a small proportion of the total generation. Marine and tidal energy will be confined to a few developments on the Scottish coastline, and will not be widely deployed, while photovoltaic technology will remain too costly for wide application.

The majority of generation will be in the form of large CCGT stations, accounting for between 40 per cent and 50 per cent of the total. This generation will be located at existing generation sites, with preference being given to locations close to load centres. This generation will tend to be concentrated in the Midlands and South-East to balance the exploitation of renewable energy resources in Scotland and the North. About 10 per cent of the CCGT fleet in 2050 will be equipped for carbon capture and sequestration. These will be the more recently constructed units, which are at convenient locations for access to carbon storage facilities. In the early twenty-first century nuclear generation technology remains expensive and continues to suffer difficulties with public acceptance, while the problems of long-term waste storage are not resolved. No new nuclear generation is built in this scenario: by 2050 all nuclear generation capacity has been eliminated.

The remaining 20 per cent of generation will be accounted for by small CHP generation, although initial development is slow, because capital costs reduce only slowly. However, as the constraints on the electricity network brought about by rising demand become increasingly onerous and costly, and it becomes clear that disappointing techno-logical progress means that environmental aspirations cannot be met by the large-scale deployment of renewables or carbon capture, incen-tives and market modification are put in place to encourage greater investment in small-scale generation and CHP. Such plants will take the form of small natural-gas-fuelled turbines or Stirling Engines. Oper-ationally, CHP will generally be run to meet heat demand, and many new urban development schemes will include larger CHP systems asso-ciated with district heating schemes operated by energy service pro-viders. Some small-scale wind and biomass generation will also be connected to local electricity networks.

Existing interconnectors are refurbished and renewed as necessary, but the pace of technological change means that expansion of capacity is unattractive to investors. Thus, there is no large-scale extension of interconnector capacity. A relatively small-capacity increase to the Re-public of Ireland is, however, developed with support from public bodies, in order to integrate Ireland better into the European electricity market.

Demand for electricity transmission increases as a consequence of load growth, this effect being increased at those times of the year when there is strong availability of renewable energy in the North. At such times, full exploitation of these resources may be prevented by lack of transmission capacity. Transmission capacity will be maximised through the extensive application of advanced control systems, in conjunction with strategic deployment of power electronic FACTS-like devices. Some strategic transmission routes may be converted to HVDC in order to increase capacity without unacceptable environmental impact. The geographical location of new generators becomes considerably more important in controlling demands made on the network.

Superconductors may be deployed in one or two key instances where increased density of power flow in a constrained space is necessary – for example, in central London – but will remain too expensive and technically complex for more general application.

There will be increased concern over the potential environmental impact of leaks from oil-filled plant, together with the risk of safety hazards. These issues will be applicable at all levels of the power network, but will be particularly acute at transmission level. While there will be some replacement of this plant with oil-free equipment at lower voltages, technical and cost issues will prevent such substitution at transmission level. Comprehensive condition-monitoring systems will therefore be developed and applied to transmission transformers and other large oil-filled equipment in order to detect developing problems.

Energy storage systems will be restricted to devices aimed at improving power quality for specific sensitive customers; any increased requirement for large strategic systems will be met by intelligent generation dispatch systems incorporating reserve management capabilities and demand-side control schemes.

Microgrids will be relatively widely applied, but will use relatively simple devices and control systems. A combination of generation dispatch and local demand-side control schemes will attempt to ensure approximate system balance, but as local energy storage systems will be technically complex and too expensive for general application there will be significant import and export of energy from the microgrid to the national network, depending on local loading conditions.

Regulatory policy remains liberalised and market-based, but modifications are progressively made to permit network operators to exert greater control by sending much stronger market signals to electricity generators and consumers in respect of both their location and their day-to-day behaviour. As a result, participation in demand-side control schemes is strongly encouraged. There is increasing liberalisation of European markets and regulation along similar lines to that in the United Kingdom, which results in the development of markets in energy and services spanning multiple countries. However, the limited ability to import and export electricity restricts the ability of the United Kingdom to participate in these markets. Nevertheless, there is strong participation in a single European market in CO_2 emissions.

Within the United Kingdom, a series of linked local and national markets will coordinate the activities of individual customers and generators, local networks and the national transmission network. As with the

Table 2.6 *Technology application in the* Technological Restriction *scenario*

Chapter	Technology	Scope of application
3	Wind generation	Mainly restricted to onshore wind; large in absolute but not relative terms. Installed capacity around 45–50GW, accounting for 20 per cent of electrical energy generated.
4	Photovoltaic generation	Little application because of high cost.
5	Biomass electricity generation	Tends to appear as relatively large-scale plants. Moderate contribution to electricity supply, accounting for 15–20 per cent of electrical energy produced. Installed capacity is around 20GW.
6	Wave generation	Applied in a few niche opportunities. Installed capacity is around 3GW, producing 1–2 per cent of total electrical energy.
7	CO_2 capture	Around 5GW of newest CCGT capacity equipped by 2050.
8	Nuclear generation	No nuclear generation.
9	Microgeneration	Becomes more important later in scenario; gas-fired using developments of current technology. By 2050 installed capacity is around 20GW, supplying 20 per cent of electrical energy consumption.
10	Superconductivity	Very limited network application in a few constrained locations.
11	Power electronics	Applications include advanced network control and compensation systems, renewal or refurbishment of interconnectors and HVDC; also some application in microgrids.
12	Hydrogen	Little influence on electricity network.
13	Energy storage	Confined to small-scale systems focusing on power quality improvement.
14	End-use technologies	Energy efficiency develops progressively; distributed generation and community heating schemes develop later.
15	Industrial electricity use	Improvements in energy efficiency tend to make use of incremental developments of existing technologies; more radical technologies are expensive or present reliability problems. Small-scale generation and cogeneration develops first in industry, using turbine and reciprocating engine technology, achieving significant penetration as a means to improve energy efficiency.
16	Transport	Some increase in rail electrification, but otherwise little influence on electricity network; fossil-fuelled hybrid road vehicles increase in popularity.
17	Smart metering	Regional application in support of market and tariff schemes reflecting network congestion; automated management of selected devices to reduce consumption when costs are high.

Strong Optimism scenario, there will be two main levels of electricity market. A series of local markets corresponding to microgrid and local networks with participation by small-scale demand and generation will underpin a single national market, in which large-scale renewables and 'conventional' plants will participate, as will larger-scale consumers and the limited interconnector capacity. Much of the back-up generation capacity to support intermittent renewable sources is provided by participants in this market, although market mechanisms to encourage the use of small-scale generation and CHP for this purpose are progressively developed.

2.10.3 Scenario summary

The *Technological Restriction* scenario represents a case in which strong economic growth and growth in the demand for electricity are not matched by strong technological progress. Restrictions in the flexibility and capability of the power network impose significant constraints on the nature and location of generators. Renewable generation technologies are deployed in relatively large absolute volumes, but make up a comparatively small proportion of overall capacity and use relatively simple technology; other technologies are adopted in order to manage the pressure of increased demand on a technologically relatively undeveloped electricity network. Market mechanisms are also important in this regard. The influence in 2050 of each of the technologies described in the various chapters is summarised in table 2.6. For each of the generation technologies mentioned, the table gives the expected installed generation capacity, and the proportion of annual electrical energy demand supplied by that technology.

2.11   Central Direction

2.11.1 Scenario background

This scenario takes the replacement of current liberal regulatory attitudes with a more prescriptive approach by central government as its focus. A strongly centralising approach is one possible outcome of an increased level of governmental involvement and intervention in the electricity industry. Other possibilities might include a more regional or local model, in which government bodies at those levels exercise strong directive control over the industry, or a mixed approach, in which different aspects of the industry (such as the exploitation of renewable energy resources, or the planning and regulation of transmission and distribution networks, for example) are controlled at different levels of decentralisation.

The centralised approach presented here has been selected for particular examination since it might plausibly be presented as an approach that reflects the importance of the electricity system to the United Kingdom as a whole, and that would be expected to lead to improved planning processes to give a better allocation and deployment of available energy resources and network capabilities in the national interest.

Pressure for more prescriptive government involvement and control may arise as a result of perceived inadequate responses of the liberalised industry to major events or the apparently inefficient use of resources, and could be compared to current government attitudes towards the railway industry. Notwithstanding the effects of the triggering events, general economic growth continues at broadly the same rates as in the recent past, and the economy as a whole remains liberalised; there is no move towards increased government control over industry in general. As a result, growing personal wealth and industrial activity tend to drive up the demand for energy-consuming appliances and energy services. This trend is counteracted by energy efficiency initiatives promoted by government incentives and regulations. Electricity demand therefore increases by a small amount.

Technologically, government policy is to focus on relatively low-risk, well-proven technologies, rather than highly innovative strategies. As a result, technical development of power network equipment is focused on the evolution of existing technologies and the application of those in development.

Environmental awareness sharpens somewhat in comparison to the current situation and is reflected in government actions. Public acceptance of the environmental impact of electricity networks continues to decline, with corresponding changes in government policy. There is, therefore, a tendency to invest in higher-capacity technology when refurbishing existing facilities and to require the undergrounding of existing circuits in environmentally sensitive areas. Government direction is used to concentrate circuits into a smaller number of corridors. The geographical location of new generation becomes increasingly important in managing constraints on the network and becomes the subject of strong government direction in order to balance the direct environmental impact of new generation against its effects on the network.

In addition to directing the development of the electricity network, the government exercises considerable influence and control over the United Kingdom's generation mix, and over the technical standards required of generators. Rather than approving or rejecting proposals for new generators created and put forward by investors and generating companies, tenders are invited for the construction, operation and ownership of generators of particular types in general geographical locations. Where such a requirement is commercially unattractive, financial support for capital or running costs may be offered. Such schemes may be coupled to initiatives in other areas, such as agricultural incentives to promote the farming of biomass feedstocks. The preference of the government is generally for a smaller number of projects at a larger scale. Embedded generation is encouraged through other approaches. CHP at medium scale develops strongly as part of district heating schemes for new office and housing build, driven by planning requirements.

Strong regulation of local electricity networks is a feature of this scenario, with operators being obliged to meet strict quality-of-supply measures. There are also targets in relation to the connection of embedded generators to these networks. However, such generators will be regulated so as not to give rise to serious problems of network management, since the government will wish to favour simple and well-established approaches, which may include requiring some measure of compulsory participation in demand-side control initiatives. Overall, there will be little scope for increased local network autonomy.

While energy markets continue to exist, they become subject to greatly increased government intervention in both their structure and in the behaviour of participants. As government focus is likely to be on simple and robust solutions that reliably deliver expected outcomes, there will be a simplification of market structures, with a series of markets focused on single commodities or services. Participants in these markets will be subject to compulsory licensing, and behaviour will be closely scrutinised by regulators. Certain participants in some markets may be obliged to participate in others as well; for example, operators of some generators in an energy market may be obliged to offer balancing services. Companies encountering financial difficulty exchange government financial support for an increased measure of government control.

There is increased EU and bilateral governmental intervention in cross-border European energy transport and trading. There is some government-supported investment in interconnector capacity, but political uncertainty over long-term prospects means that focus is primarily given to gas interconnectors; electricity interconnectors tend to be the subject of EU-supported development. Markets for emissions trading tend to be replaced by prescriptive limits imposed by national governments to meet EU requirements, operating on per-plant and per-company bases.

Changes to market structures favour the concentration of ownership into a small number of vertically integrated companies, each having a diverse portfolio of assets in order to minimise market and regulatory risk. Emerging companies specialising in particular technologies and activities are likely to be short-lived and will either fail or be absorbed into large organisations.

2.11.2   2050 electricity network

In this scenario, economic growth tends to cause an increase in the demand for energy services. However, effective energy efficiency incentives and regulations mean that growth in demand for electricity is more restricted, and averages around 0.5 per cent annually over the scenario period to approximately 430TWh in 2050, mostly within current geographical patterns. Demand-side control schemes do not attract general favour, while CHP tends to operate to meet heat load; thus, the variability of electricity demand is largely unchanged. Peak load is approximately 70GW.

In this scenario, renewable generation rises to between 50 per cent and 60 per cent of total generation, and is divided equally between onshore wind, offshore wind, biomass and marine generation. The geographical areas of application of these forms of generation are decided centrally by the government and are illustrated in figure 2.7. Offshore wind is mainly located in relatively shallow water in the Irish Sea and off East Anglia. Large developments of between 500 and 1,000MW are favoured, with machine size progressively increasing to around 30MW. There is strong development of onshore wind resources in Scotland, together with sites in central Wales. Individual wind farms of around 300MW are preferred, with machines restricted to about 15MW on the grounds of environmental impact.

Biomass generation is located in rural areas, in which the growth of energy crops is encouraged by agriculture policy. In order to limit problems related to the transport of biomass, preference is given to small- to medium-scale plants. Initially, combustion-based generation will be preferred, possibly co-firing with fossil fuel. As technology develops, most plants operating in 2050 will make use of gasification processes feeding combined-cycle turbines.

Wave generation will be deployed extensively along the west coast of Scotland, in the Western Isles and in south-west England. Policy will favour the use of large numbers of small generation systems in preference to expensive and more technically adventurous large units. Tidal

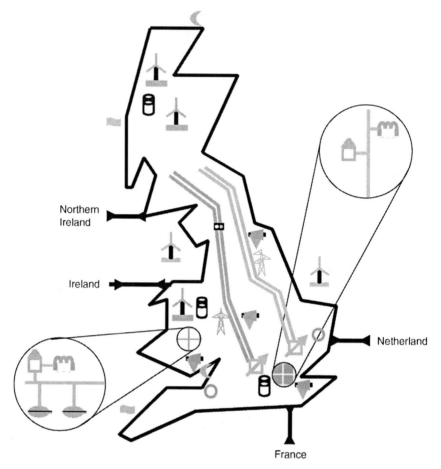

Figure 2.7. *Central Direction* scenario: electricity network in 2050.

generation developments will be located in the Bristol Channel and the Pentland Firth. Other forms of renewable generation are not favoured by government policy, on the grounds of perceived value for money or technical risk, and do not see significant application.

Large central power plants will account for 25 per cent to 30 per cent of generation. Most of these power plants will take the form of large CCGT generators, which will be required to participate in government-sponsored carbon capture and sequestration schemes. The construction of carbon transportation and storage infrastructure will be facilitated by government in harmony with planned generation development, which will in general be located close to major load centres and in areas in which renewable resources are not strongly developed. As new nuclear technologies mature there is increased interest in the construction of nuclear power stations, and a small number of new facilities, promoted on the grounds of energy security, are constructed on existing sites, beginning as the last of the current fleet is decommissioned. The remaining 10 per cent to 20 per cent of generation is composed of CHP systems, as described further below.

Existing interconnectors to mainland Europe will be retained and increased in capacity as renewal is required. A second European interconnector of similar capacity will be constructed to permit increased participation in European energy markets and to gain additional energy security benefits from increased access to a greater diversity of generation. An interconnector of modest capacity to the Republic of Ireland will extend these energy security benefits to that country. Long interconnectors to Iceland and Scandinavia will be eschewed as a result of the technical risk associated with their length and depth.

The result of these changes in the level of demand and the pattern of generation is that there is strongly increased demand for the transmission of electricity. Government preference is for this challenge to be met using mature, low-risk technological solutions. Therefore, transmission capacity along existing corridors is increased by the construction of new transmission assets. There may be some rationalisation of transmission corridors in cases of particular environmental impact, but movement in this direction is likely to be very limited as a result of risk-averse attitudes to system security. The undergrounding of sensitive sections of route is regarded as a more appropriate response in most cases.

Large-scale strategic energy storage systems using pumped storage, electrolytic or hydrogen technology according to local conditions will be used to alleviate peak transmission loads, and to enhance system security in conjunction with advanced control and compensation equipment installed at a significant number of sub-stations. With the exception of a few power-quality-driven small-scale installations, this is the only application of energy storage technology.

In a few cases, complete transmission routes will be converted to HVDC in order to maximise capacity and to eliminate otherwise unavoidable constraints on the operation of the system. Superconductors will be used in specific cases where space constraints require particularly high energy transmission densities. However, concerns over their long-term reliability and cost constraints prevent their wider application; the installation of additional conventional transmission assets is felt to be a more robust solution.

As noted above, CHP will account for between 10 per cent and 20 per cent of total generation. Planning regulations will require that new commercial and residential developments above a stipulated size in urban areas must either include integrated CHP – which will be relatively large – or participate in a district heating scheme. Smaller developments and those in rural areas will feature domestic-scale CHP systems. There will be modest support for retrofitting such systems to existing properties. Most of these CHP systems are likely to be natural-gas-fuelled turbine or Stirling Engine units; by 2050 the general adoption of fuel cell technology will have begun, but the vast majority of the CHP fleet will use a development of current technology and will be operated to meet heat demand. Many small biomass generators will also connect to local electricity networks.

Microgrid technology will not see widespread deployment, as the government will place strong emphasis on the benefits of an integrated national electricity network. Microgrid deployment will therefore be restricted to 'power parks' associated with technology-based companies having particular power quality requirements.

Demand-side control schemes will develop in a relatively small number of cases where local demand rapidly outstrips the capacity of the distribution network. However, the preferred approach in such cases will be limited network reinforcement in combination with more generalised incentives to reduce consumption. Plant recovered from network reinforcement schemes will be deployed elsewhere, either to replace life-expired equipment or to provide further reinforcement.

Government policies on social inclusion and fuel poverty are supported by novel energy pricing strategies and tariffs, facilitated by advanced metering. Such tariffs feature the automated management of 'essential services' such as space and water heating; these benefits are available to all at a reduced cost in exchange for a reduction in energy use at peak times. Smart meters also provide improved information to support the responsible use of energy for other purposes and in other pricing plans. Metering becomes a nationally regulated monopoly.

The extension of railway electrification is promoted by the government to achieve environmental benefits and an improved quality of service. However, while main routes benefit, cost constraints preclude universal electrification. The effect on the electricity system is in any case relatively small. Increasingly stringent emissions regulations for

Table 2.7 *Technology application in the* Central Direction *scenario*

Chapter	Technology	Scope of application
3	Wind generation	Strong application. Total wind generation capacity is 35–40GW, equally divided between onshore and offshore, and supplying 25 per cent of electrical energy generated.
4	Photovoltaic generation	Not favoured by government policy: very little deployment.
5	Biomass electricity generation	Many small to medium-sized facilities plus small CHP. Total capacity is around 8GW, accounting for 10–15 per cent of electrical energy produced.
6	Wave generation	Strong application in many relatively small developments. Including tidal generation total installed capacity is around 15GW, meeting 10–15 per cent of electrical energy demand.
7	CO_2 capture	Applied to all new CCGT plant (around 15GW, 20–25 per cent of energy).
8	Nuclear generation	A small number of power plants, using new technology if feasible. Installed capacity is approximately 5GW, accounting for 5–10 per cent of electricity produced.
9	Microgeneration	Applied for rural CHP and small or retrofit developments. Most CHP in the form of larger multi-user systems. Total microgeneration capacity is around 10–15GW, and supplies 10–20 per cent of electricity demand.
10	Superconductivity	Little application: viewed as poor long-term value in network applications.
11	Power electronics	Applications include advanced network control and compensation systems, interconnector upgrading and microgeneration; little application in microgrids.
12	Hydrogen	Primary application is energy storage.
13	Energy storage	A few large strategic hydrogen and pumped storage systems are built. Little small-scale storage.
14	End-use technologies	Energy efficiency promoted by government; distributed generation and community heating schemes encouraged by planning regulations.
15	Industrial electricity use	Government and European incentives and regulations promote the adoption of technological measures to increase efficiency. Planning and economic incentives to integrate cogeneration with wider community heating schemes where possible.
16	Transport	Some increase in rail electrification, but otherwise little influence on electricity network; fossil-fuelled hybrid road vehicles increasingly promoted by government.
17	Smart metering	Strong application, supporting policies on fuel poverty and responsible energy use; metering activities undertaken by a regulated monopoly.

road vehicles are addressed by the development of more efficient and flexible fossil-fuelled hybrid vehicles.

2.11.3   Scenario summary

The *Central Direction* scenario represents a case in which central government imposes a strongly interventionist regulatory regime on the electricity industry. A mix of generator types, in which renewables are strongly represented, is deployed, with generation technologies being concentrated in specific geographical areas. Network reinforcement, careful siting of generation and large strategic energy storage systems are the preferred approach to accommodating the increasing demands on the electricity network. The influence in 2050 of each of the technologies described in the various chapters is summarised in table 2.7. For each of the generation technologies mentioned, the table gives the expected installed generation capacity, and the proportion of annual electrical energy demand supplied by that technology.

2.12   Conclusions

The development of the electricity network in the United Kingdom over the years to 2050 will be influenced by a number of uncertain factors. Some of these factors are economic in character, such as the rate of growth or change in demand for electricity, or the availability of finance for investment in electricity infrastructure. Others, such as the system of regulation or the level of environmental consciousness in society, are of a more political nature. A third group of influences is technological: the rate at which the technologies discussed in this book, and others, are developed and applied.

This chapter has presented six scenarios of possible future electricity systems that may develop in Great Britain in the years to 2050. The main features of each are presented in tables 2.8 and 2.9.

While these scenarios might not appear to be particularly radical or adventurous, many of them nonetheless represent a significant but plausible shift away from current network structures and practices. Given the long life and relatively high cost of electricity network plant, particularly at transmission level, it is likely that considerable and sustained effort may be required over the coming decades for electricity networks to meet some of the possible challenges of the twenty-first century. The technologies discussed in this book will have an important role to play in these changes.

Table 2.8 *Summary of key scenario features (I)*

Scenario	Average annual demand growth	2050 electricity demand (TWh)	2050 peak electricity demand (GW)	Important network technologies
Strong Optimism	+1.25%	600	80	Advanced control and FACTS Energy storage Superconducting transmission Microgrids
Business as Usual	+1%	540	80	Advanced control and FACTS Strategic energy storage Asset management
Economic Downturn	−0.5%	275	45	Remote control of local networks Life extension Condition monitoring
Green Plus	+0.25%	390	50	Interconnectors and offshore HVDC Network control and compensation systems Large- and small-scale energy storage Microgrids Demand-side participation
Technological Restriction	+1.5%	680	100	Advanced control and FACTS HVDC Simple microgrids Condition monitoring
Central Direction	+0.5%	430	70	Large-scale energy storage HVDC Network control and compensation systems Demand-side participation

Table 2.9 *Summary of key scenario features (II)*

Scenario	Total generation capacity (GW)	Renewable generation (% of total capacity)	Renewable generation (% of total energy)	Central generation (% of total capacity)	Central generation (% of total energy)
Strong Optimism	145	60–70%	50%	10–20%	10–20%
Business as Usual	110	40–50%	30%	45%	50%
Economic Downturn	55	20–30%	10–20%	65%	75%
Green Plus	110	90%	80%	0%	0%
Technological Restriction	135	50–60%	40%	30%	40–50%
Central Direction	100	60%	50–60%	20–25%	25–30%

2.13   References

As noted previously, a large number of information sources have been consulted in the preparation of the scenarios described in this chapter. Although they are not individually referenced in the text, this section lists the principal documents that have contributed to the development of the scenarios.

Abu-Sharkh, S., R. Li, T. Markvart, N. Ross, P. Wilson, R. Yao, K. Steemers, J. Köhler and R. Arnold (2005). *Can Microgrids Make a Major Contribution to UK Energy Supply?*, Working Paper no. 70, Tyndall Centre for Climate Change Research, University of East Anglia.

British Petroleum (2003). *Statistical Review of World Energy*, London: British Petroleum plc.

Building Research Establishment (2000). *Heat Pumps in the UK – A Monitoring Report*, Watford: Building Research Establishment Sustainable Energy Centre.

Chapman, J., R. Gross et al. (2001). *Working Paper on Generating Technologies: Potentials and Cost Reductions to 2020*, London: Cabinet Office.

DEFRA (2004). *Energy Efficiency: The Government's Plan for Action*, London: Department of Environment, Food and Rural Affairs.

DGCG (2004). *Minutes of Tenth DGCG Meeting*, London: Distributed Generation Coordination Group.

DTI (2000). *Energy Projections for the UK: Energy Use and Energy-Related Emissions of Carbon Dioxide in the UK 2000 – 2020*, London: Department of Trade and Industry.

(2003a). *Options for a Low-Carbon Future*, DTI Economics Paper no. 4, London: Department of Trade and Industry.

(2003b). *Digest of United Kingdom Energy Statistics 2003*, London: Department of Trade and Industry.

(2003c). *Our Energy Future: Creating a Low-Carbon Economy*, Energy White Paper no. 68, Cm 5761, London: Department of Trade and Industry, available from http://www.dti.gov.uk/energy/whitepaper/ourenergyfuture.pdf.

(2003d). *Oil and Gas Statistics*, London: Department of Trade and Industry.

Energy Futures Task Force (2001). *Foresight: Energy for Tomorrow: Powering the 21st Century*, London: Department of Trade and Industry.

Energy Review Advisory Group (2001). *Working Paper on Energy Systems in 2050*, London: Cabinet Office.

Fergusson, M. (2001). *Analysis for PIU on Transport in the Energy Review*, London: Institute for European Environmental Policy.

Hassler, S. (ed.) (2004). Special Report: 2004 Technology Forecast and Review, *IEEE Spectrum*, 41(1): 27–74.

Ilex Energy Consulting (2002). *Quantifying the System Costs of Additional Renewables in 2020*. Oxford: Ilex Energy Consulting.

Navigant Consulting Inc. (2003). *Energy Savings Potential of Solid State Lighting in General Illumination Applications*, Springfield, VA: Department of Commerce.

Neuhoff, K., and L. De Vries (2004). *Insufficient Incentives for Investment in Electricity Generation*. CMI Working Paper no. 42, Cambridge: University of Cambridge.

Office of Power Technology (2000). *Buildings CHP Technology Roadmap*, Washington, DC: Department of Energy.

Performance and Innovation Unit (2002). *The Energy Review*, London: Cabinet Office.

Rabinowitz, M. (2000). Power systems of the future, *IEEE Power Engineering Review*, 20(3): 10–15.

Royal Commission on Environmental Pollution (2000). *Energy: The Changing Climate*, London: Her Majesty's Stationery Office.

Supergen Workshop (2003). *Future Technologies for a Sustainable Electricity System*, Cambridge: University of Cambridge.

Tsao, J. Y. (ed.) (2002). *Light-Emitting Diodes for General Illumination: An OIDA Technology Roadmap*, Washington, DC: Optoelectronics Industry Development Association.

Watson, J. (2003). *UK Electricity Scenarios for 2050*, Brighton: Tyndall Centre for Climate Change Research.

   (2004). Co-provision in sustainable energy systems: the case of microgeneration, *Energy Policy* Special Issue on System Change, 32(17): 1981–90.

World Energy Council (2003). *Global Energy Scenarios to 2050 and Beyond*, London: World Energy Council.

Part I

Renewable Generation Technologies

3 Wind power: status and perspectives

Poul Erik Morthorst

3.1 Introduction

Wind power is rapidly being developed in a European as well as a global perspective. Within the past fifteen years the global installed capacity of wind power has increased, from approximately 2.3GW in 1991 to more than 40GW by the end of 2003, an annual growth of more than 25 per cent. However, wind power is at present economically competitive to conventional power production only at a very few sites with high wind speeds. This chapter looks at how the economics of wind power has developed over the previous years and how it is expected to develop in the near future. The historical trend towards bigger machines and the impact on the cost of wind-generated power are analysed, starting with the old 95kW turbines and ranging to modern sizes of 1MW and more. The structure of onshore turbine investments is analysed and the main determining factors for the future development are outlined. The cost of power production is estimated seven to eight years ahead by using the experience curve methodology. The main conclusion is that, within this time horizon, wind power is with a high probability fully competitive economically to conventional generated power, especially if the turbines are sited in *roughness class 1* areas – i.e. in wind regimes comparable to coast locations. Finally, the chapter touches upon the development of offshore turbines, with some preliminary calculations of the power production costs of these machines.

3.2 The development of wind power

Within the last ten to fifteen years wind power has developed globally at an extraordinary pace. In 1990 the total installed capacity of wind power in the world amounted to approximately 2.0GW; by the end of 2003 this capacity had increased to more than 40GW, equalling an annual growth rate of more than 25 per cent, and the growth rate is still high – global installed capacity increased by 30 per cent in 2002 and by approximately

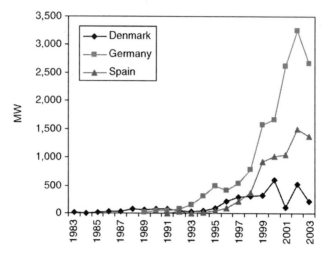

Figure 3.1. Annual increase in installed wind power capacity, 1983–2003.

26 per cent in 2003. But it is European countries that dominate the wind power scene. In 2003 approximately 65 per cent of total installed wind turbine capacity was established in Europe, and the only major contributors outside Europe were the United States, with a total installed capacity of approximately 6.4GW, and India, with 2.1GW (BTM-Consult, 2004).

Just a handful of countries are dominant, even within Europe: Germany, Spain and Denmark account for more than 75 per cent of the growth in European installed wind turbine capacity in 2003, and, correspondingly, these three countries have together installed more than 80 per cent of the total accumulated capacity in Europe; see figure 3.1. Germany in particular has experienced rapid development. In 1991 its total accumulated capacity was approximately 100MW; nowadays the annual capacity increase is around 2,700MW and total installed wind power capacity is almost 15GW. Similar developments are found in Denmark and Spain, although not to the same extent. Denmark currently has total installed capacity of almost 3.1GW and a growth rate of approximately 8 per cent in 2003, while Spain has installed a total of 6.4GW with a growth rate of more than 25 per cent in 2003. Other European contributors to be mentioned are: the Netherlands (0.9GW), Italy (0.9GW), the United Kingdom (0.8GW), Greece (0.5GW), Sweden (0.4GW) and Austria (0.4GW) (BTM-Consult, 2004).

3.3   Cost and investment structures

Wind power is used for a number of different applications, including both grid-connected and stand-alone electricity production, as well as water pumping. This section analyses the cost and investment structures of wind power, primarily in relation to grid-connected turbines, which account for the vast bulk of the market value of installed turbines.

The main parameters governing wind power economics include the following:

- investment costs, including auxiliary costs for foundation, grid-connection, etc.;
- operation and maintenance costs;
- electricity production/average wind speed;
- turbine lifetime; and
- the discount rate.

Of these, the most important parameters are the turbines' electricity production and their investment costs. As electricity production is highly dependent on wind conditions, choosing the right turbine site is critical to achieving economic viability.

The following sections outline the structure and development of land-based wind turbine capital costs and efficiency trends. Offshore turbines gain an increasingly important role in the overall development of wind power, and therefore an overview is given in a separate section. In general, three major trends have dominated the development of grid-connected wind turbines in recent years:

- the turbines have grown larger and taller, and as a result the average size of turbines sold at the market place has substantially increased;
- the efficiency of the turbines' production has steadily increased; and
- the investment costs per kW have, in general, decreased.

Figure 3.2 shows the development of the average size of wind turbines sold each year for a number of the most important wind power countries. As illustrated in figure 3.2, the average annual size has increased significantly over the last ten to fifteen years, from approximately 200kW in 1990 to almost 2,000kW in Germany, the United Kingdom and Denmark in 2003. But, as shown, there is quite a difference between the individual countries. In Spain, the average size installed in 2003 was approximately 900kW, significantly below the levels in Denmark and Germany of 2,000kW and 1,650kW, respectively. In recent years the large increase in Denmark and the United Kingdom has stemmed

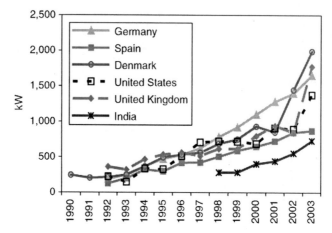

Figure 3.2. Development of average wind turbine size sold, 1990–2003.
Source: BTM-consult (2004).

mainly from establishing offshore wind farms that are mostly equipped
with 2MW turbines or larger.

In 2003 the best-selling turbines on the world market had a rated
capacity of 750 to 1,500kW and more than a 50 per cent share of the
market. But turbines with capacities of 1.5MW and more had a share of
35 per cent and are increasing their market shares. By the end of 2005,
turbines with a capacity of 2MW and above were becoming increasingly
important, even for on-land sitings.

The development of electricity production efficiency owing to improved equipment design, measured as annual energy production per
swept rotor area (kWh/m^2) at a specific reference site, has correspondingly improved significantly over the last few years. Taking into account
all three of the above-mentioned issues of improved equipment efficiency, improved turbine siting and higher hub height, overall efficiency
has increased by 2 per cent to 3 per cent annually over the last fifteen
years.

The capital costs of wind energy projects are dominated by the cost of
the wind turbine itself (ex works).[1] Table 3.1 shows a typical cost
structure for a 1MW turbine in Denmark.[2] The turbine's share of total

---

[1] 'Ex works' means that no site work, foundation or grid connection costs are included.
Ex works costs include the turbine as provided by the manufacturer, including the
turbine itself, blades and tower, and transport to the site.
[2] Based on Danish figures for a 1MW turbine, using the average 2001 exchange rate of
€1 = DKK 7.45.

Table 3.1 *Cost structure for a 1MW wind turbine*

	Investment (€ thousand)	Share (%)
Turbine (ex works)	748	81.9
Foundation	44	4.8
Electric installation	10	1.1
Grid connection	60	6.6
Control systems	2	0.2
Consultancy	8	0.9
Land	27	2.9
Financial costs	8	0.9
Road	7	0.7
Total	914	100.0

cost is approximately 82 per cent, while grid connection accounts for around 7 per cent and foundation for some 5 per cent. Other cost components, such as control systems and land, account for only minor shares of total costs.

3.4   Economics of land-sited wind turbines

Changes in investment costs over the years are shown in figure 3.3. All costs on the left axis are calculated per kW of rated capacity, while those at the right axis are calculated per swept rotor area. The data reflect turbines installed in the particular year shown and all costs are converted to 2001 prices. As shown in the figure, there was a substantial decline in per kW costs between 1989 and 1999. During this period turbine costs per kW decreased in real terms by approximately 4 per cent per annum. At the same time, the share of auxiliary costs (i.e. foundation, grid connection, etc.) as a percentage of total costs also decreased. In 1987 almost 29 per cent of the total investment costs were related to costs other than the turbine itself. By 1999 this share had declined to approximately 20 per cent. The trend towards lower auxiliary costs continues for the last vintage of turbines shown (1,000kW), where other costs amount to around 18 per cent of total costs.

A little surprisingly, investment costs per kW have increased for this last-mentioned machine compared to a 600kW turbine. The reason has to be found in the dimensioning of the turbine. With higher hub heights and larger rotor diameters, the turbine is equipped with a relatively small generator even though it produces more electricity. This is illustrated in figure 3.3 on the right axis, where total investment costs are divided

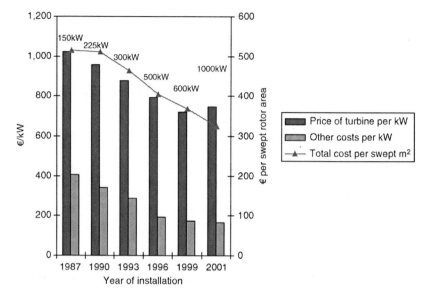

Figure 3.3. Wind turbine costs.

by the swept rotor area.[3] As shown in this figure, the cost per swept rotor area has continuously decreased for all turbines considered. Thus, over-all investment costs per swept rotor area have declined by some 3 per cent per year during the period analysed.

The total cost per produced kWh (unit cost) is calculated by discount-ing and levelising investment and operations and maintenance costs over the lifetime of the turbine, divided by the annual electricity produc-tion. The unit cost of generation is thus calculated as an average cost over the turbine's lifetime. In reality, the actual costs will be lower than the calculated average at the beginning of the turbine's life, due to low O&M costs, and will increase over the period of turbine use.

Figure 3.4 shows the calculated unit cost for different sizes of turbines based on the above-mentioned investment and corresponding O&M costs, a twenty-year lifetime and a real discount rate of 5 per cent per annum. The turbines' electricity production is estimated for *roughness classes 1 and 2*, corresponding to an average wind speed of approximately 6.9 m/s and 6.3 m/s, respectively, at a height of 50 metres above ground

---

[3] The swept rotor area is a good proxy for a turbine's power production.

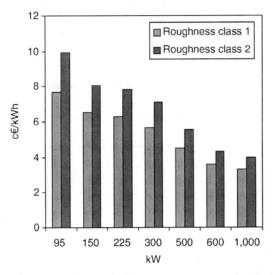

Figure 3.4. Total wind energy costs per unit of electricity produced (€/kW in constant 2001 euros).

level. A roughness class 1 position corresponds to a coastal and rather windy site, while a roughness class 2 position is an inland siting.

Figure 3.4 illustrates the trend towards larger turbines and improved cost-effectiveness. For a roughness class 1 site, for example, the average cost has decreased from over 7.7c€/kWh for the 95kW turbine (1985) to under 3.4c€/kWh for a new 1,000kW machine, an improvement of more than 50 per cent over a timescale of fifteen years (constant 2001 prices).

The turbine's production of power is the single most important factor for the cost per generated unit of power. Whether a turbine is sited at a good wind location, or not, might be the only determinant of whether the turbine is profitable or operates at a loss. In Europe, coastal positions (roughness class 1 positions) are mostly to be found on the coast of the United Kingdom, Ireland, the Netherlands, France, Germany, Spain, Denmark and Norway. A capacity factor of 25 per cent to 30 per cent can normally be achieved at coastal positions in these areas. Medium wind areas (roughness class 2 positions) are mostly to be found as inland terrain in mid- and Southern Europe – i.e. Germany, France, Spain, the Netherlands and Italy – but also at inland sites in Northern Europe – Sweden, Finland and Denmark. Here, a normal capacity factor will be in the range of 20 per cent to 25 per cent. In many cases, local conditions do significantly influence the average wind speed at the specific site, for which reason strong fluctuations in the wind regime are to be expected even for neighbouring areas.

In addition, the discount rate has a significant influence on electricity production costs and hence on wind projects' financial viability. For a 1MW turbine, changing the discount rate from 5 per cent to 10 per cent per year (in real terms) increases the production cost by a little more than 30 per cent.

Finally, it should be mentioned that the energy payback time for a wind turbine is extremely short compared to other kinds of energy-producing plants. Energy is consumed only for the construction and the erection of the turbine and, later, in small amounts during the maintenance of the turbine over its entire lifetime. Calculations carried out by the author assuming the required energy input to be generated by a conventional coal-fired power plant show that the energy payback time for a medium-sized wind turbine is less than three months.

3.4.1   *Future development of the economics of on-land turbines*

Can and will this improvement in cost-effectiveness for wind power continue in the future? Quite a number of factors are important to the future of wind power development, but the single most important one is without doubt the upscaling in the size of the turbines. As shown above, the 95kW machine was a typical size in the mid-1980s, while an average size is by now approximately 1.5MW. Thus, within a timescale of fifteen to twenty years, the size of the average turbine has grown by more than a factor of fifteen, and it seems that this upscaling is still one of the driving factors behind wind power development. Quite a number of multi-MW turbines (2 to 3MW) are sold in the market place nowadays and larger turbines still are being developed – turbines of approximately 5MW are currently being tested by the manufacturers with a view to being in serial production in 2006.

The drive towards larger machines is, especially for offshore applications, mainly to reduce the costs of foundations and cabling, which are much more expensive offshore than on land. But the large offshore machines are to an increasing extent also being used for on-land installations, especially in Germany.

Another important issue in the upscaling of turbines is the need to keep the weight down. This is especially essential for blades: the longer the blade the more important weight becomes. Therefore, new construction methods are being applied to reduce weight, and new materials, such as carbon fibre, are now being used in blade manufacturing. In a recent 3MW construction, the manufacturer managed to reduce weight to almost the same level as the previous 2MW model.

But how large will the turbines become in the future? According to experts' forecasts, there are no major physical barriers until a turbine size of over 20MW is reached.[4] A 10MW machine will have a rotor diameter of approximately 160 metres, increasing to approximately 220 metres for a 20MW turbine. Currently, the largest rotors are 110 to 120 metres in diameter (5MW turbine). If the pace of technological development is maintained, especially with regard to reducing weight, we may see turbines of a size of 30 to 40MW. The most significant future barrier might be found within the transport infrastructure.

How will continued development of the turbine, including an upscaling in size, influence the future cost of wind-produced energy? In this section, the future development of the economics of wind power is illustrated by the use of the experience curve methodology. The experience curve approach was developed back in the 1970s by the Boston Consulting Group, and the main feature is that it relates the cumulative quantitative development of a product with the development of the specific costs (Johnson and Scholes, 1984). Thus, if the cumulative sale of a product is doubled, the estimated learning rate shows the achieved reduction in specific product costs.

The experience curve is not a forecasting tool based on estimated relationships. It merely points out that, if the existing trends are maintained in the future, then we might see the proposed development. It converts the effect of mass production into an effect on production costs, and other causal relationships are not taken into account. Thus, changes in market development and/or a technological breakthrough within the field may considerably change the picture.

In a number of projects, different experience curves have been estimated (see, for instance, Durstewitz and Hoppe-Klipper, 1999, Neij, 1997, 1999, or Neij et al., 2003), but unfortunately mostly by using different specifications, which means that not all of these can be directly compared. To get the full value of the experiences gained, not only the price reduction of the turbine (the €/kW specification) should be taken into account but also the improvements in efficiency of the turbine's production. The last mentioned issue requires the use of an energy specification (c€/kWh), and this approach is used in Neij (1997) and Neij et al. (2003). Thus, using the specific costs of energy as a basis

[4] Personal communication with Flemming Rasmussen, Head of the Programme for Aerodynamics at Risø National Laboratory, Denmark, 2003.

(costs per kWh produced), the estimated progress ratios in these publications range from 0.83 to 0.91, corresponding to learning rates of 0.17 to 0.09. That is, when the total installed capacity of wind power is doubled, the costs per produced kWh for new turbines are reduced between 9 per cent and 17 per cent. In this way, both the efficiency improvements and embodied and disembodied cost reductions are taken into account in the analysis.

Wind power capacity has developed very rapidly in recent years, on average by approximately 25 per cent per year during the last ten years. Thus, it takes at present approximately four years to double the accumulated capacity of wind power. The European Union has set a target of 40,000MW wind power by 2010, compared to approximately 29,300MW installed in the Union by the end of 2003. Thus, the EU target will be exceeded several years early.

The European Wind Energy Association has recently published a target of 75,000MW for Europe in 2010. This implies that a growth rate of approximately 14 per cent per annum is required to reach the EWEA target in 2010 (a doubling time of approximately five years). In figure 3.5, the consequences for wind power production costs, according to the following assumptions, are shown: a learning rate of 15 per cent is assumed, implying that, each time the total installed capacity is doubled, the costs per kWh of wind-generated power are reduced by 15 per cent; and the growth rate of installed capacity is assumed to double, in terms of cumulative installations, every five years. The historical development of wind power costs is used as a starting point, as shown in figure 3.4.

The consequences of applying the above-mentioned results for wind power are illustrated in Figure 3.5, where a roughness class 1 position corresponds to a coastal siting, while roughness class 2 is a typical inland siting. Thus, if the accumulated capacity of wind power doubles every five years, the costs of wind-produced power around 2010 should, according to the experience curve approach, be within a range of approximately 2.4 c€/kWh to 3.0 c€/kWh (constant 2001 currency). The costs of intermittency are not included in these costs; due to fluctuations in wind speed, wind power will not always be available and, if supplying the produced power to a liberalised spot market, it will not always be possible for the wind turbine owner to fulfil the bid given to the market. Thus, other producers of power will have to step in, either increasing or decreasing their production depending on if too little or too much wind power is produced. For the conditions in the Nordic power market, Nord Pool, the cost of regulation is estimated to an average of 0.3 c€/kWh delivered by wind turbines (Morthorst, 2003). Thus, including the cost

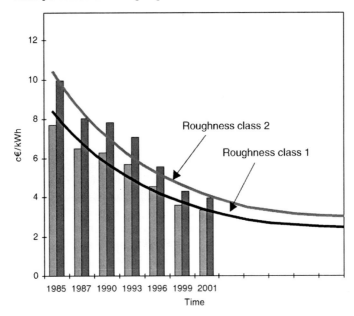

Figure 3.5. Experience curves for the development of wind turbine economics.

of intermittency, the total costs of wind-produced power by 2010 as estimated by the experience curve approach are expected to be in a range of approximately 2.7 c€/kWh to 3.3 c€/kWh (constant 2001 currency).

An implicit assumption of the learning curve approach is that the analysis is performed for essentially the same technology over time. For the period analysed, this assumption is clearly fulfilled for wind turbine development, the 95kW machine from the mid-1980s as well as the 1MW machine from 2001, both being technically classified as members of 'the Danish Concept' – that is, being upwind turbines, three-bladed and gearbox-based machines. Thus, for the period analysed and the chosen turbine sample, no technological breakthroughs have been witnessed. But the wind turbine industry is still in its infancy. As a consequence, new design concepts are to be expected, the trend going towards direct drive transmission, pitch regulation, variable speed and gearless turbines. However, these new concepts will be introduced only as a requirement by the market due to grid or regulatory conditions or because they will improve the cost-effectiveness of the turbines. Thus, even if the upscaling of turbine size as the driver towards reduced costs may slow down in the future, a considerable potential still exists for new technological developments to lower the costs per kWh for future turbines.

What, then, are the production costs of the competing conventional power producers? At present, the price of power in Nord Pool is on average approximately 3.0 c€/kWh. However, no major new investments in power capacity by the Nordic producers have been undertaken during the period, when Denmark took part in the market, and the Nordic organisation for TSOs, Nordel, expects shortage of power capacity within the next three to four years.[5] Thus, it is expected that the price will increase to induce new investments in conventional power plants. According to Danish power companies, the most promising technology to choose is natural-gas-fired combined-cycle power plants, which will produce at a cost of between 3.3 c€/kWh and 4 c€/kWh.[6] As shown in figure 3.5, this implies that around 2010 wind power should be fully competitive with new conventionally produced power, if the existing trends continue.

3.5   Development of offshore wind turbines

In a number of countries, offshore turbines are increasingly securing an important role in the development of wind power, particularly in the north-western part of Europe. Without doubt, the main reasons are that on-land sitings are limited in number and that the utilisation of these sites attracts a fair degree of opposition from the local population. This, seen in relation to an unexpectedly high level of energy production from offshore turbines compared to on-land sitings (based on experience so far), has paved the way for a huge increase in interest in offshore development.

At present a number of offshore wind farms are in operation in the northern part of Europe, the largest ones being in Danish waters. The world's largest offshore wind farm is situated off the west coast of Denmark at Horns Reef, approximately 20 kilometres off the coast of Jutland; it was established in 2002 and has a total capacity of 160MW,

---

[5] Presentation given at a meeting held at Eltra (Danish TSO) by Hans Henrik Lindboe, Fredericia, Denmark, 13 August 2002.

[6] Depending on the number of full load hours the plant is expected to produce. A utilisation time of 4,000 hours is assumed at the high cost, while the low costs implies a utilisation time of approximately 6,500 hours. Personal communication with Elsam (Danish power company), 2002.

consisting of eighty 2MW turbines. The Nysted project at Rødsand, close to the isle of Lolland, was finalised in 2003 and has a total capacity of around 160MW, generated by seventy-two 2.2MW turbines. Middel- grunden, east of Copenhagen, was put into operation in 2001, with a total capacity of 40MW from twenty 2MW turbines. The Samsø off- shore wind farm, situated south of the island of Samsø, was put into operation in 2003 and comprises ten 2.3MW turbines. Finally, the Danish parliament has just decided to tender for two new offshore wind farms, each to be approximately 200MW in size. These are expected to be in operation by 2007/8.

Offshore wind power projects are in the planning and implementa- tion phase in a number of other countries as well, notable ones among these being in Germany, Ireland, the Netherlands and the United Kingdom.

As with onshore turbines, the wind regime – i.e. where the offshore turbines are sited determining the production of power – is the single most important factor for the cost per generated unit of power. In general, the wind regime offshore is more stable than onshore, with less turbulence and higher average wind speeds. At the Danish Horns Reef wind farm, a wind speed corresponding to a utilisation time of almost 4,400 hours per year has been measured (adjusted to a normal wind year), thus giving a capacity factor of approximately 50 per cent, which is comparable to many smaller conventional power plants. For most offshore wind farms, a utilisation time of more than 3,000 hours per year is to be expected – significantly higher than for onshore turbines and therefore, to a certain extent, compensating for the additional costs of offshore plants.

An important concern for the Danish government is to ensure that future offshore development is based on market conditions in an eco- nomically efficient way. The government has therefore investigated the possibilities and conditions for tendering future offshore wind farms in Danish waters. By applying a tendering procedure, competition among the bidders will be ensured and the most cost-effective offshore turbine developments will be undertaken. As part of the governmental investi- gations, a scenario was worked out for the development of a new wind farm at Horns Reef utilising 3MW turbines in preference to the 2MW devices at the existing site. The economic consequences of this scenario are briefly summarised below.

The number of full load hours is assumed to be 4,190 per year, and investment and O&M costs are modified to a 3MW farm, using cost data from the existing 2MW farm as a starting point. As shown in

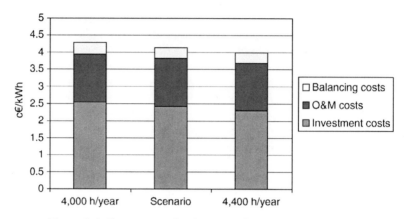

Figure 3.6. Forecast production costs for 3MW turbine scenario.

figure 3.6, total production costs are calculated at some 4.2 c€/kWh, including 1.4 c€/kWh as O&M costs and 0.3 c€/kWh for balancing the power production in the market place. Not unexpectedly, the assumption on full load hours is important. If the assumed utilisation time is reduced to 4,000 hours per year, costs will increase to 4.3 c€/kWh, while a utilisation time of 4,400 hours per year corresponds to a cost of only 4.0 c€/kWh.

The above costs are calculated as simple national economic costs using a real discount rate of 5 per cent per annum, and they will, therefore, not be the costs of a private investor, who will have higher financial costs and require a risk premium and, eventually, a profit. How much a private investor will add on top of the simple costs will depend, among other things, on the perceived technological and political risk of establishing the offshore farm and, ultimately, on the competition in the bidding process for such an offshore farm.

3.6   Conclusions

Wind power is one of the most promising new renewable technologies, currently undergoing rapid technological development and possessing environmental characteristics that make it well suited for contributing to sustainable development in the future. This chapter has addressed issues related to the market and economic development of wind power, in the process highlighting the following issues.

- Wind power is developing rapidly on a global scale, showing growth rates of installed capacity of more than 25 per cent annually. Nevertheless, the development is vulnerable, because it is dominated by just a few countries: Germany, Spain, the United States and Denmark.
- The size of the average turbine sold in the market place is continually increasing. In 2003 the best-selling turbines on the world market had a rated capacity of 750 to 1,500kW and more than a 50 per cent share of the market. But turbines with capacities of 1.5MW and above had a share of 35 per cent and are increasing their market shares. At present turbines with a capacity of 2MW and above are becoming increasingly important, even for on-land sitings.
- Within the last fifteen years there has been a consistent trend towards larger and more optimised turbines, and thus towards more cost-effective machines. For a coastal location, for example, the average cost decreased from over 7.7 c€/kWh for a 95kW turbine (1985) to under 3.4 c€/kWh for a new 1,000kW machine (2001) – an improvement of more than 50 per cent over a fifteen-year timescale (at constant 2001 prices).
- New and larger turbines are continually being developed, one of the most important issues being that of keeping the weight of the turbines down. New materials, such as carbon fibre, are used and new construction methods are applied to reduce weight. If the current pace of technological development continues, there seem to be no major physical barriers to exceeding a turbine size of 20MW, and even larger turbines of 30 to 40MW may eventually be constructed. In the final analysis, it may be the transport infrastructure that emerges as the constraining factor.
- If growth in installed wind power continues at its present rate until around 2010, the costs of wind-produced power should – according to the experience curve approach – be within a range of approximately 2.4 c€/kWh to 3.0 c€/kWh. In the Nordic power market, a natural-gas-fired combined-cycle power plant, to be constructed and on-stream within five to seven years, will produce at a cost of between 3.3 c€/kWh and 4 c€/kWh. This implies that, by 2010, onshore wind turbines should be fully competitive with new conventionally produced power, if existing trends are maintained.
- Offshore wind power is being allocated an increasingly important role in the development of wind power overall, and a future offshore farm equipped with 3MW turbines could produce at a cost of approximately 4.2 c€/kWh, including 1.4 c€/kWh as O&M costs and 0.3 c€/kWh for balancing its power production in the market place.

3.7   References

BTM-Consult (2004). *International Wind Energy Development: World Market Update 2003*, Ringkøbing, Denmark: BTM-Consult.

Durstewitz, M., and M. Hoppe-Kilpper (1999). *Wind Energy Experience Curve from the German '250MW Wind' Programme*, IEA International Workshop on Experience Curves for Policy Making, Stuttgart, 10–11 May.

Johnson, G., and K. Scholes (1984). *Exploring Corporate Strategy*, Upper Saddle River, NJ: Prentice Hall.

Morthorst, P. E. (2003). Wind power and the conditions at a liberalised power market, *Wind Power*, 6(3): 297–308.

Neij, L. (1997). Use of experience curves to analyse the prospects for diffusion and adoption of renewable energy technology, *Energy Policy*, 23(13): 1099–107.

(1999). Cost dynamics of wind power, *International Journal*, 24(5): 375–89.

Neij, L., P. Dannemand Andersen, M. Durstewitz, P. Helby, M. Hoppe-Kilpper and P. E. Morthorst (2003). Experience Curves: A Tool for Energy Policy Assessment, Environmental and Energy System Studies Report no. 40, Department of Technology and Society, Lund University, Sweden.

4 Solar energy: photovoltaic electricity generation

Asim Mumtaz and Gehan Amaratunga

4.1 Introduction

The Sun, the largest object in the Solar System, is positioned some 150 million kilometres from the Earth's surface and generates its electricity through fusion reactions, converting its hydrogen into both helium and emitted energy. The solar radiation is emitted at a temperature of about 6,000K and a power density of 63.1MW per metre squared from its surface. This is attenuated and dispersed significantly, until it is received by the Earth's atmosphere at approximately 1,300W per metre squared. The amount of energy received from the Sun in just one hour is actually more than the world consumes in an entire year. Figure 4.1 shows the global solar radiation distribution. The light received is an entire spectrum of wavelengths, ranging from 300 nanometres (ultraviolet region) to about 2 micrometres (infrared region). The peak of the spectrum is in the visible region (McDaniels, 1979).

Nature has derived energy from the Sun for millions of years, mainly through the process of photosynthesis. Other forms of renewable energy are also dependent on the Sun – for example, hydroelectricity and wind and wave power. The generation of electricity from solar energy has come into fruition only since the 1950s. Today there are a multitude of applications, broadly categorised into two types: in remote areas (off-grid), or in supplying grid electricity (on-grid). To convert solar energy into electricity, a solar cell is required. A solar cell can be simply understood as a battery whereby the charge at the two electrodes is maintained by the absorption of light, rather than through chemical reactions in the electrolyte of the battery.

4.2 History of solar cell development

The generation of electricity from the Sun is usually referred to as solar photovoltaics, or PV (not to be confused with solar thermal, which refers to heating water). The flow of electric current in the presence of light,

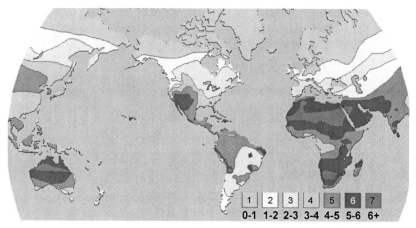

Figure 4.1. Global solar irradiation distribution (kWh/m^2 per day).

known as the photovoltaic effect (see box 1 for further details), is known to have been discovered by Edmond Becquerel in 1839. The discovery was made whilst he was experimenting with an electrolytic cell consisting of platinum electrodes coated with silver chloride, contained in an aqueous solution. Becquerel found that when the cell was exposed to light the electrical power generated increased. In 1876 two members of Cambridge University, William Grylls Adams and his student, Richard Evans Day, observed the photovoltaic effect in a solid material for the first time. They observed that when a selenium rod that had platinum contacts was exposed to light a change in its electrical characteristics occurred. This led to a selenium photocell being produced by Charles Edgar Fritts in 1883, which used selenium sandwiched between an iron plate and a semi-transparent gold top layer. Although these devices were inefficient (<1 per cent) they became the basis of photographic exposure meters. In these early photocells there was no insulating (or charge-depleted material) between the two materials with different equilibrium energies for the conduction charge. The modern photovoltaic cell with an intermediate-charge free region was first proposed at Bell Laboratories by Russell Ohl in 1941, and then further developed by Darryl Chapin and his colleagues Calvin Fuller and Gerald Pearson (Archer and Hill, 2001).

In modern solar cells the two regions with different energies of conduction charge are obtained by using semiconductors that have been doped with trace elements of other materials, such that they have either an excess amount of negative (n-type) or positive (p-type) charge carriers for conduction of electric current. When an n-type and a p-type semiconductor are metallurgically combined, a charge-depleted region (akin to an insulator) is established at the interface, referred to as the junction, between the two regions. Chapin and his colleagues produced their solar cell based on a diffused p–n junction in crystalline silicon (Si) in 1954. This cell had a light-to-electricity conversion efficiency of 4.5 per cent. All modern solar cells follow the basic principle invented by Chapin and co-workers, and are based on the use of p–n junctions (see figure 4.3) or p–i–n junctions ('i' standing for 'insulator') in semiconductors.

Within a short period of Chapin's work solar cells were being used in space to power satellites. The technology of solar cells for space applications has improved to the point where laboratory samples currently attain conversion efficiencies of around 30 per cent. This is close to the theoretical limit of what can be achieved with the gallium arsenide (GaAs) type of semiconductor that is used in space. In the early 1970s, with the realisation of the finite nature of fossil fuel reserves and the implications therein for global energy supply, photovoltaic solar energy conversion was proposed as an *alternative* process for electricity generation. Unlike the application in space power generation, for terrestrial power generation solar cell production cost has to be balanced against conversion efficiency. This resulted in the wide use of Si for solar cells, due to its dominant use as the standard semiconductor material in common electronic devices and integrated circuits, despite its lower conversion efficiency than GaAs. More recently a number of solar cells based on different materials have been proposed.

Box 1: The photovoltaic effect

The term 'Photovoltaics' refers to the conversion of light energy directly into electricity. The photovoltaic effect occurs when two materials with different equilibrium potentials for electrical charge available for conduction (also referred to as the chemical potential or work function) are separated from each other by a small distance (ranging from 0.05 to 10 micrometres). The distance between them is occupied by an insulating or a depleted region, which has no free charge carriers to conduct electricity under dark conditions. The difference in equilibrium potential for charge carriers on either side of the insulating layer leads to a 'built-in potential' across the insulating layer. When exposed to light above a specified energy, positive and negative charge carriers are created through the absorption of light energy in the insulating (depleted) region, or close enough to

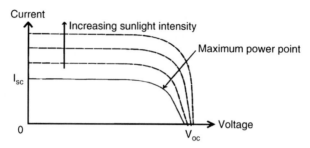

Figure 4.2. Generic solar cell characteristics.

diffuse to the depleted region. The photo-generated negative (electrons) and positive (holes) charges are separated by the built-in potential in the two different materials with different equilibrium potential. The charge separates, enabling these positive and negative charges to enter into the material in which their respective equilibrium energies are lower. Such charge separation continues until the collection of extra charge in the two materials leads to a voltage being established between them, which is equivalent to their original difference in energy. The development of a voltage across two materials with different equilibrium potential due to the collection of electric charge carriers created by absorbing light is termed the photovoltaic effect. A material system, that exhibits a photovoltaic effect is analogous to a battery cell.

Generating power. A voltage alone is insufficient for generating electric power. An electric current must flow from the positive to the negative terminal of the photovoltaic cell, while a positive voltage difference between the terminals is maintained, for there to be electric power output. An extreme condition is the application of a short circuit across the two terminals. In this case a photocurrent will flow between the electrodes of the cell, as long as it is exposed to light, with zero volts across the terminal. There is no power output from the cell, due to the zero-voltage condition. This is referred to as the short-circuit current condition. The opposite, when no current flows, is termed the open-circuit voltage condition. In this case there is no power output due to the zero-current condition. The open-circuit voltage (V_{oc}) and short-circuit current (I_{sc}) are fundamental performance parameters for a solar photovoltaic power cell (solar cell). The quantity $V_{oc} \times I_{sc}$ represents the absolute power limit for the photovoltaic cell (see figure 4.2). When delivering power to an electrical circuit connected to its terminals, the cell will have voltage and current values that are always lower than the V_{oc} and I_{sc}. The greater the intensity of light that shines on a solar cell the greater the magnitude of the short-circuit current I_{sc} and hence the electric power available from the solar cell. The open-circuit voltage, on the other hand, is virtually independent of light intensity and is governed only by the properties of the materials used to construct the solar cell (Nelson, 2003).

4.3   Commercially available solar cells

Over the past few decades much research and development has been directed at reducing the cost and improving the efficiency of solar cells. The phases of development can be categorised in three generations of solar cells.

The first generation was based on crystalline wafer technology (Green, 1995). This is based on the production of a crystalline semiconductor (Si or GaAs), which is then sliced into thin wafers. Subsequently dopants are implanted or diffused into the wafer. Silicon solar cells, as briefly described earlier, are first-generation solar cells, and retain the largest share of the solar cell market. To reduce the cost, another cell, referred to as a multi-crystalline Si solar cell, was developed. These cells are based on producing multi-crystalline ingots, as opposed to high-quality single crystalline material. The sawing process used is the same for both, but the lower-cost method has the drawback of producing lower-quality silicon. Examples of single and multi-crystalline solar cells are shown in figure 4.4. Another method to reduce the cost was to grow the silicon in ribbon form, so as to make it much easier for cutting purposes. The efficiency of the solar cells produced from such methods is about 80 per cent of that achieved using single-crystal silicon. The main method of enhancing efficiency has been to reduce the defects in the materials by hydrogen implantation.

Included in the first-generation solar cells are those based on gallium arsenide. As explained, gallium arsenide has been used in solar cells in space due to its higher efficiency than silicon. The higher efficiency is partly due to band gap of GaAs being more closely matched to the peak of the solar energy spectrum as compared to Si. As well as this, GaAs is a direct band gap semiconductor, which means that light is absorbed much more efficiently than it is by silicon, which is an indirect band gap semiconductor. Another advantage is that the temperature degradation effects in GaAs are less than that found in Si. The disadvantages of GaAs in relation to Si are its high cost, heavy weight and brittle nature. As only the top few microns are used in light absorption, only a thin layer

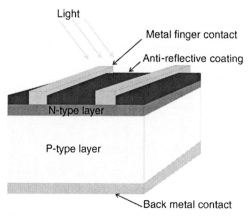

Figure 4.3. Cross-section of a solar cell.

of GaAs is required. However, a thick germanium (Ge) substrate is used in the GaAs solar cell to give added strength. The crystal lattice constant and coefficient of thermal expansion of Ge are well matched with those of GaAs.[1] The Ge–GaAs can also be made into an active p–n junction, thus having a single device with a double junction. Having multiple junctions simply allows more light to be absorbed, therefore resulting in an increase in efficiency. Multi-junction (or tandem) cells use a wider portion of the solar energy spectrum by stacking materials with different band gaps. Triple junctions are also used commercially to attain efficiencies of up to 35 per cent (Hardingham and Wood, 1998).

Thin films can be considered as the second generation of solar cells. They were invented to reduce costs further through the reduction of substrate costs and by making production a high-volume throughput process, as shown in figure 4.5 (Shah et al., 1999). Some commonly used thin-film materials are amorphous silicon (a-Si:H), micro-crystalline thin-film silicon, poly-crystalline cadmium telluride (CdTe) and poly-crystalline copper indium diselenide ($CuInSe_2$). These materials can be deposited, using either physical or chemical deposition techniques, at lower temperatures compared to the first-generation solar cells. Of the above materials, hydrogenated amorphous silicon is the most-used thin film in commercial production, with efficiencies of a-Si:H around 10 per cent (an example is shown in figure 4.6). Amorphous silicon is different from crystalline silicon in that it does not possess any long-range order

---

[1] The term 'lattice constant' defines the distance between atoms in cubic-cell crystals and is also a measure of the structural compatibility between various crystal structures, in this case between Ge and GaAs.

Multi-crystalline silicon

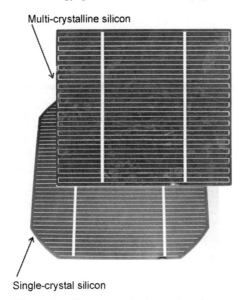

Single-crystal silicon

Figure 4.4. Images of single- and multi-crystalline silicon solar cells.

and hence has a number of dangling bonds. These are passivated by hydrogen during the chemical vapour deposition. The fabrication processes are at lower temperatures, which imply a low energy requirement for the manufacture of the cells. The incorporation of hydrogen during the fabrication also increases the size of the band gap relative to that of crystalline silicon solar cells. The operating principle of amorphous silicon solar cells is different from that of crystalline silicon solar cells in that an intrinsic layer is used in the amorphous cells, which allows for field-assisted carrier collection. Another advantage of these solar cells is the ability to produce tandem solar cells with ease. One major disadvantage of a-Si:H solar cells is that they tend to degrade over time with exposure to light. Over an operational lifetime of ten years the efficiency of conversion may degrade typically by around 20 per cent.

The third generation of solar cells is discussed in section 4.7, our future vision for solar photovoltaics.

4.4   The overall photovoltaic system

The technology of Si solar cells has developed to the point where conversion efficiencies of greater than 24 per cent have been demonstrated at the cell level (Zhao et al., 1995). The open–circuit voltage of a single

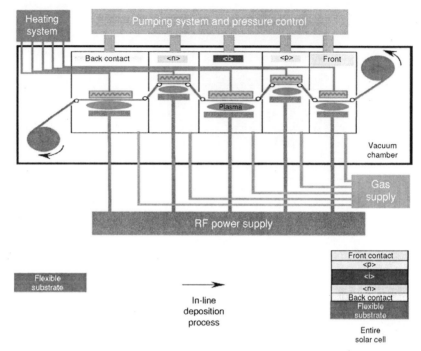

Figure 4.5. Roll-to-roll deposition process for amorphous silicon solar cells.
Source: Shah et al. (1999).

solar cell is low, typically 0.7V. This requires the series connection of many cells to realise practical solar cell *modules* with output voltages of, typically, 12V or 24V. An example of such a module is shown in figure 4.7. Such series connection leads to a degradation of conversion efficiency. The high-end Si solar modules available at present have conversion efficiencies of 18 per cent to 20 per cent.

In general, to make use of the power generated a power-conditioning unit is employed. The PCU is a component that links directly to a PV module or PV array, as shown schematically in figure 4.7 (Wenham et al., 1994). The PV module produces a DC voltage, and depending on the application the PCU will have to perform different tasks. In remote-area applications where there is no consumer mains supply (230V 50Hz, 110V 60Hz), more commonly referred to as off-grid applications, there is a need for the PV system to be interfaced to a battery. In this case the PCU acts as a charge controller. Batteries can add significant cost to off-grid systems. The other, now more common,

Figure 4.6. Examples of amorphous silicon solar cells.

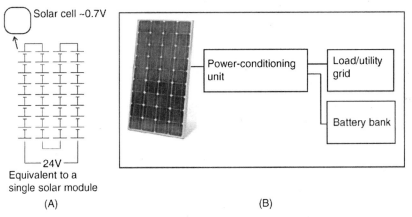

Figure 4.7. Representation of solar module and overall system.
Source: Wenhom et al. (1994).

application is when the PV system is connected to the consumer mains
supply (referred to as a grid-connected system). In these systems the
PCU acts as an inverter, to convert the DC electricity supplied by the
photovoltaic modules into AC electricity that is compatible with the mains.

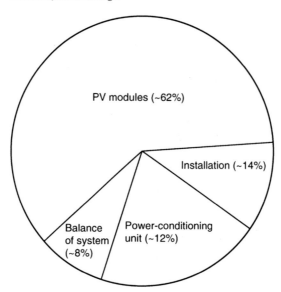

Figure 4.8. Cost breakdown for a grid-connected PV system.
Source: Thomas et al. (1999).

Inverter PCUs have a more complex task of continuously matching the voltage and frequency characteristics of the grid. Another task of the PCU is to perform maximum-power point tracking. This is essential, in order to ensure that maximum power is always obtained from the solar cells, as the sunlight available is continually changing. The PCU and the battery show lower reliability than the PV modules. The actual lifetime of the PCU is typically less than five years, compared to twenty-five years for the PV module. Significant developments in PCUs, allowing the solar module to be viewed from a new perspective, are discussed in section 4.7.

It is useful to examine the relative cost of the various components of a typical domestic PV system as shown in figure 4.8 (Thomas et al., 1999). The cost of the PV modules comprises the largest single element of the costs, followed by the installation costs. The next largest cost is that of the PCU. This is followed by the balance of the system, which in this case relates to the wiring, metering and other parts of the PV system.

4.5   Global applications: the broad landscape for solar power

There is now a whole spectrum of applications for solar energy, which are briefly discussed in this section. The solar PV industry was valued at over $7 billion in 2004 and has been growing at an annual rate of 30 per cent since 1996 (Lysen, 2003; Benner and Kazmerski, 1999). It is expected that installed capacity worldwide by 2020 will be 207GWp, with the industry growing in value to $30 billion per year by 2010. Multinational companies and governments have pledged to increase PV installations. For example legislation has recently been passed in Germany allowing homeowners to use PV to generate electricity for their own usage; any excess can be sold back to the electricity suppliers at up to five times (up to 62.4 c€/kWh for PV façade installations) the normal purchase price (approximately 12 c€/kWh) (Wagner, 2000). This type of green pricing, which is a tax on general consumers, is widely accepted by the public in Germany as a measure for protecting the environment. This has boosted the installation of domestic solar PV systems in Germany. Ironically, Sharp, the Japanese electronics company, has recently opened a new factory producing solar panels in south Wales (in July 2004), with the entire output allocated to the German market. Production doubled in 2005. PV programmes have been planned by several countries, including the installation of many hundreds of thousands of PV systems over the next few years. A recent example is, a small village in the Netherlands some 30 kilometres south of Amsterdam, consisting of 5,000 homes and other buildings, each having the facility to generate electricity by means of PV (Benner and Kazmerski, 1999).

Why is there so much interest in PV? One reason is because PV is a renewable energy source and therefore environmentally friendly. It does not produce any harmful gases such as those produced by fossil fuels. The recent Kyoto Protocol, ratified by a number of industrialised countries, has committed them to reduce their carbon emissions. One way to contribute to lower carbon emissions is to shift to PV for electricity generation.

Also, some 2 billion people (400 million homes) in the less developed regions of the world are not connected to conventional distribution systems for electricity supply, and as such have inadequate energy supplies. The provision of a basic electricity system through solar PV systems is much more cost-effective than extending grid systems to remote and isolated hamlets. Substantial health and economic benefits are brought about by having a basic electricity system. One of the main advantages is having lighting, which enables activity after dark (although this necessitates a battery in order to store power for use at night, when solar systems otherwise do not work). At present, most houses in villages without electricity use oil-burning lamps; the inhalation of fumes from these lamps is a major health hazard. PV is being promoted in these

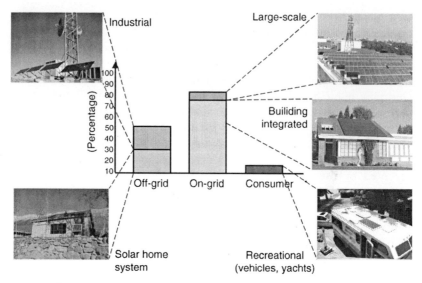

Figure 4.9. The full range of PV applications, 2002.

countries and regions through different programmes, promoted and funded by institutions such as the World Bank.

Other reasons – explained later – include the ease with which this form of electricity can be used in different types of buildings. A remarkable characteristic of PV energy generation is that it can be used in a wide range of applications, from small calculators at the milliwatt level up to large megawatt installations in open fields or desert areas.

PV systems in 2003 accounted for around 1,300MW of global electrical power. Applications of PV in 2002 were 430MW peak power and could be broken down into three broad areas, which are illustrated in figure 4.9. As shown off-grid comprised just under 40 per cent, on-grid applications accounted for about 60 per cent and the remainder was associated with consumer applications. Further details of these three areas are given below.

4.5.1   Remote power

Off-grid application, also known as remote or stand-alone, has traditionally been the largest area of applications for PV, but now occupies approximately 40 per cent of the world market. Usually grid lines are too far from the PV location, and the cost to extend the grid would be uneconomical. Figure 4.10 shows a more detailed analysis of this. The

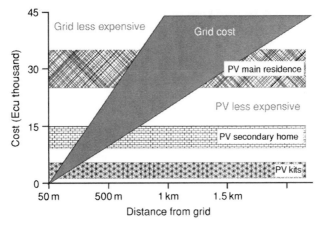

Figure 4.10. Cost of grid supply compared to PV for isolated dwellings. Source: Grubb and Vigotti (1997).

figure shows how the cost of grid supply increases with distance and also compares this with PV at different levels. At the small-scale level, PV kits such as those used in telecommunication repeaters or in cathodic protection are common, and these are found to be more cost-effective than the grid, or any other alternative, at distances in the range of a few hundred metres from the grid supply cables. The remote PV-powered secondary homes and main residences occupy a 100W to 10kW power range. These are also found to be cost-effective at distances above 500 metres and 1.5 kilometres from the grid for the respective system sizes even today. They require between six months and two years to cover the initial investment.

Remote power covers two main sectors: off-grid habitation and off-grid industrial, each occupying approximately 50 per cent of the off-grid market.

- Off-grid habitation refers to solar systems that are used in houses with no access to the grid. The majority of these systems are installed in the developing world. The solar home system is one of the most popular products, with installations currently in over 1.1 million locations. The SHS consists of a PV module (approximately 50–100W power), a charge controller, an inverter and a battery; this is sufficient to power a few fluorescent lights, a radio and – possibly – a small television. Other remote buildings, such as schools, community halls and clinics, can all benefit from electrification with solar energy. This can power radio, TV, video, telephones and refrigeration equipment. Apart from

SHS on individual dwellings, it is also possible to configure central village power plants. This can either power homes using a local wired network, enabling a type of microgrid, or alternatively it can act as a battery charging station. Charging stations enable individuals to have their batteries recharged. Other off-grid facilities include solar lanterns and solar water pumping systems.

- Off-grid industrial: for many years solar energy has been the power supply of choice for remote industrial applications. Examples include powering repeater stations for TV, radio, telemetry and telephones. In these applications, solar power is economical (see figure 4.10), without any subsidies. Solar energy is also frequently used in transportation signalling – for example, in offshore navigation buoys, lighthouses, aircraft warning lights and road traffic warning signals. Solar is used to power environmental and situation-monitoring equipment and corrosion protection systems for pipelines, well-heads and bridges. For larger electrical loads it can be cost-effective to have a hybrid power system – e.g. PV with a small diesel generator. PV systems require little maintenance and are therefore ideal in remote locations. The industry has matured and a number of standards have been developed for each part of the PV system. With high-quality manufacturing methods for the PV panels, no inherent moving parts and simple connections, lifetimes in the region of twenty-five years can be expected. With regard to the panels, maintenance is restricted to cleaning the surfaces in order to remove accumulated dust; if they are not cleaned annually a small decrease in performance can be observed. The main areas of failure are related to the balance of the system, such as the batteries or PCU. Connections do need to be checked regularly, but a main cause of failure is incorrect operation by inappropriate overloading.

4.5.2   Grid-connected systems

Grid-connected systems, also known as utility interactive, constitute the fastest-growing sector of the PV market, currently taking 60 per cent of the overall market. Building-integrated systems have just over 95 per cent of this sector, large-scale systems occupying the remaining 5 per cent.

- Building-integrated systems: PV modules are usually integrated into the roof or façades of buildings, or even on walkways. In such cases the PV system supplies energy to the building (residential or commercial).

Figure 4.11. Building-integrated PV on residential homes in Japan.
Photograph: courtesy Hakushin Corporation.

If it is not utilised then the energy is supplied to the grid, thus earning the owner credit. After a number of years the cost of the system can be paid back. The amount of credit earned can vary depending on local schemes and tariffs. The grid payback is very high in certain countries; for example, in California the current payback time (the time over which the energy generated by the solar cells in operation equals the energy consumed in their production) is just over five years. The central driving force for building-integrated systems comes from the desire of individuals or companies to obtain their electricity from a clean, non-polluting, renewable source for which they are prepared to pay a small premium. An example of building-integrated PV is shown in figure 4.11.

- Large-scale plants. The other type of grid-connected system is the large-scale central PV plant. These are central PV plants that produce energy in the range of a few hundred kWp to multi-MWp. A few of these systems have been established in Italy, the United States (see figure 4.12 for an example), Germany, Spain and Switzerland. There is also a long-term interest in very large-scale PV plants – for example,

Figure 4.12. Large installation in north-eastern Arizona.
Photograph: courtesy Tucson Electric Power.

in large installations producing many gigawatts in the deserts of the
world, such as the Gobi and Sahara.

4.5.3   Consumer applications

Consumers applications make up a very small part of the overall PV
industry. PV is frequently used in consumer product applications such as
calculators, watches and small battery rechargers. PV is also successfully
used in boats, yachting, caravans and various camping activities.

4.6   Cost-effectiveness of grid-connected systems

As shown in the previous section, remote PV systems situated at a
distance from the grid supply are found to be cost-effective even with
the high cost of the storage batteries. The analysis of on-grid PV systems
is undertaken in this section. The solar energy deposited on the Earth's
surface at the equator during daylight hours is, on average, 1 kW per
square metre. A square metre of Si solar cells (taking into consideration
efficiency) can therefore be expected to generate between 150 and 200 W
of electric power for eight to ten hours under equatorial conditions. This

translates approximately to 400 to 750kWh annually from a square meter of Si solar cells.

Surprisingly, perhaps, the reduction in the power that can be generated in northern Europe compared to equatorial regions is only about a third. This is because photovoltaic generation takes place in diffuse light as well as direct sunlight. Integrated insolation over twelve months, with short days in winter being balanced by longer days in the summer, makes solar power generation in northern Europe a viable proposition. The key consideration is the economics of how the capital installation and energy generated from solar panels is costed. If one views solar only as an alternative source for electricity, the costs are unfavourable at present. If one assumes the best figure of 500kWh per metre squared of annual output in northern Europe, then the electricity cost saved at a retail price of €0.075 per kWh is €37.50. Taking the twenty-five-year guarantee provided by solar cell manufacturers at face value, this translates into a saving of €555 (assuming a 5 per cent discount rate) over the lifetime of the cells. If one assumes that inflation in retail energy prices over the twenty-five-year period is offset by the loss of revenue from the capital invested in the solar panels, then the baseline cost has to be €4.5 to €6 per W peak before solar becomes economic. The fully installed cost of a solar system in the United Kingdom at present, assuming fitting onto an existing roof with power conversion electronics and cabling, is about double this – £7 per W. This type of economic calculation leads to the common perception that solar power is too expensive for the United Kingdom.

There are, however, a number of assumptions on costing that influence the calculation. The first is that there are alternative and cheaper solar cell technologies, which are less costly. However, they are also less efficient compared to standard Si solar cells. The best example of this is amorphous Si (a-Si) panels (described in section 3). This technology allows for large-area panels to be manufactured directly, minimising the cost of the assembly and interconnection of individual cells. With the technologies currently available it is also possible to series- and parallel-connect individual cell elements in a-Si panels with ease in order to obtain higher-voltage power output. The energy payback time is about two years for a-Si solar cells. For crystalline (conventional) Si solar cells it is about five to six years. This fact and the other advantages translate into a-Si solar cells costing 40 per cent to 50 per cent less than standard Si for the solar cell elements alone. If the cost of installing a solar system is the same, then with a-Si the cost per watt comes down to about £5 per watt in the United Kingdom. However, because the lifetime of a-Si solar cells is expected to be half that of Si solar cells, the question of recovering capital expenditure through savings on electricity charges alone remains problematic.

4.6.1   *PV as a part of the building fabric*

One way in which the economics of an installed watt of solar electricity changes is when solar panels are integrated into the fabric of a building in its construction as an architectural feature. Many examples of building-integrated PV can be seen in different parts of the world today. Solar panels can be integrated into a roof of a house, and they can be offset against the cost of an alternative roof. Other possibilities are the use of PV as wall cladding or for window use. The labour costs of installation, a major factor in the United Kingdom, would be partly offset against normal building costs. With such a scheme solar starts to become economic even under the worst-case conditions, where a kWh of solar electricity is priced, hence valued, at the same price as a kWh generated from a gas – or oil-burning power station. To make a general comparison, the cost of a cladding of polished stone such as marble, as used on the front of company headquarters and large homes, can be up to £1,000 per square metre. This compares with £300 per square metre for PV modules. A lot of progress has been made in the area of building-integrated PV. A wide range of products are now available that can easily be integrated into the building. At the same time, architects have become more confident with using these products in their projects.

4.6.2   *Peak demand and PV cost*

It also important to take into consideration the variability of demand for electricity at different times of the year. Peak demand in certain countries is known to occur during the solar peaks, because this is when air-conditioning units are most often used. The cost of electricity during these peak times can be found to be higher. Using electricity generated using PV during these periods makes economic sense. In certain locations, of course, peak demand occurs during the winter periods at night.

4.6.3   *Environmental considerations*

In the past ten years there has been rising awareness of the dangers posed by the emission of greenhouse gases into the environment. This has brought about a revised costing for a kWh generated from fossil-fuel-burning power stations, such that it includes an element for the environmental cost. With the probable levels of charging proposed in the European Union for standard electricity, its true cost starts to become higher than that of solar electricity, which involves no CO_2 emission at the generation stage.

There is, of course, the question of whether the costs of the production of the solar cells should also increase if the energy used in their manufacture involves the consumption of electricity generated through conventional means. Even with such an increase in energy costs for production, solar cells lend themselves to cost reduction through volume production as in other sectors of semiconductor electronics – ranging from standard product integrated circuits to active matrix LCD displays, which use a-Si:H transistors on glass.

4.7   Future vision of solar photovoltaics

Significant developments are being made both in the areas of the solar cells and in the balance of the system. Third-generation solar cells are currently at the laboratory development phase. Dye-sensitised solar cells are one area in which significant work is being undertaken at present (Gratzel, 2001). These are usually referred to as photoelectrochemical solar cells. In solid-state solar cells such as silicon, all tasks – the absorption of photons, the creation of electron-hole pairs, the action of the electric field to separate electrons/holes and the conduction of these carriers to the contacts – are performed by the same material. DSSCs are different in that separate materials are used for each of the functions. A photosensitizer (organic dye) is used to absorb and create electron-hole pairs, a nanoporous metal oxide is used to transport the electrons, and, typically, a liquid electrolyte is used for hole transportation. Currently 10 per cent efficiency is the best that has been achieved. The main attraction of such solar cells is their extremely low manufacturing costs. The materials lend themselves to the manufacture of solar cells using methods such as ink-jet printing. The notion of future solar cells coming off large rollers, much like a fast-moving newspaper press, is altogether achievable (Nuttall, 2004). Demonstrator cells are beginning to be seen, but a number of challenges remain such as reliability, scaling up for manufacturing and improved efficiency.

Other ideas for next-generation solar cells relate to quantum well solar cells, using tunable band gaps that can tap into multiple parts of the solar spectrum. It is believed that very high efficiencies (of approximately 30 per cent) can be achieved with this method. Self-assembling solar cells have also been proposed, in which the component materials at a certain blend ratio segregate, causing a mesoscopic self-organisation

(Schmidt-Mende et al., 2001). This could, in theory, lead to a type of solar paint.

As explained earlier, a unique feature of solar photovoltaic power generation is that it is the only technology that can be deployed in dense urban environments at present, through integration in buildings. The key enabler for this has been the advances in power conversion electronics, which can now allow for solar panels – which generate DC electricity with power variations up to a factor of five or more each second – to be connected, at fixed frequency and fixed voltage, directly to the existing AC grid. This allows for microscale domestic generation in urban areas, which is a powerful argument for PV. In this model solar power is 'stored' in the AC grid during the day. In reality, the power system operates by matching generation and consumption at every instant in time. This means that houses can act as generating units during the day and consumption units during the night. If there is a balance between the energy generated during the day and the energy consumed during the night over a twelve-month period, a single house, a housing complex, could be energy-neutral in terms of its environmental impact.

The advance of electronics has also meant that the technology that allows for individual solar panels to be connected to the grid with power outputs in the 20–100W range now exists (Haeberlin, 2001). At this power range, the cost of an individual solar panel approaches that of a standard consumer electronic product (around £300). This opens up the prospect of solar becoming a consumer-electronics-based electricity generation technology. One could look at it as the reverse of the process by which energy is consumed in small units in lighting, home computers, entertainment systems, etc. The integrated effect of this small unit consumption is, of course, very significant in urban areas. As consumers become more aware of, and concerned about, the environment, there exists the possibility of encouraging people to offset their consumption by installing one or two solar panels in their homes. With a small number of panels, they can be easily mounted and directly plugged into the domestic electricity supply through the standard three-pin sockets. Each panel will have an electronic power conversion unit, which ensures that the output conforms to the regulatory requirements and allows for such direct connection. This is an extension of the very popular solar garden lamp, a consumer item that can be purchased directly in DIY stores. They are stand-alone lights, with a battery that gets charged up during the day via a solar cell, and which run off the battery at night. The individual grid-connected solar panel, termed the AC module, is a unit, which allows solar-generated power from individual houses to be pooled (see www.enecsys.com).

4.8   Summary

The photovoltaic conversion of solar light directly into electricity is an established and mature technology. It has developed over the past thirty years to the point where the reliability and efficiency of solar cells are now guaranteed by manufacturers for up to twenty-five years.

Some examples of the wide variety of applications that solar photovoltaics now enjoy has been given in this chapter. The cost-effectiveness of solar PV has also been examined: cost-effectiveness is very much dependent on location and application area. Building-integrated PV is seen as a major opportunity for European PV programmes. There are exciting opportunities to reduce costs and, potentially, increase efficiency in the next generation of solar cells, which are currently at the R&D stage.

The best architecture for the connection of existing solar cell technologies and utilising the generated power remains an open question, however. The advance of power conditioning and control electronics has enabled new architectures that connect to the grid to generate small units of power in a highly distributed manner but the potential of such systems is still to be explored. Power-conditioning electronics at present are not as developed or mature as the solar cell technology. A challenge for solar PV systems is related to realising the best connection architecture with intelligent electronics, which enable the 'release' of power from solar cells for efficient and effective utilisation.

4.9   References

Archer, M. D., and R. Hill (2001). *Clean Electricity from Photovoltaics*, London: Imperial College Press.

Benner, J. P., and L. Kazmerski (1999). Photovoltaics gaining greater visibility, *IEEE Spectrum*, 29(9): 34–42.

Gratzel, M. (2001). Photoelectrochemical cells, *Nature*, 414: 338–44.

Green, M. A. (1995). *Silicon Solar Cells: Advanced Principles and Practice*, Sydney: University of New South Wales Press.

Grubb, M., and R. Vigotti (1997). *Renewable Energy Strategies for Europe*, Vol. II, *Electricity Systems and Primary Energy Sources*, London: Earthscan.

Haeberlin, H. (2001). *Evolution of Inverters for Grid–Connected PV Systems from 1989–2000*, paper presented at the 17th European Photovoltaic Solar Energy Conference, Munich, 22–6 October.

Hardingham, C., and S. P. Wood (1998). High-efficiency GaAs solar arrays in space, *GEC Review*, 13(3).

Lysen, E. (2003). Photovoltaics: an outlook for the 21st century, *Renewable Energy World*, 6(1): 42–53.

McDaniels, D. K. (1979). *The Sun: Our Future Energy Source*, New York: John Wiley and Sons.

Nelson, J. (2003). *The Physics of Solar Cells*, London: Imperial College Press.

Nuttall, W. J. (2004). The sunny side of solar power, *The Engineer*, 24 September–7 October: 23.

Schmidt-Mende, L., A. Fechtenkotter, K. Mullen, E. Moons, R. H. Friend and J. D. MacKenzie (2001). Self-organized discotic liquid crytals for high-efficiency organic photovoltaics, *Science*, 293: 1119–22.

Shah, A., P. Torres, R. Tscharner, N. Wyrsch, and H. Keppner (1999). Photovoltaic technology: the case for thin-film solar cells, *Science*, 285: 692–8.

Thomas, R., T. Grainger, B., Gething, and M. Keys (1999). *Photovoltaics in Buildings: A Design Guide*, London: Max Fordham & Partners in association with Feliden Clegg Architects for the Department of Trade and Industry.

Wagner, A. (2000). Set for the 21st century: Germany's New Renewable Energy Law, *Renewable Energy World*, 3(2): 79–83.

Wenham, S. R., M. A. Green and M. E. Watt (1994). *Applied Photovoltaics*, Sydney: Bridge Printing.

Zhao, J., A. P. Wang, P. Altermatt and M. A. Green (1995). 24% efficient solar cells with double layer anti-reflection coatings and reduced resistance loss, *Applied Physics Letters*, 66: 3636–8.

5 Bioenergy: future prospects for thermal processing of biomass

Tony Bridgwater

5.1 Introduction

Renewable energy is of growing importance in satisfying environmental concerns over fossil fuel usage. Wood and other forms of biomass, including energy crops and agricultural and forestry wastes, are some of the main renewable energy resources available. These can provide the only source of renewable liquid, gaseous and solid fuels. Biomass is considered the renewable energy source with the highest potential to contribute to the energy needs of modern society for both the developed and developing economies worldwide (European Commission, 1997; IEA, 2000). Energy from biomass based on short-rotation forestry and other energy crops can contribute significantly to meeting the objectives of the Kyoto Agreement in reducing greenhouse gas emissions and addressing the problems related to climate change (IEA Bioenergy, 1998).

Biomass fuels and residues can be converted to energy via thermal, biological and physical processes. Each process area is described with the greatest emphasis on the technologies that are attracting the most attention in research, demonstration and commercial arenas. In advanced thermal conversion, biomass gasification has attracted considerable interest in the last twenty years as it offers potentially higher efficiencies compared to combustion, although combustion offers much lower risks for commercial implementation and thus continues to be the technology of choice, including co-firing. Liquids from the fast pyrolysis of biomass have recently attracted much more interest as a fuel for heat and power, as a potential energy carrier for feeding high-capacity transport fuel synthesis plants and as a source of chemicals for integration into a biorefinery.

There are three main thermal processes available for converting biomass to a more useful energy form: combustion, gasification and pyrolysis. Their products and applications are summarised in figure 5.1.

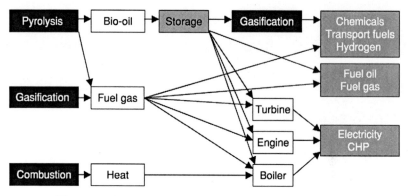

Figure 5.1. Products from thermal biomass conversion.

5.2   Combustion

The combustion of biomass and related materials is widely practised commercially to provide heat and power. The technology is commercially available and presents minimum risk to investors. The product is heat, which must be used immediately for heat and/or power generation as storage is not a viable option. Overall efficiencies to power can be as low as 15 per cent for the smaller and older plants, up to 35 per cent for larger and newer plants. Costs are competitive at present only when wastes are used as feed material, such as from pulp and paper, and agriculture. Emissions and ash handling remain technical problems. The technology is, however, widely available commercially and there are many successful working examples throughout North America and Europe, frequently utilising forestry, agricultural and industrial wastes.

5.3   Gasification

Fuel gas can be produced from biomass and related materials, either by partial oxidation, to give a mixture of carbon monoxide, carbon dioxide, hydrogen and methane, or by steam or pyrolytic gasification, as illustrated in table 5.1.

Gasification occurs in a number of sequential steps:

- drying to evaporate moisture;
- pyrolysis to give gas, vaporised tars or oils and a solid char residue; and
- gasification or partial oxidation of the solid char, pyrolysis tars and pyrolysis gases.

Table 5.1 *Modes of thermal gasification*

Partial oxidation with air	Main products are CO, CO_2, H2, CH_4, N_2, tar. This gives a low heating value gas of $\sim$5MJ/m^3. Utilisation problems can arise in combustion, particularly in gas turbines.
Partial oxidation with oxygen	The main products are CO, CO_2, H_2, CH_4, tar (no N_2). This gives a medium heating value gas of $\sim$10–12MJ/m^3. The cost of providing and using oxygen is compensated for by a better-quality fuel gas. The trade-off is finely balanced.
Steam (pyrolytic or allothermal) gasification	The main products are CO, CO_2, H_2, CH_4, tar. This gives a medium heating value gas of $\sim$15–20MJ/m^3. The process has two stages, with a primary reactor producing gas and char and a second reactor for char combustion to reheat sand, which is recirculated to provide the thermal energy for high-temperature pyrolysis. The gas heating value is maximised due to a higher methane and higher hydrocarbon gas content, but at the expense of lower overall efficiency due to loss of carbon in the second reactor, where it is burned to provide heat for the primary reactor.

When a solid fuel is heated to 300–500°C in the absence of an oxidising agent, it pyrolyses to solid char, condensable hydrocarbons or tar, and gases. The relative yields of gas, liquid and char depend mostly on the rate of heating and the final temperature. Generally in gasification, pyrolysis proceeds at a much quicker rate than gasification, and the latter is thus the rate-controlling step. The gas, liquid and solid products of pyrolysis then react with the oxidising agent – usually air – to give permanent gases of CO, CO_2, and H_2, and lesser quantities of hydrocarbon gases. Char gasification is the interactive combination of several gas–solid and gas–gas reactions in which solid carbon is oxidised to carbon monoxide and carbon dioxide, and hydrogen is generated through the water gas shift reaction. The gas–solid reactions of char oxidation are the slowest and limit the overall rate of the gasification process. Many of the reactions are catalysed by the alkali metals present in wood ash, but still do not reach equilibrium. The gas composition is influenced by many factors, such as feed composition, water content, reaction temperature and the extent of the oxidation of the pyrolysis products.

Not all the liquid products from the pyrolysis step are completely converted, due to the physical or geometrical limitations of the reactor and the chemical limitations of the reactions involved, and these give rise to contaminant tars in the final product gas. Due to the higher temperatures involved in gasification compared to pyrolysis, these tars tend to be refractory and are difficult to remove by thermal, catalytic or physical processes. This aspect of tar cracking or removal in gas clean-up is one of the most important technical uncertainties in the implementation of gasification technologies, and is discussed below.

A number of reactor configurations have been developed and tested, with their advantages and disadvantages summarised in table 5.2. A recent survey of gasifier manufacturers found that 75 per cent of gasifiers offered commercially were downdraft, 20 per cent were fluid beds (including circulating fluid beds), 2.5 per cent were updraft and 2.5 per cent were other types (Knoef, 2000).

The fuel gas quality requirements, for turbines in particular, are very high. Tar is a particular problem and remains the most significant technical barrier. There are two basic ways of destroying tars (Bridgwater, 1994), both of which have been and continue to be extensively studied:

- by catalytic cracking using, for example, dolomite or nickel; and
- by thermal cracking, for example by partial oxidation or direct contact.

The gas is very costly to store or transport so it has to be used immediately. Hot gas efficiencies for the gasifier (total energy in raw product gas divided by energy in feed) can be as high as 95 per cent to 97 per cent for close-coupled turbine and boiler applications, and up to 85 per cent for cold gas efficiencies. In power generation, using combined-cycle operation, efficiencies of up to 50 per cent for the largest installations have been proposed, falling to 35 per cent for smaller applications. A number of comprehensive reviews have been published, such as Maniatis (2001) and Bridgwater (1995).

5.3.1   Status

There is still very little information on costs, emissions, efficiencies, turn-down ratios and actual operational experience. In particular, no manufacturer is willing to give full guarantees for the technical performance of its gasification technology – i.e. offer substantial financial penalties if the performance targets are not met. This confirms the limited operating experience and the relatively low level of confidence in the technology.

Figure 5.8 suggests a relationship between gasification technologies in terms of their strength and their market attractiveness for power generation.

Atmospheric circulating fluidised bed gasifiers have proved very reliable with a variety of feedstocks, and are relatively easy to scale up from a few MWth up to 100MWth. Even for capacities above 100MWth there is confidence that the industry will be able to provide reliable gasifiers. This appears to be the preferred system for large-scale applications and

Table 5.2 *Gasifier reactor types and characteristics*

Downdraft – fixed-bed reactor (figure 5.2)

- Solid moves slowly down a vertical shaft and air is introduced and reacts at a throat that supports the gasifying biomass.
- Solid and product gas move downwards in co-current mode.
- The technology is simple, reliable and proven for fuels that are relatively uniform in size and have a low content of fines (below 5mm).
- A relatively clean gas is produced with low tar and usually with high carbon conversion.
- There is limited scale-up potential to about 500kg/h feed rate.
- There is a maximum feed moisture content of around 35% wet basis.

Examples
Biomass Engineering (Walker et al., 2001), Rural Energy (DTI, 1998), BTG&KARA (Knoef et al., 2000), Fluidyne (see www.fluidynenz.com), Johanssen (see www.eskomenterprises.com).

Updraft – fixed-bed reactor (figure 5.2)

- Solid moves down a vertical shaft and contacts a counter-current upward-moving product gas stream.
- The technology is simple, reliable and proven for fuels that are relatively uniform in size and have a low content of fines (below 5mm).
- The product gas is very dirty with high levels of tars, although tar crackers have been developed.
- Scale-up potential limited to around 4 dry t/h feed rate.
- There is high thermal efficiency and high carbon conversion.
- Intolerant of high proportion of fines in feed.
- The gas exit temperature is low.
- Good turn-down capability.

Examples
Wellman (McLellan, 2000), Volund (see www.volund.dk), Bioneer (Kurkela, 1999).

Bubbling fluid bed (figure 5.3)

- Good temperature control and high reaction rates.
- Higher particulates in the product gas and moderate tar levels in product gas.
- Good scale-up potential to 10–15 dry t/h with high specific capacity and easily started and stopped.
- Greater tolerance to particle size range.
- Good temperature control.
- Tar-cracking catalyst can be added to bed.
- Limited turn-down capability.
- There is some carbon loss with ash.

Examples
EPI (see www.energyproducts.com), Carbona (Salo and Horwath, 1999), Dinamec (De Ruyck et al., 1996).

Table 5.2. (*cont.*)

Circulating fluid bed (figure 5.4)
All the features of bubbling beds, plus:

- Large minimum size for viability, above around 15 t/h dry feed rate.
- High cost at low capacity.
- In-bed catalytic processing not easy.

Examples
Technical University of Vienna (Hofbauer and Rauch, 2001), TPS (Waldheim et al., 2001), Lurgi (Vierrath and Greil, 2001), Foster Wheeler (Nieminen, 1999).

Entrained flow (figure 5.5)

- Inherently simple reactor design, but only potentially viable above around 20 dry t/h feed rate and with good scale-up potential.
- Costly feed preparation needed for woody biomass.
- Carbon loss with ash.
- Little experience with biomass available.

Examples
Texaco, R&D.

Twin fluid bed (figures 5.6 and 5.7)

- More complex process, with two close-coupled reactors with difficult scale-up and high cost.
- The gasifier can either be a circulating fluid bed (e.g. Ferco, figure 5.6) or bubbling bed (e.g. Austrian Energy, figure 5.7) and similarly the char combustor can be either a bubbling bed or a second circulating fluid bed (e.g. Ferco and Austrian Energy).
- Complexity requires capacities of >10 t/h for viability.
- MHV gas produced with air and without requiring oxygen.
- Low carbon conversion to gas as carbon in char is lost to reheat sand for recycling.
- High tar levels in gas.
- Tar-cracking catalyst can be added to bed.

Examples
Ferco, Vermont (Paisley et al., 2001).

Other reactors

- Moving bed with mechanical transport of solid; usually lower-temperature processes. Includes: multiple hearth; horizontal moving bed; sloping hearth; screw/auger kiln.
- Rotary kiln: good gas–solid contact; careful design needed to avoid solid carry-over.
- Multi-stage reactors with pyrolysis and gasification separated for improved process control and better-quality gas.
- Cyclonic and vortex reactors: high particle velocities give high reaction rates.

Table 5.2. (*cont.*)

Examples
Rotary kiln (Heermann et al., 2000);
Two-stage pyrolysis + gasification: Thermoselect (Heerman et al., 2000), Compact Power
(Heerman et al., 2000)

Use of oxygen

- Gives better-quality gas.
- High financial and energy cost of providing oxygen and high cost of meeting extra
  process requirements, including safety.
- No evidence that benefits exceed costs.
- Can be combined with pressurise gasification.

Examples
There are no known current or recent examples of oxygen-fuelled gasifiers.

High-pressure gasification

- Significant additional cost for pressure with smaller savings from reduced
  vessel and piping sizes.
- Avoids need for fuel gas cleaning, cooling and compression in power generation as hot
  filtered gas with tars can be directly burned in gas turbine. The omission of this equipment,
  which is needed in atmospheric gasification to satisfy fuel gas quality requirements for
  compression to feed the turbine, offers some cost savings and efficiency benefits, but large
  sizes are needed to justify the additional costs, and these do not fully compensate for the
  higher cost of pressure operation.

Examples
The most recent example is at Varnamo, which finished operation
in 2000 (Ståhl et al., 2001): also Carbona (Salo and Horwath, 1999).

All biomass-fuelled gasifiers

- Feeding can give problems.
- Ash slagging and clinkering potential.

---

is used by most industrial companies, and these systems therefore have
high market attractiveness and are technically well proven.

Atmospheric bubbling fluidised bed gasifiers have proved to be reliable
with a variety of feedstocks, both at pilot scale and in commercial applications in the small to medium scale up to about 25MWth. They are limited
in their capacity size range as they have not been scaled up significantly,
and the gasifier diameter is significantly larger than that of circulating
fluid beds for the same feedstock capacity. On the other hand, they are
more economic for small- to medium-range capacities. Their market
attractiveness is thus relatively high as well as their technology strength.

Pressurised fluidised bed systems, either circulating or bubbling,
are considered of more limited market attractiveness due to the more

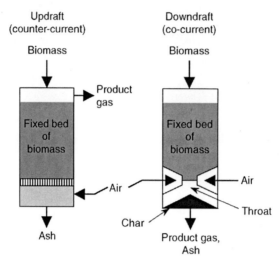

Figure 5.2. Fixed bed gasifiers.

complex operation of the installation and the additional costs related to the construction of pressurised vessels. However, pressurised fluidised bed systems have the advantage in integrated combined-cycle applications as the need to compress the fuel gas prior its utilisation in the combustion chamber of the gas turbine is avoided.

Atmospheric downdraft gasifiers are attractive for small-scale applications up to about 1.5MWth as there is a very substantial market in both

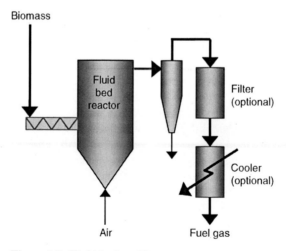

Figure 5.3. Fluid bed gasifier.

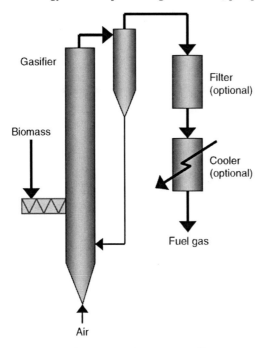

Figure 5.4. Circulating fluid bed gasifier.

developed and developing economies (Limbrick, 2000). However, the problem of efficient tar removal is still a major problem and a higher level of automation is needed, especially for small-scale industrial applications. Nevertheless, recent progress in the catalytic conversion of tar gives more credible options, and these systems can therefore be considered of average technical strength.

Atmospheric updraft gasifiers seem to have little market attractiveness for power applications. While this may be due to the high tar levels in the fuel gas, recent developments in tar cracking have shown that very low levels can be achieved from dedicated thermal/catalytic cracking reactors downstream of the gasifier (McLellan, 2000; Beld, 1997). Another possible reason is that the upper size of a single unit is around 2.5MWe, so larger plant capacities require multiple units.

Atmospheric cyclonic gasifiers have only recently been tested for bio-mass feedstocks, and although they have medium market attractiveness due to their simplicity they are still unproven. Finally, atmospheric entrained bed gasifiers are still at a very early stage of development, and since they require feedstock of a very small particle size their market attractiveness is very low. No company is known to be developing

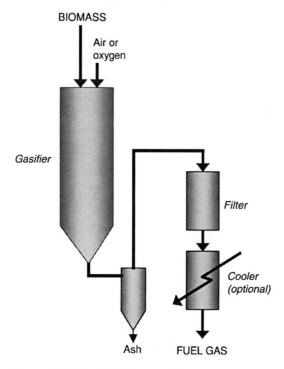

Figure 5.5. Entrained flow gasifier.

pressurised systems for downdraft, updraft, cyclonic or entrained bed gasifiers for biomass feedstocks, and it is difficult to imagine that such a technology could ever be developed into a commercial product due to the inherent problems of scale, tar removal and cost.

In conclusion, for large-scale applications the preferred and most reliable system is the circulating fluidised bed gasifier, while for small-scale applications the downdraft gasifiers are the most extensively studied. Bubbling fluidised bed gasifiers can be competitive in medium-scale applications. Large-scale fluidised bed systems have become commercial due to successful co-firing projects (see below) while moving bed gasifiers are still trying to achieve this.

5.3.2 Applications for gas

Figure 5.9 summarises the range of fuel, electricity and chemical products that can be derived from the product gas. Medium heating value gas from steam or pyrolytic gasification, or from oxygen gasification, is better suited to the synthesis of transport fuels and commodity chemicals

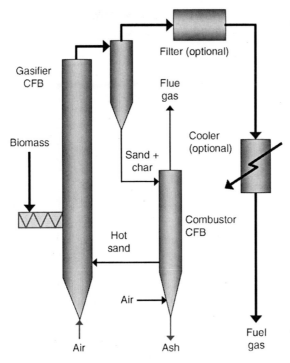

Figure 5.6. Steam or pyrolytic gasifier twin fluid bed with CFB gasifier and CFB char combustor.

due to the absence of diluent nitrogen, which would pass through unchanged but reduce process efficiency and increase costs. The exception is ammonia synthesis, when the nitrogen content derived from air gasification can be utilised in the ammonia synthesis process. In electricity generation, there is no evidence that the benefits of producing higher heating value gas with oxygen gasification justifies the cost of providing and using oxygen, which explains the low level of interest in oxygen gasification. The technology for the synthesis of commodity chemicals is commercially available but requires a very high gas quality, which is still elusive, as well as a very large scale of operation, which for biomass systems is difficult to locate.

The major interest currently is in electricity generation, on account of the ease of distributing the product and the absence of product quality requirements concerning compatibility in the market place, which remains a significant problem with many fuel and chemical products. This attraction is enhanced by the widespread incentives for electricity generation from renewable resources throughout Europe.

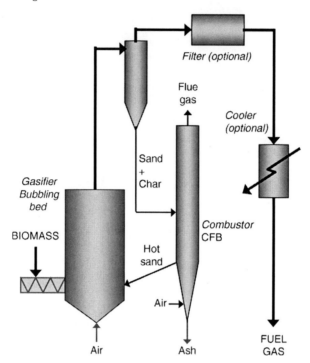

Figure 5.7. Steam or pyrolytic gasifier twin fluid bed with bubbling bed gasifier and CFB char combustor.

Co-firing is a particularly attractive option since most biofuels including gases, liquids and solids, can readily be introduced into conventional power stations, and this takes advantage of economies of scale, contributes comparable fossil fuel savings and reduces risks and uncertainties. There has been little commercial activity in this area.

5.3.3   Summary

Although biomass gasification technologies have been successfully demonstrated on a large scale and several demonstration projects are in operation or at an advanced stage of construction (Maniatis, 1999; Costello, 1999), they are still relatively expensive compared to fossil-based energy and thus face economic and other non-technical barriers when trying to penetrate energy markets (European Commission, 2000; Beenackers, 2001; Harrisson et al., 1998).

Biomass gasification will be able to penetrate energy markets only if it is completely integrated into a biomass system. Thus, the innovation in

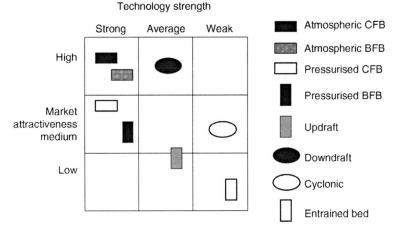

Figure 5.8. Technology status of biomass gasification.
Source: derived from Maniatis (2001).

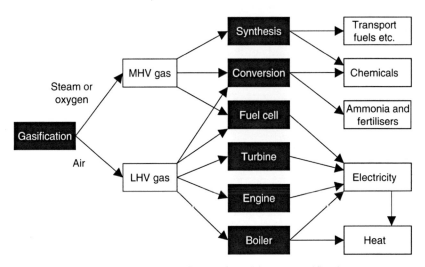

Figure 5.9. Applications for gas from biomass gasification.

practically all demonstration projects under implementation lies not only in the technical aspects of the various processes but also in the integration of the gasification technologies into existing or newly developed systems such that it can be demonstrated that the overall system offers better prospects for economic development (Maniatis and Millich, 1998).

5.4   Pyrolysis

Pyrolysis is thermal decomposition occurring in the absence of oxygen. In addtion, it is always the first step in combustion and gasification processes where it is followed by total or partial oxidation of the primary products. A lower process temperature and longer vapour residence times favour the production of charcoal. A high temperature and a longer residence time increase the biomass conversion to gas, and a moderate temperature and short vapour residence times are optimum for producing liquids.

Table 5.3 indicates the product distribution obtained from different modes of pyrolysis process. Fast pyrolysis for liquids production is of particular interest currently.

Fast pyrolysis occurs in a few seconds or less. Therefore, not only chemical reaction kinetics but also heat and mass transfer processes, as well as phase transition phenomena, play important roles. The critical issue is to bring the reacting biomass particle to the optimum process temperature and minimise its exposure to the intermediate (lower) temperatures that favour the formation of charcoal. One way this object-ive can be achieved is by using small particles, for example in the fluidised bed processes that are described later. Another possibility is to transfer heat very rapidly only to the particle surface that contacts the heat source (this second method is applied in ablative processes, which are described later). In order to illustrate the science and technology of thermal conversion in sufficient detail to appreciate the potential, fast pyrolysis is described at length.

5.4.1   Principles

In fast pyrolysis, biomass decomposes to generate mostly vapours and aerosols and some charcoal. After cooling and condensation a dark brown mobile liquid is formed, which has a heating value about a half that of conventional fuel oil. While it is related to the traditional pyrolysis processes for making charcoal, fast pyrolysis is an advanced process, with carefully controlled parameters to give high yields of liquid. The essential features of a fast pyrolysis process for producing liquids are:

- very high heating and heat transfer rates at the reaction interface, which usually requires a finely ground biomass feed;
- carefully controlled pyrolysis reaction temperature of around 500°C and vapour phase temperature of 400–450°C;
- short vapour residence times of typically less than 2 seconds; and
- rapid cooling of the pyrolysis vapours to give the bio-oil product.

Table 5.3 *Typical product yields (dry wood basis) obtained by modes of pyrolysis*

Mode	Characteristics	Liquid	Char	Gas
Fast pyrolysis	Moderate temperature, short residence times, particularly vapour	75%	12%	13%
Carbonisation	Low temperature, very long residence times	30%	35%	35%
Gasification	High temperature, long residence times	5%	10%	85%

The main product, bio-oil, is obtained in yields of up to 75 per cent wt on a dry feed basis, together with by-product char and gas, which are used within the process with the result there are no waste streams other than flue gas and ash.

A fast pyrolysis process includes drying the feed, typically to less than 10 per cent water, in order to minimise the water in the product liquid oil (although up to 15 per cent can be acceptable), grinding the feed (to around 2 millimetres in the case of fluid bed reactors) to give sufficiently small particles to ensure rapid reaction, pyrolysis reaction, the separation of solids (char) and collection of the liquid product (bio-oil).

Any form of biomass can be considered for fast pyrolysis. While most work has been carried out on wood due to its consistency, and comparability between tests, nearly a hundred different biomass types have been tested by many laboratories, ranging from agricultural wastes such as straw, olive pits and nut shells to energy crops such as miscanthus and sorghum and solid wastes such as sewage sludge and leather wastes.

5.4.2 Reactors

At the heart of a fast pyrolysis process is the reactor. Although it probably represents at most only about 10 per cent to 15 per cent of the total capital cost of an integrated system, almost all research and development has focused on the reactor. The rest of the process consists of biomass reception, storage and handling, biomass drying and grinding, product collection, storage and, when relevant, upgrading. The key aspects of these peripheral steps are described later. A comprehensive survey of fast pyrolysis processes has been published that describes all the pyrolysis processes for liquids production that have been built and tested in the last ten to fifteen years (see Bridgwater and Peacocke, 1999).

Table 5.4 *Fast pyrolysis reactor types and characteristics*

Bubbling fluid bed (figure 5.10)

- Simple construction and operation.
- Good temperature control.
- Very efficient heat transfer to biomass particles due to high solids density.
- Easy scaling.
- Well-understood technology.
- Good and consistent performance, with high liquid yields of typically 70–75% wt from wood on a dry feed basis.
- Heating can be achieved in a variety of ways, as shown in figure 5.3.
- Residence time of solids and vapours is controlled by the fluidising gas flow rate and is higher for char than for vapours.
- Char acts as an effective vapour-cracking, catalyst at fast pyrolysis reaction temperatures, so rapid and effective char separation/elutriation is important.
- Small biomass particle sizes are needed to achieve high biomass heating rates of less than 2–3mm.
- Good char separation is important; usually achieved by ejection and entrainment, followed by separation in one or more cyclones.
- Heat transfer to bed at large scale has to be considered carefully due to scale-up limitations.

Examples
Waterloo (Scott et al., 1985), Union Fenosa (Cuevas et al., 1995), Dynamotive (Robson, 2001), Wellman (McLellan, 2000).

Circulating fluid bed and transported bed (figure 5.11)

- Good temperature control can be achieved in reactor.
- Residence time for the char is almost the same as for vapours and gas.
- CFBs are suitable for very large throughputs.
- Well-understood technology.
- Hydrodynamics more complex.
- Char is more attrited due to higher gas velocities; char separation is by cyclone.
- Closely integrated char combustion in a second reactor requires careful control.
- Heat transfer at large scale has to be proven.

Examples
Ensyn (see www.ensyn.com), CRES (Boukis et al., 2001).

Ablative pyrolysis (figure 5.12)

- High pressure of particle on hot reactor wall, achieved due to centrifugal force (NREL) or mechanically (Aston).
- High relative motion between particle and reactor wall.
- Reactor wall temperature should be less than 600°C.
- Large feed sizes can be used.
- Inert gas is not required for fluidisation or transport, so the processing equipment is smaller (in case of mechanically applied pressure).
- The reaction system is more 'intensive', in that there is no fluidising gas, very little transport gas (as the biomass is moved mechanically), the high heat transfer rates reduce the area of heat transfer equipment, and higher throughputs are achieved per unit reactor volume compared to fluid and related systems.

Table 5.4. (*cont.*)

- Reaction rates are limited by heat transfer to the reactor, not to the biomass.
- The process is surface-area-controlled, so scaling is more costly.
- The process is mechanically driven, so the reactor is more complex.

Examples
CNRS Nancy (Lédé et al., 1985), NREL (Diebold and Scahill, 1988), Aston University (Peacocke and Bridgwater, 1995).

Entrained flow

- Simple technology.
- Poor heat transfer.
- High gas flows result in large plant and cause difficult liquid collection.
- Good scale-up.
- Lower liquid yields.

Examples
GTRI (Kovac and O'Neil, 1989), Egemin (Maniatis et al., 1993).

Rotating cone (figure 5.13)

- Centrifugation (at around 10Hz) drives hot sand and biomass up a rotating heated cone.
- Vapours are collected and processed conventionally.
- Char and sand drop into a fluid bed surrounding the cone, from where they are lifted to a separate fluid bed combustor where char is burned to heat the sand, which is then dropped back into the rotating cone.
- Char is burned in a secondary bubbling fluid bed combustor; the hot sand is recirculated to the pyrolyser.
- Carrier gas requirements in the pyrolysis reactor are much less than for fluid bed and transported bed systems, as the biomass is mixed with the sand heat carrier and transported up the rotating cone by centrifugal action; however, some gas is needed for transporting the char and sand to the char combustor.
- Complex integrated operation of three subsystems is required: rotating cone pyrolyser, riser for sand recycling, and bubbling bed char combustor.
- Liquid yields of 60–70% on dry feed are typically obtained.

Examples
Twente University (Prins and Wagenaar, 1997), BTG (Wagenaar et al., 2001).

Vacuum pyrolysis

- Not a true fast pyrolysis process, as solids residence time is very high.
- It can process larger particles than most fast pyrolysis reactors.
- There is less char in the liquid product due to lower gas velocities.
- There is no requirement for a carrier gas.
- Liquid yields of 35–50% on dry feed are typically obtained with higher char yields than fast pyrolysis systems; conversely, the liquid yields are higher than in slow pyrolysis technologies because of the fast removal of vapours from the reaction zone.
- The process is relatively complicated mechanically.

Example
Pyrovac (Yang et al., 2001).

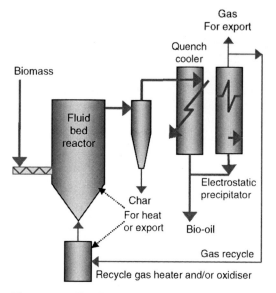

Figure 5.10. Bubling fluid bed reactor.

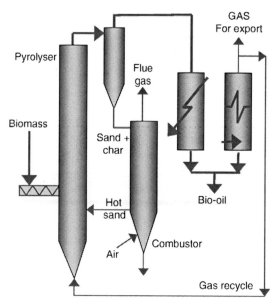

Figure 5.11. Circulating fluid bed reactor.

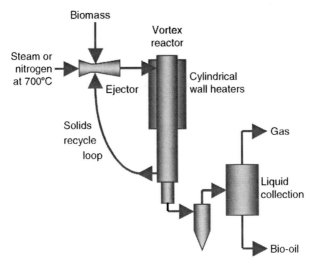

Figure 5.12. NREL vortex ablative reactor.

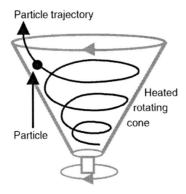

Figure 5.13. Principle of rotating cone pyrolysis reactor.

5.4.3   Char removal

Char acts as a vapour-cracking catalyst, so rapid and effective separation from the pyrolysis product vapours is essential. Cyclones are the usual method of char removal, but some fines always pass through the cyclones and collect in the liquid product, where they accelerate ageing and exacerbate the instability problem, which is described below. Hot vapour filtration, analogous to hot gas filtration in gasification processes, gives a high-quality char-free product (Diebold et al., 1994), but the liquid yield is reduced by about 10 per cent to 20 per cent by the char accumulating on the filter surface that cracks the vapours.

Pressure filtration of the liquid is very difficult because of the complex interaction of the char and the pyrolytic lignin, which appears to form a gel-like phase, rapidly blocking the filter. Modification of the liquid's microstructure by the addition of solvents, such as methanol or ethanol, that solubilise the less soluble constituents will improve this problem and also contribute to improvements in liquid stability, as described below.

5.4.4   Liquid collection

The gaseous products from fast pyrolysis consist of aerosols, true vapours and non-condensable gases. These require rapid cooling to minimise secondary reactions and to condense the true vapours, while the aerosols require coalescence or agglomeration. Simple heat exchange can cause the preferential deposition of lignin-derived components, leading to liquid fractionation and, eventually, blockage. Quenching in product oil or in an immiscible hydrocarbon solvent is widely practised. Orthodox aerosol capture devices such as demisters and other commonly used impingement devices are not very effective, and electrostatic precipitation is currently the preferred method at smaller scales up to pilot plant. The vapour product from fluid bed and transported bed reactors has a low partial pressure of collectible products due to the large volumes of fluidising gas, and this is an important design consideration in liquid collection.

5.4.5   Pyrolysis liquid: bio-oil

Pyrolysis liquid is referred to by many names, including pyrolysis oil, bio-oil, bio-crude-oil, bio-fuel-oil, wood liquids, wood oil, liquid smoke, wood distillates, pyroligneous tar, pyroligneous acid and liquid wood. The crude pyrolysis liquid is dark brown and approximates to biomass in elemental composition. It is composed of a very complex mixture of oxygenated hydrocarbons with an appreciable proportion of water, from both the original moisture and the reaction product. Solid char and dissolved alkali metals from ash (Huffmann et al., 1993) may also be present.

5.4.5.1 Liquid product characteristics   The liquid is formed by rapidly quenching and thus 'freezing' the intermediate products of the flash degradation of hemicellulose, cellulose and lignin. The liquid thus

Table 5.5 *Typical properties of wood-derived crude bio-oil*

Physical property	Typical value	Characteristics
Moisture content	15–30%	• Liquid fuel
pH	2.5	• Ready substitution for conventional
Specific gravity	1.2	fuels in many static applications, such
Elemental analysis C	55–58%	as boilers, engines, turbines.
H	5.5–7.0%	• Heating value of 17MJ/kg at 25% wt
		water is about 40% that of fuel oil/diesel.
O	35–40%	• Does not mix with hydrocarbon fuels.
N	0–0.2%	• Not as stable as fossil fuels.
Ash	0–0.2%	• Quality needs definition for each
HHV as produced	16–19MJ/kg	application.
Viscosity (at 40°C and 25% water)	40–100cP	
Solids (char)	1%	
Vacuum distillation residue	up to 50%	

contains many reactive species, which contribute to its unusual decomposition products, and stabilizes the discontinuous phase of pyrolytic lignin macro-molecules through mechanisms such as hydrogen bonding. Ageing and instability are believed to result from a breakdown in this emulsion. In some ways it is analogous to the asphaltenes found in petroleum.

Fast pyrolysis liquid has a higher heating value of about 17MJ/kg as produced with about 25 per cent wt water, which cannot readily be separated. The liquid is often referred to as 'oil' or 'bio-oil' or 'bio-crude', although it will not mix with any hydrocarbon liquids. It is composed of a complex mixture of oxygenated compounds, which provide both the potential for and a challenge to utilisation. There are some important characteristics of this liquid, summarised in table 5.5 and discussed briefly in table 5.6. Bio-oil can be considered a micro-emulsion in which the continuous phase is an aqueous solution of holocellulose.

5.4.5.2 Upgrading pyrolysis liquid The most important properties that adversely affect bio-oil fuel quality are incompatibility with conventional fuels, the solids content, high viscosity and chemical instability. The field of chemical and physical upgrading of bio-oil has been reviewed thoroughly (see Diebold, 1999). Hot-gas filtration can reduce the ash content of the oil to less than 0.01 per cent and the alkali content to less than

Table 5.6 *Typical properties and characteristics of wood-derived crude bio-oil*

Appearance	Pyrolysis oil typically is a dark brown free-flowing liquid. Depending upon the initial feedstock and the mode of fast pyrolysis, the colour can be almost black through dark red–brown to dark green, being influenced by the presence of microcarbon in the liquid and by the chemical composition. Hot vapour filtration gives a more translucent red–brown appearance due to the absence of char. High nitrogen contents in the liquid can give it a dark green tinge.
Odour	The liquid has a distinctive odour–an acrid, smoky smell, which can irritate the eyes if exposed for a prolonged period to the liquids. The cause of this smell is due to the low-molecular-weight aldehydes and acids. The liquid contains several hundred different chemicals in widely varying proportions, ranging from formaldehyde and acetic acid to complex high-molecular-weight phenols, anhydrosugars and other oligosaccharides.
Miscibility	The liquid contains varying quantities of water, which forms a stable single-phase mixture, ranging from about 15% wt to an upper limit of about 30–50% wt water, depending on how it was produced and subsequently collected. Pyrolysis liquids can tolerate the addition of some water, but there is a limit to the amount of water that can be added to the liquid before phase separation occurs; in other words, the liquid cannot be dissolved in water. It is miscible with polar solvents such as methanol, acetone, etc., but totally immiscible with petroleum-derived fuels.
Density	The density of the liquid is very high at around 1.2kg/litre, compared to light fuel oil at around 0.85kg/litre. This means that the liquid has about 42% of the energy content of fuel oil on a weight basis, but 61% on a volumetric basis. This has implications for the design and specification of equipment such as pumps.
Viscosity	The viscosity of the bio-oil as produced can vary from as low as 25cSt to as high as 1,000cSt (measured at 40°C) or more, depending on the feedstock, the water content of the oil, the amount of light ends that have been collected and the extent to which the oil has aged. Viscosity is important in many fuel applications (Diebold et al., 1997).
Distillation	Pyrolysis liquids cannot be completely vaporised once they have been recovered from the vapour phase. If the liquid is heated to 100°C or more to try to remove water or distil off lighter fractions, it rapidly reacts and eventually produces a solid residue of around 50% wt of the original liquid and some distillate containing volatile organic compounds and water. The liquid is, therefore, chemically unstable, and the instability increases with heating, so it is preferable to store the liquid at room temperature. These changes do also occur at room temperature, but much more slowly, and they can be accommodated in a commercial application.
Ageing of pyrolysis liquid	The complexity and nature of bio-oil causes some unusual behaviour, specifically that the following properties tend to change with time: • viscosity increases; • volatility decreases; and • phase separation and deposition of gums can occur.

10ppm – much lower than reported for biomass oils produced in systems using only cyclones.

A process for producing stable micro-emulsions with 5 per cent to 30 per cent of bio-oil in diesel has been developed at CANMET (Ikura et al., 1998), and the University of Florence in Italy has been working emulsions of 5 per cent to 95 per cent bio-oil in diesel (Baglioni et al., 2001). The addition of polar solvents, especially methanol, gave a significant positive effect on the oil stability (Diebold and Czernik, 1997).

Chemical/catalytic upgrading processes to produce hydrocarbon fuels that can be conventionally processed are more complex and costly than physical methods but offer significant improvements, ranging from simple stabilisation to high-quality fuel products (Maggi and Elliot, 1997). Full deoxygenation to high-grade products such as transportation fuels can be accomplished by two main routes: hydrotreating and catalytic vapour cracking over zeolites, both of which have been reviewed (see Bridgwater, 1996, and 1994).

5.4.6   Applications for bio-oil

Bio-oil can substitute for fuel oil or diesel in many static applications, including boilers, furnaces, engines and turbines for electricity generation. The possibilities are summarised in figure 5.14. There are also a range of chemicals that can be extracted or derived, including food flavourings, specialities, resins, agrichemicals, fertilisers and emissions control agents. Upgrading bio-oil to transportation fuels is feasible but currently not economic. At least 400 hours' operation has been achieved on a specially modified 250kWe dual-fuel engine and limited experience has been gained on a modified 2.5MWe gas turbine.

A range of chemicals can also be produced, from specialities such as levoglucosan to commodities such as resins and fertilisers – as summarised in table 5.7. Food flavourings are commercially produced from wood pyrolysis products in many countries. All chemicals are attractive possibilities due to their much higher added value compared to fuels and energy products, and lead to the possibility of a bio-refinery concept in which the optimum combinations of fuels and chemicals are produced.

5.4.7   Summary

The liquid bio-oil product from fast pyrolysis has the considerable advantage of being storable and transportable as well as the potential to supply a number of valuable chemicals, but there are many challenges

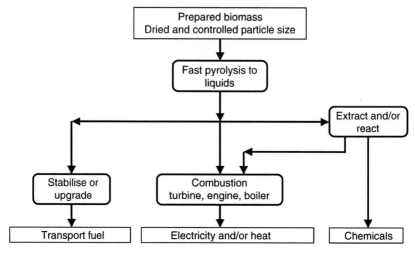

Figure 5.14. Applications for bio-oil.

Table 5.7 *Chemicals from fast pyrolysis*

Acetic acid	Adhesives	Calcium-enriched bio-oil	Food flavourings
Hydrogen	Hydroxyaceladehyde	Levoglucosan	Levoglucosenone
Preservatives	Resins	Slow-release fertilisers	sugars

facing fast pyrolysis relating to technology, product and applications. The problems facing the sector include the following:

- the cost of bio-oil, which is typically 10 per cent to 100 per cent more than fossil fuels;
- availability: there are limited supplies for testing;
- a lack of standards for the use and distribution of bio-oil, and inconsistent quality inhibits wider usage; considerable work is required to characterise and standardise these liquids and develop a wider range of energy applications;
- bio-oil is incompatible with conventional fuels;
- users are unfamiliar with this material;
- dedicated fuel-handling systems are needed; and
- pyrolysis as a technology does not enjoy a good image.

The most important issues that need to be addressed seem to be:

- scale-up;
- cost reduction;
- improving product quality, including setting norms and standards for producers and users;
- environment health and safety issues in handling, transport and usage;
- encouragement for developers to implement processes, and for users to implement applications; and
- information dissemination.

5.5   Economics of thermal conversion systems for electricity production

Comparisons of costs of electricity production between combustion (Combust), atmospheric pressure gasification (GasEng), integrated gasification in combined cycle (IGCC) and fast pyrolysis with an engine (PyrEng) are shown in figures 5.15 to 5.17. Capital costs for plants constructed now (i.e. first plant costs for gasification and pyrolysis and n'th plant costs for combustion, all costs in euros 2000) are shown in figure 5.15. The resultant electricity production costs for the four systems are shown in figure 5.16, while the benefits of learning about reducing capital costs as more plants are built – i.e. the longer-term costs – are shown in figure 5.17. Processes start with wood delivered as wet chips and include all steps and costs needed to produce electricity by turbine (Combust and IGCC) or engine (GasEng and PyrEng). Full details of the methodology can be found in Bridgwater et al., 2002, from which this data is derived.

The effect and benefits of scale are clearly shown, with a broad consensus view that 2.5MWe is about the minimum size of plant that might be economically viable, but the bigger the better within the constraints of biomass availability and supply. The higher capital costs of IGCC are compensated for by the higher efficiencies, so that delivered electricity costs, particularly at higher scales of operation, are competitive with the other technologies. Comparison of figures 5.16 and 5.17 shows that there are benefits from technology development or so-called learning but that these are relatively small. Comparison of electricity production costs with current industrial prices paid suggests that biomass-based power might be competitive with purchasing conventionally produced power, but it must be remembered that the latter are prices not costs, so the comparison becomes interesting only for embedded generation in which own-produced power replaces purchased power. It also confirms the current practice whereby renewable electricity requires

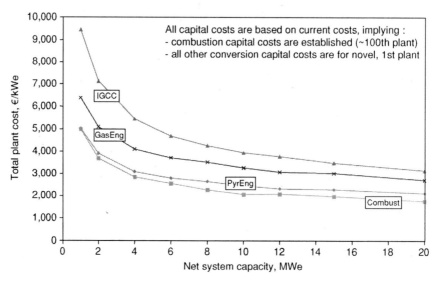

Figure 5.15. Comparison of total plant costs for biomass to electricity systems, 2000.

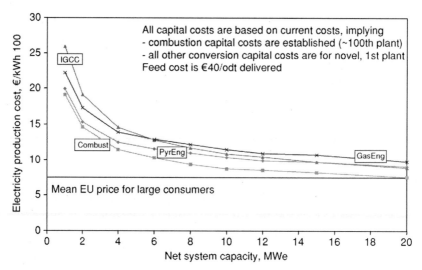

Figure 5.16. Comparison of electricity production costs for biomass to electricity systems, 2000.

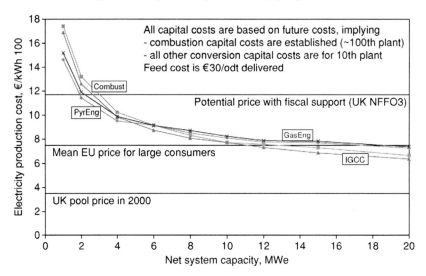

Figure 5.17. Potential electricity production costs using future system conditions.

support or incentives for it to succeed commercially. More detailed comparisons show that, while the performance of the GasEng and PyrEng options are similar, the substantial derating of the engine in the GasEng case requires a significantly larger engine for the same power output, thereby increasing the capital costs and power production costs of this option.

5.6   Barriers

The technologies have to overcome a number of technical and nontechnical barriers before industry will implement their commercialisation. The technical barriers have been described above, while some of the more important non-technical barriers are summarised below.

5.6.1   Economics

All biofuels have to compete with fossil fuels. For those countries that have made commitments to reduce fossil-fuel-derived carbon emissions, the current disincentive to implementation of bio-energy on simple cost grounds will have to be overcome; no company is going to invest in ventures that are guaranteed to lose money, regardless of the environmental benefits that may accrue. Industry will invest only in technology that has an acceptable return at an acceptable risk (Thornley and Wright, 2001). Acceptable returns will come from incentives for capital expenditure or product purchase, or from disincentives to orthodox options by, for example, the taxation of fossil fuels or legislation. This is one of the major roles that governments have to play.

5.6.2   Perceptions

There is widespread public approval of the interest in, and move towards, renewal energy and bioenergy – as long as it is not near me! Many projects are suffering from lengthy and hence costly planning and permitting delays, and increasing attention will need to be placed on 'selling' the idea to the populace where the plant is to be built. This problem could be exacerbated by the need to build smaller, and thus many more, plants than the present stock of plants than conventional power stations and refineries. Early plants may benefit from the curiosity factor and may enjoy popularity as attractions in their own right, or as part of the attraction of a 'green' site.

5.6.3   Policy

For industry to implement renewable energy technologies in order that commitments made to mitigate greenhouse gases can be met, investment has to be attractive. Without some fiscal incentives (or disincentives to fossil fuels), companies will invest only in those projects that are sufficiently profitable, and most of these will be in niche markets and special opportunities. As commented above, only governments can create the necessary instruments.

5.6.4   Scale

Economies of scale are a vital feature of the development of an industry and technology in which the larger a process can be built the cheaper it becomes. This is particularly important in the energy and process industries that will shoulder the responsibility for technology development and implementation. However, in the bioenergy industry, biomass is a diffuse resource that has to be harvested over large areas. A modest 10MWe power station operating at a modest efficiency of 35 per cent will require about 40,000 dry t/y of wood on a dry basis, which will require about 4,000 ha of land or 40 square km. This could reduce to 3,000 or even 2,000 ha (30–20 square km) if the promise of high-yielding, short-rotation forestry or annually harvested perennial crops is realised. Neither figure makes any allowance for non-productive land. There are, therefore, finite sizes that bioenergy processes can be built in, considering the costs and logistics of transporting biomass to a processing plant. The maximum size that has been suggested in Europe ranges from 30 to 80MWe in the short to medium term, and 100 to 150MWe in North America. This places a practical upper limit on the benefits of scale.

An alternative option is to consider massive trading in biomass, such as the suggested 3GWe power plant in Rotterdam, which would require some 10 million t/y of biomass, imported from countries such as Brazil. Italy is already importing 2.5 million t/y of biomass for co-firing, and most UK-based co-firing activities rely on imported biomass. Biomass is also traded extensively around the world for pulp and paper, so an extension to energy applications would require no more than the establishment of a market and acceptable economics.

5.6.5   Risk

Investors are generally risk-averse and always prefer low-risk investments, but, if risks have to be accepted, an appropriately higher return is expected. Technology developers can do much to minimise technical risk, and this topic has been thoroughly described and discussed (see Thornley and Wright, 2001).

5.6.6   Vested interests

The established energy suppliers and providers have considerable investments in orthodox energy systems and will always seek to maximise their returns and maintain their competitive edge. Most major energy companies have their own programmes of supporting renewable energy, but there have always been concerns over the extent to which they will seek to protect their interests by matching or bettering renewable power prices. The Renewable Energy trading scheme now mitigates against this practice by defining incentives and penalties.

5.7   Conclusions

There is substantial and growing interest in the thermal processing of biomass for biofuels, to make both energy and chemicals. Gasification and pyrolysis are complementary processes that have different market opportunities and should not be viewed as competitors. In both technologies considerable progress remains to be made in achieving the optimal interfacing of conversion and utilisation of the primary products from conversion, as well as the important interface between biomass production and conversion, which has been left largely to market forces.

The main challenges lie, first, in bringing the thermal conversion technologies closer to the power generation or chemicals production processes, with both sides of the interface moving to an acceptable middle position; and, second, in fully appreciating that – with rare exceptions – bioenergy systems will always be relatively small and must therefore be technically and economically competitive at much smaller scales of operation than the process and power generation industries are used to handling.

The integrated production of higher-value chemicals and lower-value fuels offers the most interesting commercial opportunities. These are widely referred to as biorefineries, and there are already a variety of examples around the world where local opportunities are being realised. Interest is growing both in new biomass-derived chemicals and in replacements for fossil-fuel-derived chemicals, particularly with the increases in crude oil prices in recent years. This is an area of significant growth prospects in which at least some of the non-technical barriers are capable of resolution.

5.8   References

Baglioni, P., D. Chiaramonti, M. Bonini, I. Soldaini and G. Tondi (2001). BCO/diesel oil emulsification: main achievements of the emulsification process and preliminary results of tests on diesel engines, in A. V. Bridgwater (ed.), *Progress in Thermochemical Biomass Conversion*, Oxford: Blackwell, 1525–39.

Beld, L. van de (1997). *Cleaning of Hot Producer Gas in a Catalytic, Reverse-Flow Reactor*, final report for NOVEM (EWAB Programme, report no. 9605) and European Commission (AIR Programme, AIR-CT93-1436).

Beenackers, A. A. C. M. (2001). Bio-energy implementation: constraints for large scale commercialisation, conclusions of workshop, in S. Kyritsis, A. A. C. M. Beenackers, P. Helm, A. Grassi and D. Chiaramonti (eds.), *Proceedings 1st World Conference and Exhibition on Biomass for Energy and Industry*, London: James and James.

Boukis, I., M. E. Gyftopoulou and I. Papamichael (2001). Biomass fast pyrolysis in an air-blown circulating fluidized bed reactor, in A. V. Bridgwater (ed.), *Progress in Thermochemical Biomass Conversion*, Oxford: Blackwell, 1259–67.

Bridgwater, A. V. (1994). Catalysis in thermal biomass conversion, *Applied Catalysis A*, 116(1–2): 5–47.

(1995). The technical and economic feasibility of biomass gasification for power generation, *Fuel*, 74(5): 631–53.

(1996). Production of high-grade fuels and chemicals from catalytic pyrolysis of biomass, *Catalysis Today*, 29: 285–95.

Bridgwater, A. V., and G. V. C. Peacocke (1999). Fast pyrolysis processes for biomass, *Renewable and Sustainable Energy Reviews*, 4(1): 1–73.

Bridgwater, A. V., A. J. Toft and J. G. Brammer (2002). A techno-economic comparison of power production by biomass fast pyrolysis with gasification and combustion, *Renewable and Sustainable Energy Reviews*, 6(5): 181–248.

Costello, R. (1999). An overview of the US Department of Energy's biomass power program, in K. Sipila and M. Korhonen (eds.), *Power Production from Biomass III: Gasification and Pyrolysis R&D&D for Industry*, Symposium 192, Technical Research Centre of Finland (VTT), Espoo, 35–56.

Cuevas, A., C. Reinoso and D. S. Scott (1995). Pyrolysis oil production and its perspectives, in *Proceedings of the conference on Power Production from Biomass II*, Symposium 164, Technical Research Centre of Finland (VTT), Espoo.

De Ruyck, J., G. Allard and K. Maniatis (1996). An externally fired evaporative gas turbine cycle for small-scale biomass CHP production, in P. Chartier (ed.), *Proceedings 9th European Bioenergy Conference, Copenhagen*, Oxford: Pergamon.

Diebold, J. P. (1999). *A Review of the Chemical and Physical Mechanisms of the Storage Stability of Fast Pyrolysis Bio-Oils*, report for Pyrolysis Network.

Diebold, J. P. and S. Czernik (1997). Additives to lower and stabilize the viscosity of pyrolysis oils during storage, *Energy and Fuels*, 11: 1081–91.

Diebold, J. P., S. Czernik, J. W. Scahill, S. D. Philips, and C. J. Feik (1994). Hot-gas filtration to remove char from pyrolysis vapours produced in the vortex reactor at NREL, in T. A. Milne (ed.), *Biomass Pyrolysis Oil Properties and Combustion Meeting*, Golden, Co.: National Renewable Energy Laboratory, 90–108.

Diebold, J. P., T. A. Milne, S. Czernik, A. Oasmaa, A. V. Bridgwater, A. Cuevas, S. Gust, D. Huffman and J. Piskorz (1997). Proposed specifications for various grades of pyrolysis oils, in A. V. Bridgwater and D. G. B. Boocock (eds.), *Developments in Thermochemical Biomass Conversion*, London: Blackie, 433–47.

Diebold, J. P., and J. Scahill (1988). Production of primary pyrolysis oils in a vortex reactor, in E. J. Soltes and T. A. Milne (eds.), *Pyrolysis Oils from Biomass*, Washington, DC: American Chemical Society, 31–40.

European Commission (1997). *Energy for the Future: Renewable Sources of Energy*, EUCOM (97)599, Brussels: European Commission, Directorate-General for Energy and Transport.

(2000). *Proposal for a Directive on the Promotion of Electricity from Renewable Energy Sources in the Internal Electricity market*. COM (2000)279, Brussels: European Commission, Directorate-General for Energy and Transport.

Harrisson, G., D. A. Fell, N. M. McDonald, A. J. Limbrick and D. C. Pike (1998). *A Study of Market Constraints on the Development of Power from Biomass*, final report of EC THERMIE contract STR-1125-96/UK, Green Land Reclamation, Twiekenham.

Heermann, C., F. J. Schwager and K. J. Whiting (2000). *Pyrolysis and Gasification of Waste*, Vol. II, Sheppards Hill, United Kingdom: Juniper Consultancy Services.

Hofbauer, H., and R. Rauch (2001). Stoichiometric water consumption of steam gasification by the FICFB-gasification process, in A. V. Bridgwater (ed.) *Progress in Thermochemical Biomass Conversion*, Oxford: Blackwell, 199–208.

Huffman, D. R., A. J. Vogiatzis and A. V. Bridgwater (1993). The characterisation of RTP bio-oils, in A. V. Bridgwater (ed.), *Advances in Thermochemical Biomass Conversion*, London: Elsevier.

Ikura, M., M. Slamak and H. Sawatzky (1998). Pyrolysis liquid-in-diesel oil microemulsions, US patent no. 5820640.

IEA (2000). *World Energy Outlook 2000*, Paris: International Energy Agency.

IEA Bioenergy (1998). *Position Paper: The Role of Bioenergy in Greenhouse Gas Mitigation*, Rotorun, New Zealand: IEA Bioenergy.

Knoef, H. A. M. (2000). *Inventory of Biomass Gasifier Manufacturers and Installations : Final Report to European Commission*, Biomass Technology Group, University of Twente, Enschede, Netherlands (see http://btgs1.ct.utwente.nl/).

Knoef, H. A. M., A. V. vanHunnik, A. Pourkamal and G. J. Buffinga (2000). *Value Engineering Study of a 150kWe Downdraft Gasification System*, final report for Shell Renewables and NOVEM.

Kovac, R. J., and D. J. O'Neil (1989). The Georgia Tech entrained flow pyrolysis process, in G. L. Ferrero, K. Maniatis, A. Buekens and A. V. Bridgwater (eds.), *Pyrolysis and Gasification*, London: Elsevier, 169–79.

Kurkela, E. (1999). PROGAS – gasification and pyrolysis R&D programme 1997–1999, in K. Sipila and M. Korhenon (eds.), *Power Production from Biomass III: Gasification and Pyrolysis R&D&D for Industry*, Symposium 192, Technical Research Centre of Finland (VTT), Espoo, 57–62.

Lédé, J., J. Panagopoulos, H. Z. Li and J. Villermaux (1985). Fast pyrolysis of wood: direct measurement and study of ablation rate, *Fuel*, 64: 1514–20.

Limbrick, A. J. (2000). *Task 281:* Annual Report, Rotorun New Zealand: IEA Bioenergy.

Maggi, R., and D. Elliott (1997). Upgrading Overview, in A. V. Bridgwater and D. G. B. Boocock (eds), *Developments in Thermochemical Biomass Conversion*, London: Blackie, 575–88.

Maniatis, K. (1999). Overview of EU THERMIE gasification projects, in K. Sipila and M. Korhonen (eds.), *Power Production from Biomass III: Gasification and Pyrolysis R&D&D for Industry*, Symposium 192, Technical Research Center of Finland (VTT), Espoo, 9–34.

(2001). Progress in biomass gasification: an overview, in A. V. Bridgwater (ed.), *Progress in Thermochemical Biomass Conversion*, Oxford: Blackwell, 1–32.

Maniatis, K., J. Baeyens, H. Peeters and G. Roggeman (1993). The Egemin flash pyrolysis process: commissioning and results, in A. V. Bridgwater (ed.), *Advances in Thermochemical Biomass Conversion*, London: Blackie, 1257– 64.

Maniatis, K., and E. Millich (1998). Energy from biomass and waste: the contribution of utility-scale biomass gasification plants, *Biomass and Bioenergy*, 15(3): 195–200.

McLellan, R. (2000). *Design of a 2.5MWe Biomass Gasification Power Generation Module*, Harwell: United Kingdom Atomic Energy Agency.

Nieminen, J. (1999). Biomass CFB gasifier connected to a 350 MWth steam boiler fired with coal and natural gas – THERMIE demonstration project in Lahti, Finland, in K. Sipila and M. Korhenon (eds.), *Power Production from Biomass III: Gasification and Pyrolysis R&D&D for Industry*, Symposium 192, Technical Research Centre of Finland (VTT), Espoo.

Paisley, M. A., R. P. Overend and M. C. Farris (2001). Preliminary operating results from Battelle/FERCO gasification demonstration plant in Burlington, Vermont, USA, in *Proceedings 1st World Biomass Conference*, London: Elsevier.

Peacocke, G. V. C., and A. V. Bridgwater (1995). Ablative plate pyrolysis of biomass for liquids, *Biomass and Bionergy*, 7(1–6): 47–154.

Prins, W., and B. M. Wagenaar (1997). Review of the rotating cone technology for flash pyrolysis of biomass, in M. Kaltschmitt and A. V. Bridgwater (eds), *Biomass Gasification and Pyrolysis: State of the Art and Future Prospects*, Newbury: CPL Scientific, 316– 26.

Robson. A. (2001). *PyNe Newsletter no. 11*, Birmingham: Pyrolysis Network, Aston University.

Salo, K., and A. Horwath (1999). Minnesota agri-power project (MAP), in K. Sipila and M. Korhonen (eds.), *Power Production from Biomass III: Gasification and Pyrolysis R&D&D for Industry*, Symposium 192, Technical Research Centre of Finland (VTT), Espoo, 141– 50.

Scott, D. S., J. Piskorz and D. Radlein (1985). Liquid products from the continuous flash pyrolysis of biomass, *Industrial and Engineering Chemistry Process Design and Development*, 24: 581–8.

Ståhl, K., M. Neergaard and J. Nieminen (2001). Final report: Värnamo demonstration programme, in A. V. Bridgwater (ed.), *Progress in thermochemical Biomass Conversion*, Oxford: Blackwell, 549– 63.

Thornley, P., and E. Wright (2001). *Evaluation of Bio-Energy Projects*, PyNe final report to the European Commission.

Vierrath, M., and C. Greil (2001). Energy and electricity from biomass, forestry and agriacultural waste, in S. Kyritsis, A. A. C. M. Beenackers, P. Helm, A. Grussi and D. Chiaramonti (eds.), *Proceedings 1st World Conference and Exhibition on Biomass for Energy and Industry*, London: James and James.

Wagenaar, B. M., R. H., Venderbosch, J. Carrasco, R. Strenziok and B. J. van der Aa (2001). Rotating cone bio-oil production and applications, in A. V. Bridgwater (ed.), *Progress in Thermochemical Biomass Conversion*, Oxford: Blackwell, 1268– 80.

Waldheim, L., M. Morris and M. R. L. V. Leal (2001). Biomass power generation: sugar cane bagasse and trash, in A. V. Bridgwater (ed.), *Progress in Thermochemical Biomass Conversion*, Oxford: Blackwell, 509– 23.

Walker, M., G. Jackson and G. V. C. Peacocke (2001). Small-scale biomass gasification: development of a gas cleaning system for power generation, in A. V. Bridgwater (ed.), *Progress in Thermochemical Biomass Conversion*. Oxford: Blackwell, 441– 51.

Yang, J., D. Blanchette, B. de Caumia and C. Roy (2001). Modelling, scale-up and demonstration of a vacuum pyrolysis reactor, in A. V. Bridgwater (ed.), *Progress in Thermochemical Biomass Conversion*, Oxford: Blackwell, 441– 51.

6 Wave energy

Tom Thorpe and Robin Wallace

6.1 Introduction

Work on wave energy began in earnest during the early 1970s as a response to the oil crisis. There were several government-sponsored programmes around the world, particularly in Japan, Norway and the United Kingdom. While these programmes advanced the technology considerably and their achievements were impressive, many were discontinued before any marine energy conversion technology could be widely or reliably demonstrated at sea. The failure of these programmes to deliver economic supplies of electricity from wave energy reduced the credibility of the technology for a number of years.

Since the mid-1990s there has been a resurgence of interest in wave energy, brought about by the need to find sustainable low-carbon energy resources. Research, development and demonstration programmes are again under way. A number of mainly small development companies are building devices all over the world (as shown by the squares in figure 6.1, which also indicates the average annual gross wave power levels per metre of wave front).

Accumulated experience has reduced the predicted cost of wave energy (compare Thorpe, 1992, with Thorpe, 1999) to such an extent that there is now considerable endorsement of the technical and economic potential of wave energy (e.g. OST, 1999, and Ove Arup, 2000), as well as strong recommendations to explore and exploit wave energy from the House of Commons Select Committee (2001), the Royal Commission on Environmental Pollution (2000) and the Scottish Executive's Forum for Renewable Energy Development (2004). More recently, an independent assessment of wave energy for the US government (Bedard et al., 2005) concluded that their study 'made a compelling case' for investment in this technology.

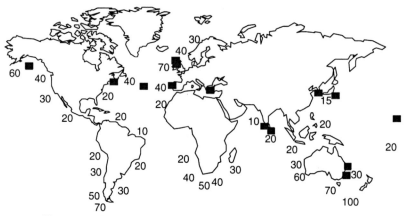

Wave power levels are approximate and given as kW/m of wave front

Figure 6.1. Distribution of wave power levels and new wave energy schemes.

6.2   The resource

The United Kingdom has one of the most energetic wave climates in the world, as shown in figure 6.1. Figure 6.2 shows the wave power levels in deep water around the United Kingdom and Ireland (wave power levels on east- and south-facing coasts are much lower, typically 10 to 20kW/m).

With these high power levels, the total UK resource is approximately 120GW (Thorpe, 1992), which is far greater than the country's current total generating capacity. However, technical and economic factors reduce this to much lower levels. These include:

- the suitability of the sea bed for the deployment of the wave energy 'farms';
- leaving areas of sea free for shipping or other prior use;
- the preservation of environmentally sensitive regions;
- areas with low wave energy levels being uneconomic to exploit;
- far offshore wave energy resources giving high costs for long submarine cables and overhead lines to connect to the electricity network; and
- the capture and delivery efficiencies of the various devices.

These factors reduce recoverable incident wave power in deep water around the UK coastlines amounts to nearly 10GW, corresponding to a technical resource of up to 50TWh/year (see table 6.1). Economic considerations reduce the economic resource still further, to, at best, a

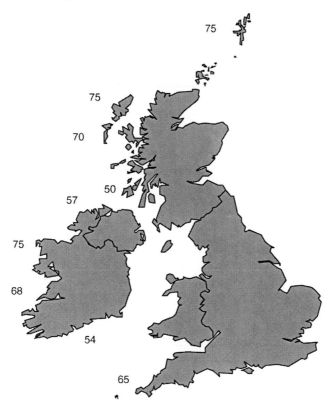

Figure 6.2. Average annual wave power levels around the United Kingdom and Ireland (kW/m).

maximum of 31 TWh/year – *assuming* that various wave energy technologies achieve their full potential (see table 6.1 and Thorpe, 1999). This corresponds to a market of up to £20 billion in capital expenditure. The near-shore and shoreline resource is reduced further due to the loss of wave energy as the waves approach the shore (due to friction with the sea bed and turbulence) and limitations on publicly acceptable sites for deploying these schemes.

The global wave energy resource is very large, with a natural resource of at least 1.3 TW. The natural, technical and economic resource has been estimated as shown in table 6.2, which corresponds to a potential offshore market of £34 billion to 210 billion in capital expenditure (Wavenet, 2003). This will be located primarily in Europe, North America, Southern Africa and Australia, as well as on islands and in other isolated communities.

Table 6.1 *UK wave energy resource*

Location	Natural resource (TWh/year)	Technical resource (TWh/year)	Economic resource (TWh/year)
Shoreline		0.4	0.0
Nearshore	400–500	2.1	2.1
Offshore	880–1,050	50.0	31.0

Table 6.2 *Global wave energy resource*

Location	Natural resource (TWh/year)	Technical resource (TWh/year)	Economic resource (TWh/year)
Shoreline		5–20	2–10
Offshore	11,400	140–750	80–510

One important fact to recognise is that the power produced by wave energy devices is predictable from one day to the next. This is because the waves that are travelling towards the shore take time to reach there and can be measured whilst out at sea. This is exemplified by one entrepreneur, who uses freely available satellite data on wave heights to predict the times and places for the best surfing around the world and sells this information to surfers worldwide! The accuracy with which wave power levels can be predicted twenty-four hours ahead is thought to be ±10 per cent, but this has yet to be confirmed in terms of the predictability of outputs from wave energy devices. This will be an important factor in determining the economic attractiveness of wave energy in markets, where electricity producers can bid for their generated energy to be bought some time in the future (typically between a few hours and a few days).

6.3   The design challenge

To be successful, wave energy devices must overcome a number of design challenges.

6.3.1   *Design waves versus production waves*

To operate its mechanical and electrical plant efficiently, a wave energy device must be rated for wave power levels that occur much of the time (e.g. in the United Kingdom this would be 20–70kW/m). However, the device also has to withstand extreme waves that occur only rarely, and these could have power levels in excess of 2,000kW/m. This poses a significant challenge, because it is the lower power levels of the commonly occurring waves that produce the normal output of the device (and hence the revenue) while the capital cost is driven by the civil structure that is designed to withstand the high power levels of the extreme waves.

6.3.2   Variability of waves

Waves vary in height and period from one wave to the next and from storm to calm conditions. While the gross average wave power levels can be predicted in advance, this inherent variability has to be converted to a smooth electrical output if it is to be accepted by the local electrical utility. This usually necessitates some form of energy storage (e.g. the flywheel effect, transmission fluid accumulators or electrical capacitors).

All wave devices have parts that move in response to wave action. The natural frequency of this movement can be quite different from that of the incident waves. Power capture is maximised when the frequency of oscillation is controlled and maintained by adjustment of the reaction forces to provide resonant conditions. A further design challenge is to control the wave energy converter to operate efficiently over a range of conditions that are changing continuously.

6.3.3   Variability in wave direction

Normally, offshore waves travel towards a wave energy device from a range of directions, so a wave energy device has to be able to interact with this variability either by having compliant moorings (which allow the device to point into the waves) or by being symmetrical. Another approach is to place the wave energy device close to the shore, because waves are diffracted as they approach a coastline, with the result that most end up travelling at right angles to the shoreline.

6.3.4   Wave characteristics

Many of these devices operate by the oscillatory part-rotation of working surfaces, with periods typically in the range five to fifteen seconds. This relatively slow oscillation has to be transformed into a unidirectional output that can turn electrical generators at high speed, which requires a gearing mechanism or the use of an intermediate energy transfer medium. High-pressure oil systems with pumps (either conventional or digitally controlled), hydraulic motors and intermediate storage (accumulators) can produce a nearly constant, unidirectional drive power for generators. Several devices use water or air as the transfer medium, while one device adopts direct generation from a reciprocating linear generator.

6.4   The technology

Currently there are a number of different wave energy technologies being built worldwide that adopt various methods of overcoming these design challenges. For convenience, wave energy converters may be classified by location into far-shore and near-shore/shoreline devices. This chapter presents a brief summary of those deployed or at an advanced stage of development. There are many other technologies at earlier stages of research and development.

6.4.1   Shoreline devices

Being located in shallow water these are thought to be easier to construct and deploy, but they see lower wave power levels than devices deployed in deeper waters. This reduces both the difference between the design and operational wave power levels and the variability in wave direction. The major class of shoreline device (for shallow waters) is the oscillating water column (OWC), as shown schematically in figure 6.3. It consists of a partially submerged, hollow structure (usually concrete), which is open to the sea below the water line, thereby enclosing a column of air on top of a column of water. As waves impinge upon the device they cause the water column to rise and fall, which alternatively compresses and expands the air column. If the air column is allowed to flow to and be drawn from the atmosphere through an air turbine, energy can be extracted from the system and used to generate electricity. By having a large surface area of water within the OWC and a relatively small orifice for the airflow, this turns the slow movement of the water into a fast movement of air (suitable for powering a turbine). In this way, the air column acts as a pneumatic transmission and gearbox. Because of the bidirectional airflow, OWCs normally use Wells turbines to drive the generators, because these rotate in the same direction regardless of which way the air is flowing. Power smoothing can be engineered either by the flywheel effect of the turbine or by the use of power electronics.

A number of OWC devices have been installed worldwide, with several commercial schemes currently being built. These include the following.

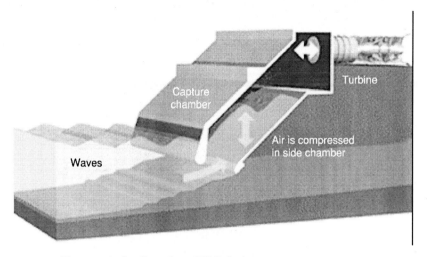

Figure 6.3. Outline of an OWC device.
NB: The arrows show the movement of water and the faster movement of air.
Drawing: courtesy Green Energy.

- *The European Pilot Plant* on the island of Pico in the Azores (Falcão, 2000). This plant is already built, with the intention of being used as a test bed for various technologies associated with OWCs as well as for supplying electricity to the island network.
- *The Wavegen Limpet* on the island of Islay in Scotland, which used a novel construction method in an attempt to reduce construction costs and ease installation (see Heath et al., 2000, and Wavegen's website: http://www.wavegen.com). This 2 × 250kW device started to generate electricity in November 2000, and has proved its reliability since then. However, the specific requirements of this device (the type of cliff, the water depth next to the cliff, etc.) reduce the replication potential of this technology.
- *The Sri Lanka OWC*. This is a 150kW demonstration scheme using a unidirectional turbine funded by the Sri Lankan Ministry of Science and Technology. It follows on from the success of a prototype tested in February 2000.
- Other, smaller devices have been deployed worldwide (Thorpe, 2004).

These conventional OWCs offer the advantage of onshore construction and maintenance, but the cost intensity of civil work and relatively low inshore wave energies are likely to make these devices permanently uneconomic. A second-generation OWC device has been built by

Figure 6.4. The Energetech OWC.
Artist's impression: courtesy Energetech.

Energetech (website: http://www.eneregetech.com.au) in Australia (figure 6.4). This uses a novel, variable-pitch turbine (which potentially offers a higher conversion efficiency than the Wells turbine), as well as a parabolic wall behind the OWC to focus the wave energy onto the OWC collector (resulting in a 300 per cent increase in energy capture for about a 50 per cent increase in capital costs). The current design is for a tethered structure, which should allow for its deployment in waters up to 30 metres deep, where the waves are more energetic than those at the coastline. These evolutionary changes are hoped to make the OWC concept economic.

6.4.2   *Offshore devices*

This class of device exploits the more powerful wave regimes available in deeper water (typically at 40 to 80 metres depth). Unlike shoreline devices, there are several completely different designs and technologies currently being developed. The wave energy is converted in a number of ways, according to device topography. Those that have been deployed or that are being constructed at the time of writing include the following.

Figure 6.5. Ocean Power Delivery's Pelamis.
Images: courtesy Ocean Power Delivery.

- *The Pelamis.* The Pelamis device (illustrated in figure 6.5) is being developed by Ocean Power Delivery (website: http://www.oceanpd. com). It is composed of cylindrical steel main tubes linked to power conversion modules between the tubes. The device is lightly moored so that it points into or slightly across the waves. As the wave moves down the length of the device, the various sections move with respect to each other. There are two degrees of freedom, which are mutually rotated by a small roll-bias angle to the conventional pitch and yaw directions. The resulting up-and-down and side-to-side motions are constrained by hydraulic rams at the joints, which can 'tune' the device to the current sea state and also extract energy from the movement. This kind of system uses the aggregated wave forces on one part of the

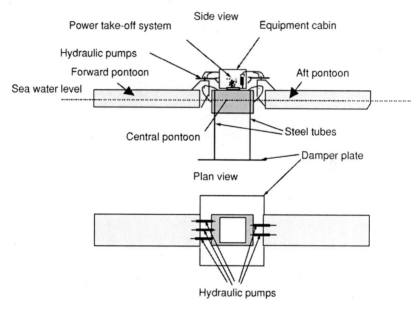

Figure 6.6. Outline of the McCabe Wave Pump.

system to react against those on another part to do work and produce power. The device is designed to avoid loading from large waves by presenting only a small cross-section to oncoming waves and being able to dive through large waves. A device is being tested at the time of writing (2005) at the European Marine Energy Centre in Orkney following an extensive and continuing R&D programme. The device is rated at 750kW, is 120 metres long and 3.5 metres in diameter and is designed for water depths of 50 metres or more. At the time of writing it has accumulated over a thousand hours of operation.

- *The McCabe Wave Pump.* This device has been constructed by Hydam Technology (website: http://wave-power.com) in Ireland. In this, three narrow steel pontoons are hinged together across their beam and are flexibly moored so that they point into the incoming waves (figure 6.6). As waves pass along the device, the front and back pontoons move up and down ('pitching') in relation to the central pontoon (which is stabilised by having a large damper plate under-neath) by rotating about the hinges. Energy is extracted from the ar-cing motion by controlled hydraulic rams (McCormick et al., 1998). The pressurised transmission fluid can be used to power hydraulic motors to drive generators up to around 400kW rating. Another

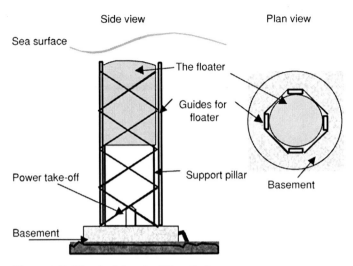

Figure 6.7. The Archimedes Wave Swing.

application is to produce potable water by supplying pressurised sea water to a reverse osmosis plant. An early 40 metre long prototype of this device was deployed off the coast of Kilbaha, County Clare, Ireland. It failed because of the unexpectedly high capture efficiencies, which led to overpressurisation of the hydraulics. A new demonstration scheme has recently been deployed.

- *The Archimedes Wave Swing.* The AWS (see website: http://www.wave-swing.com), as shown in figure 6.7, consists of a cylindrical, air-filled chamber (the 'Floater'), which is constrained to move vertically with respect to the 'Basement', which is fixed to the seabed. The air within the 9.5 metre diameter Floater provides controlled buoyancy. A wave passing over the top of the device alternately pressurises and depressurises the air within the Floater (due to the variation in the head of water over the device), changing its buoyancy and causing it to move up and down with respect to the Basement. This relative motion is used to produce energy using a novel, linear generator. This is the most powerful device currently under evaluation. A 2MW pilot scheme has been built for Portugal, and, following significant setbacks and problems with deployment, it was finally installed and initially tested in 2004. The company has started design work on larger devices that will produce at least 4MW.
- *The Wave Dragon.* The Wave Dragon (see website: http://www.wave-dragon.net) is an overtopping device with adjustable floating height.

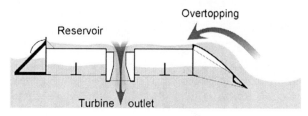

Figure 6.8. The Wave Dragon.
Images: courtesy Wave Dragon.

It has reflector walls to concentrate the incoming waves onto a central ramp, so that they overtop into a reservoir above sea level, from which the seawater is discharged to sea through a number of low-head turbines, which power separate generators (figure 6.8). During 2003 a 20kW prototype device was deployed at Nissum Bredning, a relatively sheltered coastal site in Denmark (see figure 6.8). It functioned with great reliability until January 2005, when, after more than 15,000 hours of operation, the prototype system suffered some damage following a mooring failure during a severe storm. However, the device was soon repaired and operation recommenced.

There are many prototype devices in development and many more ideas at the proof-of-concept stage. They have a wide range of technical feasibility and promise. It can be seen from the few designs described above that the best way of extracting energy from waves has not yet been proved (or possibly not even yet found). The difficulties of achieving this in a reliable and economic fashion should not be underestimated.

6.5   Current status of the technology

Generic R&D is being carried out at a number of organisations around the world. Europe in general – the United Kingdom in particular – is in a unique position to develop the marine energy resource and establish an international marine energy industry base. Europe's western coasts are at the end of the Atlantic fetch, which gathers some of the most energetic waves in the world.

6.5.1   Current UK R&D

In addition to the various companies in the United Kingdom that undertake their own R&D, nuclei of experience are forming to collaborate and meet the challenge. The UK Research Councils, the Carbon Trust, the Department of Trade and Industry and the Scottish Intermediary Technology Institute (Energy) are all committing significant resources to long-term interdisciplinary collaborations along the development chain – from generic research to pre-commercial activity. The funding available for wave and tidal current energy has increased significantly in the past few years. This covers several activities.

- The Sustainable Power Generation and Supply Initiative (Supergen) includes a large, collaborative programme of research based on an assembly of research 'consortia', which are tackling the large challenges of sustainable power generation and supply. Under this umbrella, the SuperGen Marine Energy Research Consortium conducts research into marine energy conversion and network delivery (see SuperGen Marine's web page: http://www.supergen-marine.org.uk/public/home.html).
- Excellent test facilities exist to validate designs and prove performance and reliability. There are numerous small-scale wave test tanks around the country, in universities and at developers' premises. This extends to intermediate scale in Blyth Harbour at the New and Renewable Energy Centre (NaREC) (see website: http://www.narec.co.uk/technologies-wave-tidal.php). Finally, the test facilities are completed at full scale at the European Marine Energy Centre (EMEC) for testing offshore devices in real seas in Orkney (see website: http://www.emec.org.uk).

There are four fully instrumented, network-connected berths that can accommodate wave devices each producing up to 2.4MW, and work is under way to extend the complex to include tidal current test facilities, with completion expected in 2006.

- The South-West of England Regional Development Agency has announced its decision to establish a 'Wave Hub'. This will be the United Kingdom's first offshore multi-connection wave farm, extending the range of facilities from those at EMEC to demonstrate and prove arrays of wave energy converters (Halcrow, 2005).

- The University of Edinburgh, Robert Gordon University in Aberdeen, EMEC in Orkney and NaREC in Northumberland have formed the UK Centre for Marine Renewable Energy. The partnership aims to provide a coherent approach and ensure a sustained and properly equipped research, development, test and certification base to help the emerging marine energy industry.

- The Marine Energy Challenge has been established by the Carbon Trust (see its website – http://www.thecarbontrust.co.uk – to find out when reports become available) in order to identify if, and to what extent, the cost of the energy from existing wave power and tidal current power generation technologies can be reduced. Where such reductions are possible, it will give support to marine energy technology developers of 'next-generation' prototype designs in order to help them succeed commercially. It will also highlight the generic requirements of wave and tidal stream devices that would benefit from development outside particular design concepts and that could lead to new businesses providing ancillary equipment or services.

6.5.2   Overall status of wave energy

For shoreline and near-shore applications, the OWC is a proven technology that has been deployed in numerous locations. However, it has yet to be optimised and developed to a stage where it is economically competitive with other renewable energy sources. This is likely to take up to six years of research and development, including the building of more demonstration schemes as well as more basic R&D. Offshore wave energy devices are currently being deployed. Some devices require further fundamental R&D, and all devices require R&D to: optimise their output; quantify and mitigate risk; and prove their long-term performance and reliability. This is likely to take up to eight years (including the deployment of further demonstration devices), followed (possibly) by new, second-generation devices. Both these timescales are predicated on adequate funding being available.

Some of the more successful developers have availed themselves of the opportunity to transfer knowledge and technology from the offshore oil and gas industry; the potential opportunities for this have been noted elsewhere (Ove Arup, 2000). The United Kingdom's indigenous engineering heritage is a result of the expertise and infrastructure that supported the offshore oil and gas industries. In the United Kingdom a manufacture and service infrastructure extends from the north-east of England, through central Scotland and Aberdeen, up to Orkney and Shetland – providing extensive and entirely appropriate skills, experience and facilities.

6.5.3   Funding for wave energy

The comparatively underdeveloped status of wave energy is a reflection (in part) of a lack of funding. With no single approach having been proved the best (as yet), the available funds for wave energy have been split across numerous devices and companies. Publicly available information gives some indication of the level of investment in development companies to take them through to the deployment stage: Hydam, $2 million; Energetech, $5 million; Wave Dragon, $8 million; Ocean Power Delivery, $10 million. Hence, the situation is that wave energy companies have been trying to *develop and deploy* a completely new technology for the same order-of-magnitude cost as the *deployment of* large-scale wind turbines, the latter representing a mature technology with billions of dollars of cumulative investment (in terms of both R&D and public funds to encourage deployment).

For most wave energy companies, their funding has come from both the private and public sectors. This ranges from companies such as Hydam and Energetech, which have had a small investment from government bodies (typically 10 per cent to 15 per cent of the cumulative investment, with the rest being composed of private investors, venture capitalists, etc.), through to Wave Dragon, which has received about 50 per cent of its funding from public sources (e.g. the European Union and the Danish Energy Agency). Some companies have received higher levels of public funding (e.g. from military sources), but this is rare.

The limited availability of funding and the apparent perception that a viable and competitive technology can be developed with such limited funding are the major obstacles to the more rapid development of wave energy. An independent report by a leading UK engineering consultancy (Ove Arup, 2000) concluded that 'No major technological barriers to the development of Wave Energy Prototypes have been identified'. Further development of the technology will be contingent on the best concepts finding sufficient sustained R&D and deployment funding to allow them to take their place in the renewable energy mix in future electricity markets. A major risk in trying to develop a completely new energy technology on such a low budget is that it increases the possibility of failures occurring at the demonstration stage. There have already been several failures in demonstration devices, and, given the current funding climate, more failures are very likely to occur. If they happen, it is debatable whether a viable industry can be developed in the face of the bad publicity that will ensue. This means that achieving acceptable survivability and reliability must be the main challenges facing the establishment of this technology in the near future; achieving economic competitiveness has to be a longer-term goal.

6.6   Economics of wave energy

The economics of wave energy has been a very contentious area. However, with the emergence of an independent methodology for evaluating performance, reliability and costs (Thorpe, 1992, 1999), greater confidence has been gained in this area – indeed, many private sector investors have used this methodology as the basis for their investment appraisals. It is important that all concepts should be reviewed regarding the likely technical and economic prospects at the earliest stage possible in order to avoid scarce R&D funding being allocated to unpromising devices.

The predicted upper- and lower-bound generating costs of a range of fully developed wave energy technologies (at an 8 per cent discount rate over the lifetime of the scheme) have been plotted in figure 6.9. This compares with a reduction in the generating costs of wind energy (EU average) from 3.5p/kWh to 2.5p/kWh over a similar period. The lower-bound wave energy cost is predicted to be the same as the average EU electricity price. However, it should be emphasised that these are the predicted costs for mature technologies deployed in large arrays, assuming that all the outstanding R&D is successful and that their theoretical potential is fully realised (i.e. for a 'mature technology'). At present, the generating costs for single, stand-alone devices are much higher (10–15p/kWh). Finding the funds to take the most promising devices from this 'one-off' demonstration phase to large-scale deployment (which would attract the economies of scale necessary to fulfil their economic potential) is a major problem faced by all developers (see Gross, 2004). It is questionable whether wave energy developers can make this transition on the types of funds currently available; accordingly, promising devices

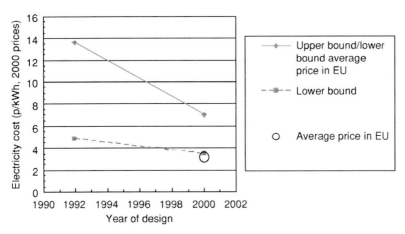

Figure 6.9. The reduction in predicted wave energy costs.
Source: adapted from Wavenet (2003).

may fail because developers have insufficient funds to secure this extent of development.

The UK government recently announced a further £50 million to fund this gap between demonstration and commercial projects for wave and tidal technologies. This decision has been greeted with enthusiasm by all developers and will undoubtedly attract inward investment in wave and tidal technologies (only Portugal is currently offering this level of incentive among the other EU members).

In the establishment of any new technology or engineered artefact, the unit costs of manufacture are highest as the technology is introduced, and then reduce as the volume supplied rises. Increased efficiency in design and manufacture combines with growing confidence in the technology's fitness for purpose as the market is supplied (e.g. IEA, 2000). Device costs will fall and capacities may rise as experience is gained; the unit capacity cost (cost/kW) will reduce to bring successive devices down the traditional cost-to-volume curve (see, for example, figure 6.10). However, if £50 million is all the funding that is going to be made available for this purpose, it will require developers to produce a far steeper reduction in costs than has been achieved in any other renewable energy technology – approximately a fourfold reduction in generating costs for an installed capacity of a few tens of MW (Gross, 2004). In comparison, the onshore wind industry required an installed capacity two orders of magnitude higher to achieve this level of cost reduction (figure 6.10). In addition, most of the development work on

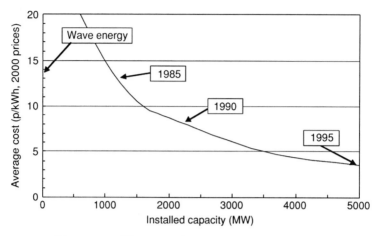

Figure 6.10. The cost reduction curve for onshore wind.

wave energy devices is device-specific and takes place mainly in the United Kingdom, so wave energy (unlike most renewable energy technologies) will not be able to benefit significantly either from generic research or from research carried out in a range of other countries. These factors present a formidable challenge that wave energy developers must meet.

6.7   Constraints to development

In order to achieve even modest levels of market penetration, there are several barriers that wave energy must overcome. After financial support and achieving economic competitiveness, the main constraints on the deployment of wave energy technology in the United Kingdom are as follows.

- The relatively high cost of connection to the electricity network. In some cases, this accounts for up to 50 per cent of the capital cost of a small scheme. The UK transmission network is heavily interconnected in the South and extends into Scotland via west- and east-coast interconnectors, ultimately projecting up the east coast of Scotland. The most energetic wind and marine energy resources are generally to be found on or off the coastlines of the least densely populated areas of the United Kingdom, such as the Western Isles or around Orkney. The electricity distribution system in these areas was originally installed to supply energy from the transmission network to these remote communities. This network is not actively managed at present; conductors are radially tapered according to the location and extent of demand, and power flows are generally unidirectionally outwards. Distribution network operators commit to statutory obligations on supply quality to customers. Injections of relatively large point sources of renewable energy into the edges of the distribution network can lead to bidirectional power flow, which, if large enough, can give rise to reductions in power quality (Kiprakis and Wallace, 2004). This imposes a limit on the capacity of the distributed renewable generation that can be connected to remote areas of the network. Indeed, limitations in the distribution and transmission networks in many of the best areas of natural resource are likely to form a major obstacle to the large-scale deployment of all renewables.

- Strategic reinforcement of the Scottish transmission and distribution network will increase the ability to deliver energy to market, but much of this additional capacity may be taken up by wind plants that are already planned. The nascent marine energy plants are of capacities that may be accommodated into the existing or evolved network alongside current wind developments. However, the large-scale development of marine energy will require bespoke reinforcement of the distribution network up to some very remote shorelines. A 2GW scheme located off the Western Isles and connecting to the nearest suitable point on the mainland transmission network has been estimated to cost in the region of £600 million (Thorpe, 1992). At present these costs will have to be borne by developers, and represent major cost centres outside their control. In general, network connection costs in other countries are low (in some cases zero, where the local utility wishes to show its support for renewables). However, network connection is an important cost centre in the United Kingdom for all offshore renewables (e.g. offshore wind farms are located as close to shore as is acceptable, near to established network grid supply points). These measures merely open the supply conduit, but, in order to access the electricity market, the energy produced must be sold in competition.

- Planning and Consent Procedures. An extensive and expensive consultation process for planning and consent is needed in the United Kingdom, because of the plethora of statutory bodies that have an involvement in the coastline and sea. The costs, delays and risks involved cannot easily be accommodated by the small companies building wave energy devices, and potential project investors are naturally wary of committing large sums to a project that might be blocked by such considerations. In other countries (not all), this process is much more streamlined (a complete planning and consent agreement has been completed in Portugal within six weeks).

- Reliability. The credibility problems following the closure of the United Kingdom's first wave energy programme are still with us. Experience of operating devices in the marine environment is accumulating but these prototype devices are but the vanguards of a new energy technology. Individual component reliability and overall device survivability have to be understood and quantified to ensure that the investment in prototype and production plant is secure. This requires extensive component and device testing, over prolonged periods, in the sea within an environment that facilitates monitoring and repair. With cautious and measured deployment of devices, confidence in the technology will grow, and a UK manufacturing base can follow. While reliability is not a criterion that may be taken for granted, it is to be expected that reliability will also increase as experience accumulates with specific devices, technologies and methodologies.

6.8   The prospects for wave energy by 2050

After many years with little funding or support, wave energy has turned a corner and more funds are now available. A number of wave energy devices are being deployed worldwide but the technology is at the advanced prototype stage, with the various approaches requiring more R&D to optimise them. However, there are still many challenges to be met (e.g. in the United Kingdom the best marine energy resources are geographically and electrically remote from the electricity markets to which they must be economically delivered). The predictability of electricity generated from marine energy is thought to be sufficiently firm to ensure that it can be sold in the market, but this is still to be proved.

If the technologies currently under development achieve their anticipated potential, there is a market in the United Kingdom for predictable and economic supplies of electricity from wave energy amounting to about 10 per cent of current electricity demand by 2050. With future designs this contribution could increase. The potential for wave energy to make a serious contribution to a portfolio of electricity supply technologies is widely accepted and supported. This represents a startling turnaround since the mid-1990s, from wave energy being considered an unlikely technology to one that looks promising. This is all the more remarkable when one considers that this has been achieved by small companies, often with small budgets and with hitherto minimal support from government. The United Kingdom is in a unique position to develop marine energy for an electricity supply industry with an increased capacity of renewable plant, harnessing extensive indigenous natural resources and making use of an established research, development and manufacturing base.

6.9   References

Bedard, R., G. Hagerman, M. Previsie, O. Siddiqui, R. Thresher and B. Ram (2005). *Offshore Wave Power Feasibility Demonstration Project*, Report no. WP009, Palo Alto, California: Electric Power Research Institute.

Falcão, A. F. (2000). *The Shoreline OWC Wave Power Plant at the Azores*, paper presented at Fourth European Wave Energy Conference, Aalborg, Denmark, 4–6 December.

Forum for Renewable Energy Development (2004). *Harnessing Scotland's Marine Energy Potential*, Edinburgh: Scottish Executive, Marine Energy Group.

Gross, R. (2004). *Innovation Systems and UK Policy Gaps*, paper presented at BWEA and Regen SW conference 'Wave and tidal energy – making it happen', Bristol, 11 February.

Halcrow (2005). *Wave Hub Technical Feasibility Project: Final Report*, London: Halcrow Group, for the South-West of England Regional Development Agency.

Heath, T., T. J. T. Whittaker and C. B. Booke (2000). *The Design, Construction and Operation of the LIMPET Wave Energy Converter*, paper presented at Fourth European Wave Energy Conference, Aalborg, Denmark, 4–6 December.

House of Commons Select Committee (2001). *Wave and Tidal Energy*, London: HMSO (see also http://www.parliament.the-stationery-office.co.uk/pa/cm200001/cmselect/cmsctech/291/29102.htm#evidence).

IEA (2000). *Experience Curves for Energy Technology Policy*, Paris: International Energy Agency.

Kiprakis, A. E., and A. R. Wallace (2004). Maximising energy capture from distributed generators in weak networks, *IEE Proceedings Generation, Transmission and Distribution*, 151 (5): 611–18.

McCormick, M, J. Murtagh and P. McCabe (1998). *Large-Scale Experimental Study of a Hinged-Barge Wave Energy Conversion System*, paper presented at Third European Wave Energy Conference, Patras, Greece, 30 September–2 October.

OST (1999). *Energies from the sea – Towards 2020*, Marine Foresight Panel report, London: Office of Science and Technology, Department of Trade and Industry.

Ove Arup (2000). *Wave Energy: Technology Transfer and R&D Recommendations*, London: Ove Arup, report for the Department of Trade and Industry.

Royal Commission on Environmental Pollution (2000). *Energy: The Changing Climate*, London: HMSO (see also http://www.rcep.org.uk/pdf/enersumm.pdf).

Thorpe, T. W. (1992). *A Review of Wave Energy*, 2 vol., ETSU Report R-72, London: Department of Trade and Industry.

(1999). *A Brief Review of Wave Energy*, ETSU Report R-120, London: Department of Trade and Industry.

(2004). Wave energy, in *The World Energy Council's 2004 Survey of Energy Resources*, Oxford: Elsevier, 401–18.

Wavenet (2003). *Results from the Work of the European Thematic Network on Wave Energy*, report ERK5-CT-1999-2001 2000-2003, Brussels: European Commission.

Part II

New Technologies for Thermal Generation

7 CO$_2$ capture, transport and storage for coal, oil and gas: technology overview

Nils A. Røkke

7.1 Introduction

Several choices are available to combat the effects of global warming, the options being the more efficient use of energy, trying to manage the atmospheric uptake of energy, the use of carbon-less or carbon-neutral fuels, the use of renewable energy sources (hydro, wind, wave, solar, etc.), the capture and storage of CO$_2$ and – last but not least – adapting to a warmer climate. Figure 7.1 depicts the various options. The last-mentioned option is one we would rather not follow, on account of the severe consequences we would face as a result: endangered species, changing patterns of wind and water, and a raised sea level – just to mention some of the effects.

This chapter will discuss the options available in the so-called carbon sequestration route, or CO$_2$ management. By capturing CO$_2$ from large point sources, transporting it by suitable means and then storing it safely underground or under the sea, we would take out CO$_2$ from the cycle and reduce the level of anthropogenic CO$_2$ emissions into the atmosphere. From a carbon exchange point of view, we would be taking the carbon found underground, using its energy content by oxidising it, and then putting the carbon back into the ground.

However, the methods that will be discussed have limitations: they add cost to the conversion of energy; it is not feasible to collect all the carbon from our operations; the storage needs to be safe for thousands of years, in terms of leaks and sudden changes in the geology; and they are less energy-efficient. Figure 7.2 shows different scenarios for storage underground with various leak rates in a 'business as usual' case. This model couples leak rates with a climate change model. Although this model makes use of a climate change model that has been questioned, the results show an effect that we clearly need to take into account: the storage site needs to be able to store the CO$_2$ for long timescales. It suggests that we would demand very long residence times for CO$_2$ underground to have a real effect on global warming. The results from

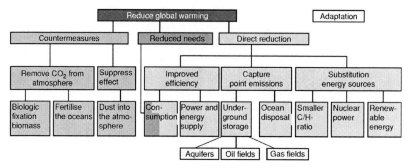

Figure 7.1. Options for reducing global warming.
Source: Bolland (2003).

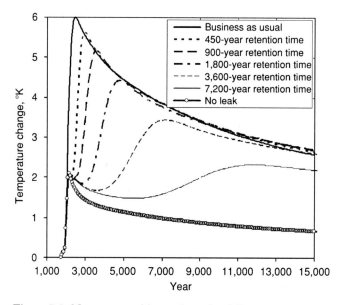

Figure 7.2. Necessary residence times for CO_2 storage.
Source: Lindeberg (2003).

this particular study indicate that residence times exceeding 7,000 years would be needed. The ability to guarantee anything over such a time-scale is highly speculative, and beyond the scope of this chapter; none-theless, putting carbon back into the ground offers a technical solution that is feasible.

7.2   Technology options

This chapter will concentrate on the capture technologies, as it is this stage in the CO_2 value chain – capture, transport and storage – that has been shown to be the most costly process. Capture usually accounts for 70 per cent to 80 per cent of the total cost. Capturing CO_2 is usually divided into the following categories: pre-combustion, post-combustion and oxy-fuel. This classification is independent of the fuel used and reflects how CO_2 is taken out of the process. A schematic is shown in figure 7.3, which is taken from Bolland's website.

7.2.1   Pre-combustion

Pre-combustion schemes are those that take the carbon out of the fuel rather than from the products of combustion in the conversion process. Reforming of natural gas in an auto-thermal reformer to make a syngas consisting mainly of H_2, CO and CO_2 (and H_2O) for a subsequent shift reaction for optimising the H_2 yield is such a technology, and is depicted in figure 7.4. The CO_2 is then removed from the fuel gas using an absorption process with a suitable liquid absorbent. The resulting fuel gas, consisting of H_2, N_2 and traces of CO_2, is then burned in a gas turbine or a boiler only, producing H_2O in the exhaust gases. In principle, the same process can be used for fuel oil, but fuel oils demand more clean-up systems because of the inherently higher content of sulphur and other toxics than in the fuel-processing system for CO_2 capture.

Using coal as fuel the process becomes more complicated, as more processes are needed to make the fuel gaseous and then to clean up the trace species that come with the coal. In principle, integrated gasification combined cycle (IGCC) plants perform these operations without the CO_2 capture. In an IGCC plant (depicted in figure 7.5) coal is gasified with steam or oxygen to produce an energy-rich fuel gas with high levels of H_2, CO and CH_4. After a clean-up process the fuel gas is fed to a gas turbine, producing power. By introducing an additional CO_2 absorption reactor the fuel gas can be made virtually CO_2-free, and can be burnt with no excess CO_2 being produced.

For both these processes, cleaning up the fuel stream has the advantage of working at an elevated pressure, and thus the absorption systems can be made more compact than systems operating at near-atmospheric conditions. Complications due to the need for process integration and high temperatures constitute more demanding issues for these processes.

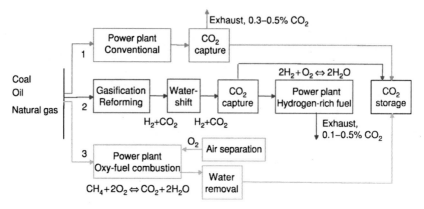

Figure 7.3. CO_2 capture routes.
NB: Route 1 = post-combustion, route 2 = pre-combustion, route 3 = oxy-fuel.

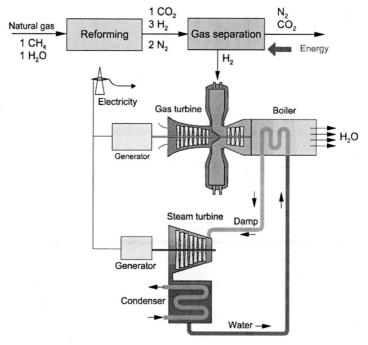

Figure 7.4. Pre-combustion system.

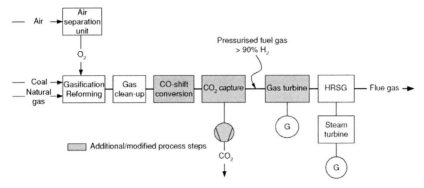

Figure 7.5. IGCC/IRCC system.

After the CO$_2$ has been captured it needs to be conditioned for further transport. In the case of pipeline transport, the gas is compressed to a level suitable for the transport distance and dried to avoid dry-icing, clogging and corrosion. Typically, pressures of 100 to 200 bar are needed. Another option is to condense the CO$_2$ to a liquid for transport by truck or by ship.

7.2.2   Post-combustion

Post-combustion technologies take the CO$_2$ out of the combustion products – i.e. the exhaust. This means that the cleaning process will need to handle much larger volumes of gas than the pre-combustion route does. The combustion of hydrocarbons demands air mass flows between fifteen and fifty times greater than the fuel flow (boilers, gas turbines), thus diluting the CO$_2$ content considerably. For a gas turbine process a CO$_2$ level of 3 per cent to 4 per cent is normal, whereas for coal-fired boilers the CO$_2$ content is 12 per cent to 14 per cent, all by volume. In addition, the process operates at near-atmospheric conditions, demanding larger process equipment. This remains, however, the most used and developed technology option, and CO$_2$ absorption is a well-known process that has been used commercially for fifty to sixty years.

Figure 7.6 shows a post-combustion capture scheme for a natural-gas-fired gas turbine. In principle, the power generation is unaffected by the capture process, as this takes place downstream of the power-generating unit. Natural gas is burnt in the gas turbine and the exhaust is collected after the fluid has done its work in the turbine(s). Sulphur, if present in significant amounts, is first removed to avoid damage to the

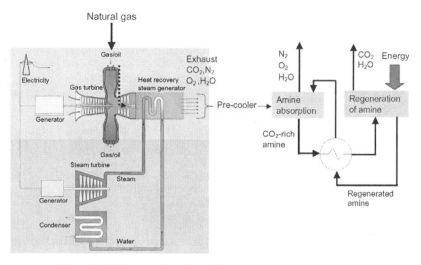

Figure 7.6. Post-combustion CO_2 capture.

catalysts in subsequent steps, and the gas is conditioned to the right temperature. It is then ducted to a packed absorption tower, where the gas is brought into contact with the liquid absorbent, absorbing the CO_2 from the exhaust gas. The fluid is pumped to the desorber, or stripper, where it releases the CO_2 and the absorbent is regenerated. Very clean CO_2 can be produced (>99.9 per cent) and food-grade CO_2 can be made from such processes. The absorber, usually being variants of amino acids, such as monoethanol amine, has a finite lifetime due to some of the amine becoming oxidised or broken down by other substances (e.g. oxides of nitrogen). Power generation based on coal or oil can use the same technology; in this instance the process benefits from the higher CO_2 content and lower flue gas volumes per power unit.

As mentioned before, this technology has been used for some time when there have been special needs for CO_2 and a value of CO_2 has been determined. Examples of the latter include CO_2 for food or beverages (soft drinks) or, on a larger scale, for enhanced oil recovery, where CO_2 is used to improve the yield and lifetime of an oilfield. This will be discussed later.

Other post-combustion capture technologies include the use of organic organisms to utilise the CO_2 for growth, such as algae. In this context it is better classified as a disposal technology than as a capture technology. It is questionable if such techniques can be seen as taking away carbon, as the algae are utilised by fish for food and by humans, thus transforming CO$_2$ into methane in the process. The same goes for the use of CO$_2$ enrichment in the atmosphere in greenhouses, to increase the growth of crops such as tomatoes.

7.2.3   Oxy-fuel

Oxy-fuel processes and power cycles are used for a variety of processes, with the aim of taking as much nitrogen as possible out of the air and then, through the oxidation of the fuel, creating pure CO$_2$ and water. These processes are sometimes referred to as denitrogenated combustion.

As the name implies, oxy-fuel processes are based on the combustion of oxygen and fuel; oxygen is, accordingly, a vital input. Traditionally, oxygen has been produced by air separation units, and the commercially dominant technique is the cryogenic distillation of oxygen, which capitalises on the different boiling temperatures of oxygen and nitrogen in air. This demands energy and adds to the cost of power. Other promising technologies for external oxygen production include the membrane separation of oxygen and the use of chemisorbents. These technologies are likely to be more suited for smaller amounts of oxygen production in a near- to medium-term scenario, reflecting their higher costs when used in large-scale operations compared to cryogenics.

For a gas turbine process, oxygen would be fed to the combustor together with the fuel. The stoichiometric combustion of natural gas in oxygen would mean temperatures in excess of 3,000°K in the combustor and a temperature at the inlet to the turbine that far exceeds the material technology of today, and for decades to come. CO$_2$ and some excess oxygen and trace species from the reaction between fuel and oxygen would then be recycled, forming a semi-closed process; water would be removed in the recycle ducting system. The only flows crossing the system boundary would be the fuel stream, oxygen stream and excess CO$_2$, which would be released from the system together with water condensed from the CO$_2$ working fluid. At present no such turbines have been built, although a design study in the United Kingdom has been undertaken by Alstom through a contract (GASZEP) with the Department of Trade and Industry.

In a boiler application CO$_2$ would also need to be recycled to control the reaction temperature; an ASU would be needed, along with modifications to the burner and boilers. It is currently the case that no such commercial plants are in operation. In figure 7.7 an oxy-boiler application schematic is provided.

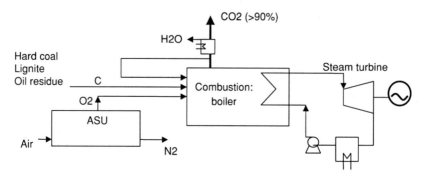

Figure 7.7. Oxy-boiler schematic – pulverised fuel system.

Novel concepts in oxy-fuel are chemical looping technology and the advanced zero-emission power plant technology (figure 7.8). In chemical looping combustion, oxygen for combustion is delivered to the fuel via a reducing – oxidising (redox) – material, the process simulating a high-speed corrosion process. Two steps are necessary, one in which the redox agent, usually nickel or iron, is oxidised to form NiO or FeO in an exothermic process, setting the stage for the subsequent reduction of the agent once in contact with the fuel in an endothermic release reaction. Pure CO_2 and water are formed in the fuel reactor. By looping the redox agent a continuous process can be achieved. More information on CLC can be found in, for instance, Brandvoll and Bolland (2004).

For the AZEP concept the combustor in a gas turbine process is equipped with an oxygen transfer membrane that transports the oxygen across to the fuel stream on the other side of the membrane. Reaction occurs and pure CO_2 is formed; recycling of CO_2 is needed in the sweep gas flow to control temperature. The challenges are mainly in ensuring the thermal stability of the membrane system and in achieving efficient high-temperature heat exchange after the combustion process has taken place.

Other oxy-fuel concepts include the zero-emission natural gas cycle, in which oxygen, fuel and steam are burnt in a closed vessel to produce a high-temperature steam/CO_2 mixture that can be expanded in steam-turbine-derived turbomachinery.

7.2.4   Other systems

A number of new systems have been proposed the last few years, many of them utilising known technologies in combinations that have not been used before. The description here will be more cursory than for the above-mentioned main classes.

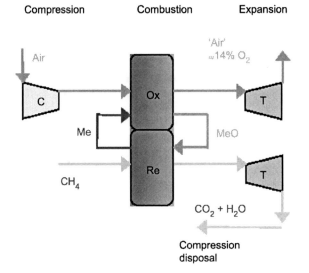

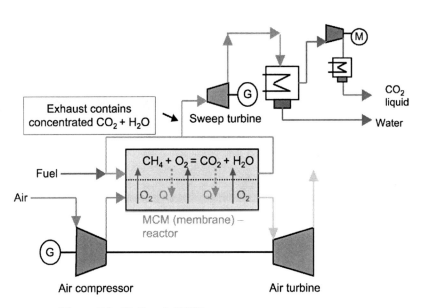

Figure 7.8. CLC and AZEP concepts.

Fuel cells utilising hydrogen (most notably the proton exchange membrane FC) can be used in a pre-combustion scheme. Efficiencies are better than for gas turbines (up to 60 per cent for an isolated FC), but the size and availability of large-scale FC systems make this system less attractive, the maximum size of the modules being typically 250kW.

Solid oxide FCs have the advantage of being able to run on natural gas, with internal fuel reforming due to the higher operating temperatures (around 700°C). By introducing a hybrid system in which the SOFC operates as a gas turbine combustor system, efficiencies of up to 70 per cent can be achieved. This alone provides a great advantage over other work machines, on account of the more efficient use of energy. Sealing systems have been developed to separate the exhaust streams to be able to capture the CO_2; how this can be made into a hybrid system is less clear, because of the air dilution in the gas turbine cycle. Tubular systems are today limited to 250kW modules, whereas planar systems are even smaller in scale, being limited to capacities in the tens of kilowatts.

7.3   Benchmarking capture technologies

For a benchmarking exercise to be useful, the various concepts need to be compared with an equal set of boundary conditions. In addition, to be fair in the assessment of costs the cost assessment uncertainty for the components comprising the system and for the system itself need to be equal. The latter requirement cannot be achieved when working with new and speculative technologies in which some of the components have not yet been developed, nor the systems. The options then are either to estimate from similar technologies and add the uncertainties into the results, or, alternatively, to start with an acceptable cost for the power to be produced and then calculate back to what would be an acceptable price for the system.

In the comparisons in figure 7.9, estimates have been made as to the maturity of the technology, the risk from a technical/economical view, the probable efficiency of the various technologies and the rate at which this is likely to improve and impact on cost estimates.

Figure 7.10 shows the efficiency potential for the various concepts discussed in this chapter, with a focus on natural gas as fuel (Bolland et al., 2002). A lag of three years is built in for all the technologies in order to allow for the erection of the plant. Typically a loss of 8 per cent to 15 per cent in efficiency is seen for the various technologies versus the baseline combined cycle plant. These calculations include compression of the CO_2 to 200 bar, and an efficiency loss of 2 per cent is attributed to this where this is applicable. From this assessment one would be

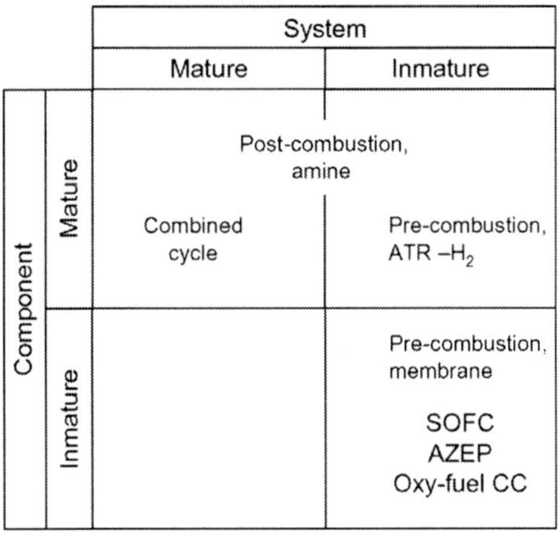

System		
	Mature	**Inmature**
Component / **Mature**	Combined cycle	Post-combustion, amine
		Pre-combustion, ATR –H₂
Component / **Inmature**		Pre-combustion, membrane
		SOFC
		AZEP
		Oxy-fuel CC

Figure 7.9. Technology classification.

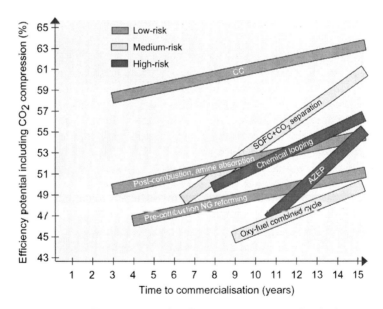

Figure 7.10. Efficiency potentials for carbon capture technologies.

tempted to focus only on the post-combustion technology, being low-risk and lowest in efficiency penalty. As a result, we need to assess the cost issue as well, and this is depicted in figure 7.11. Here we see that the picture is less conclusive, the three main routes being very competitive

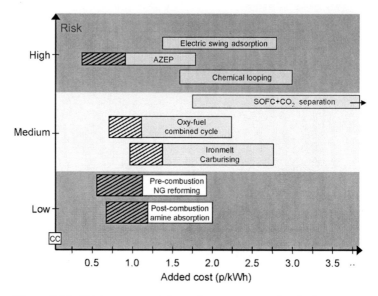

Figure 7.11. Cost assessment for carbon capture technologies.

with no clear winner evident. Recent studies, such as that by the Carbon Capture Project (see website: http://www.co2capture project.org), have indicated that cost reductions in the region of 20 per cent to 50 per cent are achievable for the capture technologies. This would imply costs of €25 to € 40 per tonne of CO_2, instead of the level of €50 to €60 that has been widely accepted up to now.

The various technologies are ranked by cost and risk in figure 7.11. The extent of the shaded boxes around the caption for each technology indicates the potential for cost efficiency for the different options. It should be noted that, for the AZEP technology, the extension indicates versions of the AZEP with reduced rather than zero CO_2 emissions. This is introduced to improve efficiency (increasing the maximum temperature in the process) and reduce costs.

7.4   Transport of CO_2

To allow for the storage or use of CO_2 it will need to be transported, either via a pipeline or via ships or trucks.

Large-scale CO_2 management dictates an infrastructure that is not yet available in Europe. As mentioned earlier, the EU15 countries have a collectable CO_2 potential of about 1Gt/year, meaning that 1 billion tonnes of CO_2 will need to be transported annually. Such large-scale systems are not currently available, and are unlikely in the near future as well. Typically, ship transport will be the most cost-effective means of transport for low transport volumes and long distances, whereas pipelines are suited to large volumes. Pipeline transport would typically demand volumes of around 1 million tonnes per year to be competitive. Other factors, such as sea depths or permits (in terms of onshore transport), will also play a major role in assessing the suitability of the different systems.

Onshore CO_2 transport has been commercially operated in the United States and Canada for some time. The experience gained from these operations is that clean CO_2 can be transported in a safe manner with the application of standard engineering practice. However, this will not be the case for the operation of pipelines under water with less clean CO_2 specifications; this is a field that is in need of research, both for the large-scale infrastructure implications and for the thermodynamics of complex CO_2/H_2O/hydrocarbon mixes.

7.5   Storage/use of CO$_2$

Studies of the storage potential of the North Sea have indicated a safe storage capacity of some 600Gt. Most of the storage potential is within aquifers, salt- or freshwater layers found deep underground. Other options are abandoned gas and oil fields or the use of CO_2 for enhanced gas or oil recovery. EOR with CO_2 is the most commercially interesting option, and has been used with great success in the United States. Studies have shown that the potential for EOR in the North Sea is substantial and that if such schemes are introduced the market for CO_2 will be sizeable. For the Norwegian oil- and gas fields a CO_2 supply of 5 to 10 million tonnes would be needed per year. This clearly shows that the CO_2 sources will have to be found outside Norway and in Europe as a whole. Studies undertaken by Kinder Morgan have shown the feasibility of using CO_2 from Danish coal power stations for EOR in the North Sea area. What remains to be settled is the price of the CO_2 at the point of delivery versus the added value of the CO_2 injection; this is still being debated. A level of between €10 and €20 per tonne has been discussed.

It should be noted that Statoil undertakes CO_2 capture and storage at the Sleipner field in the North Sea. CO_2 is removed from the produced natural gas and injected in the Utsira saline aquifer at a rate of approximately 1 million tonnes per year. A similar scheme is set to start at the Snøhvit field in the northern part of Norway, where CO_2 will be injected in a saline aquifer close to the gas field.

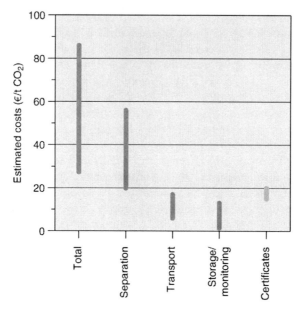

Figure 7.12. Cost of the elements in the CO_2 chain.
Source: May et al. (2002).

7.6   Research and development needs

As this chapter has shown, there is a need for a further reduction of the costs within the CO_2 chain regardless of any value that CO_2 may achieve in enhanced hydrocarbon recovery or in emission tax/quota systems that will come soon into operation. The cost distribution of capture versus transport and storage points towards focusing on reducing the capture cost as the most promising in the immediate future. For the near term, the refinement of technologies such as post-combustion and pre-combustion is needed. Improved system integration, smarter processes and reducing the capital investment and energy requirements are key items, together with improved solvents. It is believed that commercialising these technologies on a broad basis will yield substantial cost reductions, in terms of less expensive materials, designs and building codes. For mid-term technologies, such as oxy-fuel carbon capture, more research is needed into the operational aspects, as the design of new turbomachinery and safety are instrumental. Combustion technology advances are needed for both H_2-based systems and oxy-fuel systems; it is not acceptable to trade off CO$_2$ emissions with NOx emissions, for instance, and high-pressure operation for oxy-fuel is also a relatively new field.

Membranes represent a field with great promise, for oxygen production, CO$_2$ separation, H$_2$ separation and high-temperature applications. There is clearly a need for more R&D in this field, with a high potential for improvements in both cost and the efficiency of the operating cycles. The same applies to fuel cell systems.

7.7   Summary and conclusions

Carbon dioxide management technologies constitute a viable instrument for the control of man-made global warming. The capture, transport and use/storage technologies are available but not yet optimised, reflecting the fact that up to now the market has been almost non-existent. If it can be proved beyond doubt that the human contribution to global warming will reach unacceptable levels, say a global temperature increase of more than 2–6°C, such technologies will be in great demand.

A suite of capture technologies exists, the most developed being post- and pre-combustion schemes and oxy-fuel. As of today no clear winner can be announced in terms of costs, but in terms of risk and maturity post-combustion would be the preferred route.

As the technologies have not yet been applied to large-scale CO$_2$ capture from power generation (more than 1 million tonnes of CO$_2$ per year), it is believed that substantial cost reductions can be achieved by setting up such large-scale capture schemes and gaining hands-on experience in operating.

The transport link in the CO$_2$ chain can be addressed either by pipeline or by ship/surface transport. For large quantities of CO$_2$, pipelines will be the most cost-effective option; ships would be more suited for long distances and limited quantities. Interesting options exist for co-transporting LPG and CO$_2$ in ships. The experience from US/Canadian pipelines must be taken into account if comparably large-scale infrastructures are to be used in Europe. For offshore operation such experience is not available, and the thermodynamics of CO$_2$, water and trace impurities mixtures will need to be researched further in order to avoid material damage and process problems (such as dry-icing and corrosion).

The use and storage of CO$_2$ is the final link in the chain, and great opportunities exist. The North Sea offers huge potential for utilising CO$_2$ for enhanced hydrocarbon recovery. The total storage capacity of the North Sea amounts to approximately 600Gt, which could be used for storing collectible CO$_2$ from the EU15 for anything up to 500 or 600 years.

Targeted research is needed within CO_2 management studies in order to lower the added cost to electricity. The next phase would be demonstration on a semi-industrial scale, and subsequently on an industrial scale.

7.8   References

Bolland, O. (2003). Accessed at: http://www.tev.ntnu.no/Olav.Bolland/pdf/ Emergidagen_NTNU_3.3.2003_Bolland.pdf

Bolland, O., R. I. Hagen, O. Maurstad, G. Tangen, O. Juliussen and H. Svendsen (2002). *Gasskraftverk med CO_2-håndtering: Studie av alternative Teknologier*, Report TR A5693, Trondheim: Foundation for Scientific and Industrial Research at the Norwegian Institute of Technology.

Brandvoll, Ø., and O. Bolland (2004). Inherent CO2 capture using chemical looping combustion in a natural gas fired power cycle, *ASME Journal of Engineering for Gas Turbines and Power*, 126: 316–21.

Lindeberg, E. (2003). The quality of a CO_2 repository: what is the sufficient retention time of CO2 stored underground?, in J. Gale and Y. Kaya (eds.), *Proceeding of the sixth International Conference on Greenhouse Gas Control Technologies*, Vol. I, London: Elsevier Science, 255–60.

May, F., P. J. Gerling and P. Krull (2002). Underground storage of CO_2, *VGB PowerTech*, 82: 8.

8 Nuclear energy

Malcolm C. Grimston

8.1 Introduction

Nuclear power differs from some other low-carbon energy options in that it faces a group of opponents who would reject its deployment in any circumstances. Though not unique in this respect – the same can be said, for example, about large-scale hydropower and other options such as tidal power, carbon dioxide sequestration and even onshore wind power, all of which face increasing public opposition – this factor has been especially significant in the development of nuclear power over the last thirty years or so. One can foresee that some of the more fundamentalist opponents of nuclear power would even oppose research to determine whether the shortcomings of nuclear technologies can be overcome.

There can be no assumption that nuclear power should necessarily be part of a future energy mix, any more than there can be over any other single option. (Energy efficiency is in a different fundamental category; for example, improvements in energy efficiency have been an integral feature of developments in energy technology since the Industrial Revolution, with the possible exception of times when energy prices have been very low. It is hard to be 'against' energy efficiency, or even to know what that would mean.) However, nor can it be assumed that the perceived drawbacks of 'traditional' nuclear technology cannot be overcome, through technological development and public engagement.

There are several barriers, or *logjams*, to determining whether a revived nuclear programme in the developed world and continued expanding programme in the developing world would represent a helpful contribution to sustainable development or not. Among the most important are:

- the research, development and commercialisation logjam – funds for R, D&C may not be forthcoming without evidence that there will be a nuclear future, but such evidence is unlikely to emerge if the R, D&C is not done;

- the skills logjam – the suitably skilled individuals necessary for a future programme of nuclear investment may not be attracted into the industry unless such a programme is already under way;
- the public perception logjam – sufficient public confidence in nuclear technology to allow for new build may not develop until the new build programme is already established; and
- the waste logjam – new techniques to deal with waste, which may be required before a new programme can be instigated, may not be developed unless there is clear evidence of a new build programme.

It is the job of research to clear away the uncertainties that prevent a proper appraisal of the role any particular technology might play. Of course, it is impossible to eliminate uncertainty, but progress can be made towards a better basis for decision than exists at present.

Some (though not all) of the uncertainties lie in the domain of the physical and engineering sciences: the levels of reliability and safety that can be attained by different potential nuclear technologies, whether more flexible nuclear technologies can be developed, the progress that can be made in developing robust models for waste disposal facilities, how a 'hydrogen economy' might affect the attractiveness of nuclear power, etc. These questions are intimately linked with the economics of new nuclear programmes.

8.2   Nuclear energy today

Nuclear energy involves converting the energy released in the course of nuclear fission (using uranium, thorium and/or plutonium) into electricity. Fission occurs in 'fuel rods', and the heat is removed using a 'coolant' – light water (in light water reactors, such as the pressurised water reactor and boiling water reactor), heavy water (e.g. the Canadian CANDU reactor), carbon dioxide gas (in the British Magnox and advanced gas-cooled reactors), helium, sodium or a lead/bismuth mixture (the last two in fast reactors). The coolant is then used either to drive turbines directly (e.g. helium in high-temperature gas-cooled reactors) or to boil water that is then used to drive turbines, in essentially the same process as is used in conventional power stations fired by coal or oil.

Nuclear technology has been deployed for over four decades, accounting for approximately 17 per cent of global electricity production during the 1990s and early 2000s – over 2,500TWh in 2002 from 440 operating units in over thirty countries. 'Traditional' nuclear technology for generating electricity is found in all continents except Australia and

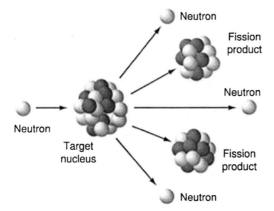

Figure 8.1. Nuclear fission.

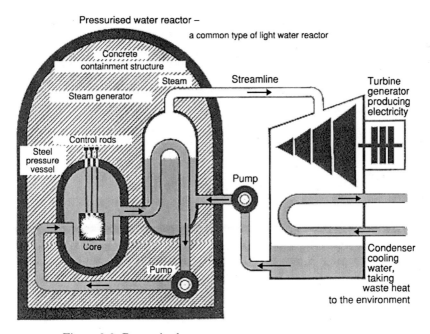

Figure 8.2. Pressurised water reactor.

Antarctica, the top ten producers in 2002 being as given in table 8.1. The data for global nuclear capacity, in GW installed, given in figure 8.3 comes from the IAEA's Power Reactor Information System database, which is available at http://www.iaea.Org/programmes/a2.

Table 8.1 *Nuclear generation*

	Generation (TWh)
United States	780
France	416
Japan	314
Germany	162
Russia	130
South Korea	113
United Kingdom	81
Ukraine	73
Canada	71
Sweden	66

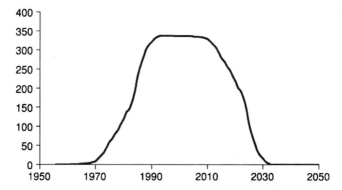

Figure 8.3. Global nuclear capacity (GW installed).

In this sense there are few major engineering obstacles to the deployment of large nuclear units within current electricity supply systems. At rates of return of 5 per cent traditional nuclear electricity has an economic edge over power generated using gas or coal in many areas of the world, though at rates of return of 10 per cent or more, more typical in liberalised power markets, this advantage is reversed (NEA, 1998).

8.3   Challenges for nuclear technology

However, despite its apparent advantages in terms of resource diversification and reducing greenhouse gas emissions, and although nuclear power was proportionally the fastest-growing of major electricity technologies in the 1970s, 1980s and 1990s, this rate of expansion has slowed in recent years, and by mid-2004 there were only some twenty-six plants under construction around the world (IAEA, 2004).

The decline in nuclear orders can be explained by reference to a number of factors, including:

- questions over economics, especially in liberalised electricity markets;
- public perceptions over issues such as waste management, safety, the proliferation of nuclear weapons etc; and
- the development of alternative electricity technologies, notably the combined-cycle gas turbine.

It was widely claimed, when major nuclear programmes were being launched in the 1960s and 1970s, that over their lifetime these nuclear plants would prove to be the cheapest option among those then available. In the event, the costs of fossil-generated electricity fell as the price of oil fell in the early 1980s and the CCGT, a technology both cheaper and more flexible than traditional nuclear designs, emerged. Major delays in nuclear construction programmes in some countries (often coupled with redesign after the building of the plant had started), caused in part by the response to the Three Mile Island accident in the United States in 1979, damaged nuclear economics enormously. (That said, the experience of nuclear construction in the 1990s, especially in the Asia-Pacific region, has been more encouraging, most major projects coming in essentially to time and cost.)

At the same time, the nuclear industry lost the confidence of significant sectors of the population in some countries (again, in part because of the accident at Three Mile Island, and also that at Chernobyl, Ukraine, in 1986), further damaging its prospects of gaining the necessary political support to flourish. This contributed, for example, to the failure to find practical solutions to the issue of waste disposal.

The introduction of competition into electricity-generating markets in the 1990s created a further difficulty for traditional nuclear technology. Very heavily capital-intensive energy sources such as traditional nuclear power designs (and, indeed, many renewables) require some realistic prospect of very long-term supply contracts at guaranteed prices in order to ensure that they will cover their initial investment costs and make a reasonable return. In command and control systems in which some utility has a monopoly over the generation of electricity, the higher economic risks associated with nuclear power can be managed: any excess costs can, in principle, be passed on to consumers. However, in competitive markets risks are inherently lower for investment in power sources that are relatively quick and cheap to build, since the initial outlay is amortised comparatively quickly.

Furthermore, nuclear economics depends significantly on economies of scale, both within plants themselves (the new reactor being built in Finland is a 1,600MW unit, perpetuating a tendency for plant size to increase) and deriving from programmes of large numbers of identical units (since 'first-of-a-kind' costs can be very high – about £700 million in the case of the PWR Sizewell B in the United Kingdom). Liberalised markets create benefits for relatively small units that are quick to build, and also for units that have flexible outputs. This is another area in which the CCGT, which can be built in smaller units than traditional nuclear power stations, can more easily increase and reduce output to follow demand. The almost complete cessation of orders for new reactors in the European Union and the United States by the mid-1990s was in part precipitated by the introduction of competitive power markets.

A revival of nuclear construction appears unlikely unless nuclear generating technologies emerge that:

- improve the relative economics of nuclear power;
- improve safety in a manner perceived and understood by the public;
- reduce waste production, especially of long-lived elements;
- improve fuel efficiency (which in turn reduces waste production); and
- ensure resistance to weapons proliferation.

In addition, progress may be needed both in ensuring sufficient fuel reserves for a major new nuclear programme and in techniques for managing nuclear waste in the long term. A number of recent studies have examined these issues in depth (e.g. MIT, 2003).

8.4   Nuclear research and development

8.4.1   *Nuclear R&D in the context of total energy R&D*

Tables 8.2 and 8.3 are taken from the IEA's statistics regarding government energy R&D expenditure in the twenty-six IEA member countries (IEA, 2001). The database does not include information about private companies' expenditure, nor funds spent by non-IEA countries, such as China, Russia or India. Figures are given in millions of 1999 dollars, except where noted otherwise.

As table 8.2 shows, the total amount of energy R&D expenditure by governments of IEA countries rose in tandem with the rise in oil prices in the mid- to late 1970s, and fell away significantly as perceptions of shortages of hydrocarbon fuels declined subsequently. The trend is even more dramatic if the figures for Japan, which maintained its R&D expenditure through the 1980s and 1990s and accounted for over a half of

Table 8.2 *Government expenditure by IEA countries on energy R&D*

Year	1975	1980	1985	1990	1995	1999
Conservation	351	977	745	530	1,081	1,141
Fossil fuels	602	2,580	1,528	1,769	941	524
Renewables	209	1,934	870	589	688	536
Nuclear fission	4,969	6,952	6,819	4,198	3,488	3,205
Nuclear fusion	611	1,226	1,487	1,080	1,003	686
Other	1,021	1,599	1,066	1,203	1,419	1,385
Total energy R&D	7,763	15,268	12,515	9,369	8,620	7,477
Total energy R&D (excl. Japan)	6,312	11,960	8,918	6,047	4,771	3,633

Table 8.3 *Government expenditure by IEA countries on fission R&D*

	United Kingdom	France	Japan	United States	Other IEA countries	All IEA countries
1990	188	385	2,407	644	574	4,198
1999	3	428[a]	2,459	19	296	3,205

Note:
[a] 1998 data.

IEA expenditure in 1999, are excluded. The table shows a consistent drop in expenditure between 1980 and 1999. Energy R&D has also represented a falling proportion of total government R&D spending in recent years. For example, in 1997 the level of energy R&D in the United States was below 10 per cent of total (non-defence) government-funded R&D.

As is often noted by opponents of nuclear power, throughout the period the expenditure on nuclear fission dominated the overall figures, though falling from 64 per cent of the total in 1975 to 43 per cent in 1999. However, even these figures can be misleading. Table 8.3 shows that in many IEA countries, with the major exceptions of Japan and France, government R&D expenditure on nuclear fission fell significantly through the 1990s, to levels below that spent on renewables.

By 1999 Japan was alone responsible for some 77 per cent of IEA R&D expenditure on nuclear fission, with France accounting for more than a half of the remainder. If the French and Japanese figures are excluded, fission R&D expenditure in the other IEA countries totalled $318 million, against $403 million for renewables.

Outside the IEA, Russia, India and China have substantial nuclear fission programmes, and as the European Union also funds an amount of fission R&D the worldwide total for fission may well be somewhat higher than the figure in table 8.3. Nonetheless, given that the bulk of government-sponsored R&D into nuclear fission focuses on waste management and other fuel cycle back-end processes, it is clear that most governments have spent relatively little on new reactor designs in recent years. The emergence of projects such as the Generation IV nuclear energy initiative (described below) may presage a change.

8.4.2   *The nature of nuclear research, development and commercialisation*

In the development of nuclear fission (and also nuclear fusion, carbon dioxide sequestration and perhaps renewables such as large geothermal or bioethanol facilities), large-scale prototype plants eventually have to be built. The costs of prototype facilities for renewables such as wind power, solar power or biomass are likely to be at least an order of magnitude less than those for nuclear power, and in some cases much less.

This tends to increase the riskiness of R, D&C into nuclear power in comparison to many of the renewables. Diversifying the research effort over a large number of small projects is very likely to lead to considerable improvements in the technology in question. Reliance on a single, large demonstration unit – all that is likely to be affordable given the cost – runs the risk of losing the whole investment if insuperable problems are encountered (although, of course, it also offers the potential for major advance). Experience of this kind in the past has contributed to a growing unwillingness to sponsor *big science*, which has accompanied the liberalisation of power markets in some countries.

8.5   Nuclear technologies

Although there is much talk of 'nuclear technology', there are many possible ways of extracting energy from uranium, just as there are many ways of extracting energy from, say, water. In both cases some of these have been pursued; others are at an early stage of consideration. It is therefore no more justified to talk of a single 'nuclear technology' than to talk of a single 'water technology'.

Even pressurised water reactors, Advanced CANDU and high-temperature approaches such as the pebble bed modular reactor are as different from each other as are hydropower, wave power and tidal power, and much more radical options (e.g. sub-critical assemblies or the Russian or Japanese microreactors) may be feasible. For this reason, it is also unjustified to talk about nuclear technology as being 'mature' – large-scale PWR technology may be 'mature' in some sense (although even here newer designs, such as the AP1000 or System-80+, are significantly different from the 'traditional' PWRs currently in operation in many countries), but for a variety of reasons, discussed below, research into other reactor concepts is at a very early stage. To talk of nuclear power as being 'mature' because there are some decades of experience of a relatively small number of design approaches would be equivalent to saying that wave power is a 'mature' technology because people have been using waterwheels for centuries. Indeed, nuclear fission as a demonstrated physical phenomenon is barely sixty years old, and it would be extraordinary if all its possibilities had been recognised, let alone demonstrated, in such a short period of time.

8.5.1   New types of reactor

Recently, the following nomenclature for reactor designs, describing four 'generations', was proposed by the US Department of Energy (see the website: http://www.gen-iv.ne.doe.gov).

- Generation I refers to the early prototype and power reactors, such as Shippingport, Magnox and Dresden.
- Generation II refers to the commercial reactors built up to the end of the 1990s, such as BWRs, PWRs, CANDU, the Russian VVERs, etc.
- Generation III (and III+) covers advanced reactors newly licensed (or ready for licensing in the near future), such as the AP600, AP1000, ABWR, EPR, VVER-640 and the South African PBMR.
- Generation IV systems are to be ready for construction during the 2020s and in operation by 2030.

Evolutionary designs are generally far less risky in economic terms than novel designs, but can still offer significant improvements over the previous generation. Generation III designs (with the exception of the more revolutionary PBMR) incorporate lessons learnt during the 1980s and 1990s from the construction, commissioning and operation mainly of LWRs (but also of gas-cooled and heavy water technologies) throughout the world. Many of the designs are ready for licensing (indeed, ABWR, AP600, AP1000 and System-80+ already have regulatory approval in the United States) and promise lower capital cost, greater speed in construction, quicker commissioning and better economic performance. Since these designs have so far not been utilised (with the exception of the ABWR in Japan), the power industry may not consider them commercially proven. In other words, although the R&D associated with these designs has largely been completed, commercialisation has not. However, there is considerable confidence within the nuclear industry that the principles, being evolutions of proven approaches, are well understood and therefore that the learning curve will not be steep.

If early means can be found to finance prototypes, Generation III reactors may well be commercially available during the second decade of this century. However, as the first unit of a kind is usually more problematic and more expensive than the following units, investment in commercial prototypes tends to be very risky. Companies are therefore reluctant, especially in a highly competitive market, to go ahead with such projects, unless there are possibilities of very large gains if the project is successful, or if the risks of building the first prototype can be widely shared or underwritten.

It can be argued, then, that there is a legitimate role for governments, either separately or perhaps in international collaboration, to provide funding or tax support for the construction of demonstration plants. Some commentators argue that this would be appropriate, as much of the regulatory uncertainty that deters private sector investment in prototypes originates with governments.

Generation III designs often make use of two important principles – simplification, leading to lower construction costs, and modularisation, leading to lower construction times – alongside other improvements. For example, the Advanced CANDU reactor, which uses light water instead of heavy water for cooling and slightly enriched uranium instead of natural uranium as fuel, might, it is claimed, be able to use spent fuel from LWRs as feedstock. A more modular approach to construction could also reduce the construction phase to forty-eight months, or less. Taken together, these changes (if achievable) could make a substantial difference to the relative economics of this type of reactor.

The South African PBMR, largely based on German and early UK R&D, is a more novel design. It is a high-temperature, helium gas-cooled reactor, power being produced by a gas turbine operating within the helium stream. If successful, the technology could have a number of advantages, which may bring substantial orders from all over the world. As an example, it has a modular design, making units as small as 100MW economically possible and reducing the costs and duration of construction. Its thermal efficiency should be significantly higher than for LWRs (some 45 per cent compared to around 30 per cent), and there could be a greatly reduced volume of spent fuel per power generated. There are some major technical issues to be addressed, such as a turbine working under severe conditions, which add to the economic risk of constructing a demonstration PBMR. However, the risks of the project were initially shared between two South African concerns (the power company ESKOM and the Industrial Development Corporation) and

BNFL of the United Kingdom (the major US power producer Exelon was a partner, but later withdrew). It is notable, however, that the major partner in the scheme is a large state-owned monopoly. China has also constructed an experimental pebble bed plant.

Generation IV and related nuclear energy initiatives There are a number of other advanced reactors under study or on the drawing board. Most of these schemes require substantial development and may not be commercially proven before the 2020s. In addition to basic research, such concepts may need a series of pilot and demonstration plants to allow in-depth study of such factors as the effects of different types of fuel, detailed study of the waste and the means of disposing it and the potential effect on proliferation of the fuel cycle associated with the envisaged reactor or assembly.

To explore opportunities for such research, the US Department of Energy has initiated international studies into possible ways of achieving these aims. Ten countries (Argentina, Brazil, Canada, France, Japan, South Korea, South Africa, Switzerland, the United Kingdom and the United States) are involved in debating possible future developments of nuclear energy. The main purpose of the study will be the delineation of the next generation of nuclear energy systems, and for that purpose the Generation IV International Forum has been formed.

The technological goals for GIF have been agreed.

- To provide sustainable energy generation that meets clean air objectives and promotes the long-term availability of systems, as well as effective fuel utilisation for worldwide energy production.
- To minimise and manage nuclear waste and, notably, reduce the burden of the long-term stewardship of waste.
- To increase confidence that the waste streams are highly unattractive for diversion into weapons programmes.
- To excel in safety and reliability.
- To have a very low likelihood and degree of reactor core damage.
- To eliminate the need for off-site emergency response.
- To have a clear life cycle cost advantage over other energy sources.
- To have financial risks comparable to other energy projects.

So as to meet the required timetable, the US Department of Energy and GIF published a 'technology roadmap' in December 2002, with the aim of evaluating potential nuclear energy concepts, selecting the most promising line for further development and defining the required R&D to bring the project to commercialisation within the proposed time.

Initial work has largely concentrated on reactors, but the full fuel cycle will also have to be considered.

Among the concepts being considered in various forms are the following.

- The rival HTGR under development by General Atomic Corporation in conjunction with France, Japan and Russia.
- Advanced light water reactor systems, such as IRIS, a modular design of 100 to 300MW unit capacity, a longer core reloading schedule (five to eight years) and enhanced safety features and proliferation resistance.
- Renewed interest in FRs, though not necessarily as breeders. (It is said that new designs of fast reactor are simpler and safer than the 'thermal' reactors that make up almost all of today's operating nuclear designs, and that they can destroy plutonium and other actinides better and more effectively than via a MOx route making use of LWRs. This may become important in view of the need to destroy surplus weapons-grade plutonium as well as material from civil reprocessing.) Much of the work on FRs has made use of sodium cooling, but more recently another coolant, a lead/bismuth mixture originally developed for Russian submarine reactors, has caused interest. However, widespread use of plutonium fuels could lead to concerns over proliferation.
- Substantial advances in the design and use of powerful accelerators, making it possible to consider accelerator-driven systems. (In such systems assemblies containing fissile material operate in subcritical mode – i.e. they do not produce sufficient neutrons to keep the nuclear reaction going, and require additional neutrons from an outside source, such as an accelerator. For the present, the interest in ADSs is largely connected with the treatment of waste (see below), but it is possible that such subcritical reactors may have advantages over critical fast reactors, especially with regard to the fuel composition, although they also require an external source of neutrons, which may be very expensive.
- A number of other, perhaps more specialised, reactors that are under development, including high-temperature reactors providing high-temperature heat for the production of hydrogen from hydrocarbons, and for use in water desalination (a process already demonstrated through the BN350 fast reactor in Kazakhstan, and the subject of an eleven-member IAEA technical cooperation project), both such uses being likely to become important during this century.
- The Russian very small reactors, possibly down to 15MWe, with sealed fuel lasting the lifetime of the reactor, for use as the energy source in isolated areas.

The IAEA has also established the International Project on Innovative Nuclear Reactors and Fuel Cycles, initially with nine members – Argentina, Brazil, China, Germany, India, Russia, South Korea, Spain and Turkey (later joined by Bulgaria, Canada, Indonesia, the Netherlands, Pakistan, Switzerland, South Africa and the European Union) – who contribute either money or cost-free technical expertise (IAEA, 2004). INPRO's focus is on:

- identifying the needs and requirements of a spectrum of developing and developed countries; and
- contributing explicitly to the debate on the global acceptability of nuclear power.

8.5.2   *Uranium and the fuel cycle*

Alongside work on new reactor concepts, there is a need to review assumptions about the fuel cycle.

When during the 1970s it was believed that nuclear energy would expand rapidly, the availability of conventional uranium reserves was regarded as a potential bottleneck. It was assumed that a fuel cycle involving recycling uranium and plutonium from spent fuel could use the latter in a programme of fast breeder reactors (thereby, in effect, using the otherwise useless uranium-238 in natural uranium). The overall effect would be to increase the amount of energy that could be extracted from a certain quantity of natural uranium by a factor of sixty.

In the event, exploration for uranium revealed many more deposits, the fast breeder turned out to be more difficult and expensive than had been assumed and nuclear energy failed to expand as rapidly as had been expected. The dismantling of nuclear weapons programmes in recent years has created a new source of non-mined uranium (or, rather, uranium that was mined some years or decades ago). As a result, there is now no shortage of uranium, and neither of the world's two working fast reactors is operating in breeder mode. This situation is unlikely to change significantly without a major expansion of nuclear power.

That said, the global use of uranium has outstripped production since 1990 and the spot price of uranium doubled between 2000 and 2003 (though it is still a long way below its peak in the mid- to late 1970s). Should a major expansion of nuclear power take place, questions over the availability of conventional uranium reserves will eventually re-emerge. Even in a more modest nuclear future, some countries, such as Japan and India, with plans for a major role for nuclear energy but no indigenous

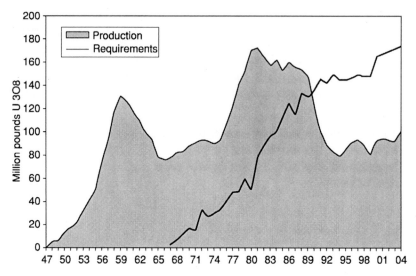

Figure 8.4. World uranium production versus requirements, 1947–2004.
Source: Combs (2004).

uranium reserves, may be concerned about long-term over-dependence on imports.

In principle, there could be three ways of extending fuel reserves for nuclear stations without pursuing the fast reactor route:

• the better use of uranium from existing reserves;
• the development of new uranium reserves; or
• the use of alternative reactor fuels.

One area of research interest associated with the first of these options is the possible use of lasers in separating isotopes. At present, two techniques are in use for the separation of fissile uranium-235 from natural uranium (which consists mainly of uranium-238): gaseous diffusion and centrifuging. Although the latter requires far less energy than the former, in absolute terms it is still costly and energy-intensive. It is predicted that the use of laser technology will be far more energy-efficient, thereby increasing the amount of useful energy to be extracted from a given amount of natural uranium. Such a process would also reduce the cost of producing enriched uranium for reactor fuel, but there could well be substantial proliferation dangers if a simple and cheap way of separating isotopes were to be developed.

Undoubtedly, should the uranium price grow, new reserves would be discovered, and the extraction of uranium from unconventional reserves such as uranium phosphates might become economically attractive. Furthermore, better mining techniques continue to develop, allowing greater yields from existing reserves. Research has an important part to play in all these areas, although it is likely that the funding will come from companies involved in the fuel cycle rather than from governments, as commercial returns might be achieved relatively quickly.

More speculative is the possibility of extracting uranium from seawater, which is being pursued in Japan. Should the extraction of uranium from seawater become economically feasible, perhaps in association with desalination as world water supplies come under pressure, then the lifetime of uranium reserves could increase by two orders of magnitude. Should a major revival in nuclear power be contemplated, uranium from seawater could well be an important area of R&D (JAERI, 1999).

India is looking into the possibility of utilising thorium (of which it has large reserves) as the main fuel for its nuclear programme. Thorium (unlike uranium) has no fissile isotope, but its main isotope, thorium-232, is *fertile* because on the absorption of a neutron it decays into the *fissile* uranium-233. The thorium fuel cycle has advantages and disadvantages when compared to the uranium cycle, and considerable research would be needed even before a realistic comparison between the two could be made. Most commentators believe that uranium will remain the basis of civil nuclear energy in most countries (see the section on thorium on the World Nuclear Association's website: http://www.world-nuclear.org/info/inf62.htm).

Alternative fuel cycles and reprocessing As noted earlier, between the mid-1950s and the mid-1970s it was assumed that reprocessing plants would be required to recover plutonium from spent reactor fuel, and fast breeder reactors would be used to extract the maximum possible energy from natural uranium reserves. The United States and some other countries abandoned this fuel cycle because of fears that its use might greatly increase the risk of proliferation. Since then, they have used a 'once-through system'. The spent fuel that arises is classified as high-level waste, which, after some time in on-site storage while its rate of heat production falls, is to be disposed of in deep waste repositories. (In 2001 the National Energy Policy Development group recommended a re-examination of reprocessing options in the United States.)

An associated reason for the move against reprocessing in some countries may have been a recognition of the difficulties associated with the development of the fast breeder reactor and of the complexity and high costs of reprocessing plants.

A number of other countries – Japan, France, Russia, China and India – did not follow the US lead, and are still officially committed to developing reprocessing plant and fast breeders. However, at present only the French Phénix and Russian BN600 fast reactors are in operation, neither being used to breed fresh plutonium. The world's only commercial-scale fast reactor, the French Superphénix, was closed in 1998. The Monju prototype plant in Japan, although closed at present, is expected to reopen for experimentation, and the 400MW Fast Flux Test Facility at Hanford, Washington State, has been kept ready for possible recommissioning in due course.

However, a fuel cycle including fast (breeder) reactors also requires the reprocessing of spent nuclear fuel to separate out the plutonium, and possibly uranium for reuse. Present reprocessing plants use modernised versions of the Purex process, originally developed for nuclear weapons production during the 1950s. Today's rationale for reprocessing is quite different (and highly contentious), and there are doubts as to whether the present process, which is complex, expensive and generates aqueous waste streams that are difficult to handle, would be appropriate should reprocessing or partitioning (see below) be required in the future. That said, at present only Japan is constructing a reprocessing plant, and it seems unlikely that the commercial plants in the United Kingdom and France will be replaced when they reach the end of their working lives. A revival in the case for reprocessing, presumably because of a significant growth in nuclear generation and a failure to develop new fuel resources, might require the use of new approaches to reprocessing. Initial research has been carried out into novel approaches to separation, ranging from new aqueous processes to pyrochemical and electrochemical methods, mainly in the context of partition and transmutation (see below). More R&D would be required to determine their suitability for large-scale reprocessing.

8.5.3   Managing radioactive waste

This has been called the 'Achilles heel' of the nuclear industry. Early on it was assumed that high-level waste would have to be disposed of in deep underground repositories, which would have to be kept safe for 100,000 years or longer. The first task was to find a site that was technically suitable and acceptable to the public. Thirty years later no such site had been found anywhere, although progress had been better in some countries – notably Finland, Sweden and the United States – than others. During this period the costs of investigation have soared: in 1982 technical site characterisation was projected to cost some $80 million per site in the United States; on the basis of experience at the Yucca Mountain site, the estimate has now increased to $5 billion. In the United Kingdom a 1997 proposal for an underground research facility as part of a site characterisation was rejected because of doubts about the scientific methods used in the analysis. There is some debate as to whether the type of uncertainties involved in long-term waste management are amenable even in principle to scientific research.

Whilst this argument rages, spent fuel and high-level waste from reprocessing is mostly being stored in surface storage on the sites where it was produced, but available storage is getting short in a number of cases. With the exceptions of Olkiluoto in Finland and Yucca Mountain in the United States, and possibly Sweden, it seems unlikely that underground repositories will be available within the next twenty years (although the events of 11 September 2001 have affected perspectives on this issue). If this proves to be the case, the only possible solutions are to build more intermediate storage (on- or off-site, on- or near-surface) or to close down reactors as their storage becomes full. This latter course would imply the abandonment of nuclear energy and is unlikely to be acceptable to a number of countries.

The question then arises as to what the potential lifetime of such stores should be. Bearing in mind today's uncertainties about the availability of final repositories and, indeed, the future scale of nuclear energy in the world, it may make sense to plan for intermediate storage with a relatively long lifetime, say of 100 years, in the expectation that within that period the future of nuclear energy will have been clarified and that there will have been more technological advances to resolve the long-term waste problem. Research must have an important input into this debate, because information will be required about the behaviour of the waste over time and what conditioning (if any) and packaging the waste should receive. This is likely to vary according to the origin and age of the waste; some of it will arise only long after the closure of individual facilities during the time of site clearance.

Should nuclear power be in global decline, an important question would arise over how to retain the necessary levels of expertise for such tasks within the industry for the several decades – or longer – between the closure of the last power plants and the eventual disposal of waste materials.

Partitioning and Transmutation   One highly speculative possibility that has attracted much attention over the years since nuclear power began is P&T, the purpose of which is to transmute components of waste streams with long half-lives (mainly minor actinides) into elements having far shorter half-lives, and by so doing to reduce the volume to be disposed of in deep repositories. Both these factors should make final disposal simpler. Proponents suggest that it should be possible to reduce the time of having to keep repositories secure to less than 500 years and to reduce the quantity of waste to the repository by a factor of twenty-five. The process consists of separating the waste into a series of different streams, one of which contains all the material to be transmuted in an accelerator-driven assembly or fast reactor. The resulting spent fuel would again be partitioned into material to be recycled and material to be sent, after conditioning, to a repository (Venneri et al., 1998).

Information from the United States indicates that research into the various processes for P&T would take some six to eight years and cost some $280 million, but that the total R, D&C might cost some $11 billion, with the first prototype being ready within about twenty years. This may lead to a dilemma, similar to those found elsewhere in the nuclear debate. P&T may make sense only in the context of an expanding nuclear industry, but the nuclear industry may be able to expand only if a waste management route such as that offered by P&T becomes available. Collaboration among those researching the field, including the United States, France, Japan, the European Union and possibly Russia, may be a way forward (DOE, 1999).

8.6   Conclusions

The fact that nuclear power accounts for some 16 per cent of global electricity supplies demonstrates that it is already a technical option both for diversifying energy production away from fossil fuels and for reducing emissions of greenhouse gases, as revealed by looking at the carbon dioxide emissions per unit of electricity generated in a number of countries.

There are several possible future paths that the nuclear fission industry could take. Some might involve an evolutionary approach from the traditional reactors of the 1970s and 1980s, large-scale plants employing more modern approaches to project management and to passive safety, thereby allowing simplified designs that are considerably cheaper and quicker to build. The research requirements for such designs are relatively modest – indeed, some have been licensed in the United States – and the issue is more one of finding resources to build pilot units. In a future characterised by large, centralised generating units and long-term

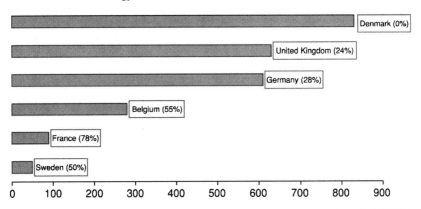

Figure 8.5. CO$_2$ emissions per unit of electricity produced (t/GWh) and nuclear generating share, 2002.
Source: Eurelectric (2004).

power contracts, these designs could well be attractive in competitive markets as hydrocarbon reserves become depleted.

At the opposite extreme lie the more speculative designs being considered in the Generation IV initiative. By their very nature these options are more difficult to appraise and will require considerably more research before they can be properly evaluated. However, it may well be that smaller and more flexible nuclear designs will be required in future scenarios more characterised by small-scale generation in competitive markets.

Though liberalisation has been the dominant theme in most electricity supply markets since the early 1990s it is not certain that this trend will continue (Grimston, 2004). As a result, the challenge for the research community is to pursue the more promising of these paths, while recognising that the nature of nuclear technology is likely to be such that large-scale prototype units may be built (in the case of at least some more speculative options) with no subsequent deployable technology emerging.

There is a further research issue. Even the apparently 'technical' issues cannot be judged without reference to the relationship between nuclear technologies and society, in fields such as public reactions to various technologies, decision-making procedures, economic performance and the role of the political community. One of the problems with traditional nuclear technology (and with several others) is that it developed in an atmosphere in which it was broadly assumed that the only important questions were technical ones, amenable to technical solutions.

In the event, society has moved on. Public involvement in decision making has increased alongside a 'decline of deference' towards the 'expert' and those in 'authority'. The dominance of a utilitarian ethic and probabilistic appraisal and decision making has been eroded, to the benefit of a more rights-based approach coupled with a growing importance of perception through anecdote and personal case study. Many of the obstacles to nuclear development have not, therefore, been purely technical, but have been located in the mistrust with which the technologies and the industry itself are regarded by significant sectors of public opinion. This, in turn, has emerged in part because the industry has failed to give the impression of being aware of the concerns held by the people who were ultimately both its paymasters and its customers – or, to put it another way, was not sufficiently sensitive to issues in the intellectual domain covered by the social sciences.

It is essential, then, that ongoing research integrates 'hard' and 'social' sciences rather more closely than has been the case in the past (Grimston, 2003). Furthermore, the evaluation of nuclear technology cannot be carried out in a vacuum; it must be done against a background of the demand for clean and economically acceptable energy, and the progress with other options such as carbon dioxide sequestration and renewables.

8.7   References

Combs, J. (2004). *Fueling the Future: A New Paradigm*, paper presented at World Nuclear Association Annual Symposium, London, 8–10 September.

DOE (1999). *A Roadmap for Developing Accelerator Transmutation of Waste Technology*, Washington, DC: Department of Energy.

Eurelectric (2004). *Statistics and Prospects for the European Electricity Sector*, Brussels: Eureletnic.

Grimston, M. (2003). *Nuclear Power*, paper presented at Economic and Social Research Council Energy Research Conference 'Projects and Policies for Step Changes in the Energy System: Developing an Agenda for Social Science Research', London, 31 March, available at http://www.psi.org.uk/docs/2003/esrc-energy-grimston-nuclear.doc.

(2004). *Liberalised Power Markets*, paper presented at World Nuclear Association Annual Symposium, London, 8–10 September.

IAEA, (2004). *International Project on Innovative Nuclear Reactors and Fuel Cycles (INPRO)*, Vienna: International Atomic Energy Agency, available at http://www.iaea.org/OurWork/ST/NE/NENP/NPTDS/Projects/INPRO.

IEA (2001). *Energy Technology R&D Statistics*, Paris: International Energy Agency/Organisation for Economic Co-operation and Development.

JAERI (1999). Uranium recovery from seawater, *JAERI News* no. 43, Kashiwa: Japan Atomic Energy Research Institute, available at http://www.jaeri.go.jp/ english/ff/ff43/topics.html.

MIT (2003). *The Future of Nuclear Power: An Interdisciplinary MIT Study*, Cambridge, MA: Massachusetts Institute of Technology, available at http://web. mit.edu/nuclearpower/.

NEA (1998). *Projected Costs of Electricity Generation: 1998 Update*, Paris: Nuclear Energy Agency/Organisation for Economic Co-operation and Development.

Venneri, F., N. Li, M. Williamson, M. Hours and G. Lawrence, (1998). *Disposition of Nuclear Waste Using Subcritical Accelerator-Driven Systems: Technology Choices and Implementation Scenario*, Los Alamos, NM: Los Alamos National Laboratory.

9 Miniaturisation of the electricity generation industry: issues, technologies and potential

Andreas Biermann

9.1 Introduction

During the past half-decade new technologies have emerged and old technologies have been developed further, which together have further strengthened the already existing trend towards the reduction of economies of scale in power generation.

These new technologies now, or will soon, allow individual households to change their boilers to micro-CHP units, or to generate electricity from sunlight through photovoltaic cells. Should micro-CHP technologies prove their ability to withstand the demands of domestic heating operating regimes, and should the cost for solar PV come down further, then it is possible that the UK domestic sector will change from its current position as a significant importer of electricity to a sector with a portfolio that is much more balanced between generation and consumption. The implications of this change for networks, generators, investors in the power sector, the United Kingdom's security of supply and the environment could be significant.

This chapter will provide a background and an overview to the technological change underlying the rise of micropower during the last few years, and will then discuss the potential impact on markets and electricity systems that this rise may have. It argues that the introduction of micropower is not only a technological revolution but also a socio-economic one.

9.2 Background

Until the late 1980s power generation benefited from increasing economies of scale. It was a *big engineering* technology, using large turbines in

The author would like to thank the Energy Saving Trust for its support for the work on this chapter, which was begun when he worked at the EST. Nevertheless, the opinions in this chapter are those of the author alone, and do not necessarily reflect the opinions of either the Energy Saving Trust or its members.

steam plants that burnt coal or ran on a nuclear fission process. This trend of increasing economies of scale rapidly accelerated from the middle of the twentieth century, when new technologies, and the development of integrated grid systems, supported larger and then even larger plants, with the standard turbine size in the United Kingdom growing from around 125MW to 500MW within less than twenty years (Newbery and Green, 1996).

This development came to an end in the late 1980s, when the introduction of combined-cycle gas turbine plant made smaller plant sizes economic, and when changing financing arrangements in some of the newly liberalised markets no longer supported the development of power stations that took a decade to build and were large enough to supply half of London with electricity single-handedly. The last of these stations was the 4GWe Drax, a coal-fired station that became a symbol of the plight of traditional generators in the liberalised markets, with the American owner AES walking away from the highly indebted plant as it could no longer sell its output in a depressed electricity wholesale market (see the Electricity Forum Website: http://www.electricityforum.com/news/avg03/aes.html).

Instead, in the 1990s, a range of single- or multi-turbine CCGT stations were built, with individual plant sizes of no more than 5 per cent to 10 per cent (200–400MWe) of Drax. Additionally, combined heat and power plants were built that were even smaller, designed to supply industrial steam load and some electricity to an industrial site. Both these developments signified a noticeable boost in the efficiency of primary energy conversion, with CHP plant easily being twice as efficient as Drax, and CCGT plant about 50 per cent more efficient.[1] As an additional benefit, natural gas as a fuel for power generation does not give rise to the emission of sulphur dioxide and particulates.

At the same time, mini-turbines in the 100kWe range were developed, and these could be used to supply, for example, a single block of flats, or a small commercial site, with heat and some electricity. In Germany, internal-combustion-engine-based CHP units of up to 50kWe were developed for use in multi-occupancy housing.

At the same time, solar PV received more and more government support across the world, while the manufacturing cost for solar cells fell, leading to increased deployment of solar technology for power generation, in markets where the right incentives and government support exist, such as Germany and Japan (IEA, 2003).

---

[1] Drax reaches an efficiency of around 35 per cent to 37 per cent, modern CCGTs reach 55 per cent to 60 per cent and gas-fired CHP can exceed 80 per cent.

These developments created a new technological environment in which, for example, network engineers had to become accustomed to having a few small-scale power stations on their lower-voltage grid systems, where previously only demand load connections had existed. At the same time, the changes were limited in scope, so while they raised issues of competition, market access and safety these were not significant enough to necessitate a resolution through government involvement. One reason for this may have been the diversity of technologies and companies operating them.

We are now at the stage of development at which it is essential to address these issues urgently in the United Kingdom. The very advanced regulatory structure of the UK electricity supply industry has led to a highly unusual process being set up, which should lead to regulatory outcomes that are robust enough to last for the foreseeable future.

9.3   Technology overview

For ease of classification, small-scale generators are often broken down into micro- and mini-generators. For the purposes of this chapter, a microgenerator has a capacity up to 3.7kWe on a single-phase connection, and a mini-generator has a capacity of up to 11kWe on a three-phase connection. These are the limits currently chosen for simplified connection arrangements to the UK networks. Technically speaking, these types of generators could go up to 25 or even 100kWe, depending on what one would like to choose as a technical boundary. For mass applications, though, smaller generator capacity is more likely to see higher numbers of installations, and it is no accident that the domestic generator size tends to be less than 3kWe. Large installations are significant investment projects, and will always be handled on a bespoke basis. More significant potential exists at the micro end, where generators become products rather than projects.

Microgenerators can be fossil- or renewably fuelled. The following sections give an overview of the currently existing, or developing, technologies.

9.3.1   Fossil fuel

Fossil-fuel-fired microgenerators are usually CHP units that run on natural gas, although some have the technical potential to run on LPG or liquid fuels as well. For the foreseeable future, fuel cells should be classed as fossil fuel, due to the absence of renewably produced hydrogen. In a country with a well-developed gas grid and a long heating period, these products have significant potential, because they can be deployed as an alternative to traditional central heating systems, producing heat as the primary output and electricity as a by-product. This will provide them with an existing market to break into, unlike pure electricity generators, which have to create a market in the domestic sector. It also has a particular advantage in reducing the opportunity cost for installations. If a boiler has to be installed, installation costs have to be borne by the customer; CHP systems are usually not much more expensive to install, and a heating system is, unlike an electricity microgenerator, not an optional extra for the customer but an integral part of the building.

These generators therefore include external combustion (Stirling) engines, which have a very low power-to-heat ratio (1:6), or fuel cells, which have a 1:1 power-to-heat ratio, as well as internal combustion engines, Rankine-cycle engines and – potentially – steam cells. Fuel cells (fuelled by natural gas) need to reform the fossil fuel to hydrogen, and this is usually done through on-board reformers, considerably adding to the cost and complexity. The projected cost differential for fuel cells, compared to Stirling engines, is 10:1 at the time of writing. For a 1kWe Stirling engine the extra cost of the generator could be as low as £500, while for a fuel cell a cost of £5,000/kWe is currently expected.

9.3.2   Renewables

Renewable microgenerators use either solar power or renewable fuels to produce electricity and, in some cases, heat. The most versatile generator both in terms of scaleability and scope for application is the photovoltaic solar cell (see chapter 4 on solar power). These cells can be used in a range of applications, and benefit from a high flexibility of installations and almost infinite scaleability. The technology suffers from very high costs of production and installation, however, and it is not expected that this will come down to levels at which competitiveness with grid-delivered electricity is achieved before 2020 (IEA, 2003).

At the moment, wind generators are still a bit too large to be deployed easily in urban settings. Very small-scale wind generators are becoming available now, and these could introduce a level of siting flexibility that is comparable to solar PV cells.

Liquid or gaseous biofuels, such as biodiesel or biogas, could be used in internal or external combustion engines, run as CHP or pure generators. At the time of writing, it does not appear that there are plans for the imminent introduction of such products.

Most of the microgenerators described in this chapter are designed for grid-parallel connection, although some can operate as stand-alone generators too. Grid-connected, they will contribute to the baseload requirement of a dwelling or site, and at times export surplus electricity to the grid. For peak- and most of the shoulder-load requirements, the site will draw on the grid supply. Installing generators that are covering the whole supply requirement of a site, or storing electricity on-site, is comparatively expensive, and inefficient, because of the lower value of exported electricity compared to on-site use. It would lead to significant oversizing of the generator unit, in particular when it is also supposed to supply heat to the site, and increase capital cost significantly.

Theoretically, every household in the United Kingdom could install a microgenerator, or be part of a shared mini-generator installation. Many dwellings could install a range of technologies that complement each other – e.g. solar PV and micro-CHP. The main limiting factor will usually be cost, but this will reduce over time when the various technologies mature. The real market potential is critically dependent on getting the cost right, and most potential customers will accept only a very low, or no, mark-up over the price of grid-delivered electricity. Additionally, they will apply a very short payback time calculation to any investment they undertake. Being able to supply an uncomplicated product with a range of values to consumers is the key for success for the products in this market.

9.4   Current status

The technologies described in this chapter are at different stages of development, from technologically proven, such as solar PV, to new product, such as micro-CHP, to technologically under development, such as small-scale fuel cells.

The UK market has seen varied activity, ranging from high in the micro-CHP field to almost non-existent in the fuel cell field. Small gas engines are being sold on a commercial basis by Baxi/Senertec, and solar PV is benefiting from a small government grant programme. Various energy suppliers are offering buy-back rates for electricity from microgenerators, usually only to their own customers, and at prices that are not in relation to the market value of the electricity they buy in. The highest observed price is £0.1/kWh, but it is possible that individual owners of generators have been able to negotiate better prices.

9.4.1   Micro- and mini-CHP

This comes in three basic forms of technology: internal combustion engine, external combustion engine and fuel cells. Internal combustion engines are well proven, and have been installed around 10,000 times on the European continent. The internal combustion engine is a tried technological concept, and in the right type of application the economics work reasonably well. With a very limited level of government support - e.g. by guaranteeing feed-in minimum price levels for exported electricity - the market for these products can be expanded significantly in the United Kingdom, as it already has been in Germany.[2]

External combustion engines are an old theoretical concept, invented in 1816 by Robert Stirling, but it has only been recent advances in material science that have made it possible to produce them with the lifetime and reliability needed in modern standard applications. The developmental requirements were in particular focused on increased longevity of the core engine parts, which are sealed for life, with no possibility to maintain/replace them on-site. Four hundred of the Powergen/Whispertech Whispergen product are currently being installed under commercial conditions in the United Kingdom, and there are plans to install 80,000 of them by 2010.[3] External combustion engines are combined with the mature standard condensing boiler technology to produce heat for the site. Because they are at an early stage in their development, they will require recognition of their energy efficiency potential, and similar support to that received by the internal combustion engine, to help them overcome the disadvantage of the price differential with conventional boilers. Both internal and external combustion engines produce AC electricity that can be used in electricity systems straightaway.

Fuel cells are less advanced, and have so far seen only a relatively small number of trial installations. In terms of combining different technological parts, the fuel cell is the most complex of the technologies described here, relying on newly developed processes, such as reforming natural gas into hydrogen, for its operation. This increases the cost, and raises questions about the longevity of the product. The prices for fuel cells are currently so high that they are viable only in very specialist applications, where price is not relevant (e.g. military), or in trial situations. Fuel cells produce DC electricity that, conventionally, needs to be inverted to AC before it can be used.

Even if fuel cells are run on a direct hydrogen feed, it is unlikely that this hydrogen will be produced using renewable energy for at least the next decade, in the United Kingdom. Fuel cells are therefore a long-term option. This is also confirmed by the development of fuel cells in

---

[2] See Senertec's website: http://www.senertec.de/ine/pdf.php?file=61&verzeichnis=vero effentlichung&readsave=0.

[3] See Whispertech's website: http://www.whispertech.co.nz/main/WTNews.

Table 9.1 *Products currently available or in testing*

Technology	Capacity in kWe	Companies involved	Status
Fuel cell	4.5	Vaillant/Plug-power	Under development
	1	Osaka University	Unknown
	2.5	Baxi/EFC	Research/under development
Stirling engine	1.2	Whispertech	Limited commercial sales
	1.2	Microgen/Sunpower	Under development
	3	Dias/Sigma	Under development
	1	Enatec	Unknown
IC engine	5.5	Baxi/Senertec	Full commercial
	4.5	Vaillant/Ecopower	Limited commercial
	1	Honda	Full commercial
Rankine-cycle	1	Baxi/Energetix Micropower/Batelle Institute	Under development

the automotive sector, where recently the focus has shifted to more conventional hybrid technology. In both sectors, a strong argument can be made for the need for an intermediate technology; Stirling engines could be that intermediate technology in the stationary sector.

Rankine-cycle engines are under development for use in domestic heating applications in the United Kingdom at the moment. They have the advantage of being very cheap to produce, using standard materials and parts from refrigeration technology. Because of this, and their low thermal mass, which leads to low response times, they have very good potential in domestic applications. Some products that are currently available or in testing are shown in table 9.1.[4] As this list shows, there is considerable scope in the technologies, company size and countries in the market, and this in itself is a strong indication that the underlying concept is sound, even if particular technologies or companies may fail on their way to the market.

9.4.2   Solar PV

Solar PV technology depends on a match with a good site. Even in very good locations, solar PV has low load factors due to the low conversion efficiency of the solar cells. Solar PV therefore requires good solar irradiation and the right direction and angle on the surface where it is to be installed. It will benefit significantly from being installed at a site

---

[4] See, for example, http://www.microgen.com, http://www.whispertech.co.nz or http://www.senertec.de.

where demand load coincides with generation – e.g. an office building with high electricity consumption during the day, and cooling needs in the summer. (For another perspective, see chapter 4.)

Total worldwide capacity installed is growing rapidly from a small base in recent years, on the back of generous grant programmes in Japan, Germany and California. The cost of solar installations is still so high that, without this support, installations may never pay back. The IEA currently does not estimate that solar PV will become competitive with grid-delivered electricity before 2020.

9.4.3   Micro-wind

Micro-wind is primarily constrained by locational restrictions that make it hard to utilise the resource in urban environments. The cost is also relatively high, although not as high as for solar PV, and recent developments may make it possible to reduce cost to a level where payback times reduce significantly.[5]

The UK government is supporting the technology through grant programmes, and these have had some effect on the market, although it is likely that further technological development needs to occur with respect to the building integration of micro-wind.

Overall, the potential for micro-wind is extremely difficult to assess, due to changing technological circumstances and the absence of a study or modelling of the technical and realistic potential for the technology.

9.5   Further technological development

Microgeneration technology, with the possible exception of solar PV and fuel cells, has been progressed primarily by private sector investment in all the potential markets. The technologies have now been brought to market, and various companies are competing in these markets, selling either microgenerators of various technologies or established technologies, such as boilers, that compete directly with them.

This makes public involvement in the further development of these technologies somewhat awkward, unless the research is focused on an area that is of benefit to all technologies – e.g. research of a very fundamental nature.

In the case of solar PV, investment in researching more efficient production processes has high potential, and it is arguable that government support may be better employed there than in the creation of feed-in

---

[2] http://www.proven.co.uk has much information on small wind turbines.

tariffs or other support for the large-scale installation of current technologies.

In the case of micro-CHP, advanced materials will probably be able to contribute to the long-term success of the technology, by ensuring the increased longevity of 'sealed-for-life' parts and helping to reduce noise and vibration during operations. In the case of fuel-cell micro-CHP, further research and development of basic components is required, with a view to reducing costs to one-tenth of their current level.

9.6   Market potential

As outlined above, cost and payback considerations will limit the potential for the widespread use of microgenerators for the foreseeable future. The realistic market potential for them is therefore far more limited than the technical market potential, and technically promising combined installations will be restricted the most by the economics.

The most significant market potential exists for technologies with the lowest marginal cost over the traditional alternative, and the highest utility for the operator. This is likely to be some form of micro-CHP, where the alternative is a conventional boiler (itself a capital-intensive product), and the utility is highest, and additional installation costs are low or non-existent. At the other end of the scale, solar PV has a very high cost, and the added utility is relatively low, because it does not produce anything but electricity, which could easily be drawn from the grid (unlike the heat provided by a micro-CHP), while the installation cost is fully additional.

The market potential for micro-CHP is essentially the market for boilers. In the United Kingdom, this is a market with some 20 million units installed, and a replacement rate of 5 per cent to 6 per cent per year. The market is very cost-sensitive, and micro-CHP technologies will, at least at the beginning, be restricted to the upper end of this market. Powergen/E.ON UK have stated that they expect that total penetration of micro-CHP in the domestic heating appliance population could reach 30 per cent by 2020. This is rather ambitious, as it would imply (assuming unchanged replacement rates) that micro-CHP reaches a very significant share of the domestic boiler market in the United Kingdom by 2020, and starts with a high market share immediately. The UK market for domestic gas boilers reaches some 1.2 million units sold per annum – about 90 per cent of them in the replacement market. Around 20 million homes are connected to gas, and about 18 million of these are estimated to have a gas central heating system. 30 per cent of this population would be between 5.5 and 6 million units installed, from a current number that is somewhere between zero and 100. Between 2005 and 2020 all 18 million gas central heating units will be replaced once, on average. In order to reach the predicted penetration rate of 30 per cent, micro-CHP will have to be a very successful technology.

In the absence of experience with domestic micro-CHP installations on a significant scale, and a consequent lack of knowledge about consumer interest and acceptance, it is very difficult to predict the potential for these units in the UK market. What can be said is that the recent regulatory developments, which were mostly aimed at and called for by micro-CHP developers, will secure a base for all microgenerators to use in penetrating the UK electricity generation markets.

To understand the potential impact in terms of contribution to the electricity demand of the domestic sector in the United Kingdom, it is necessary to start from a number of well-defined assumptions. The ones that follow are, intentionally, at the optimistic end of what could be forecast. Assuming that Powergen's scenario comes to pass, and 6 million units are installed, and that these are on average 2.5kWe (starting with 1.2kWe units now, and moving to higher generating capacity in the 2010s), with a load factor of 24 per cent (a Stirling engine producing 9kWth will have to run 2,000 hours to heat an average house with an 18,000kWth annual demand), these units will produce 30TWh per year, contributing more than a quarter of the domestic sector demand for electricity – about 115TWh at present – and reducing transmission and distribution system losses in the United Kingdom by a further 1.6–3TWh.[6] This scenario is not assuming a significant introduction of fuel cells.

9.6.1   Case study: Stirling engine micro-CHP versus conventional boiler

The United Kingdom introduced new building regulations in April 2005, ordering the installation of condensing boilers with a minimum heat efficiency of 86 per cent. Under the regulations, total efficiency – i.e. the joint efficiency of electricity and heating – is not considered. The cost for such a boiler is currently assumed to be £1,250, plus installation. This cost does to some degree depend on who is buying, and how many are bought. For a Stirling engine micro-CHP, the cost differential, at the current low production numbers, is likely to be £1,000 to £1,250.

The predicted annual savings range from £125 to £250, depending on where in the country the unit is installed and how high the heat load of the property in question is. At the lower end this is assuming a 1.2kWe

---

[6] System losses in the UK networks run between 6 per cent and 10 per cent on average, depending on the region (Ofgem, 2003).

unit running 2,000 hours a year, generating 2.4MWh of electricity, 2MWh of which is displacing imports, which are costing the household £60 to £70 per MWh. This is roughly 50 per cent of the average (not electrically heated) UK household's consumption, which is currently around 4MWh per year.[7] This is before any income from exported electricity (around £8 to £16 per year, at £20/MWh exported) and potential support for the energy efficiency properties of such a micro-generator (some £150 to £225, with the 50 per cent uplift proposed for units meeting specific requirements under the next round of the 'Energy Efficiency Commitment' under which electricity and gas suppliers have to achieve targets for the promotion of improvements in domestic energy efficiency).

At the upper end of the range, break-even could therefore be as short as three years, while at the lower end of the range, and with no additional support, it could be as long as eight to nine years. This example shows that the success of micro-CHP in the United Kingdom will be dependent not just on government support and the achievement of reimbursement for spilled electricity but also on commercial success by the micro-CHP developers, in driving down their cost of manufacturing and in targeting the right part of the market, because the predicted heat load of a property is going to be the major driver for electricity generated.

9.7   Addressing the barriers

Barriers to microgeneration exist on many levels, and they are of a sociological, economic and behavioural nature. Overcoming them is a long-term process that requires dealing with the group of actors who will lose most by any change to the status quo – i.e. the established energy suppliers, boiler manufacturers and network operators. It is instructive to observe that the prerequisite for success in eliminating barriers is not just political backing but also the close involvement of at least part of the 'establishment' in the project. Even with both these prerequisites achieved, it is a long process that will require significant commitment by the proponents of micropower, and may well be beyond the means of entire industry sectors among them.

A key issue here is that a silo mentality (which can come about for a number of reasons) on the part of the new technology developers may make it difficult to approach dealing with the established interests in

---

[7] Results from unpublished work done by the now defunct Electricity Association's Load Research Group, to which the author had access when at the EST.

a manner that does not make it appear like a zero-sum game for the microgenerator technologies. In other words, manufacturers of microgenerators may perceive the regulatory development to be focused on giving access to one class of generator, and/or be mistrustful of efforts by a competitor to open the framework up. The potential for this exists when microgeneration developers deal with established players on a bilateral basis.

A good example of how this process can work more positively is the United Kingdom's government-/regulator-sponsored Distributed Generation Coordinating Group, in which a specific workstream is dealing with microgeneration. This process has been discussed elsewhere (Biermann, 2003).

A more adversarial approach seems to have been employed in Germany, where the threat of referral to the competition authority is reported to have been instrumental in removing barriers to entry and connection. This approach is making it very difficult for new companies to challenge the established players, unless they have the resources to risk staking the success of their market entry on a positive and quick legal decision. Technology start-ups are often not well supplied with the financial and legal backing required to await the success of their submission to a higher authority.

Which way is taken to remove barriers in the engineering and economic realm will depend fundamentally on the existing ownership structures and levels of competition in the ESI in a country, as well as on the institutional culture of the energy politics. Removing these barriers now, even when the technologies are not yet ready for market introduction, is a prerequisite for attracting additional investment and larger players into the market for microgeneration.

The rapid introduction of microgenerators will have consequences for balances and settlement, and may necessitate the rapid development and deployment of advanced metering technology. A review undertaken by the UK market operator ELEXON examined the potential for simplified metering arrangements, and concluded that there was scope for increasing the minimum generation capacity beyond which half-hourly metering was required to 30kW.[8]

To address the technical issues in distribution networks, it may be necessary to conduct more focused research. Some of this is already happening now – e.g. the European Union's virtual power plant project, in which microgeneration developers have been involved. Overall,

[8] See http://www.eleron.co.uk/documents/Consulations/Open_Consultations/SSTPGL_01.pdf.

though, it is open to question how much public R&D will be required; – the technologies to make miniaturisation feasible exist, and are based on existing metering and control technologies. It is quite likely that metering and control manufacturers will try to become engaged in this market from an early stage. The interest shown by, for example, BEAMA, the UK metering trade association, shows this quite clearly.

9.8   Potential system-level impact

The potential impact on the electricity system is analysed separately from the potential impact on the markets. While there are strong feedback mechanisms between system and market, it appears unlikely that these will come into focus during the initial stages of the technology's deployment, on account of the very low impact that single installations will have on the system, and the markets. It is also necessary to handle these impacts separately because they are under separate governance mechanisms, and reactions to increased microgenerator penetration by system operators can have impacts on market solutions being adopted, such as the case of modification proposal P81 in the United Kingdom, when a technical limit for connection was chosen as a market limit for metering.

Despite the currently low expectations, the potential for significant cumulative impacts exists, especially where initial deployment tends to cluster in small geographic regions. This is because of the nature of the distribution networks, where a single sub-station can serve just a few hundred households, if not fewer. If a local authority, for example, decides to equip a block of flats with micro-CHP, or a number of solar PV installations, then this can have an impact on voltage levels in the area, or could lead to the area becoming a net exporter of electricity at certain times of the day and year.

This has implications for the design of distribution networks that need to be taken into account today, in order not to present a barrier to the development of microgenerators in five, ten or twenty years' time, when elements of the network installed today will still be in service but microgeneration will have a much higher penetration level. A recent study conducted for the United Kingdom's DGCG (Mott MacDonald, 2004) has found that it is unlikely that network operators will incur extra cost from microgenerators until high levels of penetration (greater than 42 per cent in the study) are reached. Most of the effort is likely to come under the ordinary O&M costs of running the network, and the work can be carried out as part of the planned maintenance of the system.

On the higher system level, a significant growth of microgeneration can leave elements of the transmission system stranded if increased wheeling below a grid supply point makes the transfer of electricity into the area covered by this GSP less necessary. This would also affect the requirement for large-scale additional generation connected at the transmission level. It has the potential to affect the viability of all new generation to be connected, including large on- or offshore wind farms.

For this impact to occur, though, significant amounts of microgeneration will have to operate. This may well be one investment cycle in the generation industry (fifteen to twenty years) away, but developers and regulators need to take account of it today, in order not to create structures inadvertently that will hinder the development of microgeneration.

In terms of security of supply, the introduction of micropower will increase this, even where it is fossil-fuelled, by introducing more diversity into the generation mix. Instead of single large plants that are vulnerable to technical failure or terrorist attack, millions of small plants across the country will generate, with a high statistical predictability. This will achieve government goals for increased security of supply.

9.9   Potential impact on market structures

The impact on market structures is very difficult to evaluate at this stage. It depends on further technical developments and consequent cost reductions, together with governmental willingness to support a market transformation process leading to a better competitive position for microgenerators, and companies' attitudes to the risk inherent in introducing a new technology into a mature market. For the purposes of this chapter we assume that the market will develop sufficiently to necessitate changes to electricity trading arrangements, and potentially to the market entry arrangements for electricity suppliers in the United Kingdom.

Electricity trading in the United Kingdom is currently on the basis of bilateral contracts with a balancing system, and a system operator able to call on generators or demand load to respond to short-term imbalances. The system is balanced at the transmission level, with distribution networks normally not actively managed. The number of players in the industry is restricted, by capital requirements for generation plant, high barriers to entry for suppliers and high demands for technical expertise and other running costs for participation in the trading. It is unlikely that individual microgenerator owners will ever want to become members of this structure, but a consolidation agent with a large portfolio consisting either in part or fully of microgeneration may choose to participate in the market, or be forced to do so, on account of its size.

It is more likely, though, that the bulk of microgenerators will be installed by the existing energy suppliers, most of which already have a reasonably balanced generation portfolio. This development can already be observed in the market, with NPower supporting PV installations by a specific installer company through a preferential tariff, and with Centrica and Powergen (E.ON) closely involved in the development and market introduction of micro-CHP in the United Kingdom. In essence, major suppliers at present see the development of microgeneration primarily in terms of generating customer loyalty, and not in terms of generating electricity. It is also possible that large boiler manufacturers may enter the energy supply market on the back of their micro-CHP technology, or subsidiaries of local authorities or housing associations with a significant generation portfolio, although in these cases a partnership with an established supplier is more likely.

There is considerable potential for, for example, lease-financing approaches (also called 'energy services'), whereby an energy supplier can use buying power to achieve lower prices, and then assemble a package consisting of energy trade/sales, maintenance/insurance and capital repayments/finance to reduce the cost of procuring a heating system for a householder, while at the same time achieving a closer relationship with the customer.

In terms of power investment, the introduction of microgeneration can change the current structure fundamentally, by bringing significant numbers of generators into the market the deployment of which is governed by decisions that are unrelated to the current investment climate in the power industry. Where now decisions to invest are made by individuals in large companies, and a single investment in a power station runs into hundreds of millions of pounds, in the future the decision will involve an investment of £2,500 by a household, and be tied to the refurbishment of its heating system or roof. That is a fundamental shift in the structure of the market for power generation finance.

9.10   Conclusions

Microgeneration is an area of electricity generation that has the potential to change fundamentally the face of the electricity system. In particular, it has the potential to change the ownership and operating structures of generation, by making them more akin to those found on the demand side – i.e. dispersed and random. This will change financing structures and increase security of supply, while decreasing centralised control.

Central planning will be replaced to some extent with forecasting based on statistical analysis.

The introduction of microgeneration has engineering and financial implications for the generation industry. The current focus of engineering is on the construction and R&D in large plants, such as CCGT or nuclear fusion. This will have to change, with networks requiring far more attention to them, in the form of R&D into advanced controls, or much more flexible switchgear and transformers. Financially, networks may not only require more investment but may also become much more risky businesses than they are now, requiring different financial management approaches.

Overall, a vision of a world in which individual consumers and communities have the power to exercise control over their electricity supply, and are able to retain significant amounts of value, instead of sending it down the wire, will resonate with many in society. Subsidiarity is not just a political concept but also an economic one. It may be about to arrive in the electricity industry.

9.11   References

Biermann, A. (2003). Distributed generation: institutional change in the UK 2000–2003, in S. Attali, E. Metreau, M. Prone and K. Tillerson (eds.), *Proceedings of Summer Study 2003*, Stockholm: European Council for an Energy-Efficient Economy, 653–63.

IEA (2003). *Renewables for Power Generation – 2003*, Paris: International Energy Agency/Organisation for Economic Co-Operation and Development.

Mott MacDonald (2004). *System Integration of Additional Microgeneration*, consulting study for the Distributed Generation Working Group, available at http://www.distributed-generation.gov.uk/documents/27_09_2004_dgcg00028.pdf.

Newbery, D., and R. Green (1996). Regulation, public ownership and privatisation of the English electricity industry, in R. Gilbert and E. Kahn (eds.), *International Comparisons of Electricity Regulations*, Cambridge: Cambridge University Press, 25–81.

Ofgem, (2003). *Electricity Distribution Losses: Initial Proposals*, report 44/03, London: Office of Gas and Electricity Markets, available at http://www.ofgem.gov.uk/temp/ofgem/cache/cmsat tach/3571_elecdistributionlosses 12june.pdf.

Part III

Electricity Conversion and Transmission

10 Superconductors in the electrical power industry

Archie M. Campbell

10.1 Historical introduction

Superconductivity was discovered in 1911 by the first person to liquefy helium, Kamerlingh Onnes. He measured the resistivity of mercury, as it could be made very pure, expecting the resistivity to continue linearly towards zero as the temperature was reduced. To his surprise (and initial disbelief) the resistivity suddenly dropped below his detection limit at 4K (the critical temperature for mercury). However, his hopes of making high-field magnets were not to be realised for another sixty years, as he soon found that the application of a relatively low magnetic field of about 20 millitesla (the critical field) destroyed the superconductivity. In contrast, iron magnets produce about 1 tesla.

A more sensitive test of the resistivity is to apply a magnetic field and measure how long it takes for the induced currents to decay. In a 1 centimetre copper sphere this happens in a few milliseconds, but in the superconductor no decay was observed over many months, and the material behaved as a perfect diamagnet – i.e. no magnetic field could enter it. This diamagnetism is sometimes erroneously called the 'Meissner effect'. The true Meissner effect, not discovered until 1933, occurs when a superconductor starts off at room temperature in a magnetic field and is then cooled to the superconducting state. As it goes through the transition, magnetic field is expelled from the superconductor by surface currents that start to flow spontaneously. The distinction is seen experimentally in the levitation of a magnet above the superconductor. Zero resistance means that a magnet lowered towards the superconductor will float above it. However, the Meissner effect means that a magnet originally sitting on the superconductor will rise into the air as the material goes superconducting, while a material with zero resistance will remain motionless. The Meissner effect shows that the superconductor is more than a material with zero resistance. The flowing currents are, in fact, the equilibrium state; that they start without any changing field to induce them shows that they must be truly resistanceless. This does not violate any laws of physics – electrons flow round atoms without resistance; what was extraordinary was that this was taking place not over a few nanometers but over many centimetres. The currents involved were also very large. A 1 millimetre wire of lead can carry 100 amps without resistance.

The cause of superconductivity remained a complete mystery until, in 1957, Bardeen, Cooper and Schrieffer produced their famous theory, the 'BCS Theory'. This showed how an interaction between the electrons and the lattice vibrations could produce a superconducting state. It was a remarkable achievement, which gained them a Nobel Prize, but in any real material, unfortunately, the equations are so complex that the theory has not been useful in predicting new superconductors, as is shown by the recent unexpected discovery of superconductivity in magnesium diboride at 39K.

In most branches of engineering the rate of progress is not determined by clever design but by the materials science, and superconductivity is no exception. Finding a material with a high critical temperature is only a starting point. The material must also carry high currents in high magnetic fields, and be made in the form of wires at a reasonable cost.

So far, MgB_2 aside, we have described the properties only of elements, or Type I superconductors, which are not of much practical interest. Alloys were called 'dirty superconductors', and little studied by physicists as the properties were very variable and the magnetisation hysteretic. This changed in the 1950s when it was discovered that niobium–zirconium and niobium–titanium could carry very high current densities in fields over 10 tesla, a hundred times higher than the highest critical field then known, which was 0.1 tesla for niobium. This coincided with the discovery of a previously neglected paper by Alexei Abrikosov, which had predicted the properties of these Type II superconductors. For this work he was somewhat belatedly awarded the Nobel Prize in 2003.

The niobium alloys (NbZr and NbTi) were ductile and easy to draw into wires, with the result that they came into use remarkably quickly for a new material. In 1964 IRD made a 3,000hp DC homopolar motor. More typical is the intermetallic compound Nb_3Sn, which has a much higher critical temperature at 18K and also a higher critical field and current density. Although it is about as ductile as Wedgwood china, materials scientists were nevertheless able to produce kilometre lengths of multifilamentary wire by a diffusion process. However, this is slow and expensive compared with drawing down a simple wire, so that, when assessed in dollars per kiloamp metre, NbTi remains the cheapest superconducting material by a large factor. This illustrates the importance of processing techniques in the economics of superconductors.

Until 1986 the highest critical temperature of a superconductor was 23K in NbGe, but the highest of a practical material was Nb_3Sn at 18K. In 1987 Georg Bednorz and Alexander Muller discovered superconductivity at 29K in La_2CuO_4, not on the face of it a large step above the 23K of Nb_3Ge, but it led very quickly to the discovery of superconductivity in yttrium barium copper oxide at 93K and bismuth strontium calcium cooper oxide at 110K. Thus the field of high T_C superconductivity was born. These are the only high-T_C materials that have been made into useful conductors, although mercury compounds have been made with a critical temperature of 164K at high pressure. This meant that, for the first time, superconductors could work in liquid nitrogen, which boils at 77K, and whole new areas of technology opened up.

10.2 General considerations

Superconductors provide a completely new technology, which has the potential to have a major effect on sustainable energy policies. However, the way this happens depends on how the subject – and, in particular, the materials – develop over the next twenty years. Superconductors have the following advantages over conventional materials, essentially copper and iron:

- zero resistance to direct currents and low losses in alternating currents;
- very high current densities, more than a thousand times that of copper;
- very high magnetic fields;
- stable passive levitation;
- reliability (cold things do not deteriorate); and
- The use of safe, inert insulating materials.

However, there are also disadvantages:

- they need cooling to temperatures of 77K or lower;
- the technology and materials are more expensive, although reductions in size may compensate for this;
- competition is with a well-established, reliable and cheap industry; and
- there are significant hysteresis losses every time a field or current is changed, and, although much less than those in copper, the fact that they occur at low temperatures makes the heat expensive to remove

Large systems are more efficient to cool, whether they are electrical machines or cryocoolers, because of the favourable surface-to-volume ratio, so the economics favours large-scale applications. The same applies to conventional electrical machines, which also get more efficient as they get larger, but the economics still favours superconductors at large powers. The American Superconductor Corporation estimates the break-even power at 100MW for generators and transformers, and 750kW for synchronous motors (Bryant, 1997). Up to the present the attraction of superconductors has not been the greater efficiency they provide, although the benefits are real. The real attraction is the high current density, which allows much smaller and lighter machines to be made. In spite of the more expensive technology the total cost can even be reduced. However, if energy becomes more expensive for any reason, this balance may change in favour of the energy efficiency arguments.

There are six main applications of superconductors relevant to energy consumption:

- motors and generators;
- energy storage;
- fault current limiters;
- power cables; and
- levitated trains.

Common to all these applications are the materials and cooling factors, which are considered next.

10.3   Materials

Great excitement was generated in 1987 by the discovery of superconductors with a critical temperature above the boiling point of liquid nitrogen at 77K, and the excitement was not misplaced as many new possibilities were opened up. There are three limiting material limits within which the superconductor is resistanceless. These are the critical temperature, the critical magnetic field and the critical current density. The two oxide superconductors of practical interest are BSCCO and YBCO. Liquid nitrogen at 77K cools both of them far enough below their critical temperature to be useful, and there has been little progress in raising the critical temperature for the last ten years. Critical fields are very high and critical currents in single crystals are also high.

However, the materials presented new problems that had not been anticipated. The most damaging was that grain boundaries act as barriers to the supercurrent, so that only single crystals would carry high current densities. Single crystals grow slowly from a seed and are limited in size to a few centimetres, and, although pellets with no grain boundaries can be used to trap magnetic flux and make very powerful permanent magnets, for most applications long lengths of wire are required.

This is because it is usually necessary to change the field and current in a conductor. Fixed fields from a single crystal are attractive for the rotors of electrical machines and for magnetic separation but there is a further problem in remagnetising them if the system warms up. Nevertheless, this is a very active area of research.

The second problem is that oxide superconductors can develop resistance in a combination of high temperatures and rather low magnetic fields, which limits the applications of the bismuth-based materials.

In spite of these problems, it has proved possible to make practical wires by aligning crystals so that only very low-angle grain boundaries are present. BSCCO can be aligned by being drawn down a silver tube packed with powder, and this is the basis of the high-T_C wires sold today. Critical currents are reasonable at liquid nitrogen temperatures but are low in a magnetic field at this temperature, so the material must be used at around 30K in applications such as motors and generators. YBCO has excellent properties in liquid nitrogen and is much less sensitive to magnetic fields, but wires of grain-aligned material are only now being developed, and the process is expensive. Methods developed from thin-film deposition techniques have produced wires several metres in length and these processes are being scaled up to an industrial level by a number of companies. At the same time, many laboratories are exploring a number of promising processes that should produce similar material much more quickly and cheaply. The economics of superconducting devices is heavily dependent on success in bringing down the price of these conductors (usually called 'coated conductors'), and, while the price will certainly come down, it is very difficult to make predictions as to by how much and when this will happen.

Surveys of the economics of superconducting devices must be based on the extrapolation of existing trends, such as those in figure 10.1 which compares the prices of a number of materials. All data are for 4.2K. The unit is the cost per kiloamp metre and it can be seen that in this respect low-T_C wires are orders of magnitude cheaper than high T_C superconductors. It is generally accepted that the costs of high-T_C wires need to come down by a factor of ten before they can compete with conventional materials in the power industry.

A recent development has been the discovery that magnesium diboride is superconducting up to 39K. This material is easy to make into wires and presents few materials problems, but it must be used around 27K and the critical fields and currents are much lower than those of YBCO at this temperature. It is, however, a serious competitor with high-T_C wires for a number of applications.

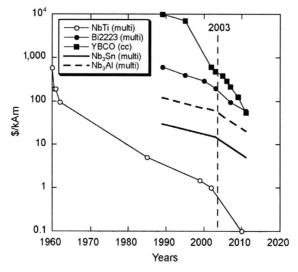

Figure 10.1. The costs of superconducting wires at 4.2K.
Source: Glowacki (2005).

10.4 Cooling

All economic assessments of the impact of superconductors must take into account the costs of cooling. There is a minimum power need set by the second law of thermodynamics. For every watt dissipated at low temperature the power needed to bring it up to room temperature is, approximately, inversely proportional to the temperature. So a 1 watt heat leak at 77K needs about 3 watts cooling power and at 4.2K needs 70 watts. However, coolers are not very efficient, and the real power requirements can be more than a factor of ten greater. This heat leak comes from a combination of heat conducted from the outside and hysteresis losses in the superconductor. It is not a problem for large DC magnets such as those used in body scanners or magnetic separators. These can be made with very low heat leaks, and only need occasional topping up with liquid helium. However, in the power industry there are inevitably thick current leads and drive shafts, which conduct heat into the cryogen. If in addition there are 50Hz currents, there will be large losses in the superconductor itself. These AC losses are unacceptable in liquid helium, a problem at 27K (the boiling point of liquid neon) but tolerable in liquid nitrogen for some applications.

Systems using helium or nitrogen can be cooled by bringing in liquid gas in tankers, which makes use of the greater efficiency of large-scale liquefiers. For operations at 27K either helium gas or liquid neon is used. Neon is very expensive so in both cases a closed-cycle refrigerator is needed. At present, coolers represent a fairly small market with specialist applications, so they are expensive. However, if a large market emerges it has been estimated that costs could be reduced by a factor of ten.

It can be seen that it is not possible to forecast the economic impact of superconductors on energy with any accuracy because of the large number of factors involved. Prototype systems have been designed to show that the technology works, not to minimise costs or maximise efficiency.

10.5   Environment and safety

In general, cryogenic systems are very safe. Once something is working at low temperatures it usually stays working, in contrast to resistive magnets, where heating can lead to the breakdown of insulation and fires. It is easier to keep a large superconducting magnet at 4.2K than a copper one at room temperature. Cryogenic fluids such as nitrogen, neon and helium are inert, although, as with any gas, it is important to make sure that not enough is allowed to escape to reduce the oxygen concentration to a dangerous level. Liquid hydrogen is more dangerous and not used much, but it is not much more dangerous than petrol or other hydrocarbons, and could certainly be used with appropriate precautions.

Superconducting magnets can 'quench' without much warning. A quench occurs if some disturbance, such as a wire rubbing against another, causes a local hot spot to become resistive. The current flowing through the resistive region increases the size of the hot spot until the whole magnet goes normal. Usually this occurs only the first few times a magnet is energised (a process known as 'training'), during which the maximum field attainable tends to increase slightly.

The sudden dumping of several kilojoules of magnetic energy into liquid helium can produce an alarming rate of boil-off and damage the magnet, but all commercial magnets are designed to cope with a quench. At liquid nitrogen temperatures specific heats are far larger than at 4.2K and thermal instability does not seem to be a problem in high-T_C superconductors.

Some of the metals in superconducting wires, such as barium and bismuth, are toxic if ingested, but provided suitable precautions are taken during manufacture they do not pose a significant risk once incorporated into wires.

10.6   Applications

10.6.1   *Motors and generators*

This is a very large market, with major implications for energy conservation. A recent article (Hartkainen et al., 2003) has analysed this in great detail, showing how much greenhouse gas emissions can be reduced on various assumptions of how superconducting generators and motors penetrate the market. All AC superconducting motors made so far use a normal stator because of the AC losses that would occur in a superconducting stator. A superconducting rotor can raise the efficiency of a large alternator from 98 per cent to 99 per cent. This gain sounds better if it is pointed out that in the process it is halving the dissipation, with a corresponding reduction in emissions. In view of the large amount of power generated and used by synchronous machines worldwide this could be an important contribution, but it will be necessary to convince the utilities that it is profitable. This is most likely to occur after the initial use of superconducting machines in ships and trains, where the reduction in size and weight makes superconductors attractive and their reliability can be established.

Another application is in renewable energy systems such as wind turbines and tidal generators, where the frequency is low and as a result the AC losses in the stator may be acceptable, and a wholly superconducting machine can become practical.

10.6.2   *Energy storage*

Energy storage techniques are crucial to a sustainable energy system as most renewable sources are unreliable and fluctuating. Superconducting magnetic energy storage is already in commercial use, although the systems are relatively small; they are used for uninterruptible power supplies and power conditioning. They consist of a niobium titanium solenoid at 4.2K in which the energy is stored as magnetic energy. The energy density is $B^2/2\mu_o$ or 40 MJ/m^3 at 10 tesla. These systems are very efficient and reliable. A number of projects are under way to investigate SMES using high-T_C superconductors, and these will become more practical as the coated YBCO conductors are developed. However, to be useful in the energy industry large magnets are needed, and even building a prototype is very expensive.

Storing energy in rotating flywheels is also a commercial technology. URENCO market a system based on carbon fibre rotors developed originally for the separation of uranium isotopes. Again, present applications are for short-term storage, but the extra efficiency afforded by the use of superconducting bearings could allow this to be used for diurnal energy storage. The Interdisciplinary Research Centre in Superconductivity in Cambridge is developing such a bearing in collaboration with URENCO, and Boeing are also developing an energy storage flywheel with superconducting bearings. Superconducting bearings are non-contact (so do not wear out), need no maintenance apart from cooling and can operate at unlimited speeds. The only disadvantage for most purposes is that they are much softer than conventional bearings, but this is not a problem in static flywheel applications.

More details about energy storage devices can be found in Wolsky (2002).

10.6.3   Fault current limiters

These relatively little-known devices are, in fact, probably the nearest thing to a commercial application in the electrical industry. This is because, in contrast to nearly all other applications of superconductors, a superconducting fault current limiter cannot be replicated by a conventional device. A limiter is designed to limit the current when a fault occurs – a function now carried out by fuses and circuit-breakers. A superconducting limiter presents almost no resistance below the critical-current, but when this is exceeded in a fault the material becomes resistive and limits the current to a safe value. The advantage of the superconductor is that the limit occurs in the first cycle, whereas circuit-breakers take several cycles to operate so the system must be robust enough to take the fault current for this time. It is also 'fail-safe', which is important for a safety measure and something that semiconducting systems cannot provide. Superconducting fault current limiters will allow embedded generation from renewable sources to be added to the existing grid without having to upgrade all the protection components.

The main technical problem with fault current limiters is that any inhomogeneity leads to hot spots and thermal instabilities, resulting in the element burning out. However, this problem is soluble with the addition of conductive layers to smooth out any temperature variations, and several working elements have been made. A commercial product will be available within a few years.

10.6.4   Transformers

Large conventional transformers are even more efficient than generators and are expected to work for many years unattended, so there is less motivation to make them superconducting, although this does have the advantage of getting rid of toxic insulating oils. Again, the first applications will be in transport, where the need to minimise the size means that conventional transformers are much less efficient than those in power networks.

10.6.5   *Power lines*

This is often the first thing people think of as an application for superconductors, as the 6 per cent loss in the transmission grid represents a huge amount of energy. However, when the numbers are put in it looks less attractive. If we consider the lifetime cost of overhead lines and a superconducting cable, the overhead line is far cheaper. A more valid comparison is with underground cables, but even here the superconducting cable is significantly more expensive. The main application is in heavily congested cities, where there is no space to bring in extra underground power lines. In the United States and Japan there are existing cables in steel conduits that can be replaced by a superconductor in the same tube, greatly increasing the power density. Several short lengths of cable have been demonstrated to work well, although there are considerable logistical problems in inserting a cryogenic cable in a long length of tubing that may well bend round corners.

Figure 10.2 is an illustration of the factors taken into account in an economic assessment by Tsukamoto (2004), assuming a cable cost of ¥10 per amp metre. It can be seen that a large number of factors are involved, many of which will inevitably vary from country to country. However, the most important factor is the capital cost of the conductor, which is projected to reach the required level by 2015. Also, the cooling cost of monocore HTS cable (the cost for the electricity to counter the AC losses and the heat leak from the environment) is higher than the cost of the transmission losses of the CV cable system.

Applications to DC cables are more attractive, but these are rare and are always very large-scale projects, such as possible links between the United Kingdom and France, and the links from the Canadian hydro-electric plants to the United States.

10.6.6   *Trains*

Perhaps the most spectacular application of superconductors is the levitated train used on Japanese railways. This contains a large superconducting magnet that generates eddy currents in coils beside the track, which lift the train several centimetres above the ground. The propulsion is from a linear motor so that there is no contact with the train, and there

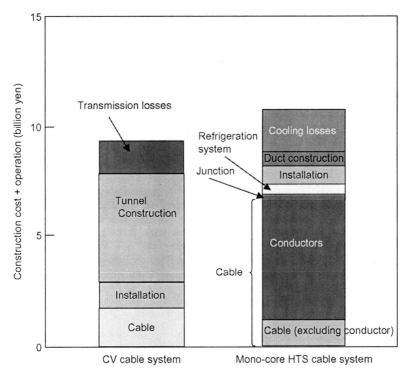

Figure 10.2. Costs of conventional and high-temperature supercon-ducting cables.
Source: Tsukamoto (2004).

are no moving parts and only wind noise. The train recently set a world speed record of 560 kmh, and at these speeds most of the energy goes into overcoming air resistance. The main drawback is the cost of the track. This is complicated in structure and has to be straight and level, thus requiring major civil engineering works. Schemes in which the air resistance is eliminated by enclosing the line in an evacuated tube, allowing speeds of 3,000 km/h, have not yet progressed beyond the stage of rough sketches.

10.7   Conclusions

Superconductors can contribute to a wide range of methods for reducing our dependence on fossil fuels. The nearest device to market is the superconducting fault current limiter, which can be used to help the introduction of embedded generation. The losses in motors and generators could be halved by the use of superconductors, and energy storage using magnets or flywheels could extend the use of renewables. The problems are not so much technical as economic. Copper, iron and fossil fuels are so cheap that it is very difficult for a new technology to compete in the current market environment.

10.8   References

Bryant, E. (1997). *Climate Process and Change*, Cambridge: Cambridge University Press.

Glowacki, B. A. (2005). Superconductivity and superconductors, *in Kirk-Othmer Online Encyclopaedia of Chemical Technology*, New York: John Wiley.

Hartkainen, T., J. Lehtonen and R. Mikonen (2003). Role of HTS devices in greenhouse gas emission reduction, *Superconductor Science and Technology*, 16: 963–9.

Tsukamoto, O. (2004). Ways for power applications of high-temperature superconductors to go into the real world, *Superconductor Science and Technology*, 17(5): S185–S190.

Wolsky, A. M. (2002). The status and prospects for flywheels and SMES that incorporate HTS, *Physica* C, 372: 1495–9.

11 The role of power electronics in future power systems

Tim C. Green and Carlos A. Hernández Arámburo

11.1 Introduction

Power electronics is a technology that has brought enormous benefits in terms of the flexibility and controllability with which electrical power is used by consumers. The basis of the technology is the use of semiconductor devices that can switch large currents from large voltages. A key feature is that high-frequency switching can be used to provide fast regulation of the waveforms applied to the loads.

Some of the important features of power electronics are as follows.

- Many renewable energy technologies are not 50/60Hz voltage sources and need frequency and voltage transformation in order to connect to the network. Power electronics is the most versatile transformation option.
- Generators connected to local distribution systems disturb the voltage profile in the system, and generation must be limited to avoid voltage tolerances being breached. Greater control of the real and reactive power flows, not traditionally used in local distribution networks but available through power electronics, can alleviate the problem.
- New power flows arise from new generation sites, from new long-distance trades or new patterns of demand. In some cases new transmission infrastructure might be needed, and in some of those cases a traditional AC link might not offer the properties needed.
- In some other cases, new power flows might be accommodated within the power rating of the existing infrastructure but cause stability or voltage tolerance issues, which can be solved with power electronic controllers.
- Intermittent sources of generation and ill-conditioned loads can degrade the quality of supply to consumers. Power electronic controllers can correct many of these problems.

Figure 11.1 shows the equipment cabins of a reactive power compensator known as a Statcom (static compensator). Inside, as shown in

Figure 11.1. A 75MVAr gate-turn-off-based Statcom, shown in combination with a 150MVAr switched VAr compensator, located at National Grid Company's 400kV East Claydon sub-station; the equipment cabins housing the power electronic elements are relocatable.
Photograph: courtesy Areva T&D.

figure 11.2, are the power-semiconductor devices that form the power-processing elements and the heatsinks that are needed to remove the power lost in the devices during operation. The passive components (inductors and capacitors) that also form part of the power converter, together with the switchgear and coupling transformers, are visible outside the cabins of figure 11.1. The example here is of a relocatable system, with the equipment cabinets designed as container-sized portable units that could be moved from one sub-station to another if a change in system use meant that the Statcom could be better deployed at another site.

Power electronics is not a new technology, and in some areas is considered a mature technology. Power electronics is used across almost the entire power range of possible loads, from chargers for mobile phones (a few watts) to railway locomotives (in the region of 10 MW). But, whatever its successes elsewhere, power electronics has yet to realise its full potential within the electricity supply industry. Before

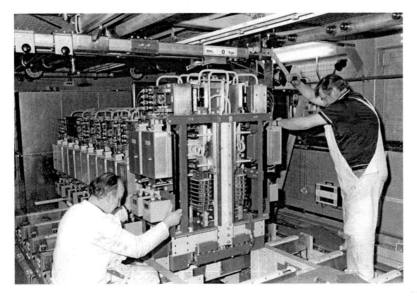

Figure 11.2. The GTOs and their heat sinks being installed.

going on to discuss that potential, it is worth a short discussion of the evolution of power electronics in a different field.

At first, power electronics was an expensive technology that was used only where the performance benefit was clear. In many application areas it now offers clear cost advantages too. In industrial drives, the DC motor was the traditional choice for variable-speed applications. The motor has attractive control features: it has a simple dynamic response and can be used with simple rectifier circuits. The drawbacks are the cost of the machine itself, the limited maximum speed and the frequent maintenance and arcing resulting from its use of a commutator and brushes. The induction machine, on the other hand, offers superior mechanical robustness, including higher maximum speeds and little need for maintenance. Its drawback is the need for a complex control algorithm (running on a sophisticated microprocessor) and a power electronic converter to produce variable-frequency waveform. The power electronic converter and control hardware initially led to a higher system cost even though the machine itself was cheaper. It took two decades for the technology to become accepted both in terms of proven operational benefits and in terms of the cost becoming competitive. Costs were improved through higher production volumes and general reductions in the costs of electronic components.

The situation today is that the brush-and-commutator DC machine has been eclipsed.

The flexible AC transmission system (FACTS) is a vision of a traditional AC transmission system supplemented by several control devices that enhance the operation of the system (Hingorani and Gyugyi, 2000). Enhancements might include increases in transfer capability through crucial transmission corridors, the improvement of transient and dynamic stability and the ability to adapt better to contingencies. The references cited here (Glavitsch and Rahmani, 1998; Edris, 2000; Hosseini and Ajami, 2002; Reed et al., 2003) are but a small sample of the literature available on this topic. FACTS is an alternative to the traditional approach of reinforcing the system with additional transmission lines and infrastructure, and a particularly useful alternative when transmission rights of way are increasingly difficult to obtain. In almost all cases, the proposed extra control is introduced through power electronic circuits.

Power systems are the last unconquered area for the electronic processing of power, and the factors holding back the technology are similar to those in the early stages of electrical drives: much of the technology has seen only trial use at the power levels concerned; uncertainty exists over how the technology will perform; the costs are considered high; and, although there are potential benefits in the control offered, these are not always realisable because of established operating practices. For many decades the utility system has been run satisfactorily using electromagnetic devices for power conversion and control. The present deployment of power electronics needs to work in sympathy with these traditional systems and function in broadly similar, but superior, ways. The future could be different. It might be desirable to reorder the system to exploit fully the features of power electronics, but much would need to change. The ability to control power flows in all the lines of a network, rather as telecoms traffic is routed, and to achieve fast dynamic control could make better use of the network infrastructure, could provide defined paths for trading power and could help cope with rapid changes in the available generation due to intermittency in some sources. However, this is not just about power electronics regulating power flows; it also requires a monitoring and communications infrastructure to support the operational decisions and the control actions affecting many thousands of pieces of plant, and it needs a control philosophy that is decentralised and distributed, that can take many control actions in harmony and is robust and flexible enough to cope with many different operating scenarios. For this to happen, a clear value chain must be established so that those operating networks and in a position to invest in new network technology will benefit financially from the improved system performance that others observe. It may well be that it becomes easier to integrate new and intermittent forms of generation within a more responsive network, but, for the network to be built, appropriate incentives will need to be put in place by the regulatory authorities.

There are some very important differences in the characteristics of power electronic power conversion when compared to traditional electro-magnetic or electrodynamic means. Semiconductor switches operate on a timescale of a few microseconds whereas electromechanical switches and relays operate on timescales of hundreds of milliseconds. Transformers, synchronous generators and transmission lines are voltage- and current-limited. The voltage limit is, by and large, a firm limit. The current limit is essentially a limit on the maximum temperature, and the temperature rise is determined by the losses caused by the current flow. Because of the large mass of these pieces of equipment, it can take up to thirty minutes for the maximum temperature to be reached. For short periods, currents 20 per cent to 50 per cent higher than the continuous limit can be allowed to flow. In principle, the same argument applies to semiconductor devices used in power electronics. However, the mass of the semiconductor is small and there is no usable short-time rating. In addition, silicon semi-conductor devices cannot be manufactured at any scale because defect rates in large devices make this uneconomic. The maximum rating of an individual device may be considerably less than that required, and so multiple devices are necessary. As a result, power electronics offers fast-acting (high-bandwidth) control but with limited power rating and no short-time rating.

An example of where these differences become important is in protec-tion systems. When a short-circuit fault occurs in a power system a large and potentially damaging current flows, but because the current is large it is readily detected and located. Circuit-breakers can be operated to isolate the faulty section of the network. The fault currents can be withstood for the fraction of a second needed to operate the breakers. Power electronics does not fit easily here. The large fault currents can not be allowed to flow through a converter and so the converter will protect itself by internally limiting its current through fast-acting control (although the development of silicon carbide devices will increase the ability of converters to withstand very high currents and the high device temperatures they create). If the amount of power processed by convert-ers is a small fraction of the system, this might be an advantage in that the fault current that the breaker has to clear is reduced. However, if converters dominate the generation then little fault current will flow and the protection system may not recognise the condition as a fault, and

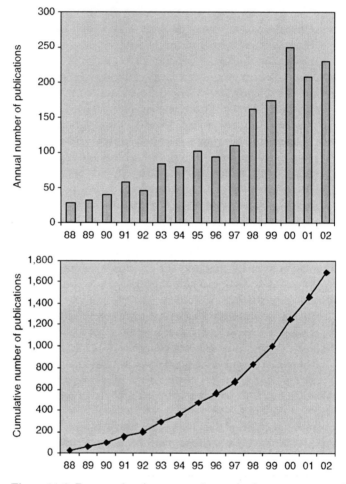

Figure 11.3. Papers related to power electronics in power systems (as at April 2004).

the faulted section of network will remain connected and degrade the supply. This suggests that aspects of power system practice will need to be rethought if power electronics becomes widespread.

As has been observed with other applications of power electronics, and other technologies, there is an explosion of academic interest in the early stages. Figure 11.3 indicates the cumulative number of papers between 1988 and 2002 in the IEEExplore database that cover this topic. This example includes papers with the indexing terms that appear later in this chapter, such as flexible AC transmission systems, FACTS, UPFC, Statcon, Statcom, static var compensator or static var compensators. There has been a huge growth in the literature, but this needs to be set against the fact that most FACTS controllers exist only in trial installations. It is also worth noting that the control schemes used in present installations are often modest in their objectives in comparison to the schemes discussed in the literature. The ability to provide damping in dynamic and transient disturbance is often not exploited and the power electronics is used only to regulate steady-state conditions. System operators do not yet have the experience, confidence or control infrastructure to exploit the transient capabilities.

The existence of a large body of literature does not guarantee that commercial exploitation will follow. The factors that will inhibit industrial deployment have been noted and they might, in fact, never be overcome. Still, it seems that power electronics has a lot to offer in facilitating new forms of generation and can offer features not available with traditional network-reinforcing measures. However, power electronics will be expensive and unfulfilling if insufficient consideration is given to its proper role.

11.2   Ratings

It was noted in the introduction that the scale, or rating, of semiconductor devices is an important factor in future prospects for power electronics. Some general trends in the deployment of power electronics are illustrated in figure 11.4. In the low-power generation systems of distributed generation (including several of the renewable forms of generation), power electronics has two advantages: it is well established at this power rating in other applications, and it has a crucial role in matching non-synchronous sources to the network. In most applications power electronics will process all the power involved. At the higher power ratings used in new wind and tidal flow generators, power electronics plays a supporting role to the doubly fed induction generator. For conventional plant, and for medium-scale combined heat and power using natural gas or biomass, it is possible to arrange for synchronous generation and obviate the need for power electronics. Variable-speed generation might bring a small efficiency improvement but is technologically very difficult and very expensive. What we see instead is power electronics playing a supporting role, but within the transmission network rather than in close association with the generation.

Figure 11.4 also shows the change in the choice of power electronic devices used across the power range. The various device technologies

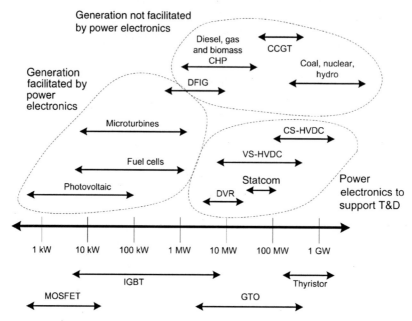

Figure 11.4. Application areas and device technologies arranged by approximate power rating.

are introduced in Mohan et al. (1995). In the lower power range, IGBT (and to some extent MOSFET) devices can be used with high switching frequencies to provide interfaces with good dynamic control and low harmonic distortion. GTO thyristors do not allow such high switching frequencies. This does have some impact on dynamic response but, more importantly, requires attention to harmonic distortion. The highest power ratings, such as HVDC links in the gigawatt range, use thyristors (without gate turn-off provision), and considerable extra design effort is required to meet distortion targets. In general, semiconductor devices have relatively low voltage and current ratings compared to typical values in distribution and transmission networks. Power ratings above 10MW cannot be met with single-element semiconductor switches. Systems have to be built from the parallel/series connection of many devices rated at a fraction of the circuit's total rating. A first approach is to use series strings of several devices (usually known as valves), which act as if they were one device of a higher voltage rating. A second approach is to use several devices as elements in a multi-level and multi-pulse circuits (Soto and Green, 2002). The multi-pulse and multi-level circuits achieve power ratings proportional to the number of devices and yield advantages over the valve approach in terms of their effective switching frequency and harmonic distortion. Some of the multi-pulse/multi-level circuits allow a modular approach to circuit construction, and this approach could be taken further, to the benefit of reliability (through the provision of redundancy) and cost advantage through production volume. The multi-level and multi-pulse methods will remain important even if individual device ratings improve, since the improvement necessary to enable single-device use is enormous.

Engineers design around certainty and design conservatively. The rating of a system is often set on the basis of the power available under worst-case conditions. For most of its life the circuit or system will run considerably away from the worst case. A different approach is sometimes taken with overhead transmission lines, where the maximum current can be set according to the actual ambient temperature rather than an assumed worst case. This approach has so far been little used in power electronics, but in this application perhaps it should. A converter's current rating could be set according to its actual heat sink temperature rather than the assumed worst case. It is also common in other application areas of power electronics to design the protection system to protect the valuable and vulnerable semiconductors by tripping (shutting down) when a fault occurs and then waiting for intervention before operation is resumed. This runs counter to power network needs. There remains a lot of thinking to be done on how to implement fault ride-through for power electronics. Soft-tripping is needed, in which some limited functionality or power is still achieved during a fault condition and automatic recovery is possible. Fault-tolerant power electronics is being developed for other application areas, notably the aerospace industry.

The history of power electronics has seen the invention of several different semiconductor devices. The trend now is towards the development of higher ratings for existing device types. However, there is the prospect of a major change. Silicon-carbide offers some significant advantages over silicon as a semiconductor material. It has a higher energy gap, leading to higher voltage rating devices. It can be run at higher temperatures without loss of its important properties, and this enables it to be run to higher current densities with less cooling provision (Johnson, 2003). After many years of research progress, devices are currently appearing that are practicable for circuit use. There is now the prospect of a step forward in device ratings.

11.3   Power electronics on the supply side

Power electronics has already made inroads into the electricity supply industry. The six areas described in the following sections chart the progress from established successes to more speculative future applications. Many new technologies have been proposed, both in terms of power electronic hardware and control systems to exploit that hardware.

11.3.1   High-voltage direct current interconnection

There has long been a need to provide power exchange between systems that cannot be synchronised. These point-to-point connections, often between distinct geographical areas, have been realised with HVDC transmission. HVDC requires AC to DC and DC to AC conversion either side of a DC link but allows the two AC systems to run at different frequencies. The frequency difference may be small (but still difficult to synchronise) or it may well be in the order of tens of hertz (a tie between a 50Hz and a 60Hz system, such as found in Japan). Whatever the differences between the AC systems, the technological advantages of power electronics in HVDC could not be matched, and, once proven, several commercial implementations have followed. A number of land and undersea connections already exist around the world but a well-known example is the tie between the United Kingdom and France, inaugurated in 1961 and expanded in stages to 2,000MW at ±270kV.[1] A more recent example is Japan's Kii-channel (500kV/2,800MW) (Hasegawa, 2002), phase I of which entered operation in 2000.

11.3.2   Reactive power compensation

The transmission system requires injection of reactive power to regulate voltage and facilitate real power transfers. It has long been recognised that power electronic switches can be used to add and control reactive components. These are the first-generation controllers known as static VAr compensators, and they are well established (Gyugyi, 1988; Hingorani and Gyugyi, 2000; Mori, 2001). They are considerably faster-acting and more flexible than mechanical devices. A second generation of controller has been developed, with a wider operating range, lower harmonic distortion and better control properties. These systems,

---

[1] See the national grid's website – http://www.nationalgrid.com/activity/other/mn_interconnectors_france.html – and the website of the Energy Systems Research Unit of the University of Strathclyde: http://www.esru.strath.ac.uk/EandE/web_sites/98-9/offshore.elec.htm.

known as static synchronous compensators (Statcoms), use DC-to-AC power converters to inject reactive current into a line or node. Small numbers have been installed and some representative examples are described in Horwill et al. (2001) Hanson et al. (2002) and Reed et al. (2002). These controllers have the potential to provide a rapid response to system disturbance and therefore maintain stable operation when otherwise the system might face problems They can also combat fast voltage variation, known as flicker, which can be a problem with some forms of renewable generation and loads such as railway traction systems and arc furnaces (Elnady et al., 2002; Tan et al., 2003).

11.3.3   Static power generators

Some generators do not employ a rotary generator and directly produce a DC voltage, such as photovoltaics and fuel cells. These sources have thus far been small, but there are already some fuel cell systems in the megawatt range being operated as utility-size demonstration units. Japan has an aggressive policy towards developing fuelcells for utility power production (Dayton et al., 2001). Photovoltaic arrays have not seen widespread use in grid-connected systems but the power electronic hardware required is well established and use in off-grid applications is growing (see chapter 4). In general, the power converters (which convert DC to AC) are well within the technology range already used elsewhere. The operating regime and the cost still need attention (Wenger et al., 1994).

11.3.4   Distributed generation using rotating power generators

Traditional large-scale generators have been built to generate at 50 or 60Hz. Many small-scale, distributed energy sources can be run more efficiently or effectively if they are free to run at a variable or higher speed/frequency. Microturbines can use direct-drive high-frequency generators which have good power densities. Some permanent-magnet-based generators may reach speeds in the tens of thousands rpm and, consequently, their output frequency is usually in the kHz range (Pullen et al., 1996). At the other end of the range, wind and marine turbines may run at a few rpm and the output frequency may be well below the utility frequency. In addition to their rated-frequency incompatibility with the grid, these generators can run at variable frequency to optimise the capture of energy from the flow. For generators up to a few hundreds of kilowatts it is feasible to use IGBT-based AC-DC-AC frequency conversion based on the technology used in industrial drives. The challenge for renewable sources such as wind and tidal flow turbines is to arrange variable-speed operation in the megawatt range. Here the current practice is to strike a compromise. Operation across a limited but adequate speed range is achieved by using power electronics rated at a fraction (20 per cent to 30 per cent) of the total power and connected to a doubly fed induction generator (Muller et al., 2002; Ekanayake et al., 2003). Although the generator is more costly, and performance is partially restricted, the significant saving in cost of power electronics is compelling.

11.3.5   Voltage-source high-voltage direct current

Traditional HVDC was built around current source technology and line-commutated thyristors. More capable (commutable) power semiconductors such as IGBTs have enabled voltage-source variants to be built. Although more limited in power rating, these technologies offer a wider range of capabilities (Ooi and Wang, 1991). They can be used to interface unsynchronised wind farms (Lu and Ooi, 2003), to provide controlled parallel links to existing AC links, to provide an alternative to AC distribution systems (Jiang and Ekstrom, 1998) and to enhance the grid performance (Venkatasubramanian and Taylor, 2000; Lu and Ooi, 2001; Huang et al., 2003). The major manufacturers all offer variations of this technology. Relatively small numbers of installations have been achieved so far. However, this is a technology that offers useful features for overcoming the problems associated with introducing intermittent renewable energy into relatively weak sections of a transmission and distribution system.

11.3.6   Flexible alternating current tansmission systems

The FACTS vision includes a range of power processing circuits to provide a greater degree of control over the operation of the transmission system. These include series compensators (to complement the shunt-connected Statcom) and power flow controllers. FACTS was conceived as a transmission system technology but the growth of distributed generation and the need to introduce control into distribution networks have seen the development of lower power distribution versions of the FACTS controllers.

11.3.7   Further development

Thus far, power electronics is seen as enhancing the operation of AC transmission and distribution systems and matching new forms of generation to these systems. Because power electronics is quite different in nature from other power technologies, this may not make the best use of the technology. At some point it might be beneficial to think again and plan the system around distributed generation and electronic power conversion, and fit the traditional forms of generation and transmission around this. To some extent, this thinking is beginning with microgrids (Marnay et al., 2001; Lasseter, 2002; Meliopoulos, 2002). Microgrids are small sections of a grid that have sufficient generation (or approximately so) to meet local needs. One of the key differences between a 'micro-grid' and the traditional view of a 'small' power system (be it an 'island' or an 'area of control') is that the microgrids envisaged may be dominated by inverter-based generators, and so operation and protection must be suited to power electronic technologies. Example microgrids exist in real physical islands and in remote systems. However, the development of microgrids as a part of, or as an adjunct to, urban distribution networks will require much work in establishing technical standards and regulatory frameworks. The London borough of Woking sought to introduce distributed generation for environmental policy reasons but has had to resort to forming a private wires network of its own (Woking Borough Council Civic Offices, 2001). The regulatory restrictions faced in Woking would, if encountered more generally, be a major impediment to the development of microgrids.

Power electronics will also be necessary to support the increased use of cables rather than overhead lines. In part, this follows from the development of offshore wind and marine energy sources where seabed cables will be used. It also arises from public pressure to avoid, or even remove, unsightly overhead lines. It is clear that new bulk transfers, such as between wind generation in north-west Scotland and load centres in England, will require new transmission infrastructure and that permission for overhead lines will be very difficult to secure. It is well known to electrical engineers, if not to the public, that cables are not a straightforward alternative to overhead lines. A cable has a large capacitance between its conductors and has a large reactive power flow even when unloaded. The management of reactive power in a cable-dominated subsystem will require Statcoms. The expense and technical difficulty of this solution favours instead voltage-source HVDC. An emerging technology here is multi-point (rather than simple point-to-point) HVDC. This is still some way short of a meshed HVDC system, but perhaps that too will develop.

11.4   Power electronics for the demand side

Power electronics is well established as a technology for conditioning electrical power prior to final use. Conditioning takes two forms: the creation of a well-regulated supply for electronic circuits, and the control of power supplied to mechanical, lighting or heating loads. The questions that arise for the future concern whether the interface between supply system and end-user system has been arranged for the best overall result. The point of interface is defined in various ways. For domestic and commercial consumers we expect, in the UK example, an AC voltage supply of 230V at 50Hz and sinusoidal wave shape. Beyond this are definitions of the allowable deviations in terms of expected interruption rates, voltage tolerance, frequency tolerance and harmonic distortion. On one side of the interface the supplier seeks to meet this standard, and on the other side the equipment manufacturers ensure that proper operation can continue for the expected range of variation in supply. So, the questions for the future are: is the interface definition well chosen for the anticipated use, and what can power electronics offer to ease the burden at either side of the interface? They will be discussed under three headings: power quality, a review of the compatibility level and managed loads.

11.4.1 Power quality and supply quality

There is room for much debate over what constitutes quality in electricity supply and how much importance is and should be attached to it. The definition used here is that the term 'power quality' refers to how accurately the power delivered conforms to definitions of its acceptable voltage, frequency, etc. The term 'quality of supply' includes consideration of interruptions to the supply of power, and is essentially an issue of reliability. Some consumers require and would value higher reliability and better waveform quality; some would be unconcerned. The prime issue is normally quality of supply. Autumn 2003 saw widespread power cuts in the eastern United States and Canada, Italy, Scandinavia and London (Bialek, 2004). They were dramatic and costly events – but they are far from being the only problem. It is also important that consumers receive a voltage that is within the acceptable limit for their equipment and is free from waveform distortion that may cause maloperation (Bollen, 2000; Schlabbach et al., 2001).

11.4.1.1 *Power quality issues arising from loads* Waveform distortion can cause problems, and there are various national and international standards on the harmonic distortion allowable in the provision of supply voltage and in the current drawn by consumers. Non-linear loads that draw non-sinusoidal current are the main cause of this problem and the main culprits are low-technology power electronic loads (David et al.,

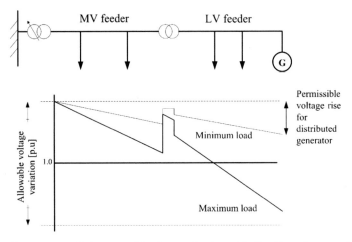

Figure 11.5. Voltage profile along a feeder with distributed generation. Source: Jenkins et al. (2000).

1997). For many years there was acceptance of diode- and thyristor-based AC-to-DC converters used in loads, and the harmonic problem grew. Now there are regulations concerning product design (e.g. IEC 1000) and better designs are mandatory. Still, however, most low-voltage consumers receive a significantly distorted voltage waveform.

11.4.1.2 Power quality issues arising from distributed generation The traditional power system has achieved good power quality through the following means.

- The transmission network is highly interconnected and operated with reserve generation capacity. Both measures allow for continuity of supply after a single or even a double equipment failure (the n-1 and n-2 contingency provisions).
- The distribution system is conservatively planned and has the ability to switch in alternative supplies and to control transformer settings to adjust voltage levels. Critical loads are continuously supplied through at least two routes. Far away from sub-station transformers, the provision of accurate voltage and low distortion relies on decisions made during system planning and the fact that the supply path is low-impedance.

During planning it was generally assumed that the power flows from sub-station to loads along the feeders and that the voltage profile drops steadily along the feeder. Figure 11.5 illustrates a typical voltage profile and shows how the introduction of a distributed generator disturbs that profile (Kojovic, 2002). This is particularly problematic with an intermittent generator, which can cause large variations (and reversals) of power flow, and hence large voltage variation. This may cause the network operator to impose restrictions on the installation or operation of distributed generators connected to remote parts of the distribution network.

11.4.1.3   Current and feasible solutions   A number of technologies have emerged to combat some or all of the power quality problems at the point of load. Those listed are all based on power electronic systems.

- Uninterruptible power supply (UPS). All designs provide a back–up power source to take over in the event of an outage (Richard et al., 2001; Roberts, 2001). Some designs can also correct over- and under-voltage problems and waveform distortion.
- Dynamic voltage restorer (DVR). A device that can inject voltage (with either reactive-only or reactive and real power) to correct sag and swell (Campbell and McHattie, 1999; Vilathgamuwa et al., 2003; Nielsen et al., 2004).
- Active power filter (APF). A device that injects series voltage or shunt current to correct harmonic distortion. Some designs can also correct unbalance between phases and compensate for reactive power flow (Grady et al., 1990; Peng, 1998; Singh et al., 1999).
- Unified Power Quality Controller (UPQC). A combination of shunt and series devices that can perform APF and DVR functions (Fujita and Akagi, 1998; Elnady and Salama, 2001; Jianjun et al., 2002).

In terms of deployment, APFs represent a technology that has received a huge amount of academic interest, with a publishing rate comparable to that of FACTS. However, there is little industrial take-up (though with some interest in Japan, in particular in relation to traction supply systems). In contrast, the UPS has been widely taken up, as there are clear benefits to individual consumers with particularly sensitive loads.

The basic hardware blocks used in all the technologies described above are similar to each other, and similar in turn to the power converters used to interface DC and variable-frequency DG. This opens up the possibility of adding power quality enhancement capabilities to the fundamental function of generating power (Yamamoto et al., 1999). In a network that has such generation it would be possible to perform APF and voltage regulation functions using the DG inverters. This would require some extra control functionality, which is relatively cheap to provide. The power processing can use the spare capacity of the inverter that is available when the DG is not running at full power. Additionally, the inverter could be rated above the power of the generation source in order to provide this capacity continuously. The questions that arise are: why would a DG operator provide these services, how would they be valued, how would they be paid for and how would they be managed? The network operator is responsible for power quality, and, although some of the problems arise from the network itself, some arise from the generators and some from the loads.

The benefits of DG for the power quality of the network are by no means restricted to improvement of the shape of the voltage and current waveforms. There are a number of ancillary services that may be provided by a DG scheme, ranging from reactive power management to system protection (Joos et al., 2000; Ackermann and Knyazkin, 2002; Kojovic, 2002). All these services can also be provided, without exception, by a DG source interfaced to the grid by power electronics. Generators could, for example, regulate the voltage at their point on the line, but at present this option is not used in the United Kingdom. The network operator has responsibility for the voltage on its network and does not have the means (technically or, perhaps, contractually) to set the way in which a third-party generator should control the voltage. For a network operator to pay for a DG to provide such a service, a value chain will need to be established.

The next development in using DG to improve the power quality of a certain region actively may rely on the microgrid concept described earlier. A microgrid could operate as a power quality island with the ability to control its local voltage. Furthermore, a microgrid may be able to disconnect itself when there are faults on the main network and run independently. It can thus avoid what would otherwise have been an outage (though perhaps it will have to shed some non-critical loads to achieve this). Attention must be given to the detachment of a certain region from the grid to avoid unintentional islands (Walling and Miller, 2002).

11.4.2 Revisiting the compatibility level

There is some overlap between the topics of power quality and electromagnetic compatibility. In an EMC context there is a more explicit expression of the need to address both sides of the question – that is, the need to provide immunity in loads as well as to avoid introducing pollution (unwanted frequency components, for instance) into the supply. All loads and generators connected to the same system share

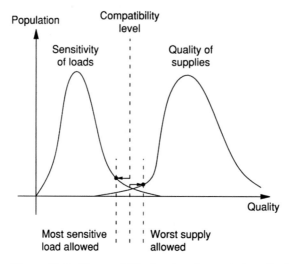

Figure 11.6. Compatibility level and population distributions of load immunity and supply quality.

the same 'power quality environment' and have rights and responsibilities in respect of this environment. The balance between providing immunity and avoiding pollution is expressed in figure 11.6 as a population distribution of various qualities of supply and various sensitivities of loads. By defining a lower limit on supply quality and an upper limit on sensitivity, the risk of maloperation is managed to a very low level. The placement of this compatibility level dictates how the cost of achieving low risk is shared between suppliers and consumers.

Most office and home loads operate at low-voltage DC and therefore include internal voltage regulation that can tolerate some error in the voltage supplied by the utility. An increasing number of portable appliances, most notably laptop computers, are labelled 'universal input' and can operate between 40 and 65Hz and 90 and 250V. Two issues arise here. First, an increasing number of the loads are constant-power loads – that is, they consume a fixed power irrespective (within reason) of the voltage supplied – whereas a simple resistive load consumes power proportional to the voltage squared. Resistive loads act to damp oscillatory disturbances and aid system stability. Constant-power loads detract from the damping in a system and cause problems for system operators. Second, these loads are immune to high degrees of under-voltage and sag.

In systems other than public electricity supply, voltage regulation is treated differently. Instead of going to considerable lengths to regulate the distributed voltage to within tight limits, wide limits are allowed. Reliance is then placed on the loads to include point-of-load regulation so as to process the distribution voltage into a well-regulated voltage for final use. On a very small scale this is seen in the distribution inside a computer system. It is also a feature of the systems proposed for future automobiles and electric aircraft.

A traditional power system has a very reliable and well-regulated voltage within the transmission system. Reliability and voltage regulation is still good, albeit somewhat less so, through the distribution system and poorest at the point of load. Could there be benefits in the ability to operate with intermittent and distributed generation if less reliance was placed on distributed voltage regulation and more on point-of-load regulation? This could be 'internal' through power electronics within the load performing the final regulation, or 'external' through a UPS or DVR performing regulation for a cluster of loads. Some loads, such as simple heat loads, might not need regulation at all. Others, such as line-connected induction machines and incandescent lights, could be very badly affected without regulation.

It is often remarked that it is difficult to differentiate the quality of supply and the power quality given to adjacent consumers. Large consumers can be provided with dedicated supplies to lessen interference and duplicated supply paths to reduce the likelihood of interruption. Point-of-load regulation could be part of a differentiated energy service. Where required, point-of-load regulation and local storage/generation could provide premium-quality supply. Some of the microgrid structures being discussed have these features (Basu et al., 2001; Liang et al., 2002; Weiss et al., 2004). Figure 11.7 illustrates a distribution network in which a subsection has been partially separated by introducing coupling impedance. This allows the voltage in the subsection to be regulated locally using an inverter to achieve enhanced power quality. The inverter could be an independent element, such as an APF or DVR, or could be a part of a distributed generator with enhanced functionality.

11.4.3 Managed loads

Balancing supply and demand is traditionally achieved almost entirely through supply-side action, but power electronics and controllable loads could open up useful possibilities for demand-side action that would allow greater use of intermittent and uncontrolled supply

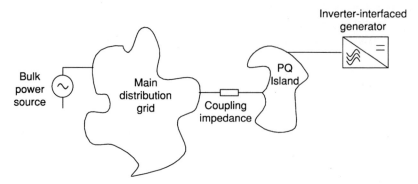

Figure 11.7. A power quality island.

sources. At present, intermittent renewable sources are compensated for by using more responsive carbon-based sources. If, during a shortfall of a renewable energy supply, demand is deferred to those periods when there is an abundance of renewable energy, there could be – in principle – savings in the cost of providing the energy and a reduction in carbon emissions.

There are existing arrangements for energy-intensive industry to contribute some demand reduction to the national grid's control of the system (McCartney, 1993). Distributed generation would benefit from a distributed demand-side management. This will need to be more than a simple pre-programmed delay of certain loads to off-peak periods. What is really sought is responsive loads that can react to network conditions or control signals with a reduction of consumption (Gardner, 1995).[2] The integration of renewable energy into buildings and the management of loads is described in De Almeida and Vine (1994), Clarke et al. (1998), Bellarmine (2000) and Clarke et al. (2002). Although loads could be disconnected with simple controllers it is perhaps more promising to use more subtle intervention in the loads use of power, and this is likely to be achieved through having power electronics in the load.

11.5   Costs

At present cost is still a barrier to the wider deployment of power electronics. This is true in both distributed generation and in networks (FACTS). Refined silicon is an expensive material (and the amount

---

[2] A proposal to control refrigerator loads to reduce their consumption at times of low system frequency is described at. http://www.responsiveload.co.uk.

used depends on the electrical ratings), large-scale devices can have a relatively low production yield and the thermal and packaging design is an important additional cost factor. Power electronic equipment does benefit greatly from high production volumes in some applications, but for most power system uses the volumes will be low and much customisation of the design is necessary. Traditional copper- and iron-based electromagnetic systems are often relatively cheap. Thus far, power electronics has been deployed where there is an overwhelming technical case (such as for connecting non-50/60Hz sources), where flexibility is a key requirement or where adopting alternative solutions (such as additional overhead lines) presents both high costs and planning consent difficulties.

An additional aspect of the cost of power electronic equipment is the power losses incurred. The capitalised value of losses can be a significant factor if the efficiency of the power conversion is not high enough. In most application areas the efficiency of conversion by electronic means is considered high, but network operators are used to efficiencies of around 99 per cent for grid transformers (National Appliance and Equipment Energy Efficiency Committee, 2001; George Wilkenfeld and Associates, 2002). Power electronic converters can suffer high losses in comparison to this. A converter operating from a 1,000V supply with two IGBTs in each current path, each with an on-state voltage drop of 4V, would suffer a conduction power loss of 0.8 per cent. There is an energy loss at each switching event, raising the power loss in proportion to the switching frequency. On top of this come the losses in the other components of the system. There is a need to reduce power losses in equipment to reduce the burden of cooling the semiconductors, but, more importantly, the power losses could be a real impediment to the introduction of power electronic equipment where the drive is to reduce energy use. So long as power electronic equipment remains relatively high-loss, it can be justified only where its control capability and flexibility can offset its losses by improving energy generation or use across the system as a whole.

11.6   Control issues

Power electronics has been deployed to solve steady-state problems in electrical networks, such as matching non-synchronous generation, providing reactive power and proving low-voltage supply to loads. Many of the possibilities discussed for the future require power electronics to solve dynamic and transient problems through control technology.

At the power systems level the challenge is how to ensure that many hundreds of actuators taking action do so in sympathy and achieve satisfactory results at thousands of points across the network. Supervisory control and data acquisition technology has had a vast impact on the operation of the transmission and distribution networks in terms of collecting data and transmitting control commands. It has facilitated the centralised operation of large and complex systems and provided great flexibility and responsiveness. However, this is largely in terms of providing better steady-state operating conditions and in reconfiguring systems around contingencies.

FACTS devices, such as SVCs, can provide damping of oscillatory power flows in a line using current or power feedback (Hingorani and Gyugyi, 2000; Cong and Wang, 2002; Xie et al., 2002). It has also been shown that a single FACTS controller can provide damping across a relatively large area provided suitable feedback signals are available from that area (Chaudhuri et al., 2003). This requires a wide-area measurement system that is able to collect and transmit data with only a short delay or latency. Phasor measurement units with time-stamped data transmission are an emerging technology that might pave the way for wide-area control (Burnett et al., 1994; Bertsch et al., 2003; http://www.epri.com/).

When there are many FACTS controllers and generation sources, central control is not an attractive option on account of the large volume of data to be processed and the complexity of the control design. The alternative is decentralised control: each section of network gathers local data, and local controllers are used. Devolved or autonomous control would be a radical change for network operators. There are candidate technologies of interest, such as intelligent agents, for implementing such cooperative but autonomous controllers (Macken et al., 2004). A large and comprehensive verification study would be needed before a move to operate a system in this way could be made.

Traditional synchronous generators suffer a dynamic stability problem that may result in a loss of synchronism following a fault or disturbance. This is a relatively low-frequency problem (considerably less than the system frequency) governed by the acceleration of the inertia of the generator and prime mover. Inverter-interfaced power sources do not have inertia as such. Synchronisation is maintained by a control loop, often through a phase-locked loop. The dynamic stability issue for an inverter is maintaining the stability of control loops governing the current output.

Shown in relation to the frequency spectrum of the output voltage of an inverter, the control bandwidth is related to the sample rate and

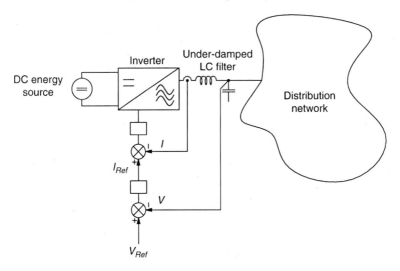

Figure 11.8. An inverter-based power source with output filter and current and voltage control loops.

switching frequency of the inverter. Inverters and other power electronic circuits tend to use a set of nested control loops, as illustrated in figure 11.8. There is a major restriction on the design of these control loops: the faster loop (normally an inner current control loop) cannot have a control bandwidth greater than the switching frequency of the circuit. The problem is that high-power circuits need to use low switching frequencies because of the characteristics of high-power semiconductors. The low switching frequency also dictates the use of low-cut-off frequency filtering, which affects the control bandwidth that can be achieved. Figure 11.9 illustrates the relationship between the switching frequency and the bandwidth achievable in the inner current loop and outer voltage loop. The bandwidth has two sets of implications. First, one can provide active suppression of harmonic distortion only within the bandwidth of the controller. Second, one can shape the dynamic response, and thereby influence the interaction with other controllers in the system, only within the control bandwidth. Generally, and following the practice in DC power supplies (Sudhoff and Glover, 2000; Sudhoff et al., 2000; Feng et al., 2002), the designer needs to control the output impedance of the source converter over the frequency range over which the load converters might exhibit negative damping. Negative damping arises from the constant-power nature of some loads, illustrated in figure 11.10 such that their input current

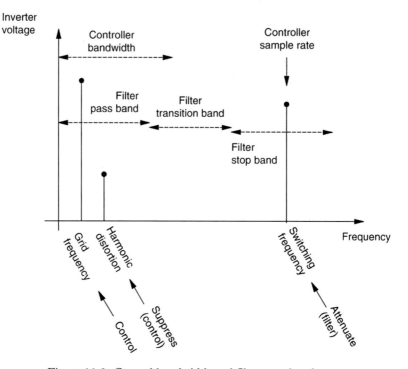

Figure 11.9. Control bandwidth and filter pass band.

rises if the input voltage falls. The problem is that the source converter, serving many loads, might use a lower switching frequency and smaller bandwidth than the loads, and therefore allow undesirable interaction outside the bandwidth of the source converter.

11.7   System design

The technologies of power electronics and power systems have followed separate development paths but are now being pressed together to facilitate the desired changes in electricity generation and use. There is an enormous challenge in making this work effectively. Power systems have evolved in a particular direction for very good reasons, and have a huge body of accepted practice and large capital assets from their long service life. The problem is that power electronics does not fit comfortably into that body of practice and yet is too small a part of the system at present to justify the upheaval that would be necessary to provide a better fit. It will take imaginative thinking to find ways of easing the

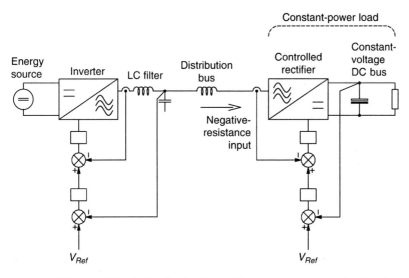

Figure 11.10. A distribution bus with a constant-power load and controlled source.
NB: The stability of the source can be adversely affected by the negative small-signal resistance of the load.

burden of making the fit happen. It is possible to imagine very different power systems in which power electronics is dominant and cheaper by virtue of its widespread use. The system would be designed and run very differently. But is that a desirable and realisable outcome? What intermediate positions would bring significant benefit and how might those positions be achieved?

Several issues must be tackled to ease the introduction of power electronics, and they have already been touched upon.

- It is not sensible (because it will lead to greatly increased cost) to require power electronic equipment to mimic the fault response of conventional plant. Instead, fault protection and fault ride-through must be rethought. In some circumstances, the less onerous fault current interruption that results might lead to overall cost benefits.
- To gain maximum advantage, given the cost, it should be possible to use a piece of power electronic equipment for multiple functions. Ancillary services provided by distributed generators could expand into many fields (such as power quality) at little extra equipment cost. However, this will require control infrastructure and a suitable regulatory and commercial environment.

- The relationship negotiated with consumers (indirectly via new standards, perhaps) must address the optimisation of a system that includes the consumers' equipment. Are we sure that the product that is being supplied is what is actually wanted by consumers, now and in the future?

11.8   Conclusions

Power electronics is an enabling technology that offers flexibility and control opportunities in power processing well beyond that achievable through traditional means. The questions are: what do we want to do with it, and is it cost-effective in that role?

If future electricity production depends heavily on small-scale renewable sources then we will see the widespread use of power electronics as an interface means. Having installed such power converters in large numbers we shall probably see use made of them to manage and control the networks into which they are embedded. This could be achieved by providing ancillary services in a distribution network based on the existing network. A variant could be the development of microgrids that are largely autonomous but exist in federations for the well-established principles of sharing reserves and increasing reliability.

The development of the larger-scale renewable resources, such as offshore wind and marine energy will require substantial changes to the transmission infrastructure, which will be achieved through a blend of traditional AC equipment supported by power electronics and a greater use of HVDC. The large-scale use of biomass will perhaps cause less change because it more closely resembles traditional thermal plant, but there will be a change of scale requiring more active control of distribution networks.

In scenarios that retain the use of large central plant (such as CCGTs) there is still a role for power electronics as FACTS controllers to allow the transmission system to be run at greater capacity while maintaining stability.

An optimist looking at this greater use of power electronics would note that:

- inverter-interfaced generation does not have the rotor synchronisation problem of rotary generators;
- FACTS controllers can facilitate better utilisation of other plant;
- voltage regulation and transient damping can also be improved by adopting FACTS; and
- inverter-based DG can provide active control of power quality.

A pessimist would note that:

- power electronics cannot support the fault current needed to operate traditional protection systems;
- multiple FACTS or DG units could have unplanned controller interaction;
- with many switch-mode devices on a system the frequency spectrum will be contaminated and congested;
- power electronic devices will have relatively high losses, which have to be paid for; and
- however attractive the control offered, power electronic systems are expensive.

Imagination and innovation should allow us to overcome the pessimistic view, and the natural conservatism of engineers will guard against over-optimism. This is an exciting time to be involved with electricity system development, because – for the first time in a generation – the future is wide open.

11.9   References

Ackermann, T., and V. Knyazkin (2002). Interaction between distributed generation and the distribution network: operation aspects, in *Transmission and Distribution Conference and Exhibition 2002: Asia Pacific*, Vol. II, New York: IEEE Press, 1357–62.

Basu, M., Das, S. P. et al. (2001). Experimental investigation of performance of a single phase UPQC for voltage sensitive and non-linear loads, in *Proceedings of the 4th IEEE International Conference on Power Electronics and Drive Systems*, New York: IEEE Press.

Bellarmine, G. T. (2000). Load management techniques, in *Proceedings of the IEEE Southeast Conference 2000*, New York: IEEE Press, 139–45.

Bertsch, J., C. Carnal and A. Surányi (2003). Detecting power system instabilities and optimizing asset utilization with Inform!T Wide Area Monitoring, *ABB Review*, 4: 32–6.

Bialek, J. (2004). Are blackouts contagious?, *Power Engineer*, 17(6): 10–13.

Bollen, M. H. J. (2000). *Understanding Power Quality Problems: Voltage Sags and Interruptions*, New York: IEEE Press.

Burnett, R. O., Jr., M. M. Butts and P. S. Sterlina (1994). Power system applications for phasor measurement units, *Computer Applications in Power*, 7(1): 8–13.

Campbell, A., and R. McHattie (1999). Backfilling the sinewave: a dynamic voltage restorer case study, *Power Engineering Journal*, 13(3): 153–8.

Chaudhuri, B., Pal, B. C. et al. (2003). Mixed-sensitivity approach to H/sub /spl infin//control of power system oscillations employing multiple FACTS devices, *IEEE Transactions on Power Systems*, 18(3): 1149–56.

Clarke, J. A., S. Conner, J. W. Hand, N. J. Kelly R. Moore, T. O'Brien and P. Strachan (2002). Simulation-assisted control in building energy management systems, *Energy and Buildings*, 34(9): 933–40.

Clarke, J. A., C. M. Johnstone and I. Macdonald (1998). Integrated modelling of low energy buildings, *Renewable Energy*, 15: 151–6.

Cong, L., and Y. Wang (2002). Co-ordinated control of generator excitation and STATCOM for rotor angle stability and voltage regulation enhancement of power systems, in *IEE Proceedings: Generation, Transmission and Distribution*, 149(6): 659–66.

David, A., J. Lachaume, P. Rioual and M. Bisson (1997). How to conciliate demand side management and electromagnetic compatibility? in *14th International Conference and Exhibition on Electricity Distribution*, Part 1 *Contributions*, Vol. V, Conference Publication no. 438, New York: IEEE Press, 25/1–25/6.

Dayton, D. C., R. Bain and M. Ratcliff (2001). *Fuel Cell Integration – A Study of the Impacts of Gas Quality and Impurities: Milestone Completion Report*, Report no. MP-510-30298, National Renewable Energy Laboratory, Golden, CO.

De Almeida, A. T., and E. L. Vine (1994). Advanced monitoring technologies for the evaluation of demand-side management programs, *IEEE Transactions on Power Systems*, 9(3): 1691–7.

Edris, A. (2000). FACTS technology development: an update, *Power Engineering Review*, 20(3): 4–9.

Ekanayake, J., L. Holdsworth and N. Jenkins (2003). Control of DFIG wind turbines, *Power Engineer*, 17(1): 28–32.

Elnady, A., W. El-khattam and M. M. A. Salama (2002). *Mitigation of AC Arc Furnace Voltage Flicker Using the Unified Power Quality Conditioner*, paper presented at Power Engineering Society Winter Meeting, New York, 27–31 January.

Elnady, A., and M. M. A. Salama (2001). New functionalities of the unified power quality conditioner, in *Transmission and Distribution Conference and Exposition 2001*, Vol. I, New York: IEEE Press, 415–20.

Feng, X., J. Liu and F. C. Lee (2002). Impedance specifications for stable DC distributed power systems, *IEEE Transactions on Power Electronics*, 17(2): 157–62.

Fujita, H., and H. Akagi (1998). The unified power quality conditioner: the integration of series and shunt-active filters, *IEEE Transactions on Power Electronics*, 13(2): 315–22.

Gardner, E. (1995). *Load Management DSM: Past, Present and Future*, paper presented at the 39th Annual Conference on Rural Electric Power, Nashville, TN, 30 April–2 May.

George Wilkenfeld and Associates (2002). *Regulatory Impact Statement: Minimum Energy Performance Standards and Alternative Strategies for Electricity Distribution Transformers*, report prepared for the Australian Greenhouse Office, George Wilkenfeld and Associates, Newtown, NSW.

Glavitsch, H., and M. Rahmani (1998). Increased transmission capacity by forced symmetrization, *IEEE Transactions on Power Electronics*, 13(1): 79–85.

Grady, W. M., M. J. Samotyj and A. H. Noyola (1990). Survey of active power line conditioning methodologies, *IEEE Transactions on Power Delivery*, 5(3): 1536–42.

Gyugyi, L. (1988). Power electronics in electric utilities: static VAr compensators, *Proceedings of the IEEE*, 76(4): 483–94.

Hanson, D. J., C. Horwill, B. D. Gemmell and D. R. Monkhouse (2002). *A STATCOM-Based Relocatable SVC Project in the UK for National Grid*, paper presented at Power Engineering Society Winter Meeting, New York, 27–31 January.

Hasegawa, T. (2002). *Expectation for Power Conversion Technologies from the Electric Power Company*, paper presented at Power Conversion Conference, Osaka, 2–5 April.

Hingorani, N. G., and L. Gyugyi (2000). *Understanding FACTS*, New York: IEEE Press.

Horwill, C., A. J. Totterdell, D. J. Hanson, D. R. Monkhouse and J. J. Price (2001). Commissioning of a 225 Mvar SVC incorporating A /spl plusmn/75 Mvar STATCOM at NGC's 400kV East Claydon substation, in *7th International Conference on AC-DC Power Transmission*, Conference Publication no. 485, New York: IEEE Press, 232–7.

Hosseini, S. H, and A. Ajami (2002). Transient stability enhancement of AC transmission system using STATCOM, in *Proceedings of the 2002 IEEE Region 10 Conference on Computers, Communications, Control and Power Engineering*, Vol. III, New York: IEEE Press, 1809–12.

Huang, Z., B. T. Ooi, L. A. Dessaint and F. D. Galiana (2003). Exploiting voltage support of voltage-source HVDC, *IEE Proceedings on Generation, Transmission and Distribution*, 150(2): 252–6.

Jenkins, N., R., Allan, P. Crossley, D. Kirschen and G. Strbac (2000). *Embedded Generation, Power and Energy series no. 31*, London: Institution of Electrical Engineers.

Jiang, H., and A. Ekstorm (1998). Multiterminal HVDC systems in urban areas of large cities, *IEEE Transactions on Power Delivery*, 13(4): 1278–84.

Jianjun, G., X. Dianguo, L. Hankui and G. Maozhong (2002). Unified power quality conditioner (UPQC): the principle, control and application, in *Proceedings of the Power Conversion Conference, 2002*, Vol. I, New York: IEEE Press, 80– 5.

Johnson, C. M. (2003). Current state of the art and future prospects for power semiconductor devices in power transmission and distribution applications, *International Journal of Electronics*, 90(11/12): 667–93.

Joos, G., B. T. Ooi, D. J. McGillis, F. D. Galiana and R. J. Marceau (2000). *The Potential of Distributed Generation to Provide Ancillary Services*, paper presented at Power Engineering Society Summer Meeting, Seattle, 16–20 July.

Kojovic, L. (2002). *Impact DG on Voltage Regulation*, paper presented at Power Engineering Society Summer Meeting, Chicago, 21–5 July.

Lasseter, R. H. (2002). *Microgrids*, paper presented at Power Engineering Society Winter Meeting, New York, 27–31 January.

Liang, J., T. C. Green, G. Weiss and Q.-C. Zhong (2002). Repetitive control of power conversion system from a distributed generator to the utility grid, in *Proceedings of the International Conference on Control Applications 2002*, Vol. I, New York: IEEE Press, 13–18.

Lu, W., and B.-T. Ooi (2001). *Simultaneous Inter-Area Decoupling and Local Area Damping by Voltage-Source HVDC*, paper presented at Power Engineering Society Winter Meeting, Columbus, OH, 28 January–1 February.

  (2003). Optimal acquisition and aggregation of offshore wind power by multi-terminal voltage-source HVDC, *IEEE Transactions on Power Delivery*, 18(1): 201–6.

Macken, K. J. P., K. Vanthournout, J. Van den Keybus, G. Deconinek and R. Belmans (2004). Distributed control of renewable generation units with integrated active filter, *IEEE Transactions on Power Electronics*, 19(5): 1353–60.

Marnay, C., F. J. Robio and A. S. Siddiqui (2001). *Shape of the Microgrid*, paper presented at Power Engineering Society Winter Meeting, Columbus, OH, 28 January–1 February.

McCartney, A. I. (1993). Load management using radio teleswitches within NIE, *Power Engineering Journal*, 7(4): 163–9.

Meliopoulos, A. P. S. (2002). *Challenges in Simulation and Design of /spl mu/Grids*, paper presented at Power Engineering Society Winter Meeting, New York, 27–31 January.

Mohan, N., T. M. Undeland and W. P. Robbins (1995). *Power Electronics: Converters, Applications and Design*, New York: John Wiley.

Mori, H. (2001). *Optimal Allocation of FACTS Devices in Distribution Systems*, paper presented at Power Engineering Society Winter Meeting, Columbus, OH, 28 January–1 February.

Muller, S., M., Deicke and R. W. De Doncker (2002). Doubly fed induction generator systems for wind turbines, *Industry Applications Magazine*, 8(3): 26–33.

National Appliance and Equipment Energy Efficiency Committee (2001). *Minimum Energy Performance Standards*, Energy Efficiency Team, Australian Greenhouse Office, Canberra.

Nielsen, J. G., M. Newman, H. O. Nielsen and F. Blaabjerg (2004). Control and testing of a dynamic voltage restorer (DVR) at medium voltage level, *IEEE Transactions on Power Electronics*, 19(3): 806–13.

Ooi, B.-T., and X. Wang (1991). Boost-type PWM HVDC transmission system, *IEEE Transactions on Power Delivery*, 6(4): 1557–63.

Peng, F. Z. (1998). Application issues of active power filters, *Industry Applications Magazine*, 4(5): 21–30.

Pullen, K. R., M. R. Etemad and A. Fenocchi (1996). The high speed axial flux disc generator – unlocking the potential of the automotive gas turbine, in *IEE Colloqium Digest* no. 1996/152, 8.

Reed, G., J. Paserba, T. Croasdaile, R. Westover, S. Jochi, N. Morishima, M. Takeda, T. Sugiyama, Y. Hamasaki, T. Snow and A. Abed (2002). *SDG&E Talega STATCOM project – System Analysis, Design, and Configuration*, paper presented at Transmission and Distribution Conference and Exhibition 2002: Asia Pacific, Yokohama, 6–10 October.

Reed, G., J. Paserba and P. Salavantis (2003). The FACTS on resolving transmission gridlock, *Power and Energy Magazine*, 1(5): 41–6.

Richard, T., R. Belhomme, N. Buchheit and F. Gorgette (2001). 'Power quality improvement case study of the connection of four 1.6MVA flywheel dynamic UPS systems to a medium voltage distribution network, in *Transmission and Distribution Conference and Exposition 2001*, Vol. I, New York: IEEE Press, 253– 8.

Roberts, B. P. (2001). Energy storage applications for large scale power protection systems, in *Transmission and Distribution Conference and Exposition 2001*, Vol. II, New York: IEEE Press, 1157– 60.

Schlabbach, J., D. Blume and T. Stephanblome (2001). *Voltage Quality in Electrical Power Systems*, Power and Energy series no. 36, London: Institution of Electrical Engineers.

Singh, B., K. Al-Haddad and A. Chandra (1999). A review of active filters for power quality improvement, *IEEE Transactions on Industrial Electronics*, 46 (5): 960–71.

Soto, D., and T. C. Green (2002). A comparison of high-power converter topologies for the implementation of FACTS controllers, *IEEE Transactions on Industrial Electronics*, 49(5): 1072–80.

Sudhoff, S. D., and S. F. Glover (2000). Three-dimensional stability analysis of DC power electronics based systems, in *31st IEEE Anuual Power Electronics Specialists Conference*, New York: IEEE Press, 101–6.

Sudhoff, S. D., S. F. Glover, P. T. Lamm, D. H. Schmucker and D. E. Delisle (2000). Admittance space stability analysis of power electronic systems, *IEEE Transactions on Aerospace and Electronic Systems*, 36(3): 965–73.

Tan, P.-C., R. E. Morrison and D. G. Holmes (2003). Voltage form factor control and reactive power compensation in a 25-kV electrified railway system using a shunt active filter based on voltage detection, *IEEE Transactions on Industry Applications*, 39(2): 575–81.

Venkatasubramanian, V., and C. W. Taylor (2000). *Improving Pacific Intertie Stability using Slatt Thyristor-Controlled Series Compensation*, paper presented at Power Engineering Society Winter Meeting, Singapore, 23–7 January.

Vilathgamuwa, D. M., A. A. D. Ranjith Perera and S. S. Choi (2003). Voltage sag compensation with energy optimized dynamic voltage restorer, *IEEE Transactions on Power Delivery*, 18(3): 928–36.

Walling, R. A., and N. W. Miller (2002). *Distributed Generation Islanding – Implications on Power System Dynamic Performance*, paper presented at Power Engineering Society Summer Meeting, Chicago, 21–5 July.

Weiss, G., Q.-C. Zhong, T. C. Green and J. Liang Zhong (2004). H/sup /spl infin//repetitive control of DC-AC converters in microgrids, *IEEE Transactions on Power Electronics*, 19(1): 219–30.

Wenger, H. J., T. E. Hoff and B. K. Farmer (1994). Measuring the value of distributed photovoltaic generation: final results of the Kerman grid-support project, *Proceedings of the First World Conference on Photovoltaic Energy Conversion*, Vol. I, New York: IEEE Press, 792–6.

Woking Borough Council Civic Offices (2001). *Woking Energy Station*, PDF file at http://www.woking.gov.uk/:PDF file.

Xie, X., G. Yan and W. Cui (2002). STATCOM and generator excitation: coordinated and optimal control for improving dynamic performance and transfer capability of interconnected power systems, in *Transmission and Distribution Conference and Exhibition 2002: Asia Pacific*, Vol. I, New York: IEEE Press, 190–4.

Yamamoto, F., A. Kitamura, N. Fujita, Y. Nakanishi and M. Nagasawa (1999). A study on optimal locations and sizes of active filters as an additional function of distributed generation systems, in *Proceedings of the IEEE International Conference on Systems, Man, and Cybernetics 1999*, Vol. VI, New York: IEEE Press 515–20.

12 Sustainable hydrogen energy

Peter P. Edwards, Vladimir L. Kuznetsov, Simon R. Johnson, Matthew T. J. Lodge and Martin Owen Jones

12.1 Hydrogen in our energy future

A major challenge – some would argue the major challenge facing our planet today – relates to the problem of anthropological-driven climate change and its inextricable link to our global society's present and future energy needs (Hoffman, 2001; Roberts, 2004; Hasselman et al., 2004; May, 2004; King, 2004).

The growth of tangible environmental concerns is providing one of the major driving forces towards sustainable energy development. All modern-day assessments of energy futures take the view that the growth in demand must now be met by a diverse energy mix, including renewable or sustainable energy sources. These sources (e.g. solar, wind and wave) are abundant throughout the world but are most often intermittent and regional, and sustainable energy can become a major feature of any total energy picture only if we can find effective ways to store and transport this intermittent energy.

Hydrogen, the most abundant chemical element in the Universe and the third most abundant chemical element in the Earth's crust, has the potential to realise the vision of a renewable-based system (Roberts, 2004; Hoffmann, 2001; Momirlan and Veziroglu, 2002; POST, 2002; Gosselink, 2002; Kennedy, 2004). The intrinsic value of hydrogen lies in its ability to store and transport energy produced from intermittent sources; for example, the electrolysis of water to produce hydrogen using electricity at times of low demand can deliver its latent energy via the subsequent production of electricity in a hydrogen-powered fuel cell or via direct combustion. Hydrogen as an energy carrier can thus neutralise

We are most grateful to David Book, Rex Harris, Paul Bellaby, Malcolm Eames, Paul Ekins, Rob Flynn, William McDowell, Keith Ross and Jim Skea for many important discussions and comments relating to future UK hydrogen scenarios, and to Paul Bellaby, Rob Flynn and Keith Ross for the preparation of figure 12.4. We thank the EPSRC for support through the UK Sustainable Hydrogen Energy Consortium. Peter P. Edwards is coordinator of the Consortium, which is part of the EPSRC Super Gen initiative: see http://www.uk-shec.org and http://www.supergen.co.uk.

the vexing issue of intermittency in the generation and transportation of sustainable energy. It is this key element of energy storage capacity for hydrogen that provides the potent link between sustainable energy technologies and the sustainable energy economy, generally placed under the umbrella of 'the hydrogen economy'. We follow the accepted convention whereby the hydrogen economy is defined as the production, storage, distribution and use of hydrogen as an energy carrier (Kennedy, 2004; Fuelcelltoday.com, 2004; Hydrogen.co.uk, 2003; Spacedaily. com, 2004; DTI, 2003; Department of Energy, 2004; Pricewaterhouse Coopers, 2002; HyNet, 2004; Joint Research Centre, 2003).

However, the challenges and barriers attendant on a transition to a sustainable hydrogen economy encompass the diverse areas of production, storage, distribution and end usage; these challenges are daunting, complex and strongly interrelated (Nicoletti, 1995; Harris et al., 2004; Hart, 2003; National Academy of Engineering and Board on Energy and Environmental Systems, 2004; Office of Science, 2004). This notwithstanding, hydrogen is now seen by many as the clean energy source of the future; for example, the European Commission (European Commission, 2003) now expounds the view that hydrogen will ultimately power our cars and generating plants, replacing the current hydrocarbon energy base (an overview of the European Commission vision is presented in section 12.3). A sustainable hydrogen energy vision therefore derives from the requirements for a reduction in carbon dioxide emissions, an enhancement of urban (local) air quality, a move towards the use of local resources for energy, an abiding concern about fossil fuel resources and a transition towards the sustainable and long-term security of energy supplies. Hydrogen is also beginning to be piped into the mainstream of energy policies and strategies, both in the developed and the developing worlds. Perhaps the most telling argument for a sustainable hydrogen economy is the potential – globally – to reduce greenhouse gas emissions drastically.

12.2   Hydrogen as an energy carrier

Even though hydrogen is highly abundant on Earth in numerous chemically bound forms (e.g. water, hydrocarbons, biomass, etc.), free, unassociated molecular hydrogen exists only in trace amounts, since (a) it is so light it can easily reach escape velocity and exit the Earth's atmosphere, and (b) it is also highly chemically reactive – most notably in its (dissociated) atomic form – and thus readily forms compounds with almost all other chemical elements. Combined with oxygen it forms water, the most abundant hydrogen-containing compound on our planet.

Table 12.1 *Specific quantities of polluting matter in combustion fumes (kg/kg of fuel)*

	CO_2	SO_2	NO_x	Dust and unburnt matter	H_2O
Hydrogen	0	0	0.016	0	9
Coal	1.893	0.012	0.008	0.1	0.633
Natural gas	2.75	0.03	0.0075	0	2.154
Petrol	3.09	0.010	0.0115	0.85	1.254

Source: Nicoletti (1995).

Hydrogen, produced from renewable resources such as sun, wind, waves, etc., has the potential to be the clean, sustainable and therefore climate-neutral energy source of the future. Thus, when burned with oxygen from the air, the main combustion product is water with traces of nitrogen oxides, NOx, formed from the reaction of radicals with nitrogen and oxygen in the air. Interestingly, the assumed simplicity of the chemical reaction $2H_2 + O_2 \rightarrow 2H_2O$ is merely apparent, since in reality it is a series of complex reactions and radical intermediates such as atomic hydrogen and the hydroxyl ion OH. In table 12.1 we show the concentration of polluting matter in various fumes originating from combustion at standard conditions during the burning of a kilogram of coal, natural gas (methane), petrol and hydrogen (Nicoletti, 1995).

Hydrogen has several features that set it apart from other common fuels such as petrol and natural gas that significantly influence its potential use as a fuel (Hoffmann, 2001; Dunn, 2001, 2002; Ogden, 2002; Momirlan and Veziroglu, 2002; POST, 2002). Because of its position as the lightest of all the chemical elements, hydrogen releases – gram for gram – more energy than any other chemical fuel. In respect of volumetric comparisons, however, hydrogen gas at a given pressure contains only about one-third of the energy of the same volume of methane. Liquid hydrogen has about one-quarter of the energy density of the same volume of petrol. In table 12.2 we compare the energy densities of hydrogen versus petrol on both a weight and a volume basis (Harris et al., 2004).

Compared to other fuels, hydrogen has a wider range of flammability and detonation limits (concentrations in air that will support a fire or explosion, respectively). In practical (operating) situations, perhaps the lower flammability limit is the more important parameter – for example, if the hydrogen concentration were to build up in an enclosed space through a leak. If hydrogen does catch fire, the flame spreads more rapidly than for burning methane or petrol (flame velocities in air

Table 12.2 *Energy density of hydrogen and petrol*

	Hydrogen	Petrol
Weight basis	120 MJ/kg	44 MJ/kg (LHV)
Volume basis	3 MJ/litre @ 333bar	32 MJ/litre
	8 MJ/litre (liquid H_2)	

Source: Harris et al. (2004).

(centimetres per second): hydrogen, 325–365; petrol, 37–43). Hydrogen is non-toxic compared to petrol, which is generally considered to be toxic above 50 parts per million. Liquid methanol, sometimes identified as a potential fuel, is highly toxic.

The importance of hydrogen as a potential energy carrier has increased significantly over the last decade because of rapid advances in fuel cell technology. Fuel cells are a key energy technology for the twenty-first century due to their inherent advantages, such as high efficiency and environmental friendliness. Within a fuel cell, hydrogen is combined with oxygen (without combustion) in an electrochemical reaction that is the reverse of electrolysis, to produce DC electricity. In the prototypical polymer electrolyte membrane fuel cell (also known as a proton-exchange membrane cell) a catalyst in the anode dissociates molecular hydrogen to yield atomic hydrogen and, subsequently, dissociated hydrogen – protons and electrons (figure 12.1). The electrolyte membrane in the centre of the diagram enables the transport of the protons to the cathode, leaving the excess electrons behind. These electrons then flow through an external circuit to provide electrical current and thus electrical energy (electrical load). At the cathode, another catalyst assists the combination of the incoming electrons and protons with molecular oxygen from the air. When the fuel input is pure hydrogen and air, the resulting exhaust process consists of water vapour. Running a fuel cell with a hydrocarbon fuel (e.g. methanol) is also possible but now the exhaust is water and carbon dioxide.

Fuel cells can compete most effectively in energy efficiencies against a number of very low carbon dioxide and pollutant emission technologies. Hydrogen-powered fuel-cell vehicles also have virtually no emissions, even of nitrous oxides, because they operate at temperatures that are much lower than those of internal combustion engines. A hydrogen-fuelled fuel-cell vehicle emits only water vapour at the exhaust point and provides a route, in theory, to real (complete life cycle) zero emissions if the hydrogen fuel could be sourced from renewable or

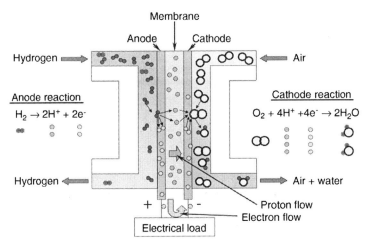

Figure 12.1. Schematic representation of a hydrogen fuel cell.
Diagram: courtesy Dr David Book, University of Birmingham.

sustainable supplies. Clearly, the headline claim 'no environmental effects – emits only water' for hydrogen fuel cells is true only for a fuel cell in relation to emissions at the exhaust, but certainly not true in a complete life cycle, or 'well-to-wheels' analysis, if the hydrogen fuel is not produced from renewable sources.

Hydrogen-fuelled fuel-cell vehicles are increasingly seen as an attractive alternative to other zero-emission vehicles such as battery-driven electric cars, because the chemical energy density of hydrogen and several hydrocarbon fuels is significantly higher than that found in electric battery materials (Winter and Brodd, 2004). Rechargeable batteries for electric cars also suffer from seemingly insuperable obstacles of a sort: battery lifetime and cumbersome recharging procedures. Hydrogen fuel cells, on the other hand, could deliver much longer operational lifetimes than could electric batteries, and the same high specific energy as traditional combustion engines. The most important performance issues facing hydrogen vehicles are the problems related to fuel storage and driving range. The use of very high-pressure hydrogen tanks is likely to increase the energy penalty and reduce the overall energy efficiency of the system due to the need to compress hydrogen to extremely high pressures. The development of solid-state materials with a high and reversible hydrogen storage capacity could be a major breakthrough, facilitating the widespread use of hydrogen and fuel cell technology in a variety of applications.

12.3 Barriers to a sustainable hydrogen energy economy

If hydrogen's benefits as an energy carrier are so clear, one might justifiably ask why it has not already made significant inroads into the issue of sustainable energy. Indeed, establishing a transition to a hydrogen economy is seen, worldwide, as a particularly worthy long-term target. Such goals call for policies and actions that will ultimately lead to the widespread use of fuel-cell vehicles and stationary fuel cell applications, with hydrogen as the only viable fuel in the long term.

In the short to medium term, however, the issues of how to advance or establish hydrogen energy as a working technology, and how such a technology would fit into society, present us with a variety of significant barriers (National Academy of Engineering and Board on Energy and Environmental Systems, 2004; Office of Science, 2004). The main obstacles to implementing sustainable hydrogen energy – and with it the hydrogen economy – fall into three categories: financial, technological and social.

12.3.1 *Financial barriers*

Creating a new hydrogen-based national energy infrastructure will require a sustained term and very substantial capital investment programme, associated with the construction of new facilities for hydrogen production, storage, distribution and utilisation and, equally, with the carbon capture and sequestration processes crucial for coping with carbon dioxide generated from non-sustainable hydrogen production methods.

To achieve any substantial amount of take-up, hydrogen must clearly become cost-competitive with other fuels. The cost of hydrogen depends significantly on the method of production. At present, the cheapest option involves the reforming of natural gas to produce hydrogen; the most expensive is the solar photovoltaic electrolysis of water. In both cases the hydrogen produced is considerably more expensive than using natural gas directly as a fuel.

Analysis of the fuel price to drive a car for the same distance using petrol, biogas, ethanol and liquid and compressed hydrogen produced from different sources was carried out recently by Air Products, LB-Systemtechnik and the Verkehrswirtschaftliche Energiestrategie–Clean Energy Partnership (VES-CEP), and the results are presented in Geiger (2004).[1] The analysis indicates that the cost of hydrogen produced

---

[1] The energy content of 1 kilogram of hydrogen is approximately equal to 1 gallon of petrol. The electric power required to electrolyse 1 kg of hydrogen using commercially

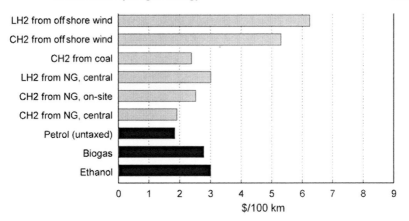

Figure 12.2. Fuel price to drive conventional and fuel-cell (Honda FCEV) vehicles for 100 kilometres.
NB: LH2 and CH2 – liquid and compressed hydrogen; NG – natural gas; central and on-side – centralised and local facilities of hydrogen production.
Source: Geiger (2004).

from renewable resources is at least 2.5 times higher than the cost of hydrogen produced by the cheapest method, that of reforming natural gas in a large centralised facility (figure 12.2). It should be pointed out that the fuel price to drive a car for a certain distance comprises both the cost of fuel and fuel efficiency. Because the fuel cells are significantly more efficient than internal combustion engines, the cost of hydrogen (produced by the steam reformation of natural gas) required to drive a fuel-cell car (a Honda FCEV) is the same as the cost of untaxed petrol needed by a conventional petrol car with a petrol consumption figure of 8l/100 kilometres or 30 miles per gallon.

The cost of hydrogen production from renewable resources must ultimately become competitive with production from carbon-based materials; this can be achieved only through major technological advances, as well as through government taxation and investment policies. Another major difficulty with hydrogen is that its storage and distribution is extremely expensive. Cost is also the greatest challenge to fuel cell development. For example, most fuel cell types require expensive, precious-metal catalysts; others require costly materials that are resistant to

available electrolysers is around 50 kWh, with the approximate cost of this power at 8p per kWh being £4.00 per 'gallon equivalent'. The amount of electricity required to produce, by electrolysis, enough hydrogen to drive a car for a year (12,000 miles at 35 miles/gallon) is around 17,000 kWh, (£1,370 at 8p per kWh).

extremely high temperatures. Many of the cost-related barriers can be overcome by sustained advances in science and technology in what is now a forefront area of intensive research activity. Most of the performance limits (and costs) that current fuel cell technologies face are in materials issues themselves.

12.3.2   Scientific and technological barriers

The scientific and technical challenges that will have to be overcome in order to achieve a transition to a hydrogen economy include many key issues, including the lowering of cost and an improvement in efficiency and reliability for all components of the hydrogen economy – namely hydrogen production, transportation, storage and conversion, and end-use applications. As in all areas of modern energy usage, financial, scientific and technological barriers are closely interlinked, and in the following sections we present a brief overview of the key issues.

12.3.2.1   The production of hydrogen   There are several ways of producing hydrogen and they can be divided into two groups, depending on whether the hydrogen production is accompanied by carbon dioxide release. For a recent review, see Turner (2004).

These are the hydrogen production methods associated with carbon dioxide release.

- The steam reformation of natural gas. This is currently the cheapest production method and provides a ready route to the large-scale production of hydrogen. It currently accounts for approximately 80 per cent of global hydrogen production.
- The gasification of coal or biomass. The gasification of coal is the oldest method for the production of hydrogen and widely used at an industrial scale. Biomass gasification is currently one of the least expensive and most advanced methods of hydrogen production from renewable resources. A wide variety of biomass sources can be used to produce hydrogen.
- Emerging reforming technologies, including advanced natural gas reforming, sorbent-enhanced reforming and partial oxidation of heavy hydrocarbons and coal. The partial oxidation process is technically well proven and realised on an industrial scale.

These are the hydrogen production methods without carbon dioxide release.

- The electrolysis of water using electricity from renewable resources (generally intermittent). Industrial-scale alkaline electrolysers are commercially available, but they require modification if powered from intermittent energy sources.

- The high-temperature pyrolysis of hydrocarbons, biomass and municipal solid waste, producing hydrogen and (solid) carbon black. There are several industrial plants utilising this process for the commercial production of carbon black used in tyre manufacturing. New types of reactors, including microchannel reactors and plasma reformers, need to be developed.
- The chemical or thermal reformation of biomass feed stocks such as crops, wood chips or methanol manufactured from biomass. This method releases carbon dioxide, but ultimately it can be recycled by the subsequent growth of more biomass – in a 'carbon-dioxide-neutral' cycle of production.
- The biological reformation of biomass using micro-organisms and fermentation. This method also releases carbon dioxide, but it can be recycled by the growth of more biomass (thereby being counted as a carbon-dioxide-neutral activity). The process of biomass fermentation is developed and commercially available (Hawkes et al., 2002).
- New methods of hydrogen production using the catalytic pyrolysis of hydrocarbons and the reaction of methane with bromine.
- The direct photolytic splitting of water using light with special catalysts. The technology is currently at the point of laboratory system development.
- Nuclear production via, for example, the high-temperature thermal decomposition of water using direct thermochemical processes. The next generation of fission reactors includes designs that can provide the necessary heat for the thermal splitting of water. For the future it is clear that fusion power stations (once available) would be ideal sources of heat and/or electricity to produce hydrogen.

Several methods of large scale hydrogen production are currently viable in the United Kingdom (Dutton, 2003): the production of hydrogen using the steam reformation of natural gas and the gasification of coal; among the current carbon-dioxide-free methods, the cheapest option is the electrolysis of water using electricity generated by offshore wind power.

The cost of electrolysis can be reduced by further improving electrolyser efficiency. Developing a reversible fuel cell that combines the electrolyser and fuel cell in one unit is an alternative way to advance this method. A cost reduction could also be achieved by electrolysing liquid hydrogen bromide, which is significantly more efficient than electrolysing water. Hydrogen bromide could be produced by reacting methane with bromine without producing carbon dioxide. The bromine released during the electrolysis can then be recycled for further methane processing.

The steam reformation of natural gas does produce carbon dioxide – but no more than burning it. Hence the development of advanced catalysts and reactors is required to improve the process efficiency. Cost-efficient gas-cleaning technology (such as membrane separation) for the removal of trace components of gases (CO, SO_2, NO, C, etc.) is necessary. In these processes, carbon dioxide can be captured and sequestered at an energy expense, and, in theory at least, this process could lead to a viable carbon-free technology for hydrogen production. Carbon dioxide sequestration involves the capture, pressurisation, transportation and injection of liquid carbon dioxide under the ocean (usually at depths of more than 2 kilometres) or underground (e.g. depleted natural gas wells or geological formations) (see chapter 7 on carbon capture in this volume). The key risk results from the uncertain long-term ecological consequences of carbon dioxide sequestration. An interesting development centres on an economically viable process for the production of hydrogen and elemental carbon (chemically reduced carbon dioxide) via the so-called thermocatalytic decomposition of natural gas or other hydrocarbon fuels.

Gasification of coal with zero emissions using carbon capture and sequestration would offer a rapid route to a hydrogen economy, allowing the proving and testing of technologies relating to hydrogen storage, distribution, safety and use. At the initial stages of the development of a hydrogen economy, the gasification of coal could provide a significant part of the required hydrogen until the hydrogen production from renewable energy sources becomes price-competitive. This technology has huge potential given that estimates of the world's coal reserves range from 200 to 500 years at the present rate of use. One of the conservative estimates indicates that, at 2003 production levels, world coal reserves are sufficient to last for 200 years, compared to forty years' reserves of oil and seventy years' reserves of natural gas; for the United Kingdom these figures are fifty-three, 5.4 and 6.1 years, correspondingly (British Petroleum statistics, 2003; Rudrum Holdings, 2001). Even if a significant part of coal is used for hydrogen production, the already available coal reserves will last much longer than those of oil, especially in the case of the United Kingdom.

The economic viability of any hydrogen production method will be strongly affected by regional factors (the availability of renewable energy sources, delivery approaches, taxation, etc.). In any fully developed hydrogen economy, one anticipates that hydrogen will be produced both centrally in large energy complexes, distributed at renewable power facilities, and also locally – in refuelling stations, communities, and on-site at customers' premises. The development and implementation of such a diverse range of hydrogen production techniques requires substantial technological advances, and the social acceptability of any such development. As noted by Turner, 'The vision of using energy from electricity and electrolysis to generate hydrogen from water for transportation and energy storage . . . is compelling, but as yet remains unrealized' (Turner, 2004).

12.3.2.2 The storage of hydrogen One of the greatest technological barriers to the widespread use of hydrogen is the lack of a safe, low-weight and low-cost storage method with a high energy density (Schlapbach and Züttel, 2001; Kennedy, 2004; Harris et al., 2004). Viable hydrogen storage is often cited as the key to an effective hydrogen economy. Whilst this is a highly focused problem for hydrogen-powered fuel cell vehicles, which have to store hydrogen on board, the storage problem is certainly not limited to that use; large-scale storage also represents a major challenge in the transportation and the use of high-volume quantities of hydrogen. Various hydrogen storage methods are summarised below.

Non-solid-state storage methods:

- compressed hydrogen gas;
- liquid cryogenically cooled hydrogen; and
- hydrogen storage through liquid ammonia, where hydrogen can be subsequently released through dissociation (this requires high temperature and/or pressure and catalysts; another drawback is that some fuel cells are highly sensitive to ammonia).

Solid-state storage methods:

- transition and lanthanide metal hydrides (including new ternary/quaternary transition metal hydrides);
- light metal hydrides and complex alanates (e.g. MgH_2 and $NaAlH_4$, respectively);
- various forms of carbon, encompassing porous (high-surface-area) carbons, nanotubes and nanostructures;
- open-framework (porous) organic and inorganic structures; and
- new materials.

At present, conventional hydrogen storage solutions include liquid hydrogen and compressed gas cylinders. However, a substantial energy input is necessary for either liquefying or compressing the hydrogen.

There are also major safety concerns associated with these techniques (high pressure and liquid hydrogen boil-off). The most likely short-term solution is the use of composite pressure vessels for both stationary power plants and for portable and mobile power systems, although legitimate safety concerns will need to be addressed before any such high-pressure storage technology could be widely adopted – and widely accepted by the public.

The development of new solid-state hydrogen storage systems using advanced materials could herald a breakthrough in the technology of hydrogen storage and would have a major impact on the transition to a hydrogen economy (Harris et al., 2004; National Academy of Engineering and Board on Energy and Environmental Systems, 2004; US Department of Energy, Office of Science, 2004; Turner, 2004; Schlapbach and Züttel, 2001; Sandrock and Bowman, 2003; Grochala and Edwards, 2004). For transportation uses, a suitable solid-state storage material should be able to store a high weight percentage of hydrogen and contain a high volume density of hydrogen, absorb and desorb hydrogen at – or close to – room temperature, and pressure and possess rapid absorption and desorption kinetics. Ideally, such a material should be made from cheap and readily available materials with a straightforward, low-energy preparation method, be resistant to poisoning by trace impurities, have a good thermal conductivity in charged and uncharged conditions, be safe and reusable on exposure to air and have the ability to be regenerated and readily recycled. These represent a particularly challenging set of credentials for an ideal storage material; at present no single material meets all these requirements. Substantial efforts worldwide now focus on a detailed understanding of the chemical and physical processes governing the all-important hydrogen–material interactions as a prelude to the required 'step change' advances necessary in this area.

Hydrogen stored at large power plants would also offer a method of longer-term and larger-scale energy storage and could be used for load balancing to smooth out the mismatch between the fluctuating electrical load in the grid and power output from renewable energy sources. When there is a surplus of electricity from renewable sources, hydrogen could be produced by the electrolysis of water and subsequently stored. During a shortfall of power from renewable sources, the stored hydrogen can be used for electricity production via, for example, fuel cells.

12.3.2.3   The transportation and distribution of hydrogen   New concepts will be needed to reduce delivery costs whilst retaining high safety standards from the point of production through to refuelling stations and distributed power facilities. Although producing hydrogen on a large scale can be done at a reasonably acceptable financial cost (for example, by the steam reformation of methane), the same hydrogen costs at least ten times as much as petrol when delivered to the customer by current methods, such as compressed gas in tube cylinders. In addition, there is clearly a high environmental or 'damage' cost associated with hydrogen produced from hydrocarbon precursors (with concomitant carbon dioxide production).

The current transportation system for delivering conventional fuels to consumers cannot be used for hydrogen. The construction of a new hydrogen pipeline system would require significant investment in connection with the necessary research and development of materials with a low diffusivity to hydrogen and alloys that do not become brittle after contact with hydrogen. Also, the development of a low-cost compressor technology, seals, sensors and controls, as well as refilling stations' infrastructure, is required to ensure the safety of any hydrogen delivery system. Major potential advances in all these areas are highlighted in the European Union's *Hydrogen Energy and Fuel Cells* review from the final report of the High Level Group (European Commission, 2003).

Interestingly, at an early stage, certainly before specialised hydrogen pipelines have been built, the existing natural gas pipelines could possibly be used to carry a mixture containing up to 20 per cent of hydrogen in the natural gas, and this method is already used in the United States. This mixture can also be used to run natural gas fuel cells, or can be chemically reformed at the point of use (obviously at an energy cost) to give pure hydrogen for ultimate use in hydrogen fuel cells. This gas injection/hybrid gas carrier approach could offer an early route to market for the initial small-scale production of hydrogen before separate hydrogen pipelines are built. When hydrogen does become the main energy carrier, sections of the natural gas grid could possibly be changed to pure hydrogen, and the existing local gas appliances would then have to be adjusted to burn hydrogen. This is somewhat similar to events that occurred when the United Kingdom changed from town gas, which was over 50 per cent hydrogen, to natural gas (Hydrogen.co.uk, 2003). During the transition from town gas to natural gas the main part of the country's urban distribution networks (running at low-pressure town gas) was harnessed, with minor modifications, to the new natural gas supply; as a result the cost was not significant. However, this will not be the case for the transition from natural gas to hydrogen, because of its significantly different physical and chemical properties, including the high diffusivity of hydrogen in many materials and alloys, which become brittle after contact with hydrogen. For example, the existing natural gas high-pressure pipelines cannot be used for the transportation of a large amount of hydrogen at high pressure. The low-pressure urban distribution networks should also be modified to accommodate hydrogen, including the development of new sealing materials, gas meters, taps, etc. to operate safely in a hydrogen atmosphere. The majority of appliances will also require modification. All these issues will bring the cost of switching to hydrogen to a significant level.

12.3.2.4 The utilisation of hydrogen   The widespread acceptance of hydrogen as an energy carrier will, obviously, depend on the availability of clean, efficient and economic techniques for its utilisation and conversion to electricity/heat. Using hydrogen in fuel cells or using the natural gas itself in fuel cells produces at least twice as much useful energy for a given amount of fuel as does direct combustion. Therefore, one view is that to get the best use from natural gas it is necessary to use it in fuel cells, either directly or after reforming it into hydrogen. Natural gas fuel cells could possibly develop as an effective bridging technology to a hydrogen-powered economy; similarly, methanol fuel cells have created considerable interest.

The key scientific and technical challenges facing fuel cells are cost reduction and increased durability. These require intensive research in the development of improved or new materials and could lead to the commercial viability of fuel cells in both stationary and mobile applications. The development of new thin-film solid-state fuel cells and hydrogen PEM fuel cells could expand the application of fuel cell technology to small-scale – but large-volume – applications such as laptop batteries and power supplies for other portable electrical equipment. Taking into account the potentially much higher efficiency of fuel-cell-based portable power supplies, this technology could lead to a marked reduction in the future use of electrical batteries.

For transport purposes, hydrogen would be burnt in an internal combustion engine, or would be used to power fuel cell vehicles. Using hydrogen in a fuel cell is twice as efficient as burning it in an internal combustion engine. The development of hydrogen or dual-fuel combustion engines for vehicles can be regarded as a promising intermediate step before the widespread adoption of hydrogen-fuel-cell-powered vehicles (this is the current strategy of BMW).

In summary, the developed hydrogen economy would use hydrogen-powered fuel cells for the full range of applications associated with electric power/heat generation, including large-scale energy generation systems, distributed energy facilities, automotive applications, local power generation, domestic combined heat and power applications, and even portable applications.

12.3.3 Hydrogen safety and public awareness

Safety is not only a technological issue but is also the major psychological and sociological issue facing the adoption of a hydrogen economy. Consumers need to have complete confidence in the safety of hydrogen. A central factor in promoting public confidence will be the development and adoption of internationally accepted codes and standards. Developers will need to optimise carefully new fuel storage and delivery systems for safe, everyday use, and consumers must become familiar with hydrogen's somewhat unfamiliar properties and risks as a fuel. For example, basic programmes on the transport, kinetics and hydrodynamics of hydrogen gas in enclosed structures and on its combustion properties, as well as the development of highly efficient and gas-selective sensors for detecting hydrogen leaks, all form part of the major schemes currently in force in the United States.

This confidence building is necessary for transportation and for stationary residential and portable applications, where consumers will interact directly with both hydrogen and fuel cell technology. Consumers will undoubtedly have concerns about the safety and dependability of fuel-cell-powered equipment, new dispensing technology and so on, just as they had about other modern devices when they were introduced. Education projects, product exposure and marketing methods should be developed in order to facilitate a successful introduction of hydrogen as an alternative fuel (Schulte et al., 2004).

12.4 A European strategy for the transition to the hydrogen economy

These many and significant challenges – encompassing technological through socio-economic issues – will have to be overcome in any transition to a hydrogen economy. The timescale and evolution of such a development is the focus of many 'road maps' emanating from the United States, Japan, Canada and the European Union (amongst many others). For example, a major EU initiative was the establishment of the High Level Group for Hydrogen and Fuel Cells in October 2002. An ambitious – and challenging – proposal for the main elements and timescale of the European road map on the production and distribution of hydrogen and fuel cells has been developed for the period 2000–2005, and the skeleton proposal for the European hydrogen and

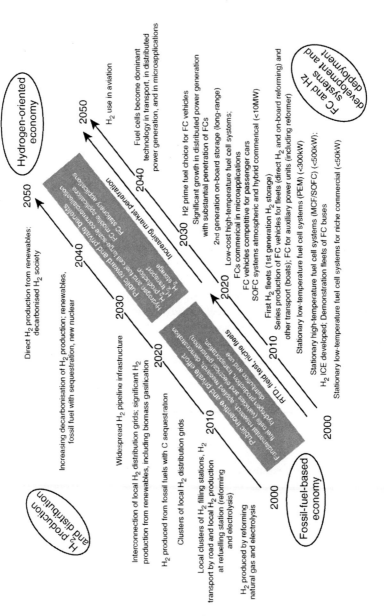

Figure 12.3. The skeleton proposal for the European hydrogen and fuel cell roadmap. Source: European Commission (2003).

fuel cell roadmap is shown here. Within the European hydrogen vision, the transition to a hydrogen economy will be executed along broad (but clearly defined) time lines. The key components in this hydrogen vision relate to hydrogen production, storage and distribution and the fuel cell/hydrogen interface, and encompass many of the scientific issues and challenges outlined earlier. Key highlights and scenarios from this major European perspective are noted below and summarised in figure 12.3 (European Commission, 2003).

12.4.1   Production

Hydrogen will be produced from a variety of sources and using a number of different technologies, both centralised and decentralised. During the transition period hydrogen would almost certainly be produced from natural gas/coal/biomass using advanced and clean reformation/gasification processes with carbon capture and sequestration, as well as by electrolysis using electricity generated by present coal-fired or nuclear power plants. This would enable a reasonably cost-effective supply chain for hydrogen to develop and enable the development and evolution of hydrogen technologies related to transportation, storage, distribution and use.

The cost-competitive technology of electrolytic hydrogen production using renewable energy sources must be developed in tandem, and will gradually replace the reformation/gasification processes. Other advanced processes (photolytic water splitting, the high-temperature pyrolysis of biomass, biological processes, etc.) also need to be rapidly developed in this transition period. Electrolyser technology could provide a central solution to meet both the power management needs of the electricity sector (production and storage of hydrogen during off-peak periods and its use in fuel cells for electricity production when more energy is required) and the needs of the transport and industrial sectors for hydrogen.

12.4.2   Storage

More compact, low-weight, lower-cost, safe and efficient storage systems will need to be developed for automotive and larger-scale applications (see figure 12.3). At the initial stage these will include high-pressure and cryogenic storage systems, which will gradually be replaced by low-cost and high-density solid-state storage systems operating at low temperatures and pressures. Note that first-generation hydrogen storage units are scheduled for around 2010, with second-generation on-board stores (for long-range transportation) by approximately 2025.

12.4.3   Distribution

The basic components of a hydrogen delivery infrastructure need to be developed, initially to supply local refilling stations. Subsequently, the components of a national hydrogen delivery and distribution network (including hydrogen pipelines) will need to be developed to provide a reliable supply of low-cost hydrogen. In some areas it will be cheaper to produce hydrogen locally – for example, at refilling stations – by the electrolysis of water or by effective (small-scale) reformation units.

12.4.4   Utilisation and applications

Fuel cells will be widely used, for which hydrogen will be extracted directly from a hydrocarbon source, such as natural gas, methanol or petrol, and using the existing infrastructure for the distribution of fossil fuel. Low-cost and durable hydrogen-powered fuel cells, engines and turbines will have to be developed and become mature technologies in mass production for use in cars, houses and factories. The European vision has hydrogen fuel cell vehicles becoming competitive with existing technology by approximately 2018 (see figure 12.3).

To realise a positive environmental impact, fuel cell vehicles must be sold in large quantities. The use of hybrid vehicles, which comprise both a fuel cell and a conventional or hydrogen combustion engine, may be an intermediate step to fuel cell commercialisation.

Before the development of a large-scale national hydrogen infrastructure, the introduction of hydrogen into the economy could start from 'islands' of hydrogen availability – for example, building and expanding the network of hydrogen filling stations. In the European vision, clusters of local hydrogen distribution grids begin to appear about a decade from now. Vehicular transportation represents one of the main sources of air pollutants. Transferring even a part of the vehicle fleet from petrol to hydrogen would have a significant environmental impact.

At the next step, hydrogen and fuel cell technology will be used to provide combined electricity and heat for households, businesses and industrial processes. Fuel cells will play a key role in large-scale electricity generation and as a means of backing up intermittent renewable power sources. Significant growth in distributed power generation – with substantial penetration of fuel cells – is envisaged by the late 2020s. A recent report by Pricewaterhouse Coopers (2002) projects global demand for all fuel cell products (in portable, stationary and transportation power applications) to reach \$46 billion per year by 2011 and to grow to more than \$2.5 trillion per year by 2021.

12.5 Specific comments relating to the United Kingdom

The general plan for the transition to the hydrogen economy in the United Kingdom was formulated in the government's White Paper no. 68 *Our Energy Future: Creating a Low-Carbon Economy* (DTI, 2003). To address the environmental, political and economical reasons for the transition to the hydrogen economy, the White Paper formulates four long-term goals (paragraph 1):

- to cut the UK's carbon dioxide emissions by some 60% by about 2050 with real progress by 2020;
- to maintain the reliability of energy supplies;
- to promote competitive markets in the UK and beyond, helping to raise the rate of sustainable economic growth and to improve our productivity; and
- to ensure that every home is adequately and affordably heated.

There are also several documents issued by Parliamentary Committees on subjects related to the hydrogen economy and renewable energy, including *Prospects for a Hydrogen Economy*, published by the Parliamentary Office of Science and Technology in October 2002 (POST, 2002). In addition, there are several initiatives, including the London Hydrogen Partnership, launched in April 2002, that will develop and implement the London Hydrogen Action Plan as a road map for clean energy in the city, and may provide the experience for a national plan. In the framework of the partnership, comprehensive modelling of the infrastructure needed for the refuelling of hydrogen fuel-cell buses in London has recently been undertaken (Joffe et al., 2004). As yet, however, there is no detailed programme for the transition to the hydrogen economy, that sets targets, milestones and a time line for the United Kingdom (for comparison, see the European hydrogen and fuel cell road map: figure 12.3; European Commission, 2003).

In 2004 the DTI commissioned an analysis to identify current UK expertise in hydrogen and areas where hydrogen could meet major UK policy priorities; the final report was published at the end of that year (E4tech, Element Energy, Eoin Lees Energy, 2004). The report considers potential UK hydrogen activities up to 2030, including transport, stationary and other applications. It concludes that hydrogen energy offers an opportunity for UK innovation and growth, represents a key option for the long-term, cost-competitive reduction of carbon dioxide emissions and a means of improving the energy security of the country, and possesses a number of other benefits. The main barrier to the deployment of hydrogen in the near term is the absence of viable end users, mainly commercialised fuel-cell vehicles. Significant innovations are also required in hydrogen storage and transportation infrastructure before hydrogen can be deployed widely as an energy carrier.

The United Kingdom has internationally leading research in several areas, such as hydrogen storage and fuel cell materials, novel non-nuclear hydrogen production technologies and systems analysis related to hydrogen infrastructure (E4tech, Element Energy, Eoin Lees Energy 2004). To achieve decisive advances in these and other key areas of the developing hydrogen economy, proactive and long-term governmental backing is required with consistent funding and guidance to meet the priority targets. Five main areas were identified where the government should be involved in developing hydrogen options for the United Kingdom:

- the coordination of the country's hydrogen activities;
- support for research and development;
- support for the demonstration of hydrogen systems;
- support for product commercialisation; and
- policy changes to help create demand for hydrogen.

A recent Hydrogen Vision workshop (SHEC, 2004), held under the auspices of the SuperGen Sustainable Hydrogen Energy Consortium, identified the (emerging) key areas regarding the transition to a hydrogen economy in the United Kingdom.

- The United Kingdom has a substantial renewable energy capability, claimed by some to be sufficient to provide this country's sustainable energy needs. This represents a major incentive to provide the country with a primary medium-long-term hydrogen economy objective.
- There is a need for technology development not just through research but, equally importantly, through the integration of research with *large-scale* demonstration and utilisation projects.
- Hydrogen derived from fossil fuels, especially natural gas, will be an important part of any transition, both for demonstration projects and early applications.
- Public engagement and acceptance – at the broadest level – is now vital. In relation to this, the issue of safety and public awareness of the benefits of utilising hydrogen energy are key to the adoption of the new energy technologies based on hydrogen.
- The development of comprehensive technical safety and performance standards for hydrogen technologies suitable for mainstream applications is crucial (rather than the standards developed solely for the chemical/gas production industry).

- The government will need to play a strong role in coordinating and funding research – most notably in the short term – and in providing a long-term regulatory framework to identify and deliver the sources of revenue for early hydrogen development. Similar efforts will need to be made to develop the United Kingdom's renewable energy base, widely recognised as being essential to the long-term vision of sustainable hydrogen energy.

12.6   Concluding remarks

Hydrogen has outstanding potential for becoming a major element in catalysing the transition of the global energy system to a sustainable future. There are multiple ways by which a hydrogen economy could evolve, depending upon many factors – regional and global.

Any assessment of the feasibility of a sustainable hydrogen-energy economy will involve an appraisal of the many steps that will have to be taken on the road to that future – not only steps in sciences and technology but also social and economic considerations. The 'systems approach' of looking at the future of hydrogen energy, outlined in the recent *Strategic Framework for Hydrogen Energy in the UK* (E4tech, Element Energy, Eoin Lees Energy, 2004), also concludes that there is not one single route to a hydrogen economy but, rather, that many factors/variables are involved in determining its direction. It may therefore be not just rather difficult but, indeed, limiting to attempt to establish a single path to the hydrogen economy at this juncture.

In figure 12.4, developed by Bellaby et al.,[2] we see just some of the key issues that have to be confronted; as shown, the challenges and problems are many, complex and intertwined. Bellaby et al. note:

In a nutshell, the viability of a hydrogen future depends on the combination of long-term (concerted) political will and short-term competition in the market from other energies. Other 'alternative energies' are not necessarily competitors for hydrogen, because hydrogen is an energy carrier and not sustainable in the future if the primary energy sources are fossil fuels. Even though fossil fuels are going to run out, it is not entirely clear when that will happen (since not all reserves are known) and until that point is approached, fossil fuels are likely to remain highly competitive with all alternatives, not least hydrogen.

It is abundantly clear that a multitude of factors will work, at national and international levels, to influence any possible transition to a hydrogen economy; these are the great unknowns – the backdrop against

---

[2] Personal communication from P. Bellaby, K. Ross and R. Flyan to P. P. Edwards at SHEC Technical Meeting, London, 28–9 October 2004.

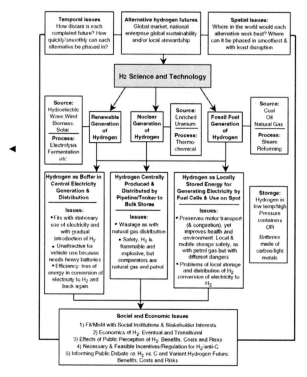

Figure 12.4. The challenges and problems of a possible hydrogen economy.

which the unfolding story of hydrogen will be played out.[3] *This will be quite a compelling story!*

12.7   References

British Petroleum (2003). *BP Statistics*, London: British Petroleum, available from: http://www.bp.com/genericarticle.do?categoryId=113&contentId= 2014980.

Department of Energy (2004). *Hydrogen Posture Plan: an Integrated Research, Development, and Demonstration Plan*, Washington, DC: Department of Energy, available from http://www.eere.energy.gov/hydrogenandfuelcells/pdfs/hydrogen_posture_plan.pdf.

---

[3] Personal communication from M. Eames to P. P. Edwards at SHEC Technical Meeting, London, 28–9 October 2004.

DTI (2003). *Our Energy Future: Creating a Low-Carbon Economy*, Energy White Paper no. 68, Cm5761, Department of Trade and Industry, London: available from http://www.dti.gov.uk/energy/whitepaper/ourenergyfuture.pdf.

Dunn, S. (2002). Hydrogen futures: toward a sustainable energy system, *International Journal of Hydrogen Energy*, 27: 235–64.

Dunn, S. (2001). *Hydrogen Futures: Towards a Sustainable Energy System*. Worldwatch Paper no. 157, Oxon Hill, MD: World Watch Institute.

Dutton, A. G. (2003). The hydrogen economy and carbon abatement: implications and challenges for wind energy, *Wind Engineering*, 27: 239–55.

E4tech, Element Energy, Eoin Lees Energy, (2004). *A Strategic Framework for Hydrogen Energy in the UK*, final report to the Department of Trade and Industry, London: E4 tech, available from http://www.dti.gov.uk/energy/sepn/hydrogen.shtml

European Commission (2003). *Hydrogen Energy and Fuel Cells: a Vision of Our Future*, Brussels: European Commision, available from http://www.europa.eu.int/comm/research/energy/pdf/hydrogen-report_en.pdf.

Fuelcelltoday.com (2004). *How soon for Hydrogen?*, fuelcelltoday.com, http://www.fuelcelltoday.com/FuelCellToday/IndustryInformation/IndustryInformationExternal/NewsDisplayArticle/0,1602,4820,00.html.

Geiger, S. (2004). *Fuel Cell Market Survey: Automotive Hydrogen Infrastructure*, Fuel Cell Today. http://www.fuelcelltoday.com/FuelCellToday/FCTFiles/FCTArticleFiles/Article_805_hydrogensurvey0504.pdf.

Gosselink, J. W. (2002). Pathways to a more sustainable production of energy: sustainable hydrogen - a research objective for Shell, *International Journal of Hydrogen Energy*, 27: 1125–9.

Grochala, W., and P. P. Edwards (2004). Thermal decomposition of the non-interstitial hydrides for the storage and production of hydrogen, *Chemical Reviews*, 104: 1283–315.

Harris, I. R., D. Book, P. A. Anderson and P. P. Edwards (2004). Hydrogen storage: the grand challenge, *Fuel Cell Review*, 1(1) 17–23.

Hart, D. (2003). Hydrogen – a truly sustainable transport fuel?, *Frontiers in Ecology and the Environment*, 1: 138–45.

Hasselman, K. H., J. Schellnhuber, and O. Edenhofer (2004). Climate change: complexity in action, *Physics World*, 17: 31–5.

Hawkes, F. R., R. Dinsdale, D. L. Hawkes and I. Hussy (2002). Sustainable fermentative hydrogen production: challenges for process optimisation, *International Journal of Hydrogen Energy*, 27: 1339–47.

Hoffman, P. (2001). *Tomorrow's Energy*. Cambridge, MA: MIT Press.

Hydrogen.co.uk (2003). *The Likely Development of Hydrogen Supplies for the UK and Sequence of Events for Developing UK Hydrogen*, hydrogen.co.uk, http://www.hydrogen.co.uk/h2/h2_page2.htm.

HyNet (2004). *Towards a European Hydrogen Energy Roadmap*, hynet.info, http://www.hynet.info/hyactiv/docs/HyNet_HTP_Launch_Conference_21_01-04.pdf http://www.hynet.info/publications/docs/HYNETroadmap_ABSTRACT_MAY2004.pdf.

Joffe, D., D. Hart and A. Bauen (2004). Modelling of hydrogen infrastructure for vehicle refuelling in London, *Journal of Power Sources*, 131: 13–22.

Joint Research Centre (2003). *Hydrogen Storage: State-of-the-Art and Future Perspective* Brussels: available from http://www.jrc.nl/publ/P2003-181= EUR 20995EN.pdf.

Kennedy, D. (2004). The hydrogen solution, *Science*, 305: 917.

King, D. A. (2004). Climate change science: adapt, mitigate, or ignore, *Science*, 303: 176–7.

May, R. (2004). Anniversary presidential address to the Royal Society, available from http://www.royalsoc.ac.uk/publication/asp?id=2181.

Momirlan, M., and T. N. Veziroglu (2002). Current status of hydrogen energy, *Renewable and Sustainable Energy Reviews*, 6: 141–79.

National Academy of Engineering and Board on Energy and Environmental Systems (2004). *The Hydrogen Economy: Opportunities, Costs, Barriers and R&D Needs*, Washington, DC: National Academies Press.

Nicoletti, G. (1995). The hydrogen option for energy: a review of technical, environmental and economic aspects, *International Journal of Hydrogen Energy*, 20: 759–65.

Office of Science (2004). *Basic Research Needs for the Hydrogen Economy*, Report of the Basic Energy Sciences Workshop on Hydrogen Production. Washingdon, DC: Department of Energy, available from http://www.sc.doe.gov/bes/hydrogen.pdf.

Ogden, J. M. (2002). Hydrogen: the fuel of the future?, *Physics Today*, 55: 69–75.

POST (2002). *Prospects for a Hydrogen Economy*, London: Parliamentary Office of Science and Technology, available from http://www.parliament.uk/post/pn186.pdf.

Pricewaterhouse Coopers (2002). *Fuel Cells: the Opportunity for Canada*, London: Pricewaterhouse Coopers.

Roberts, P. (2004). *The End of Oil*. London: Bloomsbury.

Rudrum Holdings (2001). *Global Hard Coal Statistics*, Bristol: Rudrum Holdings, available from http://www.rudrumholdings.co.uk/second_level_pages/ff2.htm.

Sandrock, G., and R. C. Bowman (2003). Gas-based hydride applications: recent progress and future needs, *Journal of Alloys and Compounds*, 356: 794–9.

Schlapbach, L., and A. Züttel (2001). Hydrogen-storage materials for mobile applications, *Nature*, 414: 353–8.

Schulte I., D. Hart and R. van der Vorst (2004). Issues affecting the acceptance of hydrogen fuel, *International Journal of Hydrogen Energy*, 29: 677–85.

SHEC (2004). *Hydrogen Visions Workshop Report*, London: Sustainable Hydrogen Energy Consortium, available from: http://www.uk-shec.org/files/UKSHECHVWR.pdf.

Spacedaily.com (2004). *Cool Fuel Cells*, available from: http://www.spacedaily.com/news/energy-tech-04zz.html.

Turner, J. A. (2004). Sustainable hydrogen production, *Science*, 305: 972–4.

Winter, M., and R. J. Brodd (2004). What are batteries, fuel cells, and super-capacitors?, *Chemical Reviews*, 104: 4245–69.

13 Electrical energy storage

Alan Ruddell

13.1 Introduction

The supply of electrical power to a network of consumers involves continuously matching the supply of generated power to the load demand. This has to be achieved economically, while maintaining high levels of supply security and reliability, and high quality of supply in terms of voltage and frequency regulation. National power networks have generally been designed with large centralised generators, situated near fuel resource centres, with a high-voltage transmission grid and low-voltage distribution (T&D) network to supply the load centres. Overall demand is smoothed in the short term by diversity, with diurnal and seasonal variations, and is approximately predictable on an hourly basis. Demand prediction allows power generation plant to be optimally scheduled according to the plant economics and response time; and the demand deviations are balanced by governor control of on-line generators, together with fast-response generators and spinning reserve that can be brought on-line at short notice.

Although the energy source can be stored for some forms of renewable generation, such as hydro and biomass, and power is despatchable according to load demand, other forms, such as wind and solar photovoltaics, are responsive to instantaneous meteorological conditions such as wind speed and solar irradiance. There is also likely to be increased generation by combined heat and power systems (CHP), which offer efficiency improvements, improved economics and reduction of CO_2 emissions, but are generally driven by heat demand. In general, it is desirable to be able to control generated power on demand, and, indeed, the economics of electricity trading places a premium on predictability.

The nature of generation from dispersed renewable sources and CHP means that generators are relatively small (for example, less than 10MW) and connected into the distribution network, where the power is used locally. While modest penetration of distributed generation of the order of 10 per cent to 20 per cent may be possible within existing T&D

303

structures, it is widely believed that power systems will have to evolve to accommodate increased utilisation of distributed generation (DTI, 2003). Existing supply networks are basically unidirectional, delivering power from a few central power generating nodes, through the T&D network branches to individual loads. A high level of distributed generation may require bidirectional power flow networks, with control of power routing. It is not yet clear how large existing networks will be adapted for new requirements; however, some aspects are being actively investigated, including the possible benefits of microgrids or 'quasi-autonomous operation', and, on the other hand, the possible opportunities for Europe-wide transmission and trading networks. Meanwhile, there is a pressing need for rural electrification schemes in developing countries, where multiple autonomous networks in geographically dispersed areas may be more economic than a single, large interconnected grid network.

A simple calculation illustrates the challenge of incorporating high levels of renewable generation in the United Kingdom, where 10 per cent (or approximately 40TWh per annum) of electricity generation would mean 10–15GW of wind generation capacity, assuming capacity factor in the range 30 per cent to 45 per cent (Jenkins and Strbac, 2000). The minimum summer loading in the United Kingdom is less than 20GW, and to ensure stability when maximum wind generation coincides with minimum loading it may at times be necessary to reduce wind generation output, or to trade on a large interconnected European grid or to store bulk electrical energy. A full analysis of the impact and economics of storage in an electricity system requires knowledge of the storage technology performance and lifetime, which can be used in simulation models to consider various scenarios of generation mix and distribution network topology.

13.2   Energy storage applications

A group of experts in the United States identified and defined applications for electricity storage in power systems, ranging from power quality improvement ('high power' storage, in the range of seconds), to the replacement of spinning reserve for grid stability and the need for generation scheduling (in the range of minutes), and to load levelling, peak shaving and energy management ('high energy' storage, in the range of hours), as summarised graphically in figure 13.1. Here the term 'storage time' is defined as the discharge time at rated power (calculated as storage capacity divided by rated power), rather than the storage interval or period.

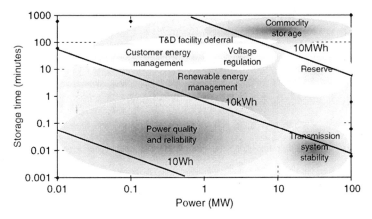

Figure 13.1. The electricity storage spectrum.

The study by Butler et al. (2002) suggests that the management of renewable energy generation in electric power utility applications can potentially benefit from storage over a very wide spectrum of power (10kW to 100MW), storage time (0.1 seconds to 10 hours) and energy. A report by the European Commission (2001) suggests that the integration of renewable energy into the electricity grid requires a range of storage systems with rated power greater than 10kW, and storage times from around 0.1 hours up to twenty-four hours. The rated power and the storage time (discharge time at rated power) are key parameters, which categorise storage requirements and appropriate storage technologies. The ratio of rated power to energy capacity (P/E) (or its inverse, the storage time) leads to categories of 'high power' and 'high energy' storage, as summarised in table 13.1.

Early studies by Davidson et al. (1980) reviewed the potential for large-scale bulk energy storage in the United Kingdom, while Infield (1984) studied the role of electricity storage and central electricity generation. The latter study concluded that there was an economic case for increased levels of efficient storage, and that T&D losses could be reduced if storage was distributed rather than centralised.

At the 'power' end of the spectrum (storage times in the region of seconds to minutes), storage is applicable for power quality improvement and for transmission grid stability applications. Power quality improvement measures applied at the distribution network level include the mitigation of voltage dips and sags caused by faults elsewhere in the transmission system, and the reduction of voltage fluctuations (including 'flicker') and voltage rise caused by distributed generators. The wide

Table 13.1 *Summary of power/energy requirements*

P/E (hour $^{-1}$)	Storage time	Applications
< 1 'energy' storage	> 1 hour	• Load levelling
		• Peak shaving
60 to 1	1 minute to 1 hour	• Spinning reserve
		• Frequency and voltage regulation
> 60 'power' storage	< 1 minute	• Power quality improvement
		• Transmission grid stability

spectrum of power and energy requirements means that a range of storage technologies may be needed.

The categories in table 13.1 are applicable to large power systems. Stand-alone or hybrid power systems with high levels of renewable energy penetration may also require short-term storage for power bridging when scheduling or starting generating sets, in addition to power quality improvement.

Other key technical parameters include the cycling requirements (or lifetime energy throughput), the response time and the in–out efficiency. Environmental issues include the safety of materials, emissions during manufacture and operation, and end-of-life recycling and waste management.

13.3   Utilisation of storage worldwide

Worldwide, the total power of utility-scale storage in 1996 was 90GW, representing less than 3 per cent of total generation capacity (Price, 1998). Some countries have considerably higher levels of storage, as shown in table 13.2. The storage technology is mainly pumped hydro, providing both high power and high energy storage for load levelling and peak lopping, and fast-response spinning reserve.

At the other end of the energy spectrum, there is considerable interest in 'high power' storage for power quality improvement and stability, and applications are emerging for flywheel, superconducting magnetic energy storage (SMES) and supercapacitor technologies.

The application of bulk storage in a power system depends on the generation mix and the load profile. Davidson et al. (1980) identified a requirement for bulk storage in the United Kingdom in which nuclear generation was expected to provide baseload capacity, together with slow-response thermal power stations. The increasing use of fast-response gas turbines has dramatically changed the characteristics of the generation mix, and there is now no clear economic case for additional bulk storage in the existing system.

Table 13.2 *Utilisation of utility-scale storage worldwide, 1996*

	Total installed capacity (MW)	Storage installed capacity (MW)	Penetration of storage (%)
United States	778,000	19,000	2.4
South Africa	39,000	1,500	3.8
United Kingdom	73,000	2,800	3.8
South Korea	34,000	1,700	5.0
Belgium	14,000	1,200	8.4
Italy	56,000	5,400	9.5
Japan	219,000	21,000	9.6

Source: Price (1998) and Utility Data Institute.

Storage is viewed differently in Japan, where approximately 80 per cent of primary fuel is imported and where there is continuing development of nuclear power generation as a baseload power source. Energy policy in Japan has been driven by considerations of energy security and the need to minimise dependence on imported fuels, as well as the need to achieve greenhouse gas reduction; a ten-year energy plan submitted in 2001 called for an increase in nuclear power generation of around 30 per cent. A study by Tanaka and Kurihara (1998) has considered the future social structure change factors affecting demand, and the future generation mix, assuming various growth scenarios. The study predicts that the optimum capacity of energy storage in Japan by 2050 will be in the range 40–65GW, about 10 per cent to 15 per cent of the predicted generation capacity. This should be compared with the storage capacity in 1996 of around 20GW, which was 9.6 per cent of the generation capacity. The main drivers appear to be the increased difference between maximum daytime and minimum night-time loading caused by social structure changes, and the future generation mix favouring nuclear operating as baseload.

Utilisation of storage worldwide is mainly pumped hydro, and for environmental and economic reasons the potential for future development is limited. Therefore, it is clearly important to develop energy storage systems based on new technologies.

13.4 Storage technologies

Electrical energy may be stored by transforming it into another form of energy, categorised into electrochemical, electromechanical or electrical energy forms.

Table 13.3 *General suitability of storage technologies*

Technology:	Application	'Energy' storage, load levelling, peak shaving	Spinning reserve, frequency and voltage regulation	'Power' storage, power quality improvement, transmission grid stability
	Storage time:	> 1 hour	1 minute to 1 hour	< 1 minute
Electrochemical storage	Batteries	●	●	●
	Flow cells	●	○	
Electromechanical storage	Pumped hydro	●		
	CAES	●		
	Flywheel		○	●
Electrical storage	SMES		○	●
	Supercapacitor			●

NB:
● = suitable; ○ = possible.

Electrochemical storage:

- batteries (where the electrodes are part of the chemical reaction) – lead–acid, lithium ion, nickel cadmium, sodium sulphur;
- flow cells (where the electrodes are catalysts for the chemical reaction) – polysulphide bromide, vanadium, zinc bromine; and
- hydrogen electrolysers and fuel cells.

Electromechanical storage:

- pumped hydro;
- compressed air energy storage (CAES) and small compressed air storage; and
- flywheels.

Electrical storage:

- superconducting magnetic energy storage (SMES); and
- supercapacitors (which may also be considered as electrochemical storage).

The storage technologies have distinctly different characteristics, including the feasibility of implementation at various power or energy ratings, and they are at different states of technical and commercial maturity. Therefore, it is possible to make only general observations of their suitability for applications categorised according to storage times, as shown in table 13.3. The information presented in table 13.3 has been drawn from various sources, which also contain more details of the individual technologies (European Commission, 2001; Butler et al., 2002; Electricity Storage Association (technologies and applications: http://www.electricitystorage.org/)).

The overall cost of energy storage, including capital costs, O&M costs and losses, is a key factor. The choice of technology also depends on the size of the storage units and the operational profile. Cost comparisons are difficult, because costs may be quoted in terms of kWh or kW installed, while the operational cost per kWh throughput over the whole lifetime may be application-dependent and not quoted by manufacturers.

Batteries such as lead–acid and nickel cadmium are suitable for a wide range of applications, while advanced batteries with enhanced characteristics are under development but have not reached the same level of maturity. Reviews of nine storage technologies (lead–acid batteries; lithium batteries; nickel batteries (nickel zinc, nickel cadmium, nickel metal hydride); metal–air batteries; electrolysers, hydrogen storage, and fuel cells; redox flow cells; flywheels; compressed air; and supercapacitors) have been completed as part of the INVESTIRE network, and the Storage Technology Reports are available from http://www.itpower. co.uk/investire. The reports include a comparison of commercial systems and references for further information. The reports also include discussion of other factors that define performance, such as reliability, availability, ease of maintenance and service infrastructure, and safety. Information on storage technologies has been further expanded as part of the GreenNet project (European Commission, 2003).

13.4.1 *Electrochemical storage technologies*

Electrochemical storage can be subdivided into batteries, where the electrodes are part of the chemical reaction, and flow cells, where the electrodes are catalysts for the chemical reaction. Recent developments and installations of electrochemical energy storage have been reviewed by Price (2003).

13.4.1.1 Batteries Batteries are generally used as the storage technology in the mid-range of the energy spectrum. Large battery systems with storage times of one to several hours have been installed worldwide in peak shaving, load levelling, frequency control and spinning reserve applications, usually to provide security of supply in remote areas.

Lead–acid battery systems (flooded and valve-regulated) include the 20MW, 14MWh system installed in Puerto Rico in 1994 and the 1.4MWh system installed at Metlakatla, Alaska, in 1997. The largest battery is the 27MW, 6.75MWh (0.25 hours) nickel cadmium system installed at Fairbanks, Alaska, in 2003 (see chapter 11 on power electronics in this volume).

Batteries such as lead–acid and nickel cadmium are suitable for a wide range of applications, while advanced batteries with enhanced characteristics are under development but have not reached the same level of maturity. Nickel cadmium batteries have a long lifetime, and provide a wide operating temperature range, but have a higher initial cost. Although other battery technologies are being used for specialised applications, the lead–acid battery is the most economic choice for utility storage applications and is likely to be the standard choice for some time.

The overall reaction in a lead–acid battery is

$$PbO_2 + Pb + 2H_2SO_4 \qquad <=> \quad 2PbSO_4 + 2H_2O$$
$$\text{(charged)} \qquad\qquad\qquad \text{(discharged)}$$

However, it is informative to describe the reaction at each electrode, both of which are partially converted to lead sulphate during discharge:

positive electrode: $PbO_2 + 4H^+ + SO_4^{2-} + 2e^- <=> PbSO_4 + 2H_2O$
negative electrode: $Pb + SO_4^{2-} \qquad\qquad\qquad <=> PbSO_4 + 2e^-$
$$\text{(charged)} \qquad\qquad\qquad\qquad \text{(discharged)}$$

The lifetime of lead–acid batteries is limited by various ageing processes, including irreversible sulphation of the plates, degradation of the active mass, and corrosion.

13.4.1.2 Flow cells

The electrodes in regenerative flow cells are catalysts for the chemical reaction, and energy is stored in electrolytes that can be stored externally to the cell, as shown in figure 13.2. The most obvious advantage of flow cells compared with other electrochemical storage systems is the possibility of independently specifying power and energy ratings. A large number of charge–discharge cycles are possible; there is no degradation for deep discharge, and no memory effect. Various electrolyte couples can be used, and the main technologies under development are as follows.

(a) Vanadium redox. The electrochemistry of the vanadium redox battery involves vanadium at different valence states, and the reactions at each electrode are

positive electrode: $V^{4+} \qquad <=> V^{5+} + e^-$
negative electrode: $V^{3+} + e^- \quad <=> V^{2+}$
$$\text{(discharged)} <=> \text{(charged)}$$

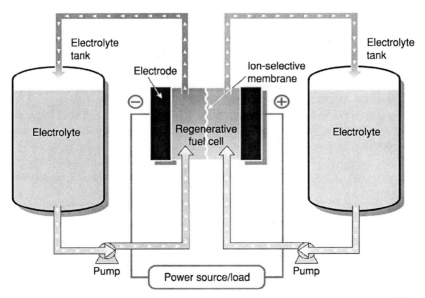

Figure 13.2. The principle of a regenerative flow cell.
Source: VRB Power Systems, Vancouver.

In 2004 VRB Power Systems (Vancouver) acquired all worldwide patents for vanadium technology, other than Australian patent rights, from the technology developer Pinnacle (Australia). Pinnacle and VRB Power Systems have installed two large systems. A 250kW, 8 hour system in a remote location in Utah was completed in 2004, and is used to supply peak power by load levelling/peak shaving. A 200kW, 4 hour system in a remote wind–diesel power system on King Island, Australia, was completed in 2003, and is used to smooth wind power and load fluctuations, ensuring optimum performance of the diesel and wind generation systems. Sumitomo Electric Industries (Japan) is licensed to use and market the technology, and has installed several systems in Japan up to 500kW, 10 hours.

A separate company, Cellennium (Thailand) Company Limited, is developing vanadium technology based on the intellectual property owned by Squirrel Holdings, and has been licensed to proceed with commercialisation in Thailand; it is the intention that the licence will be expanded in the future to cover the rest of Asia. The key advantages claimed by Cellennium for its technology include a novel cell architecture based on a stack of series flow cells and a method of electrolyte production by dissolving vanadium pentoxide in acid. Cellennium received grant funding from the Thai government in 2004, to develop 5–100kW demonstration systems for various applications, including solar, wind and load levelling applications.

(b) Polysulphide bromide. The electrolytes are concentrated solutions of sodium bromide (NaBr) and sodium polysulphide (Na_2S_4). The simplified overall chemical reaction for the cell, where electrical balance is maintained by the transport of sodium ions across the ion-selective membrane, is given by

$$3NaBr + Na_2S_4 \quad <=> \quad NaBr_3 + 2Na_2S_2$$
(discharged)   (charged)

Regenesys (UK) developed this technology to an advanced stage, and two demonstration plants of 15MW, 120MWh capacity were constructed but not commissioned. The technology rights were acquired by VRB Power Systems (Vancouver) in 2004 to complement its own technologies, providing products for very large utility-scale applications from 10–100MW, with eight to ten hours' storage time.

(c) Zinc bromine. When discharged, the electrolytes consist of zinc and bromine ions in solution. During charge, metallic zinc is deposited on the negative electrode, and bromine evolves at the positive electrode and becomes thick bromine oil, which sinks to the bottom of the electrolyte tank. During discharge, the bromine oil is mixed with the electrolyte and is reduced to bromine ions at the positive electrode, while the metallic zinc is oxidised to zinc ions at the negative electrode. The reactions at each electrode are

positive electrode: $2Br^-$ $\qquad <=> \quad Br_2 + 2e^-$

negative electrode: $Zn^{2+} + 2e^-$ $\quad <=> \quad Zn$
$\qquad\qquad$ (discharged) $\qquad\qquad$ (charged)

ZBB Energy Corporation (United States and Australia) produces a containerised 250kW, 500kWh product, and several systems have been installed in the United States in order to provide reinforcement in weak distribution networks and for power quality improvement in industrial applications. The company also markets 50kWh modules that can provide peak shaving, power quality improvement and uninterruptible power supply functions in an integrated energy management system.

13.4.1.3 Hydrogen fuel cells   Hydrogen can be used for energy storage, using an electrolyser to produce hydrogen, and a fuel cell to produce electricity. The key advantage is the ability to specify power and energy independently but the capital cost of components is high and the system has a low overall efficiency of 25 per cent to 30 per cent. Storage of hydrogen may be provided at large scale in low-pressure underground caverns, or at medium to small scale in compressed tanks or bottles (between about 70 bar and 300 bar). The liquefaction of hydrogen gas uses 30 per cent of the original energy, and requires cryogenic storage at around 20K. Other methods under development include the use of metal hydrides, which can currently store 1 per cent to 2 per cent content by weight (% w/w), and carbon structures, which potentially could store 30 per cent to 40 per cent w/w. The current development objective for metal hydrides for hydrogen storage in vehicles is 7 per cent w/w.

13.4.2 Electromechanical storage technologies

13.4.2.1 Pumped hydro The main utility storage worldwide is pumped hydro. The principle is simple: two reservoirs at different altitudes are used, and the upper reservoir is used as a potential energy store for water pumped from the lower reservoir. Pumping usually takes place overnight, when electricity demand and the marginal cost are both at their lowest, while regeneration provides load levelling, peak lopping and fast-response spinning reserve for frequency control in the event of load or generation disturbances.

Pumped hydro storage has many advantages, including fast response, large amounts of stored energy and high efficiency. Disadvantages include the high capital cost, the time to complete construction and the availability of suitable sites.

The total installed storage capacity in the United Kingdom is 2,800MW, provided by several plants at Festiniog, Foyers, Cruachan and Dinorwig. The plant at Dinorwig was completed in 1983 after ten years' construction, and is particularly impressive. It is rated at 1,800MW for five hours' storage time, with a response time of sixteen seconds to full power (or two minutes from a cold start), and 78 per cent average cycle efficiency. Pumped storage in the United Kingdom represents 3.5 per cent of the total installed generation capacity. This is lower than the European Union average, which in 1999 had 32GW pumped storage capacity (out of a total of 188GW of hydropower), representing 5.5 per cent of total generation capacity.

13.4.2.2 Compressed air energy storage CAES operates by supplying compressed air to a gas turbine (Davidson et al., 1980), and is a mixture

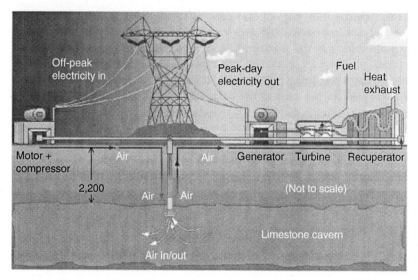

Figure 13.3. Compressed air storage and generation.
Image: courtesy CAES Development Company.

of storage and generation technologies. The air is first compressed, using off-peak electricity, then stored in underground caverns and used later to supply a gas turbine, as shown in figure 13.3. The principle is that a gas turbine fed with compressed air is very efficient. A normal gas turbine uses around two-thirds of the gross output to compress air; for example, when the gross output is 300MW the compressor consumes 200MW, leaving a net output of 100MW to drive the electric generator. Therefore, in discharge mode CAES systems are highly efficient, and have high specific power output, and like conventional gas turbines have a fast response. The main problem is that a suitable geological formation is required for the underground storage of compressed air. Various geological structures can be utilised, such as aquifers, solution-mined salt caverns, the reuse of existing mines, and hard rock caverns.

The measures of performance are charge energy factor and fuel heat rate (Davidson et al., 1980), defined as

$$\text{charge energy factor (c.e.f)} = \frac{\text{electrical energy output}}{\text{electrical charge energy}}$$

$$\text{fuel heat rate (f.h.r)} = \frac{\text{combustion fuel consumed}}{\text{electrical energy output}}$$

The fuel cost of generation is given by

$$\text{fuel cost of generation} = \frac{\text{charge energy cost}}{\text{c.e.f.}} + \text{fuel cost} \times \text{f.h.r.}$$

CAES can be developed for various combinations of c.e.f and f.h.r., according to the economic requirements, and a full evaluation of the energy and capital costs is required at the design feasibility stage.

Energy is used to charge the compressed air store, and some energy is lost as heat from compression intercooling, which is necessary to prevent damage to the compressors and the storage cavern. The system economics depends on the relative values of the electricity used to charge the store and that generated when discharging. There is interest in improving the efficiency by using thermal storage during compression and thermal recovery during the extraction of compressed air from the store, which could potentially reduce fuel use. Theoretically, the process could be made adiabatic – i.e. no exchange of heat between the system and external surroundings takes place.

Until recently there were just two systems in the world, the best-known being the first ever built, at Huntorf in Germany, constructed in 1978 and rated at 290MW for two hours' storage (Crotogino et al., 2001). The compressed air is stored at pressures in the range 70 bar to 43 bar in a salt cavern with a maximum depth of 650 metres. The first system in the United States was constructed at McIntosh, Alabama, in 1991. There is considerable interest in developing new systems; in 2001, for example, the CAES Development Company announced plans to develop a 2,700MW system at Norton, Ohio, using an existing limestone mine. There are also several feasibility studies under way of the integration of wind generation with CAES; for example, a proposed stored energy plant in Iowa would integrate up to 200MW renewable wind generation with a 100–200MW CAES. System developers and equipment suppliers include CAES Development Company, Ridge Energy Storage, Iowa Association of Municipal Utilities, Alstom Power and Dresser-Rand.

13.4.2.3 Flywheels Flywheel systems are kinetic energy storage devices, and store energy in a rotating mass (rotor), with the amount of stored energy (capacity) dependent on the rotor mass and form (inertia) and rotational speed. The kinetic energy stored in a rotating mass, where J is the moment of inertia, and ω is the angular velocity, is:

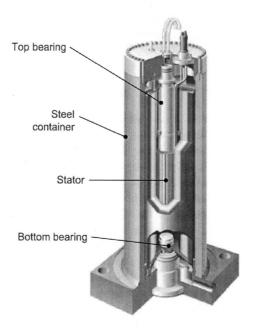

Top bearing

Steel container

Stator

Bottom bearing

Figure 13.4. Cutaway view of a flywheel.
Image: Courtesy Urenco Power Technologies.

$$E = \frac{1}{2}\mathcal{J}\omega^2$$

A flywheel made by Urenco Power Technologies (Tarrant, 2000) has a cylindrical rotor of mass 110 kg and moment of inertia around 5.2 kg m², and has an energy storage capacity of 2kWh (7.2 MJ) when operated over the speed range 27,000–37,800 rpm. A typical flywheel construction is shown in figure 13.4.

An accelerating torque causes a flywheel to speed up and store energy, while a decelerating torque causes a flywheel to slow down and regenerate energy. The storage of electrical energy is achieved by the addition of an electrical motor/generator, which may be integrated with the flywheel, and a power electronic variable-speed drive.

Flywheel energy storage technologies fall broadly into two classes depending on rotor type and speed. Low-speed flywheels, with typical operating speeds up to 6,000 rpm, have steel rotors and conventional bearings. Typical energy densities are around 5Wh/kg. High-speed flywheels, with operating speeds up to 50,000 rpm, use rotors made from advanced composite materials, and special-purpose magnetic bearings.

Energy densities up to around 100Wh/kg have been achieved, while commercial rotors typically have energy densities up to 40Wh/kg.

High angular velocity is more important than mass in achieving high stored energy. The tensile strength of the material defines the upper limit of angular velocity. For example, in the case of an ideal flywheel with mass m concentrated at the rim, and with rotor material density ρ and maximum tensile strength σ_{max}, the theoretical maximum stored energy is

$$E = \frac{1}{2}m\frac{\sigma_{max}}{\rho}$$

This means that a flywheel made from a material that combines high tensile strength with low density achieves the maximum energy that may be stored for a given mass. For example, the theoretical maximum stored specific energy of a steel rotor is 32Wh/kg, compared with 222Wh/kg for a carbon-fibre-reinforced composite rotor. Although in practice a rotor would be operated well below the theoretical maximum speed, it is clear that, to achieve high specific energy (at high speeds), composite materials are better than metal. A further advantage of composite rotors is that they fail in a less destructive manner than steel rotors, and therefore are intrinsically safer.

The high cycling capability of flywheels is a key feature, and the lifetime is not dependent on the charge or discharge rate. Full charge–discharge cycle lifetimes quoted by manufacturers range from 10^5 to 10^7 cycles. The limiting factor in most applications is more likely to be the standby lifetime, which is typically quoted as twenty years. The in–out efficiency for charge and discharge at full rated power can be up to 90 per cent. However, the standby losses are rather high, and the lowest self-discharge rates currently achieved for complete flywheel systems, with electrical interface powered, are around 20 per cent of the stored capacity per hour.

The capacity of commercially available rotors ranges from 0.25kWh to 25kWh, and power interfaces range up to around 300kW. Multiple rotor modules can be paralleled to a common DC bus, and several manufacturers can provide paralleled systems with capacity and power up to around 250kWh at 2MW. Products targeted at uninterruptible power supply systems include those by Piller, which has 500 installations worldwide, and Active Power. High-speed composite flywheel systems have been extensively tested in field trials, and commercial products are now available, notably those by Beacon Power and Urenco Power Technologies (Tarrant, 2000) – see figure 13.4. The main stationary applications are in distributed power generation, power quality systems and trackside support in traction (rail) systems. Manufacturers also foresee applications in peak shaving in electrical power systems, and for power smoothing in renewable energy systems.

Research and development efforts in flywheels are aimed mainly at reducing losses and overall costs. Advanced bearings are being actively developed, including the use of high-temperature superconducting magnetic bearings, to provide reduced losses, higher efficiency, reduced running costs and longer bearing life. It is believed that an energy-efficient flywheel could be constructed with a bearing loss equivalent to less than 2 per cent capacity loss per day. In the future it is likely that modules and systems will be offered in a wide range of powers, P/E ratios and cycling lifetimes, to meet specific market requirements.

13.4.3   Electrical storage technologies

13.4.3.1 Superconducting magnetic energy storage (SMES)   The basic principle is that energy is stored in a magnetic field created by a DC current flowing through a coil made from superconducting wire (Campbell, 2000; see also chapter 10 on superconductors in this volume). The amount of energy stored, where L is the inductance of the electromagnet and I is the current, is expressed by the following equation:

$$E = \frac{1}{2}LI^2$$

The resistance of a coil made using normal wire would result in I^2R heat losses, and economical storage of energy is made possible using superconducting wire, with virtually zero resistance at a temperature below the critical temperature T_C. The coil has to be maintained at low temperature using a cryostat. The storage system is potentially efficient for cyclic periods of several hours, with round-trip efficiencies of around 85 per cent, limited mainly by the efficiency of the power electronics interface (Kondoh et al., 2000).

Current SMES systems use niobium-based material (e.g. NbTi) with T_C of 9.2K, known as low-temperature superconducting (LTS) materials. Ceramic materials with high-temperature superconducting properties (HTS), with Tc around 77K (the temperature of liquid nitrogen), were discovered in 1986. HTS materials are brittle and have poor mechanical properties; nonetheless, they are already in use for the current leads from the outside of the SMES system to the LTS coil on the inside. This makes the interface from ambient temperature to around 4K easier to achieve with low thermal loss; see figure 13.5. SMES systems

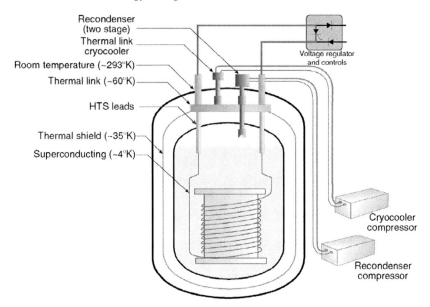

Figure 13.5. SMES with high-efficiency cryostat.
Image: Courtesy American Superconductor.

using HTS for the coil offers reduced capital and running costs, and development is being funded by the US Department of Energy.

The volumetric energy density in the magnet is proportional to the square of the magnetic flux density, and fields of up to 6T are feasible, corresponding to an energy density of $14\,MJ/m^3$. It is desirable to minimise any external magnetic field. Toroidal coil shapes confine the magnetic field much better than solenoid shapes, but use twice the length of superconductor wire and are difficult and expensive to construct. A further problem with toroids is the strong outward force (Lorentz force), which requires mechanical containment. Currently SMES designs use the more economical solenoid coils despite the comparatively large external magnetic fields.

GE Industrial Systems and American Superconductor produce a shunt-connected flexible AC transmission system device called Distributed SMES. The system is capable of injecting reactive power with sub-cycle response time, and real power injection, to compensate for disturbances on the grid network. The system is trailer-mounted for rapid installation, and is usually connected at the distribution level. The magnet current is over 1,000A, with discharge power of 3MW and energy storage of around 3MJ (0.83kWh, equivalent to one second of discharge time). Standby power is 18kW. This system is commercially available and has been installed in a number of locations, mainly in the United States.

There are many manufacturers of prototype and pilot plants. A commercial product is manufactured by Intermagnetics Corporation (the IPQ-750: 6MJ, 2MW maximum). Kyushu Electric Power Company developed and installed a SMES system (the ESK: 1kWh, 1MW) in 1998. This was planned as a first step in scaling up SMES technology to large SMES systems of up to 100kWh, 20MW, composed of twelve toroidal coils, for the compensation of voltage fluctuations at the southern end of the Japanese power grid.

ACCEL Instruments GmbH designed a 2MJ SMES in collaboration with E.U.S. GmbH, both German companies, in which the SMES was used to ensure the power quality of a laboratory plant. The coil is wound using NbTi superconductor, using a liquid helium cooler. The system is designed for a carry-over time of eight seconds at an average power of 200kW (800kW maximum). The magnet current is 1,000A, and the magnetic field strength is 4.5T.

13.4.3.2 Supercapacitors The term 'supercapacitor' refers to a new type of electrochemical storage device, more accurately referred to as a double-layer capacitor; it is also called an ultracapacitor or a pseudocapacitor. Commercial brand names include Goldcap, Powercap and Boostcap. The device stores energy electrostatically by polarising an electrolytic solution, and is therefore a direct electrical energy storage device. It is also an electrochemical device, but unlike a battery there are normally no chemical reactions involved in its energy storage mechanism.

Capacitors store electrical energy in the form of separated electrostatic charge, and the capacitance depends on the electrode area and the charge separation distance. A conventional capacitor has flat conductive plates, separated by a dielectric material such as plastic film, paper or ceramic. In contrast to conventional capacitors, supercapacitors have a significantly enlarged electrode surface area and a liquid electrolyte. The applied potential on the positive plate attracts the negative ions in the electrolyte, while the potential on the negative plate attracts the positive ions. This effectively creates two layers of capacitive storage, one where the charges are separated at the positive plate, and another at the negative plate. This mechanism is highly reversible, allowing the supercapacitor to be charged and discharged for up to 10^5 cycles. The lifetime is application-dependent but could be in excess of ten years, even when subject to a full cycle every hour.

The electrodes are made from a porous carbon-based material, which has a surface area up to 2,000 m^2/g, much greater than can be accomplished using flat or textured films and plates. The charge separation distance is determined by the size of the ions in the electrolyte, which are attracted to the charged electrode. This charge separation (less than 10Å) is much smaller than can be accomplished using conventional dielectric materials. The combination of large surface area and small charge separation distance gives the supercapacitor its outstanding capacitance relative to conventional capacitors. Organic electrolytes are often used giving a cell voltage of 2.3V. The organic solvent (acetronitrile) is hazardous, being toxic and flammable.

The maximum energy E (joules) stored in a capacitance C (farads), charged to a voltage V (volts) is given by

$$E = \frac{1}{2}CV^2$$

Power converters operate over a limited voltage range, and a realistic final discharge voltage is 0.5Vmax, which allows 75 per cent of the maximum energy to be extracted.

There are many manufacturers, including Maxwell Technologies (the Boostcap), Epcos, Saft, Bollore Technologies and Panasonic. Cells with capacitance up to 5,000 farad are now available. Acceptance in the possible markets is currently limited by the high cost compared to batteries. The cost per unit of capacitance in 2002 was in the region of €0.04–0.12 per farad, with the equivalent cost per unit of usable stored energy of €50,000–150,000 per kWh. However, cost reduction targets for 2005 were quoted as low as €0.01 per farad (equivalent to around €10,000 per kWh).

The main applications at present are for power back-up in small consumer electronic devices. Large supercapacitors have applications in the field of transport, such as regenerative braking and motor starting applications, and providing fast-response and high-power cycling in hybrid fuel cell and battery power systems. In power applications, it is necessary to integrate single cells in series to give system voltages up to 800V, when an intermediate modular structure with a cell voltage balancing system is required.

13.5   Environmental assessment

A life cycle assessment for the calculation of input energy requirements and CO_2 emissions was conducted by Denholm and Kulcinski (2003)

Table 13.4 *Life cycle input energy requirements and CO_2 emissions per unit of energy delivered for 'energy' storage systems*

	Lead–acid battery	Vanadium flow cell	Pumped hydro
Specific energy (GJ$_t$/GWh$_e$)	763	591	37.2
Specific CO_2 emissions (tonne/GWh$_e$)	80.5	64.9	3
Net energy ratio (primary energy and emissions multiplier)	1.43	1.33	1.35

Source: Denholm and Kulcinski (2003).

for pumped hydro, compressed air and battery/flow cell energy storage systems (utility or 'energy' storage applications). The scope of the study included fixed components (construction of the reservoir, capital equipment and decommissioning) and variable components (operational, in–out efficiency transmission and standing storage losses). Pumped hydro systems require large-scale earth moving, tunnelling and concrete construction operations; the resulting storage capacity is large, however, and the lifetime is long. Carbon dioxide emissions during construction are generally proportional to the energy used. There is some concern that the creation of pumped hydro reservoirs leads to the production of methane, a powerful greenhouse gas, resulting from the decay of biomass under the flooded area.

The results of the life cycle analysis by Denholm and Kulcinski (2003), shown in table 13.4, show that the battery and the vanadium flow cell have much higher energy and CO_2 emissions per unit of electricity delivered (GWhe) than pumped storage, mainly due to the greater (approximately ten to fifteen times) specific energy requirements associated with construction. These figures do not include the losses due to storage efficiency, transmission and standing losses. The losses may be accounted for by the net energy ratio, which includes the inverse of the storage efficiency and other factors, and represents the increased primary electrical energy requirements and emissions per unit of electrical energy delivered. The net energy ratio is fairly similar for the three storage technologies, as shown in table 13.4. In the case of a pumped hydro storage system, an additional loss of 0.35GWhe, or 1,260GJe, will occur for each 1GWhe delivered by a pumped hydro system. The additional thermal energy and emissions depend on the source of the primary electrical energy. For example, if the stored electricity was generated from a typical thermal source,[1] the resulting additional thermal energy due to storage and other losses could be 2,800GJth per GWhe delivered, and the additional CO_2 emissions could be 152 tonnes per GWhe delivered. A comparison of these figures with the data in table 13.4 shows how the specific energy and emissions associated with storage depend more strongly on the source of the primary electricity and the storage net energy ratio than on the construction and operation of the storage.

CAES is not a pure storage system but may be considered a hybrid generation/storage system. Calculating the overall efficiency of a CAES system is complicated, and comparison with other storage technologies is difficult. Denholm and Kulcinski (2003) have described a method of calculating the efficiency of the electrical storage process, which assigns an electrical energy value to the natural gas used, based on the performance of an alternative gas turbine generator. The calculation gives the electrical storage efficiency of peaking CAES as 74 per cent, which is comparable to the other storage technologies.

Toxic materials are used in several electrochemical batteries (for example, lead, zinc and cadmium), and, although the materials can be recycled at the end of life, environmental concerns may become a limiting factor when alternative technologies become competitive in price and performance. Flow cells use relatively low-toxicity electrolytes and materials.

An environmental assessment and comparison of 'power' storage technologies was delivered by the INVESTIRE thematic network (see http://www.itpower.co.uk/investire). The specific energy demand during the construction of a high-speed flywheel, per unit of installed capacity, is around five times greater than for a lead–acid battery, mainly due to the material used in the rotor containment. However, in applications where the high cycle lifetime of a flywheel is utilised, the energy demand per unit of energy delivered is potentially very much lower than for a lead–acid battery. The materials used in flywheels have low environmental risks.

13.6   Cost comparison

It is difficult to compare the capital costs of the various storage technologies, since costs may be quoted by manufacturers for various system sizes. The most reliable data are for existing installations of mature technologies, such as pumped hydro and CAES, although site-dependent

---

[1] For example, gas-powered generation, with thermal efficiency of 45 per cent and CO_2 emissions of 435 tonnes per GWhe.

factors have to be taken into account. In the case of emerging technologies such as supercapacitors, flywheels, SMES and flow cells, cost projections by manufacturers invariably include a large component to amortise the R&D costs, and if production volumes increase future costs can be expected to reduce rapidly. Cost projections for emerging technologies should be regarded as no more than a guideline, and reliable estimates for energy storage systems in specific applications can be obtained only by a design and tendering exercise.

One approach that allows for comparisons of technologies in systems with various power and energy levels is to split the total capital cost into a power-related cost, an energy-related cost and a balance of plant cost, which could include buildings (Schoenung, 2001). Basically, this approach assumes that the cost is a linear function of size, which is an approximation for some technologies, in particular SMES. Schoenung and Hassenzahl (2003a, 2003b) have extended earlier work on energy storage characterisation to include life cycle cost analysis, thereby providing a quantitative comparison of energy storage technologies. The analysis considers the need for full or partial replacement of system components, and indicates typical lifetimes in terms of the replacement period in years. Energy storage systems could be required to have lifetimes of at least twenty years, similar to other generation equipment, but the lifetime achieved by emerging technologies may be uncertain, and the lifetime of battery systems may be limited by their cycle performance (up to 1,500 cycles). Various applications of energy storage and the cost of supercapacitors and flywheels have been described by Wohlgemuth et al. (1999).

13.6.1 'High power' storage

Storage technologies suitable for use in 'high power' applications – for example, power quality improvement systems – are compared in table 13.5. The power and energy characteristics of the storage technologies in the table tend to favour their application in certain power ranges, such as supercapacitors from 10kW to 100kW, flywheels from 10kW to 1MW, and superconducting magnetic energy storage systems from 1MW upwards.

Flywheels are well positioned to cover the low and medium power range, with high cycling lifetime and relatively low cost. Modules can be operated in parallel to cover a range of power and energy requirements. The costs of high-speed flywheels are highly variable, depending on the manufacturer, and the cost per kWh given is a mid-figure. In the short term, a target energy-related cost of $1,000 per kWh is likely to be

Table 13.5 *Construction costs of 'high power' storage systems, 2001*

	Supercapacitor	Flywheel	Micro-SMES
Power range (kW)	10 to 100	10 to 1,000	1,000 to 10,000
Storage time (s)	10	5 to 30	1
Energy-related cost ($/kWh)	82,000	25,000	72,000
Power-related cost ($/kW)	300	350	300
Typical lifetime (years)	20	20	30

Source: Schoenung (2001); Schoenung and Hassenzahl (2003a, 2003b); http://www.itpower.co.uk/investire.

achievable, and further cost reduction is anticipated if UPS and power quality markets are penetrated and production volumes increase.

Supercapacitors and SMES are currently very expensive in their range of power and capacity that is commercially available. However, cost targets for supercapacitors down to €10,000 per kWh may make them competitive for low-energy power quality requirements.

The commercial development of HTS will enable reduced capital and operating costs for cooling in SMES, and dramatic cost reductions are possible in large SMES systems. It is possible that medium-sized to large SMES systems for 'energy' applications could be developed with much reduced costs. The economics of new design concepts reported by Taylor et al. (1999) and Schoenung (2001) indicates that an energy-related cost of less than $1,000 per kKh for a 100MWh system is achievable, which could enable SMES to commercialise a wide range of requirements, including energy trading and fast response.

13.6.2 'High energy' storage

Storage technologies suitable for 'high energy' applications – e.g. load levelling and peak shaving – are compared in table 13.6.

Lead–acid batteries generally provide the lowest-cost solution when the storage time is less than one hour. They are also the standard solution for stand-alone systems, when storage times of several hours may be required. Lead–acid battery technology is mature and batteries are manufactured in high volumes, and although further development is likely to lead to improved performance and lifetime there is little scope for significant cost reduction.

Pumped hydro is a mature technology, and proposed CAES systems have been subject to detailed studies, and the respective costs may be

Table 13.6 *Construction costs of 'high energy' storage systems, 2001*

	Batteries	Flow cells	Pumped hydro	CAES
Power range (MW)	up to 30	up to 10	up to 2,000	up to 3,000
Storage time (h)	up to 0.25	up to 8	up to 5	up to 2
Energy-related cost ($/kWh)	175–250	150	12	3
Power-related cost ($/kW)	200–300	1,500	600	425
Typical lifetime (years)	up to 10	up to 15	>50	>30

Source: Schoenung 2001; Schoenung and Hassenzahl (2003a, 2003b); http://www.itpower. co.uk/investire.

regarded as reliable current estimates. Although the costs are not likely to change significantly in the short term, the construction costs of pumped hydro and CAES are highly site-dependent, and the shortage of economic sites means that costs are likely to rise in the long term.

Flow cells are a relatively new technology, with only a few prototype systems installed. The combination of energy-related and power-related costs shows that the present cost of a flow cell system with an eight hour storage time is around $350 per kWh. While cost reduction to $300 per kWh is likely in the short term, detailed long-term projections are not available.

13.7   Outlook and conclusions

13.7.1   *Opportunities and economic factors*

The potential opportunity for energy storage in UK electricity networks is currently receiving considerable attention (DTI, 2004a, 2004b, 2004c, 2004d). Jenkins and Strbac (2000) conclude that there are several significant opportunities for increasing the value of renewable generation using energy storage. The intermittency of renewables generation gives rise to additional system costs, although this becomes significant only when the penetration of renewables exceeds around 10 per cent to 20 per cent of total electricity demand. Analysis by ILEX and UMIST (2002) shows that penetration of renewables of 20 per cent to 30 per cent results in additional costs in the ranges £3 to £9 and £4 to £11 per MWh of additional renewable generation, respectively. These costs may be compared with the assumed average wholesale price of all electricity generated of £22 per MWh in 2020, based on 2002 prices. The analysis assumed that the additional capacity costs to provide security was provided by open-cycle gas turbines, and found that the additional costs were mainly generation costs. Energy storage, as well as developments in load management and flexible generation, could reduce these costs. Strbac and Black (DTI, 2004a) analyse the inclusion of 2–5GW of storage and 26GW of wind power in systems with low-, medium- and high-flexibility generation mix, and show that the benefits of storage could be significant in terms of increased wind power utilisation, reduced costs of synchronised reserve and reduced CO_2 emissions.

Energy storage can potentially provide a wide range of benefits, ranging from power quality improvement in the distribution network (high power systems) to load levelling and energy trading in the grid network (high energy systems). Various technologies are available to suit a range of application requirements. To maximise the economic benefits, it is desirable that an energy storage system should offer a range of technical features – for example, high energy for load levelling and high power for grid stability improvement.

The cost and economics of storage are determined by both technology and market factors. Technology factors will include the cost of technology development, the cost of the raw materials and the cost of production. Market penetration would result in increased production volumes, but the effect of this would be quite different for different technologies. For example, in the case of pumped hydro and CAES, the capital costs are determined mainly by the specific geographical site, and have little to do with the number of systems. On the other hand, flow cells are built from modules, and volume production could lead to potential cost reduction via production process development. The round-trip efficiency of storage is a key parameter. A typical additional loss of 35 per cent of the energy delivered by storage translates into an additional cost of £8 per MWh delivered by storage, assuming an average price of £22 per MWh. However, this does not necessarily mean additional fuel usage and CO_2 emissions, as the storage may be operated in conjunction with, and charged from, renewable energy generation.

Investment in storage systems is currently driven by economic factors, which are sensitive to primary fuel costs. Predictions about future oil prices are notoriously unreliable; for example, the crude oil price approximately doubled during 2004, contrary to predictions of a relatively narrow trading range. There is no doubt that increasing concerns about climate change will cause the benefits of storage to be assessed with an emphasis on reduced emissions rather than solely on economic factors. In any case, it is important to conduct a life cycle assessment, including the costs of construction, operation and decommissioning.

13.7.2   Technological developments

The most promising emerging technology for 'high power' applications is the high-speed flywheel, which has a high cycle lifetime and potentially offers very low energy throughput costs. Key development priorities are improved rotor materials and bearings, to increase specific energy and reduce losses (see the INVESTIRE Storage Technology Reports, available from http://www.itpower.co.uk/investire).

Large-scale utility applications requiring 'high energy' storage invariably use pumped hydro. Further performance improvements are possible; for example, existing pumped hydro systems provide dynamic response only while generating, and improved drive systems could provide dynamic response while pumping. Pumped hydro has the drawback that suitable geological sites are required, and the limited availability of such sites will limit the development of new systems and is likely to increase costs in the long term. There are also concerns about the environmental impact of creating hydro reservoirs, including the effect of methane production resulting from the decay of biomass under the flooded area.

Two new technologies, CAES and flow cells, are particularly promising. CAES technology is attracting renewed interest more than two decades after the first system was constructed. CAES systems require suitable underground storage sites, and there are several areas in the United Kingdom where solution mining could be used on salt structures to create storage caverns. One opportunity for efficiency improvement is to store the heat generated during compression, and use it later to pre-heat the air extracted from the cavern. Flow cells are still under development, and considerable cost reduction is important to encourage large-scale deployment. The use of electrolysers, hydrogen storage and hydrogen fuel cells to store electricity is currently very expensive and inefficient; nevertheless, the low overall efficiency could be improved if the waste heat was utilised by integration in CHP systems. The development of a hydrogen economy could make electricity storage using hydrogen more attractive.

Clearly, it is important to understand the requirements for energy storage in evolving power systems, and to develop suitable new energy storage technologies. The development of innovative storage technologies and systems, in order to facilitate the large-scale penetration of distributed energy resources such as renewable energy, is an important research topic within the European Commission's Research Programme. In the United Kingdom, the Department of Trade and Industry has recognised that more research is required to identify the potential for energy storage, and organised a workshop in 2004 to consider future needs and technology options as an initial step in the development of a strategy for energy storage (DTI, 2004a).

13.8 References

Butler, P., J. L. Miller and P. A. Taylor (2002). *Energy Storage Opportunities Analysis Phase II: Final Report*, a study for the DOE Energy Storage Systems Program, Report no. SAND2002-1314, Albuquerque, NM: Sandi National Laboratories.

Campbell, A. M. (2000). Superconducting magnetic energy storage (SMES), in *Renewable Energy Storage*, IMechE Seminar Publication no. 2000–7, London: Institution of Mechanical Engineers, 45–50.

Crotogino, F., K.-U. Mohmeyer and R. Scharf (2001). *Huntorf CAES: More than 20 Years of Successful Operation*, paper presented at Solution Mining Research Institute Spring 2001 Meeting, available from http://www.solutionmining.org.

Davidson, B. J., I. Glendenning, R. D. Harman, A. B. Hart, B. J. Maddock, R. D. Moffit, V. G. Newman, T. F. Smith, P. J. Worthington and J. K. Wright (1980). Large-scale electrical energy storage, *IEE Proceedings Part A*, 127(6): 345–85.

Denholm, P., and G. Kulcinski (2003). *Net Energy Balance and Greenhouse Gas Emissions from Renewable Energy Storage Systems*, Report no. 223-1, Madison: Energy Center of Wisconsin, available from http://www.ecw.org/prod/223-1.pdf.

DTI (2003). *Our Energy Future: Creating a Low-Carbon Economy*, Energy White Paper no. 68, Cm5761 London: Department of Trade and Industry, available from http://www.dti.gov.uk/energy/whitepaper/ourenergyfuture.pdf.

(2004a). Presentations at DTI Workshop on Energy Storage, London, 13 July, http://www.dti.gov.uk/energy/sepn/energy_storage.shtml.

(2004b). *Review of Electrical Energy Storage Technologies and Systems and of their Potential for the UK*, London: Department of Trade and Industry, available from http://www.dti.gov.uk/.

(2004c). *The Future Value of Electrical Energy Storage in the UK with Generator Intermittency*, London: Department of Trade and Industry, available from http://www.dti.gov.uk/.

(2004d). *Status of Electrical Energy Storage Systems*, London: Department of Trade and Industry, available from http://www.dti.gov.uk/.

European Commission (2001). *Energy Storage: A Key Technology for Decentralised Power, Power Quality, and Clean Transport*, Brussels: European Commission.

European Commission (2003). *Cost and Technical Opportunities for Electrical Energy Storage*, Work Package Report no. 3, Brussels: European Commission, available from http://www.greennet.at.

ILEX and UMIST (2002). *Quantifying the System Costs of Additional Renewables in 2020 (SCAR Report)*, a report to the Department of Trade and Industry, Oxford: ILEX Energy Consulting and University of Manchester Institute of

Science and Technology, available from http://www.dti.gov.uk/energy/developep/080scar_report_v2_0.pdf.

Infield, D. G. (1984). *A Study of Electricity Storage and Central Electricity Generation*, Technical Report no. RAL 84045, Didcot: Rutherford Appleton Laboratory.

Jenkins, N., and G. Strbac (2000). Increasing the value of renewable sources with energy storage, in *Renewable Energy Storage*, IMechE Seminar Publication no. 2000-7, London: Institution of Mechanical Engineers, 1–10.

Kondoh, J., I. Ishii, M. Yamaguchi, A. Murata, K. Otani, K. Sakuta, N. Miguchi and S. Sekine (2000). Electrical energy storage systems for energy networks, *Energy Conversion and Management*, 41(17): 1863–74.

Price, A. (1998). Why store energy when energy is so cheap?, in *Proceedings of the Conference on Electrical Energy Storage, Applications and Technologies* Morgan Hill, CA: Electricity Storage Association, 297–304.

—— (2003). *Battery Developments and Electrochemical Storage*, paper presented at Storage of Renewable Energy: Strategies and Technologies to Meet the Challenge, Institution of Mechanical Engineers London 27 November.

Schoenung, S. M. (2001). *Characteristics and Technologies for Long- vs. Short-Term Energy Storage*, a study for the DOE Energy Storage Systems Program, Report no. SAND2001-0765, Albuquerque, NM: Sandia National Laboratories.

Schoenung, S. M., and W. V. Hassenzahl (2003a). *Long- vs. Short-Term Energy Storage Technologies Analysis: A Life-Cycle Cost Study*, a study for the DOE Energy Storage Systems Program, Report no. SAND2003-2783, Albuquerque, NM: Sandia National Laboratories.

—— (2003b). Life-cycle cost analysis of energy storage technologies for long- and short-duration applications, in *Proceedings of the Third International Conference on Electrical Energy Storage, Applications and Technologies*, available on CD-ROM from; http://www.sandia.gov/eesat/.

Tanaka, T., and I. Kurihara (1998). Market potential of utility-purpose energy storage in Japan up to the year 2050, in *Proceedings of the First International Conference on Electrical Energy Storage Applications and Technologies*, Morgan Hill, CA: Electricity Storage Association, 11–16.

Tarrant, C. D. (2000). The use of flywheel energy storage in electrical energy management, in *Renewable Energy Storage*, IMechE Seminar Publication no. 2000-7, London: Institution of Mechanical Engineers, 35–44.

Taylor, P., L. Johnson, K. Reichart, P. DiPietro, J. Philip and P. Butler (1999). *A Summary of the State-of-the-Art of SMES, Flywheel, and CAES*, Report no. SAND99-1854, Albuquerque, NM: Sandia National Laboratories.

Wohlgemuth, J., J. Miller and L. B. Sibley (1999). *Investigation of Synergy between Electrochemical Capacitors, Flywheels and Batteries in Hybrid Energy Storage for PV Systems*, Report no. SAND99-1477, Albuquerque, NM: Sandia National Laboratories.

Part IV

End-Use Technologies: Main Drivers, and
Patterns of Future Demand

14   Buildings

Wolfgang Eichhammer

14.1   Introduction

The purpose of this chapter is to investigate possible developments in building energy demand with a time horizon of 2050, and the impacts these developments might have on the technologies around which the electricity system will need to be designed in 2050. Even though a share of the building energy demand changes quite slowly over time, due to the long lifetime of the building stock (typically 100 years on average), it is not easy to describe with certainty the technological trends behind the changes. In addition, unlike the energy supply options, a multitude of technologies are generally involved on the demand side, ranging from the building shell, including windows, to technologies satisfying the demand for heat and cold, as well as all kinds of electrical appliances. For this reason, it is usually better to design scenarios of future energy demand in buildings rather than try to identify single trends. In this perspective, two main trends in building energy demand can be seen to be emerging from current developments, and these are described in this chapter. The description first takes the form of two alternative, and perhaps mutually exclusive, future worlds, while the latter part of the study attempts to look at possible synergies between the two worlds. The two worlds described in this chapter are as follows:

- The *Integrated World*: characterised by an increasing integration of energy demand and energy supply, with buildings contributing to the future power and possibly heat supply. Future technical developments such as 'virtual power plants' and 'home automation' feature here.
- The *Component World*: the second world is derived from the observation that the energy efficiency potentials of the components of the building sector (e.g. the building shell) are far from being exhausted and that, ultimately, energy demand might reach levels at which an integration with supply makes less sense due to the low consumption levels involved.

333

The following gives a brief outline of these two worlds and the innovations required to develop each of them in the future.

14.2   The *Integrated World*

The central element of the *Integrated World* is ICT. In this world, on the one hand, there are the classical and new supply technologies (such as wind power, biomass power, central CHP, heating, fuel cells and PV plants) and the distributed loads for heat and electricity. On the other hand, there are the distributed supply elements, such as distributed CHP/fuel cells (which are used in cars even when stationary) and distributed PV. In order to manage such a complex supply system, it is necessary to be able to estimate with a fair degree of certainty the fluctuations in both the central and distributed supply (the quality of weather forecasts) and the fluctuations in demand. This requires a permanent exchange of information and an optimisation of energy purchase and energy use, hence also the creation of efficient exchange markets for energy.

Currently, the first elements of an *Integrated World* are being developed in the form of small fuel cells for residential application, and increasingly by interconnecting a certain number of fuel cells in order to understand better the practical implications of such links. Suppliers of heating equipment for residential buildings, electricity and gas suppliers, research institutes, etc. are currently working on the demonstration of a virtual power plant by interconnecting some thirty to forty fuel cells in decentralised locations. For other examples, refer, among others, to the ENCORP Virtual Power Plant (see http://www.encorp.com/context.asp?.cms ID=41) and MacDonald (2003).

However, before the *Integrated World* can be realised, a variety of innovations are required with respect to technologies (component and interconnection technologies) and networking (networking technologies and networking management), as well as training/education and component supply chains. Some of the components mentioned in this chapter are described in detail in other chapters of this book, such as fuel cells and PV technologies. The following is a list of some of the necessary innovations. Its length shows that the *Integrated World* is complex to realise and the social and commercial complexities are vast, which indicates that it will take decades to introduce the required changes. Nevertheless, some of the innovations will be becoming available anyway as part of the existing drive towards the greater use of renewables, in particular wind, which already accounts for more than 20 per cent of gross electricity production in some regions of the European Union (e.g.

in northern Germany, or Navarre in Spain). By 2030, however, when fuel cells might have reached maturity and installed PV capacity in Europe could exceed 100GW (mostly decentrally installed), compared to less than 1GW in 2004, there will be strong pressure to continue with the innovations described below, as the smooth functioning of the electric supply system will depend on them by then. The main stakeholders in the development of such a world are technology providers and consumers. Governments have an indirect, but important, role through the incentives set for new technologies, in particular PV, as long as they have not reached competitiveness and externalities are not integrated into energy prices.

14.2.1   Innovations required in the Integrated World

14.2.1.1   Technologies

(a) Innovations in component technologies:
  - CHP technologies; fuel cells (stationary or mobile in cars); micro-turbines; internal combustion engines (see chapter 9 on micro-generation in this volume);
  - electricity generation incorporated in building components (e.g. PV); and
  - network-compatible supply and demand components (home automation).
(b) Innovations in interconnection technologies:
  - ICT/data communication devices;
  - storage technologies; and
  - power quality devices.

14.2.1.2   Networks

(a) Innovations in network technologies:
  - active networks at the distribution (collection) level; and
  - short-term forecasting methodologies (weather forecasts, load forecasts).
(b) Innovations in markets and in regulation:
  - correct valuation of distributed facilities (e.g. fluctuating power versus savings on network extensions);
  - creating equal conditions for both distributed and centralised generation;
  - a transformation of the role of distribution network operators; and
  - short-term markets for fluctuating generation.

14.2.1.3   *Education/training and cooperation*

(a) Innovations in the fields of education and training:
  - new educational fields in schools and universities to cover the technologies required; and
  - training for installers and skilled workers in the new technologies and the complex issues related to the interconnection of devices.

(b) Innovations in the field of cooperation:
  - cooperation between the suppliers of heating equipment, energy service companies, owners, associations, etc.; and
  - new structures in the component chain supplying equipment suppliers.

In order to get an idea of the potential of distributed electricity supply, it is instructive to look at the following orders of magnitude. Some 10 per cent of today's heating demand in Germany (half of the possible 2050 heat demand) is generated in distributed CHP plants with 45 per cent electrical efficiency – equivalent to an installed electric power of 30GW (at present, the total capacity of all stationary power plants in Germany is 115GW). In Germany there are 82 million inhabitants with 44 million cars registered with an average capacity of 70kW (around 3,000GW max). The average car runs for less than one hour out of twenty-four. Imagine that each car were equipped with a 75kW fuel cell powered by hydrogen. while stationary, these cars together would produce enough power to create a 'virtual power plant', able to supply all industrial and private consumers not only with electricity but also with heat.

14.3   The *Component World*

The *Component World* is based on a radically different view of the future development of the building sector. Its starting point is the hypothesis that energy efficiency potentials are far from being exhausted in the building sector and for electrical appliances in the buildings, so that energy demand of individual components can be reduced towards the middle of this century to the extent that the interconnection and integration of such small amounts of energy can no longer be justified economically.

What are the indications today that such a development is possible and how far is it possible to advance in the direction of reduced demand for both electricity and heat in buildings?

14.3.1   *Demand for heat in buildings*

Figure 14.1 shows the progress that has been made (on a theoretical basis) in thermal efficiency standards for new dwellings over the past

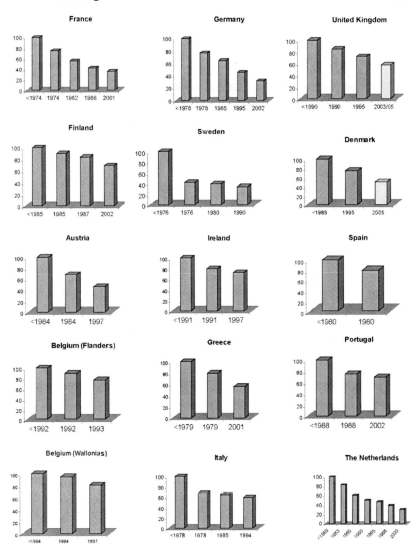

Figure 14.1. Changes in efficiency standards of new dwellings in Europe (specific consumption index).
Source: Odyssee database on Energy Efficiency Indicators (see http://www.odyssee-indicators.org).

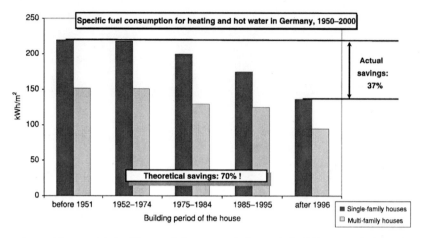

Figure 14.2. The real impact of thermal building regulations in Germany.

twenty to thirty years. In most European countries, the requirements for new buildings have decreased to between one- half and one-third of the values observed in the 1970s. Even though, in fact, around a half of the impact of the building regulations has been cancelled out by societal trends (such as higher heating temperatures, more rooms being heated for a longer period over the year: see figure 14.2), this nevertheless represents considerable progress. One major question is whether the societal trends that partially or fully cancelled out the current energy efficiency policies will continue to evolve in the future. The current indications are that at least the trend towards fewer persons per household will continue at least for some while, hampering the full realisation of the reduction possible.

The technical possibilities for reducing heat demand in buildings in the future are still considerable. Figure 14.3 illustrates this with the example of developments in Switzerland. SIA 380/1 is the current standard for new buildings, while the Minergie standard is a more advanced voluntary standard similar to the passive house standard in Germany. The latter shows that, even in the short term, major improvements are still feasible on the heat side, even taking into account grey energy for construction and renovation. For the future, this will leave electricity as the main part of energy demand (expressed in primary energy terms) in the building. How does this possible progress in the energy efficiency of buildings translate into a reduction of energy demand?

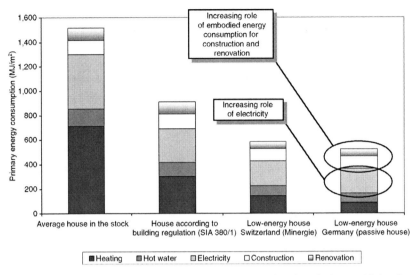

Figure 14.3. Primary energy consumption of typical Swiss multi-family houses.
Source: Jochem et al. (2002).

Figures 14.4 and 14.5 show this based on the example of Germany for the specific demand for space heating and for CO_2 emissions. Up to 2050 a reduction of more than one-third in CO_2 emissions from heating the existing building stock seems possible, even in the reference scenarios, with a similar development for energy demand. With climate protection strategies, reduction levels of at least two-thirds, if not as high as 90 per cent, could be reached in 2050. Governments are undoubtedly the main movers in driving down the energy consumption of buildings, through the continual tightening of thermal building regulation and the simultaneous encouragement of innovative building technology.

14.3.2 Demand for electricity in buildings

The electricity efficiency of household appliances has been improved by 20 per cent on average over the past decade. This is shown by the bottom-up energy indicator from the Odyssee database constructed for all appliances.[1] However, in terms of unit consumption (i.e. electricity

---

[1] The aggregate bottom-up indicator for all appliances is constructed from each indicator for the individual appliance (electricity per appliance) by weighting their different contributions to the aggregate bottom-up indicator by their share of electricity consumption.

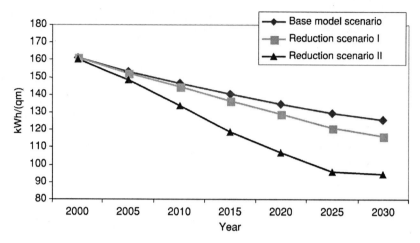

Figure 14.4. Specific heating requirements: projections in Germany for CO_2 emissions.
Source: Markewitz and Ziesing (2004).

consumed per dwelling), the decrease was less than half the expected value due to increased ownership of electrical appliances: a 21 per cent efficiency progress for large appliances since 1990 but only an 8 per cent decrease for the average consumption of large appliances per dwelling, because of the increased number of appliances. Here, again, the influence of societal and comfort factors cancelled out the technical progress in and the impact of energy efficiency policies.

Nevertheless, efficiency policies in this field *have* had an impact, in particular the labelling of electrical household appliances and minimum standards for cold appliances. While electricity demand elsewhere is still growing, the electricity share of large electrical appliances, which had been subject to such standards for a longer period, has decreased (see figure 14.6). For cold appliances and washing machines, which have the oldest efficiency policies and the highest equipment levels per household (hence a saturation of the comfort factor), even the absolute level of electricity consumption has started to decrease. For newer large appliances such as dryers, or small appliances such as IT equipment, this is not yet the case, but efficiency policies, in particular those aimed at reducing the losses when the devices are on standby, will make a clear difference in the future. The leaders in promoting this progress in the energy efficiency of appliances have been the European Commission, with a comprehensive set of labelling policies and minimum standards,

Reference scenarios for CO_2 emissions (residential and service sectors)

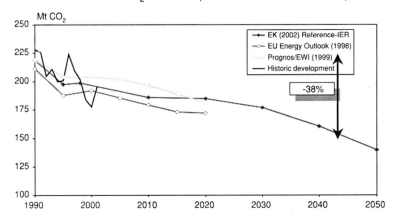

Climate protection scenarios for CO_2 emissions (residential and service sectors)

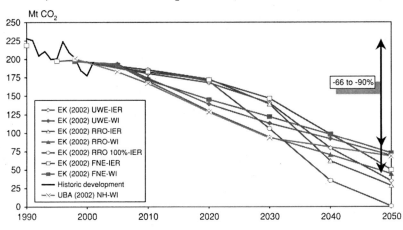

Figure 14.5. Reference and climate protection scenarios in Germany. Source: Markewitz and Ziesing (2004).

while the equipment suppliers have responded with a large number of innovations, sometimes anticipating policy action. The most decisive element however, was consumer choice, guided by the information provided from energy efficiency labels. For efficient IT appliances, procurement policies can be an important element of promotion.

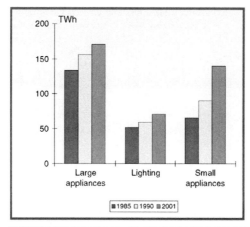

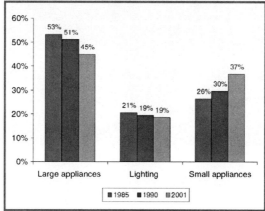

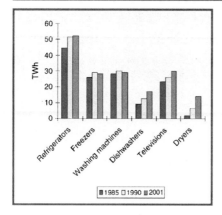

Figure 14.6. Household electricity consumption by type of appliance. Source: Odyssee Database on Energy Efficiency Indicators (see http://www.odysee-indicators.org).

What kind of new electricity demand will arise? Even if some appliances are reaching saturation levels, new appliances and electricity uses might evolve that, to some extent, can only be imagined today. Important issues for new demand could be as follows.

- Increased electricity demand for space heating. If demand levels are reduced, distribution systems in all their forms, including district heat and distribution within houses, might become too 'wasteful' and expensive compared to the small amount of energy needed for heating. It might be more sensible then to use electricity for heating. This would require, on average, high conversion efficiencies of 60 per cent and more (high-efficiency combined-cycle plants, high-efficiency fuel cells) in order to be acceptable. However, this seems feasible given a time horizon of 2050.
- Increased electricity demand for electric cars, which will partially or mainly occur in the building sector (residential and services).
- Increased demand for means of cooling buildings (in particular if the greenhouse effect drives temperatures up, but also as a result of marketing strategies).
- Increased electricity demand from 'fancy add-ons', such as Christmas decorations able to transform whole cities into 'Las Vegas'-type areas for a longer and longer period in winter, or televisions running without people watching them or to entertain pets, etc.

This list could certainly be extended. Hence the importance of a number of measures, such as early intervention when designing new applications, so that electricity efficiency is already integrated into the conception phase; strong policy with respect to standby losses (home electronics left on standby lead to increased electricity consumption for no real increase in utility); early warning systems for politicians on forthcoming electricity uses; etc.

The *Component World* as much as the *Integrated World* requires a large number of innovations, in particular in the field of energy demand and energy supply technologies, but also with respect to the R&D system for energy itself.

14.3.3 *Innovations required in the* Component World

(1) Innovations in component technologies:
  - superinsulation;
  - photo- and heat-sensitive adaptive materials; and
  - low-energy appliances (in particular low-energy ICT, including standby).

(2) Innovations in electricity supply technologies:
- very high electric efficiencies in central units (above 70 per cent);
- fuel cells, very high-temperature gas turbines, offshore wind, etc.; and
- the elimination of heat distribution in homes (all electric).

(3) Innovations in R&D: the vision of a 2,000W society:
- R&D for energy efficiency plays a primary role in the *Component World*, and the whole R&D system for energy[2] must innovate towards the vision of a 2,000W per capita society around 2050, compared with today's consumption of three times this amount; a recent report describes how such a vision could be implemented for Switzerland (Jochem et al., 2002).

(4) Societal innovations to change behaviour, innovations in component technologies:
- milieu-specific information and marketing concepts;
- empirical data and socio-economic data to identify the causal relationships between values, measures and target groups (including services and crafts) and different societal milieus or individual behaviour; and
- sustainability concepts in education and TV[3].

(5) Innovations in the building professions:
- the education of architects and craftsmen, and professional training; and
- milieu-specific social innovation.

14.4   Time-frame for important innovations in both worlds

In a recent European energy Delphi exercise, carried out in two rounds, people with different degrees of expertise were asked for their estimations of the timing for improvements in the field of energy technologies. According to this exercise, by the middle of this century a variety of these innovations should have strongly penetrated the market. Even the 5 per cent PV target, which might appear low, implies the installation of close to 100GW of PV.

---

[2] It is arguable that the system of innovation in R&D today is still not sufficiently predicated on energy efficiency and renewable supply. However, while there has been progress in the case of the latter, there is still a great deal of 'lip service' paid to financing R&D for energy efficiency innovations, both at the national and the European levels (see, for example, the lack of progress in energy efficiency R&D in the successive EU research framework programmes), while the task to be carried out is enormous.

[3] One might doubt the capacity of television to promote ideas of sustainability on anything more than an occasional basis; nonetheless, there are also examples on TV where the problems related to climate change are dealt with in an informed way.

14.5   Conclusions: synergies of the *Integrated* and *Component Worlds*

In this chapter we have explored the main drivers and patterns of future demand for buildings in the form of two alternative worlds: first, the *Integrated World*, characterised by an increasing integration of energy demand and distributed energy supply, with buildings contributing to the future supply of power and, possibly, heat; second, the *Component World*, derived from the observation that the energy efficiency potential of the components of the building sector (the building shell, but also the electric equipment and appliances) is far from being exhausted, and that ultimately energy demand might reach very low levels towards the middle of this century. These two scenarios for the energy demand of building and appliances seem to contradict each other up to a certain point, in particular if the assumption is made that energy demand for heating might become so small that integration with distributed supply appears to be less economic and that all the building sector's demand could be met using electricity, while, at the same time, the electric conversion system becomes so efficient that more than 60 per cent of the fuel input is converted into electricity.

However, the following arguments make it apparent that there are a number of synergies that could lead to a subsequent, if not parallel, realisation of both worlds.

- The *Integrated World* is compatible with an imperfect *Component World* due to the difference in investment cycles. It appears realisable to a larger degree in the timeframe 2030 to 2050. The turnover of building stock is much slower than the turnover of heating/cooling equipment (including the distributed generation of electricity and heat) and automation technology towards which the *Integrated World* is primarily directed. Technical progress for distributed energy supply in the frame of competitive markets, taking into account externalities for the different energy carriers, is an important element in such a world, but innovations are required beyond technology in many fields. The increasing penetration of distributed supply – in particular renewables, with all their fluctuations – will force a number of these innovations to be realised in the next thirty or so years in any event.
- The *Component World* is possible in combination with a highly efficient building sector based on electric heating and a very efficient central electricity supply. Governments play an essential role in promoting the *Component World* through the future development of thermal building regulations and standards for appliances. Heat demand would be

driven down considerably while electricity demand would remain at a relatively high level, due to new demand for electric heating. In addition, transport energy demand might also shift partially to electricity demand in buildings (electricity-powered vehicles). Hence, the role and consumption of electricity will certainly increase for a longer time than the consumption of heat, although strict electricity efficiency policies have started to have some impact. Therefore, managing and covering the increased electricity demand in an integrated approach will be necessary for more than half a century at least. The *Component World* has a longer time-frame to be realised, given the long investment cycles of the building stock. Only around 2050 and beyond much such types of policies expected to have an be appreciable impact. One could question whether the *Component World* will materialise, if distributed supply options penetrate to a large degree in an earlier time-frame. However, if the impact of climate change becomes more visible in the coming decades, and the need for even stronger reductions more urgent, there will be a strong push to realise this world in parallel with the *Integrated World.*

• If the *Integrated* and the *Component Worlds* are realised together in the building sector, they have the potential, in the second half of the century, to make the residential sector – if not the whole building sector (including the service sector) – self-sufficient in energy terms. First, heat demand in the buildings can be reduced by at least two–thirds, if not by 90 per cent, over half a century, even taking into account comfort factors that have cancelled out the impact of building regulation in the past. A large part of the remaining demand for heat might shift to electric heating to avoid distribution losses. For electricity, from the current perspective, self-sufficiency appears a far-off target, but one has to realise that the current captive electricity consumption of the residential sector in the EU-15[4] (excluding electricity for heating) corresponds to about 175GW of decentralised power (based on 2,200 full hours per year) (Odyssee Database). Half of this can be saved through energy-efficient electric devices on the time horizon of half a century, even taking into account some new applications. For the service sector, the captive electricity consumption is the equivalent of 230GW. Here the prospective savings are even larger, given the considerable potential for savings in the field of office appliances, as well as in the cooling and ventilation of buildings. Electricity used for heating, hot water and cooking in both the service and the

---

[4] The EU-15 are Austria, Belgium, Denmark, Finland, France, Germany, Greece, Ireland, Italy, Luxembourg, the Netherlands, Portugal, Spain, Sweden and the United Kingdom.

residential sectors corresponds today to about 350TWh, of which a large part can be saved through low-energy houses. All in all, with a decentralised generation capacity of 200–250GW in the EU-15, combined with appliances that are twice as energy-efficient as today's devices (while lowering future demand for electricity by integrating energy efficiency requirement into the design of devices) and low-energy houses, the building sector could become largely autonomous in terms of electricity demand towards the middle of this century. In the very long term, towards the end of the century, the building sector could provide the supply for all demand sectors, including industrial applications and a possible shift towards electric cars, and could become the powerhouse for the entire economy.

14.6   References

Jochem, E., D. Favrat, K. Hungerbühler, P. Rudolph von Rohr, D. Spreng, A. Wokaun and M. Zimmermann (2002). *Steps Towards a 2000Watt Society: Developing a White Paper on Research and Development of Energy-Efficient Technologies*, Zurich: Centre for Energy Policy and Economics, available from http://www.cepe.ethz.ch/download/projects/Steps_towards_a_2000_Watt%96Society.pdf.

MacDonald, A. (2003). *The Virtual Power Plant: Objectives, Concept, Components, Context, and Business Plan*, http://www.oeb.gov.on.ca/documents/directive_dsm_AlexMacdonald_vpp141103.pdf

Markewitz, P., and H.-J. Ziesing (eds.) (2004). *Politikszenarien für den Klimaschutz (Policy Scenarios for Climate Protection)*, Environment series no. 50, Jülich, Germany: Schriften des Forschungszentrums Jülich.

15 Industry

Lynn Price, Christina Galitsky and Ernst Worrell

15.1 Introduction

Globally, industry consumes nearly 40 per cent of commercial energy to extract natural resources, convert them into raw materials and manufacture finished products (Price et al., 2005). Energy-intensive industries engaged in the transformation of raw materials into manufactured goods such as cement and steel typically dominate energy demand in industrialising countries as infrastructures are built. Increasingly, industry is confronted with the challenge of moving towards a cleaner, more sustainable path of production and consumption, while maintaining global competitiveness. Technology will be essential for meeting these challenges. Opportunities to reduce industry's electricity demand are found throughout this diverse sector. In addition, there is a continuous stream of emerging technologies being developed, demonstrated and adopted by industries around the world.

Historically, global industrial primary electricity demand (including transmission and distribution losses) grew at an average annual growth rate of 2.6 per cent between 1971 and 2000 (see table 15.1). Growth was especially high in the developing countries in Asia, Latin America, the Middle East and North Africa. Growth was moderate in the industrialised countries of the Pacific and North America, while relatively flat in western Europe and the former Soviet Union states. As a region, central and eastern Europe experienced a decline in electricity use during this period.

Table 15.1 also provides projections of electricity demand to 2050 based on the Intergovernmental Panel on Climate Change's *Special Report on Emissions Scenarios* marker scenario A1, which forecasts growth associated with rapid and successful economic development enabling the global economy to expand at an average annual rate of about 3 per cent (Nakicenovic et al., 2000). This scenario projects overall global AAGR at 3.5 per cent, with high growth forecast for all developing country regions and relatively high growth in the former Soviet Union states and

Table 15.1 *Industrial sector primary electricity demand*

	1971	2000	2050	AAGR 1971–2000	AAGR 2000–2050
	EJ			%	
Pacific OECD	2.49	4.92	7.04	2.4	0.7
North America	6.43	11.59	13.80	2.1	0.3
Western Europe	5.71	7.30	17.71	0.9	1.8
Central and Eastern Europe	1.40	1.16	4.74	−0.6	2.8
Former Soviet Union	3.12	3.14	16.88	0.0	3.4
Centrally planned Asia	1.23	9.79	69.23	7.4	4.0
Other Asia	0.52	4.31	43.70	7.6	4.7
Latin America	0.73	2.89	22.37	4.9	4.2
Sub-Saharan Africa	0.67	1.34	25.03	2.4	6.0
Middle East and North Africa	0.19	1.39	53.01	7.0	7.6
World	22.47	47.85	273.49	2.6	3.5

Source: Price et al. (2005).

central and eastern Europe. This scenario projects that electricity use in Western Europe will grow at a faster pace than in the past, while slowing in the industrialised countries of the Pacific and in North America.

Table 15.2 provides a breakdown of industrial sector final electricity use in the United States, showing that the chemicals, primary metals and paper industries consumed 50 per cent of industrial electricity in 1998. The food, transportation equipment, petroleum and coal products, fabricated metals products, plastics and rubber products, and computer and electronic products industries consumed another 32 per cent of US electricity that year (EIA, 2001).

Industry is not interested in consuming electricity but, rather, in the services that the electricity-consuming equipment provides. These services are also called end uses. Electricity end uses vary from industry to industry. While some sectors use electricity mainly to drive processes (e. g. electrolysis), others use them mainly to drive pumps or compressed air systems (see chapter 13 on energy storage in this volume). Table 15.3 provides a distribution of typical electricity end uses for selected sectors. Although the table 15.3 is based on the situation in the United States, similar distributions are found in other countries around the world.

15.2 Drivers for industrial electricity efficiency

Increasingly, industry is confronted with the challenge of moving towards a cleaner, more sustainable path of production and consumption,

Table 15.2 *US final electricity demand by industrial subsectors, 1998*

Industrial sector	Final electricity use (million kWh)	Industrial share of final electricity use (%)
Chemicals	215	21
Primary metals	169	16
Paper	124	12
Food	67	7
Transportation equipment	58	6
Petroleum and coal products	54	5
Fabricated metal products	52	5
Plastics and rubber products	54	5
Computer and electronic products	40	4
Machinery	28	3
Textile mills	30	3
Wood products	23	2
Electrical equipment, appliances and components	16	2
Beverages and tobacco products	8	1
Textile product mills	5	1
Apparel	5	1
Printing and related support	15	1
Furniture and related products	9	1
Miscellaneous	12	1
Leather and allied products	1	0.1
Total	477	

Source: EIA (2001).

while attempting to maintain global competitiveness. The drivers for improving industrial electricity efficiency include the desire to reduce vulnerability to rapidly increasing electricity prices and price spikes, to maintain competitiveness through the overall minimisation of electricity prices, to respond to regulatory requirements for cleaner production (including air quality, solid waste and greenhouse gas emissions issues) and to meet consumer demand for 'greener', more environmentally friendly products.

Technology will be essential for meeting these challenges. At some point, businesses are faced with investment in new capital stock. At this decision point, new and emerging technologies compete for capital investment alongside more established or mature technologies. Understanding the dynamics of the decision-making process is important to perceive what drives technology change and the overall effect on industrial energy use. From a policy-making perspective, the better technology developments are understood the more effectively future research funds will be used.

Table 15.3 *Percentage distribution of electricity end uses in selected industrial sectors*

Sector	Process	Refrigeration	Pumps	Fans	Compressed air	Other drives	HVAC	Lighting	Other
Food and kindred products	6	23	16	9	9	16	7	7	7
Textile mill	4	6	10	8	4	36	14	10	7
Lumber and wood	8	1	12	9	5	44	5	6	9
Paper	4	1	27	16	4	36	3	3	6
Printing and publishing	3	4	8	6	3	28	20	23	5
Chemicals	1	10	25	6	2	20	7	4	9
Petroleum and coal	2	5	47	7	12	13	3	3	1
Rubber and plastics	19	8	9	7	4	31	8	10	5
Stone, clay, glass and concrete	24	2	18	14	6	21	5	5	4
Primary metals	13	0	23	18	8	27	4	4	1
Fabricated metals	14	2	9	7	12	22	10	15	10
Electrical equipment	17	6	5	4	12	10	22	13	11
Transportation equipment	10	4	7	5	14	14	18	16	12
Total	21	5	15	8	9	21	7	6	8

Source: based on data from the Energy Information Administration, US Department of Energy.

Opportunities to reduce industry's energy demand are found through-out this diverse sector (de Beer et al., 2001; ECCP, 2001; IPCC, 2001). Efficiency improvements in cross-cutting technologies are found in almost all industries, such as motor and pumping systems, typically range between 15 per cent and 20 per cent of annual facility energy consumption, often with simple payback periods of around two years and internal rates of return of around 45 per cent (Lung et al., 2003; DOE, 1998). Use of high-efficiency motor-driven systems, combined with improvements to existing systems, could reduce electricity use by motor-driven systems in the European Union by 30 per cent (De Keulenaer, 2004). The optimisation of compressed air systems can result in improvements of 20 per cent to 50 per cent (McKane and Medaris, 2003). Assessments of cost-effective efficiency improvement opportunities in energy-intensive industries in the United States, such as paper, steel and cement manufacturing, have found cost-effective savings of 16 per cent to 18 per cent (Martin et al., 1999: Martin, Anglani et al., 2000; Worrell et al., 1999, 2000, 2001; Worrell, Martin, Anglani et al., 2001); even greater savings can often be realised in developing countries, where old, inefficient technologies have continued to be used to meet growing material demands (Price et al., 1999; Price et al., 2002; Schumacher and Sathaye, 1999, WEC, 2004).

In addition, there is a continuous stream of emerging technologies being developed, demonstrated and adopted in the industrial sector. Emerging technologies, such as direct reduction and near net shape/strip casting in steel formation, separation membranes, black liquor gasification and advanced cogeneration, can bring even further savings as they are commercialised and adopted by industries (Worrell et al., 2004). Roughly 175 such technologies, applicable to industries as diverse as petroleum refining, food processing, mining, glass-making and the production of chemicals, aluminum, ceramics, steel and paper, have recently been identified. Of these, fifty-four were evaluated, and over a half of these promised high energy savings, many with simple payback times of three years or less (Martin, Worrell et al., 2000).

Analyses of energy efficiency improvements found potential savings compared to current average energy use of 35 per cent for steelmaking and 75 per cent to 90 per cent in papermaking in the long term (over two decades) (de Beer et al., 1998a, 1998b).

15.3   Emerging industrial technologies

Opportunities to reduce industrial electricity use include electricity-efficient technologies and measures, and measures that produce electricity

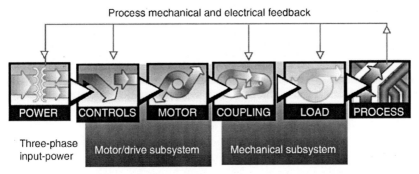

Figure 15.1. Schematic representation of a motor system.
Source: Office of Industrial Technologies, Department of Energy, Best-Practice Program website for motors: http://www.oit.doe.gov/bestpractices/motors/.

using waste gases or through co-generation. We distinguish various categories of technologies:

- electricity-efficiency improvement – i.e. more efficient use of electricity to perform the same service;
- fuel switching – i.e. to or away from electricity, but leading to an overall efficiency improvement; and
- co-generation – i.e. the co-production of heat and electricity using fossil, renewable or waste fuels, leading to increased overall energy efficiency improvement.

To understand the magnitude of possible savings, we discuss examples of emerging technologies below. These represent only a portion of the opportunities available for improving energy efficiency in this sector.

15.3.1 Electricity-efficient technologies and measures: motor systems

Motor systems consume over a half of the electricity in industry. Motor systems consist of a range of components centred around a motor-driven device, such as a compressor, pump or fan (see figure 15.1). Motor system performance improvement focuses on optimising the flows in motor-driven systems to meet end-use requirements. The opportunity for energy savings derives from the fact that the power consumption of the end user varies as the cube of the speed, while output varies linearly. As a result, small changes in motor speed can yield large energy savings, so it is important to match output closely to end-use requirements. Many of these opportunities can be implemented today, but motor operators often fail to do so. However, in the long term new motor technologies may improve energy efficiency further.

Emerging motor system improvements can be categorised into the following three areas of development opportunities: (1) upgrades to the motors themselves, including superconducting motors, permanent magnet motors, copper rotor motors, switched reluctance drives, written pole motors and very low-loss magnetic steels; (2) system design optimisation and management, such as end-use efficiency improvements, the use of premium lubricants, and advanced system design and management tools; and (3) controls on existing systems, including multi-master controls on compressors, sensor-based controls and advanced adjustable speed drives with improvements like regenerative braking, active power factor correction, better torque/speed control.

(1) *New motors.* Permanent magnet motors either have replaced the stator winding on a motor with a permanent magnet or contain a stator with three windings, producing a rotating field, and a rotor with one or more permanent magnets that interact with the rotating field of the stator. By switching the direction of current through the stator windings, the polarity of their magnetic field is reversed, causing the rotor to rotate. The most common type of PM motor is the electronically commutated permanent magnet motor, also known as the brushless DC motor (Nadel et al., 2002).

Copper rotor motors and magnetic steel motors replace aluminium in the rotor 'squirrel cage' structure of the motor, since the electrical conductivity of these materials is up to 60 per cent higher than that of aluminium and, hence, produces a more energy-efficient induction motor. In addition, copper reacts with much more stability to changing loads, especially at low speeds and frequencies, operates at a lower temperature and has fewer repairs and rewindings, increasing motor life and decreasing maintenance costs. More research is needed on the materials and methods used in pressure die-casting of the copper rotors – their last major hurdle before they can compete on cost.

Written pole motors are hybrids of induction motors, during start-up, and synchronous motors, upon reaching full operating speed. The single-phase motor combines the starting characteristics of a high-slip, high-power-factor cage motor with the energy efficiency of an AC permanent magnet motor without power electronics, reduced voltage starters or phase converters. Written pole motors can now be used in applications for which only three-phase motors were available in the past. WP motors are limited to 15–75 hp and have been used in fewer than 100 commercial applications to date. WP motors are currently being used for irrigation pumps, conveyor motors, water pumps, food-processing air dryers and process stirring (Nadel et al., 2002).

Switched reluctance drives are simple, compact, brushless, electronically commutated AC motors that offer high efficiency and torque. The stator of the motor consists of steel poles, each wound with a series of coils, connected in pairs, while the rotor is just a shaped piece of steel or iron, forming poles with no magnets or coil windings. Current is switched among the different-phased windings of the stator to rotate it. Their advantages include variable speed regulation and high efficiency in extremely high and low speed ranges, precision control, high vibration tolerance, high power density and simple construction. However, the high pulsating magnetic flux causes acoustic noise and large vibrations; therefore, these motors require considerable control to switch current properly, and the specialized design that SR motors require is non-intuitive relative to traditional motors (Paula, 1998). Switched reluctance drives are currently used in military applications, such as generators for turbine engines and pump motors for jet fighters, where high reliability is required (Paula, 1998).

Superconductivity is the ability of certain materials, when cooled to extremely low temperatures, to conduct electrical current without resistance and with extremely low losses. High-temperature superconducting motors operate at temperatures between $-173°C$ and $-195°C$, achievable through liquid nitrogen cooling. These motors are expected to exhibit a longer operating life, greater safety, higher overload thresholds, a reduction in friction and reduced noise, size, volume and weight.

Rockwell Automation, in partnership with the US Department of Energy, has successfully demonstrated and tested a cryogenically cooled 1,000hp HTS motor. A prototype 5,000hp HTS motor has been developed by American Superconductor^{TM} that utilises an off-the-shelf cryogenic cooling system. The motor successfully passed full load testing at rated voltage, rated current and rated power, sustaining a maximum load of 7,000hp at rated speed. The present barrier to marketability is cost, particularly wire costs. HTS generators are currently being used in ship propulsion generators (see the AMSC website: http://www.amsuper.com/html/).

(2) *System design optimisation and end users*. Designing a system that properly matches supply to demand is crucial to energy efficiency. All components of the motor system, including compressed air, pumps, fans and motors, should be optimised to minimise demand and increase efficiency. While the engineering associated with pump systems is well understood, many engineers are not experienced in performing the energy efficiency analyses that their system requires (Martin et al., 2000). Pump

systems may require slowing the pumps, trimming the impellers or replacing an existing pump. In addition to system management for motors and motor systems, selecting a premium lubricant for the equipment can reduce friction losses, particularly in end-use equipment such as compressors, pumps and gear drives, and increase system efficiency.

(3) *Controls.* Many controls are available for motors and motor systems, and they are continuously being updated. Today more options are available to meet more system demands, and where one control does not work another probably does. Still, adjustable-speed drives of all types have penetrated only 9 per cent of US motor systems (Easton Consultants, 1999). A new class of ASDs – magnetically coupled adjustable-speed drives – offers a greater range of possibilities for ASDs. Compared to variable-frequency drives, MC-ASDs have many advantages in addition to greater energy efficiency, including: a greater tolerance for motor misalignment; little impact on power quality; the ability to be used with regular duty motors (instead of inverters); lower expected long-term maintenance costs; and extended motor and equipment lives, due to the elimination of vibration and wear on equipment (Chvála et al., 2002). Today's ASDs are available to a wider range of applications than VFDs. MC-ASDs easily mount on the shaft of any AC motor and therefore can be applied to both new and retrofit motors. MC-ASDs are fairly new – less than ten years old.

Two particularly promising MC-ASD devices are the Magna Drive and the PAYBACK drive. In the Magna Drive, fixed rare earth magnets create an induced electromotive force to transfer torque. The physical connection between motors and loads in replaced with a gap of air, and the amount of torque transferred is controlled by varying the air gap distarce between rotating plates in the assembly. The PAYBACK drive is similar to the Magna Drive but, instead of rare earth magnets, an electromagnet is used to control the speed of the drive. Current is applied to the coil of the electromagnet rotor, and the speed is controlled by varying the strength of the magnetic field.

Three types of secondary circuits – variable resistance, inverter and magnetic switch – can be used in varying combinations. In addition to ASDs, system controls can be implemented on systems of motors or components in order to minimise energy consumption, distribute wear and tear on equipment evenly and allow for the smooth operation of entire systems. For example, advanced compressor controls can handle multiple compressors that communicate with each other. One supplier boasts the ability to control up to thirty-one drives together all at once (see the PML Flightlink website: http://www.pmlflightlink.com). Sensor

Table 15.4 *Electricity efficiency estimates for emerging motor technologies*

Technology	Electricity savings (%)	Notes
New motors		
Superconductor	2 to 10	Higher efficiencies at partial load.
Copper rotor	1 to 3	5% has been reported.
Switched reluctance	3	
Permanent magnet	5 to 10	
Written pole	3 to 4	
System and end-use improvements		
Systems management	17 to 25	Compressed air efficiency improvements are probably greater than pumping systems or motors.
Premium lubricants	3	
Controls		
MagnaDrive	Up to 60	Savings are great compared to non-ASDs. Compared to ASDs energy savings will be less.
PAYBACK drive	Up to 60	Savings are great compared to non-ASDs. Compared to ASDs energy savings will be less.
Advanced ASDs	2	Savings are great compared to conventional ASDs.

controls can monitor air quality or other end uses and provide feedback to the motor for adjustment.

15.3.1.1 Energy savings Primary specific electricity savings for particular motor applications are summarised in table 15.4. Total electricity savings will depend on the penetration rate of new motors, controls and system improvements in the market. In turn, this rate depends on the success of R&D and the impact of market transformation and technology transfer programmes. Depending on the application, some measures can be applied to retrofits of motors and motor systems and some can be applied only to new motors. Most systems can be adapted in some way for energy efficiency. A recent study estimated the total potential for energy savings from energy-efficient motor technologies in the United States by 2025 at just below 12 per cent of motor energy use (Worrell et al., 2004).

Motor systems are broad cross-cutting technologies that are used by every sector and every industry in the United States. The total energy savings potential for upgrades in motors and motor systems has been estimated to be between 15 per cent and 25 per cent in the United States (and even higher when emerging technologies are included) (Nadel et al., 2002).

15.3.1.2   Cost savings   (1) *New motors.* Depending on the new motor, relative costs vary greatly, and each has its own barriers to mass production. Superconductor motors are eventually expected to have lower capital costs, due to smaller sizes and compactness, and reduced operating costs due to increased energy efficiency (see the AMSC website: http://www.amsuper.com/html/). PM motors are easy to manufacture and costs, are comparable to conventional ASDs, about $200–400 per horsepower. Copper rotor motor commercialisation is currently cost-prohibitive because of the expensive casting of the rotor. Once this barrier is overcome, potentially lower purchase prices could be achieved due to the motors' reduced size. Operating costs for copper rotor motors are less than conventional aluminum motors. In addition, the life expectancy of the motor itself is predicted to be 50 per cent greater, increasing the overall cost-effectiveness of the motor.

WP motors are simple to manufacture, but costs are still high because of the lack of production volume (Nadel et al, 2002). The installation cost of a 20hp WP motor and controller package is about 60 per cent higher than for a conventional induction motor. Once the production volume reaches full production levels, the cost premium is expected to drop by 50 per cent, bringing the installation costs down to 30 per cent higher. SR motors and their associated controls, starters and enclosures cost about 50 per cent more than comparably sized and equipped induction motors with variable-speed controls (Martin et al., 2000). This price is likely to drop by a half when SR motors are more widely accepted and with new developments in controls. Currently shafts and bearing systems must be of higher quality than those of conventional motors, driving up the price.

(2) *System design optimisation and end users.* There are generally no system optimisation capital costs because no equipment needs to be purchased. Some fees for staff time or hiring an expert may be required. Many optimisation tools are offered free of charge and require no investment costs.

(3) *Controls.* MC-ASD installation costs are comparable to those of VFDs, when compared over a lifetime. Initial capital costs are higher, but the life expectancy of the MC-ASDs is considerably longer – thirty years compared to five to ten years for conventional ASDs. Long-term maintenance costs are expected to be reduced, and MC-ASD motor systems can be down-sized more easily than conventional ASD systems. Advanced ASD designs and advanced compressor controls will cost

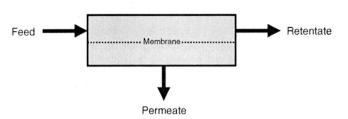

Figure 15.2. Schematic representation of a membrane separation unit.

more up-front than conventional ASDs or simpler controls, but provide operational savings due to better energy efficiency.

15.3.2 Fuel switching measures: membranes

Separation processes are a major energy consumer in industry. Distillation and drying consume large amounts of fuel in many industries. Membranes are a primary example of a technology that increases electricity use but would result in an overall reduction of primary energy use because of the large fuel savings.

Membranes selectively separate one or more materials from a liquid or gas and can replace energy-intensive separation processes in a number of industrial sectors, including food processing, chemicals, paper, petroleum refining and metals. Membranes can be used to remove dissolved or suspended solids in the waste water generated by large water-consuming industries. Membranes can also be used to purify product streams or separate gases. Energy savings, however, will depend on the specific application. Figure 15.2 gives a schematic presentation of a membrane unit.

Membranes can be made from organic or inorganic materials, or can be a hybrid of both. Organic membranes can be used for processes with temperatures below 150°C Inorganic membranes can be used in high-temperature environments, ranging from 500–800°C using metal membranes, to over 1,000°C using many ceramic membranes. Hybrid membranes have organic molecules that allow water and dissolved substances to be filtered by the membrane, and inorganic molecules that provide stability.

Based on the separation principle and the state of feed and permeate streams, different membrane technology categories are distinguished. Typical membrane separation processes include microfiltration, ultrafiltration, nanofiltration, reverse osmosis, electrodialysis, gas separation and pervaporation. Emerging membrane technologies include microporous membranes for gas separation; ion-exchange membranes for electrodialysis, diffusion dialysis, NF, membrane solvent extraction and facilitated transport; pervaporation membranes for removing trace organics from water; proton-exchange membrane fuel cells for converting chemical energy directly into electrical energy; encapsulating membranes for environmentally sensitive materials; ultrafiltration systems for oily waste streams; supported liquid membranes to extract selectively multiple elements or compounds from a mixed process stream; liquid membranes and emulsion liquid membranes for the removal of trace impurities; and a variety of other membrane technologies (Srikanth, 2004).

Membranes can be used in a wide variety of applications in the automobile, beverage, biopharmaceutical, chemical, dairy, electronic, fertiliser, food processing, metal finishing, mining, petroleum refining, pharmaceutical and textile industries and for cleaning drinking water, cleaning waste water, de-icing, dewatering and desalinisation.

In the food processing industry, membranes are used to concentrate, fractionate and purify liquid products. Four types of membrane processes are important: MF, UF, NF and RO. Gas separation is used only in the fruit and vegetable sector for packaging in a nitrogen atmosphere.

The dairy industry is an important sector using membranes worldwide, and many thousands of square metres of membranes have been installed in this industry. It is the sector with the longest history of using membranes, which are used for the desalting of whey and to separate lactose from salt and minerals (NF), the concentration of skimmed milk, for ice cream, the concentration of soy proteins (UF), concentrating lactose or whey protein in the waste stream and reclaiming it as value-added concentrates or isolates for other processors (UF), the conversion of milk into cheese and soft cheese, and the preparation of egg white and egg yolk. RO is used to concentrate milk solids prior to evaporation in making concentrated milks and to remove water from whey concentrates, isolates or lactose in cheese processing (Neff, 1999). Process water can also be recycled or used for boilers if cleaned with RO or be prepared for discharge using NF (Neff, 1999). Current developments in the dairy industry are the reduction of bacteria in milk and the clearing of dairy fluids. The application of membranes in the dairy industry is considered to be in an important phase for implementation on a large scale.

In the beverage industry, while MF is used sometimes for the clarification of juices and water purification, UF is more frequently used because it removes a wider range of compounds and can selectively remove certain proteins or sugars. Membranes are used by Coca Cola for juice concentration and for alcohol recovery in the production of non-alcoholic beers (Gach et al., 2000). A number of breweries (e.g. Miller Brewing Co.) already apply membranes for the removal of alcohol from beer, although potential exists for further application and development. Water treatment is an important application of membranes in the beverage industry (Comb, 1995). Electrodialysis for the stabilisation of wines is a new application of membranes in the food processing industry.

One of the most energy-intensive unit operations in the chemical industry is separation (Office of Industrial Technologies, 2000). Separation technologies include distillation, fractionation and extraction. Gas membranes to separate organic mixtures and liquid membranes to separate both aqueous and organic mixtures offer an alternative to liquid – liquid extraction that uses much less energy. Membrane separation technology is increasingly being utilised in the chemical industry for a wide range of applications, such as removing water from organics. The membrane-based process of pervaporation is gaining importance and is now routinely used in the chemical industry for splitting azeotropes.

The market for liquid and gas membrane separators will encompass every portion of the chemical industry. The market for membranes remains large because of the relatively few processes for which they are currently used for separation. Liquid membranes will first be used in the production of speciality chemicals in the pharmaceutical, agricultural, food and biotechnology industries, and for the production of bulk commodity chemicals and processing industrial gases, industrial waste and waste water (SRI International, 1998). Membranes are also an attractive technology for hydrogen recovery in refineries. New membrane applications for the refinery and chemical industries are under development. Membranes for hydrogen recovery from ammonia plants were first demonstrated about twenty years ago (Baker et al., 2000), and are used in various state-of-the-art plant designs. Liquid membranes are highly specific with regard to the compounds that they can separate, and therefore differing processes will require differing membranes.

Waste water is produced in a variety of industries, including the metal, metal plating, food, paper, chemical and electronics industries, and may contain different contaminants, ranging from bio-organic compounds to metal compounds. Such waste water needs to be cleaned before it can be discharged or recovered for reuse in the plant. Treatment with chemicals (sanitising, flocculation), biological treatment, ozonation, ultraviolet treatment, gravity settling, flotation and screening are conventional methods used to clean water. Membranes can also be used to remove dissolved or suspended solids, or microbes. The membrane types mostly used in waste water treatment are UF, NF and RO, while MF is mainly used to stabilise (pre-filter) the water for RO treatment. Membrane waste water treatment plant design starts with the selection of the membrane. The type of membrane material used determines the contaminant rejection characteristics (i.e. the chemicals removed from the water), the durability and the fouling characteristics. Most membranes used today are polymer membranes, as these have lower costs. Ceramic membranes are more expensive, but can be used at higher pressures and with longer lifetimes. Membrane processes (e.g. MF and RO) can be combined to remove different contaminants.

15.3.2.1 Energy savings (1) *Food processing.* The main energy-consuming industrial sectors in which membranes can be applied are fruit and vegetable processing, beverages and dairy. For specific applications, energy savings may be up to 40 per cent to 55 per cent of the energy needs for distillation and evaporation. Research is aimed at increasing the number of applications, increasing the product quality and lifetime, and increasing energy savings. A European study estimated that membranes could be used to replace 15 per cent of fuel using applications in the food industries (Eichhammer, 1995). Net energy savings of 10.2 GJ/tonne of water removed were realised when an NF unit was installed in place of a two-stage evaporation process for whey concentration at a dairy plant (CADDET, 1998). Energy savings of 66 per cent were experienced when a combination of UF and RO was used for apple juice concentration compared to an evaporation process (CADDET, 1996). Membrane microfiltration for the sterilising and filtration of beer typically uses approximately 0.04–0.07 kWh/litre. The replacement of plate membranes by new spiral membranes at the Heineken brewery in 's-Hertogenbosch, the Netherlands, reduced pumping energy and water demand, and resulted in savings of 4.6 kWh for every 100 litres of beer. Investigations into the use of oscillatory flow in cross-flow microfiltration for beer clarification found energy savings ranging from 15 per cent to 40 per cent compared to standard microfiltration, due to reduced pumping requirements (Blanpain-Avet et al., 1999).[1] Electrodialysis can be used instead of conventional energy-intensive refrigeration for stabilising wines, reducing electricity use by 80 per cent.

(2) *Chemicals.* Gas and liquid membranes offer an alternative to liquid–liquid extraction, and use much less energy. This technology can be used to separate both aqueous and organic mixtures. Membrane separation uses 60 per cent less fuel than liquid–liquid extraction for

---

[1] Nonetheless, some manufacturers believe that current cross-flow membrane filtration systems may require as much extra energy as they save; personal communication with D. Todd, of LCI Corporation.

separating a mixture of isopropyl alcohol and water. Separation processes account for one quarter of the process energy to produce isopropyl alcohol. A recent assessment found primary energy saving potentials of 20 per cent and 53 per cent, respectively, for specific applications of gas and liquid membranes as replacements in the production of methanol and isopropyl alcohol.

(3) *Waste water*. For specific applications, the energy savings of membranes for water treatment may be up to 40 per cent to 55 per cent of the energy needs for evaporation. Additional production savings are achieved through product quality, reduced water use and lower operation costs, which are site-specific. Tri-Valley Growers in Madera, California, installed an UF/RO membrane system to reduce the waste water discharge from an olive oil plant. The system allowed the operation of the plant with zero discharges. The system reduced capital costs and energy costs compared to a biological waste water treatment system. Gas use was reduced by 55 per cent and electricity use by 30 per cent (Fok and Moore, 1999). A closed-loop zero-effluent-discharge paper mill using pressurised ozone with dissolved air flotation and an ultrafiltration membrane in series allows total dissolved solids in process water to be readily converted to total suspended solids for efficient removal, saving energy through avoiding the cost to heat incoming fresh water.

15.3.2.2 Cost savings An economic assessment of membrane applications requires the evaluation of both the capital and operating costs associated with the application as well as the resulting benefits when compared to more traditional alternatives. The economic benefits in process applications include reduced operating costs relative to competitive technology, reduced product waste, recovery of by-products, and savings of water, energy and chemicals. Economic benefits related to effluent reduction include savings in transport and disposal costs, as well as the ability to increase production in situations where effluent disposal limits are imposed.

(1) *Food processing*. In the food processing industry, traditional filtration, separation and evaporation processes are typically used to separate, clarify and purify foods and beverages. Membranes can be a cost-effective alternative, especially if they increase by-product recovery. For example, capital costs of $250,000 and annual operating costs of $82,000 for a membrane treatment system were seen at a Dole Raisin plant, but annual savings of over $500,000 were realised due to the recovery of sugar concentrate (Mannapperuma et al., 1995). At Golden Town Apple Products in Canada, a combination of UF and RO was used for apple juice concentration. The payback period of the combined

system is about 2.5 years (CADDET, 1996). The investment costs for a NF unit installed for whey concentration at a dairy plant in the Netherlands, replacing a two-stage evaporation process, were $100/m^2. Energy savings, as well as reduced transport costs and emission charges, resulted in a payback period of 1.3 years (CADDET, 1998). Alcohol separation processes in breweries require an additional process step (as opposed to manipulated fermentation) and are done to improve taste. The Heineken brewery at 's-Hertogenbosch produces 120,000 hectolitres/year of non-alcoholic beer by removing alcohol and water from ordinary beer using a RO filter. In 1997 the filters were replaced by 'spiral wound' units, where the filter membranes are shaped like tubes and are configured according to the cross-flow principle. The payback period was about four years (CADDET, 1999; NOVEM, 1997). A recent study has estimated that membranes for food processing would result in a simple payback period of just over two years and an internal rate of return of 45 per cent, given a 15 per cent discount rate (Martin et al., 2000).

(2) *Chemicals.* One of the most energy-intensive unit operations in the chemical industry is separation, which can account for over 50 per cent of the plant operating costs (Tham, 2003). Separation technologies include distillation, fractionation and extraction. Certain mixtures of chemicals cannot be separated beyond a certain point by standard distillation processes and must undergo extraction. Improved gas separations involving oxygen (O_2), hydrogen (H_2) and carbon dioxide (CO_2) can lead to reduced capital and operating costs, as well as to improvements in thermal efficiency and superior environmental performance. DOE-sponsored studies indicate that technologies now in the research and development phase will offer substantial cost reduction compared to the cryogenic air separation methods currently employed (Steigel et al., 2003). Liquid and gas membranes for separation offer an alternative to liquid–liquid extraction that uses much less energy. Liquid membrane separators tend to cost about 10 per cent less than traditional separation units (Martin et al., 2000). The annual operating costs of membranes tend to run a bit higher than those of other separators, mainly because membranes foul easily and must be replaced rather frequently. In general, gas and liquid membrane applications currently have simple payback times of around ten years with low internal rates of return (Martin et al., 2000), but shorter payback times are seen in many applications.

(3) *Waste water.* Traditional waste water treatment methods include the use of chemicals (coagulants) to remove impurities, flocculation, sedimentation and fine particle (e.g. sand) filtration. The costs and energy use of waste water treatment depend heavily on the facility, differences in flow and type of pollutants, as well as the type of equipment used. The

main driver for membrane application is the cost of waste water treatment, and not energy use, although membranes can reduce energy use in relation to evaporation. Life cycle costs of new, relatively small water treatment facilities (less than 20,000 m³/day) using pressure-driven membrane processes should be less than or comparable to those of new facilities using conventional processes for particle removal or the reduction of dissolved organic materials (Wiesner and Chellam, 1999). A recent study has estimated that membrane technologies for waste water treatment average about $30,000 in capital costs and save $6,400 annually in operating costs, resulting in a simple payback period of just under five years and an internal rate of return of about 20 per cent (Martin et al., 2000). In a number of applications, the annual operating cost savings from reductions in waste-water-related fees and associated labour costs lead to simple payback periods of three years or less (Nini and Gimenez-Mitsotakis, 1994; Pollution Engineering, 2002). Where the costs of the new membrane technology at a Hunt-Wesson tomato processing plant were greater than the direct benefits, the improved effluent treatment levels enabled the plant to increase production and the resulting increase in income outweighed the membrane costs by a significant amount (Mannapperuma et al., 1995).

15.3.3 Electricity generation

Electricity demand from industry can also be reduced through self–generation, using either new gasification technologies or advanced co-generation, which is also called combined heat and power production (see also chapter 9 on microgeneration in this volume).

CHP systems generate electricity (and/or mechanical energy) and thermal energy in a single, integrated system. This contrasts with the more common practice, whereby electricity is generated at a central power plant, and on-site heating and cooling equipment is used for non-electric energy requirements. Conventional electricity generation is inherently inefficient, converting only about one-third of a fuel's potential energy into usable energy. Because CHP captures the heat that would otherwise be rejected in the traditional generation of electric or mechanical energy, the total efficiency of these integrated systems is much greater than from separate systems. The significant increase in efficiency with CHP results in lower fuel consumption and reduced emissions compared with the separate generation of heat and power. CHP is not a specific technology but, rather, an application of technologies to meet end-user needs for heating and/or cooling, and mechanical and/or electric power. Steam turbines, gas turbines, combined cycles and reciprocating engines are the major current technologies used for power generation and CHP. New technologies, such as fuel cells, are under development, while R&D also contributes to increased efficiencies and new applications of existing co-generation in industry.

(1) *Large scale (> 10MW)*. Currently, most of the installed CHP plants have capacities over 20MW. The future potential of large-scale conventional CHP systems is estimated at 48GW (Onsite Sycom, 2000). An increase in turbine inlet temperature has led to increasing efficiencies in gas turbines. Industrial-sized single-cycle turbines are available with efficiencies of 40 per cent to 42 per cent (lower heating value).[2] The current industry 'standard' is the GE LM2500 turbine, with an efficiency of 34 per cent to 40 per cent. It is expected that the efficiencies of aero-derivative and industrial turbines can increase to 45 per cent by 2010.

The higher inlet temperature also allows a higher outlet temperature. The flue gas of the turbine can then be used to heat a chemical reactor, if the outlet and reactor temperatures can be matched. One option is the so-called 'repowering' option. In this option the furnace is not modified, but the combustion air fans in the furnace are replaced by a gas turbine. The exhaust gases still contain a considerable amount of oxygen, and can thus be used as combustion air for the furnaces. The gas turbine can deliver up to 20 per cent of the furnace heat. A few plants have used the repowering option; for example, two of these installations, totalling 35MW, are installed at refineries in the Netherlands.

Another option, with a larger CHP potential and associated energy savings, is 'high-temperature CHP'. In this case, the flue gases of a CHP plant are used to heat the input of a furnace. Zollar (2002) discusses various applications in the chemical and refinery industries. The study finds total potential of 44GW in addition to the conventional CHP potential in these two sectors. The major candidate processes are atmospheric distillation, coking and hydrotreating in petroleum refineries and ethylene and ammonia manufacture in the chemical industry. High-temperature CHP requires replacing the existing furnaces. This is due to the fact that the radiative heat transfer from gas turbine exhaust gases is much smaller than it is from combustion gases, due to their lower temperature.

By 2025 large-scale applications of fuel cells are expected to consist of parallel smaller systems, which are discussed below. In the long term, the integration of industrial processes, such as reforming in the chemical and petroleum refining industries, with high-temperature solid oxide fuel cells are likely to lead to revolutionary design changes and allow the direct co-generation of power and chemicals.

---

[2] Note that the efficiency of these turbines in combined-cycle plants and utility-sized turbines is higher, at 52 per cent to 56 per cent.

(2) *Medium scale (< 20MW)*. Both in the United States and Europe, research aims at developing medium-scale gas turbines with high efficiencies. In Europe, the development and demonstration of a 1.4MW gas turbine with a single-cycle efficiency of 43 per cent (LHV) is being undertaken, as part of the CAME-GT (Cleaner and More Efficient Engines–Gas Turbines) programme. Current turbines of this size have efficiencies of around 25 per cent (LHV).

Steam-injected gas turbines (known both as STIGs and Cheng-cycle turbines) can absorb excess steam – e.g. that generated due to seasonal reduced heating needs – to boost power production by injecting the steam into the turbine, thereby boosting the turbine's power output. The size of typical STIGs starts at around 5MWe. Currently over 100 STIGs are found around the world, especially in Japan, as well as in Europe and the United States.

CHP integration allows the increased use of CHP in industry by utilising the heat in more efficient ways. This can be done by using the heat as a process input for drying or process heating (see also above), or by tri-generation (see below) through the supply of power, heating and cooling. The flue gas of a turbine can often be used directly in a dryer. This option has been used successfully for the drying of minerals as well as food products. Although NOx emissions of gas turbines vary widely, tests in the Netherlands have shown that the flue gases do not affect the drying air and product quality negatively, depending on the type of gas turbine selected (Buijze, 1998). In order to permit continuous operation, bypassing the gas turbines makes it possible to maintain the turbine and run the drying process (Buijze, 1998). A cement plant in Rozenburg, the Netherlands, uses a standard industrial gas turbine to generate power and to dry the blast furnace slags used in cement making to replace clinker. In the food industry, an Avebe starch plant in Gasselternijveen in the Netherlands uses a STIG installation to provide both power and heat for the plant. Another project has shown that it is more efficient to use the waste heat (i.e. the flue gases) from a gas turbine directly to dry protein-rich cattle feed by-product. The excess flue gas is mixed with air and used directly for the drying process. The project was expected to result in savings of 12 per cent of the total on-site fuel consumption with a simple payback period of 2.5 years (NOVEM, 1995).

Tri-generation has been used at various commercial locations in the United States, but less so in industry. Bassols et al. (2002) discuss various applications in food processing plants in Europe. Plants that have varying heating and refrigeration loads and that have a large refrigeration load are especially attractive, e.g. margarine and vegetable oils, dairy, vegetable and fruit processing and freezing, and meat processing. Bassols et al. (2002) discuss commercial applications varying from 4–9 MW capacity in the Netherlands and Spain, but do not discuss economics.

Pressure recovery turbines utilise the opportunity to recover power from the decompression of natural gas on industrial sites. Natural gas is transported in pipelines at high pressures, and decompressed for local distribution and use. Recovery turbines can recover part of this compression energy by producing power (Lehman and Worrell, 2001). Industrial facilities are very suitable for this technology as low-temperature waste heat is often available on-site to reheat the gas during decompression. Many industrial sites have excess low-temperature waste heat that is currently not utilised, due to a lack of suitable applications or due to poor economics. Lehman and Worrell (2001) estimate the technical potential in US industry at 12 TWh, while the payback period depends strongly on the electricity price. With an electricity price of $0.1/kWh the simple payback period may be as low as three years. The Corus iron and steel plant in Ijmuiden, the Netherlands, installed a 2 MW power recovery turbine in 1994. Hot water from the hot strip mill is used to reheat the recompressed gas in the system (Lehman and Worrell, 2001).

(3) *Small scale (< 1 MW)*. For small-scale industrial applications the major developments are found in improved designs for reciprocating engines, fuel cells and microturbines, and developments in the integration of the unit in processes allowing more efficient operation (e.g. the tri-generation of power, heat and cooling or drying and other direct process applications – see above). Microturbines and fuel cells are the most exciting developments in small-scale CHP technology.

Microturbines (25–500 kW) are expected to have an efficiency of 26 per cent to 30 per cent (Martin et al., 2000). Although this is lower than the efficiency of power generation in large grid-connected power plants, their use as a CHP unit can provide substantial energy savings. Martin et al. estimate the primary energy savings of a microturbine system at 17 per cent compared to separate power and heat production. Current development aims mainly at the commercial market, but small-scale industrial facilities may provide a potential application as well. Martin et al. (2000) estimate that up to 5 per cent of the industrial power market by 2015 may be technically suitable for microturbine application, resulting in power production of up to 40 TWh. However, the high costs of microturbines make the technology less attractive for most industries, and only in cases of high-quality power needs (premium power) are microturbine projects likely be implemented (see chapter 9 on micro-generation in this volume).

Fuel cells DC generate electricity and heat by combining fuel and oxygen in an electrochemical reaction (see chapter 13 on energy storage in this volume). This technology is an advance in power generation, avoiding both the intermediate combustion step and boiling water associated with Rankine-cycle technologies and the efficiency losses associated with gas turbine technologies. Fuel-to-electricity conversion efficiencies can theoretically reach 80 per cent to 83 per cent for low-temperature fuel cell stacks and 73 per cent to 78 per cent for high-temperature stacks. In practice, efficiencies of 50 per cent to 60 per cent are achieved with hydrogen fuel cells, while efficiencies of 42 per cent to 65 per cent are achievable with natural gas as a fuel (Martin et al., 2000). The main fuel cell types for industrial CHP applications are phosphoric acid, molten carbonate and solid oxide. Proton exchange membrane fuel cells are less suitable for co-generation as they produce only hot water as a by-product.

PAFC efficiencies are limited and the corrosive nature of the process reduces the economic attractiveness of the technology. Hence, MCFCs and SOFCs offer the most potential for industrial applications, even though PAFCs remain the most sold fuel cell system. Several industrial facilities currently use MCFCs in Japan (the Kirin brewery) and Germany (at Michelin's rubber processing plant) (Hoogers, 2003). These demonstration systems still cost around $11,000/kW. Stand-alone SOFCs have achieved efficiencies of 47 per cent, and in combination with a gas turbine in a pressurised system efficiencies of 53 per cent (LHV) have been achieved (Hoogers, 2003). Unfortunately, the production costs of SOFCs are still high. Dow Chemical and GM will collaborate in the installation of a large-scale PEMFC system (up to 35 MW), using hydrogen produced as a by-product from chlorine production at Freeport, Texas. It is expected that the performance of fuel cells of between 100 kW and 5 MW output will surpass the efficiency of engine-based CHP, and that costs will also come down through improved fabrication techniques, mass production and reduced catalyst loads (in the case of PEMFCs).

15.3.3.1 Energy savings The primary energy savings are determined by the efficiency of the co-generation unit used, the efficiency of the boiler or other equipment replaced and the average efficiency of electricity generation by the public grid. Martin et al. (2000) have estimated the primary energy savings at between 17 per cent for microturbine CHP applications and 33 per cent for larger-scale systems. Another study forecasts 1.03 EJ of primary energy savings in the United States by 2025 (Worrell et al., 2004).

Table 15.5 *Cost estimates for CHP technologies in 2015*

Technology	Current costs (1999, $/kW)	Investment ($/kW)	O&M ($/kWh)	Estimated simple payback period (years)	Reference
Small – gas turbine	1,400–1,700	915	0.008		Martin et al., 2000
Small – fuel cell	2,800–3,200	1,500	0.005	> 10	Onsite Sycom, 2000
Medium – gas turbine	830–965	830	0.005	5–7	Onsite Sycom, 2000
Large – gas turbine	650–700	625	0.004	3–4	Onsite Sycom, 2000
Process	650–700	650	0.004	3–5	Onsite Sycom, 2000; Worrell et al., 1997
Pressure recovery	1,300	1,300	0.008	5–8	Lehman and Worrell, 2001

15.3.3.2 Cost savings CHP is a modular technology, and costs are expected to come down as the volume produced increases. Table 15.5 provides an overview of the estimated costs of CHP technologies in 2015. The cost-effectiveness of CHP will depend strongly on the price differential between electricity and fuels (mainly natural gas). This means that the cost-effectiveness will vary by region, by site and by overtime.

Simple payback period estimates are based on an electricity price of 4–5¢/kWh and a natural gas price of $3.2/GJ.

15.4   Conclusions

Electricity is an important energy carrier for industry, being consumed by a large variety of end uses in all industries. The most important end uses are motor systems, electrochemical processes and refrigeration, followed by cross-cutting end uses such as air conditioning and lighting.

Because of its ease of use, electricity consumption has rapidly increased over time in all industries. Generally, electricity use is growing more rapidly than the overall primary energy consumption of an industry. It is expected that industrial electricity use will continue growing in every region of the world.

There are, nonetheless, many opportunities to improve the efficiency with which electricity is used in industry. Most notably, new technologies continue to emerge that will enable important energy savings in the industrial generation and use of electricity. While some electricity applications may lead to higher electricity use, they may also contribute to increased overall energy efficiency. Hence, overall energy efficiency (based on primary energy inputs) should be the guiding principle in developing energy-efficient technology.

Enhancing the efficiency of motor systems is an important area of electricity efficiency improvement in industry, as motors use more than a half of all electricity in industry. There are many opportunities to improve the total motor system, varying from reducing the losses in the motors themselves (e.g. high-efficiency motors, superconducting motors) to improving the components and controls (e.g. variable-speed drives). There is still considerable potential for further improvements in the efficiency of motor systems when using a systems approach.

The co-generation of heat and power is a well-known technology for improving on-site power generation in industry. Although it has been used in many industries and sites around the world for some years, new technologies are continually being developed to increase the overall efficiency of the system (e.g. high-efficiency gas turbines, fuel cells) and to increase the applications for co-generation (e.g. the use of flue gas from power generation for drying and furnace heating). Even with current technology there is still considerable worldwide potential for co-generation; new technologies can only increase the applicability and primary energy savings.

Membranes are a prime example of a technology to improve overall energy efficiency (expressed as primary energy used in a process), even though electricity use increases. Membranes allow a more energy-efficient separation process, and replace traditional separation processes such as distillation. Membranes are developed for specific applications or separations; new membrane applications are being developed around the world, increasing the potential for this technology. Membranes are slowly replacing other separations in niche areas, and also more and more in bulk separation processes.

In this chapter, we have discussed some of the important new technologies: improvements to electricity efficiency, high-efficiency on-site power generation and technologies that, even though they increase electricity use, lead to net primary energy savings. Beyond these examples, there are many other electricity efficiency technologies that are currently available or under development. Continued research and development, along with active technology demonstration and dissemination programmes, can ensure that future growth in electricity demand in industry is moderated through the increased application of energy- and electricity-efficient technologies.

15.5   References

Baker, R. W., K. A. Lokhandwala, M. L. Jacobs and D. E. Gottschlich (2000). Recover feedstock and product from reactor vent streams, *Chemical Engineering Progress*, 12(96): 51–7.

Bassols, J., B. Kuckelhorn, J. Langreck, R. Schneider and H. Veelken (2002). Trigeneration in the food industry, *Applied Thermal Engineering*, 22: 595–602.

Blanpain-Avet, P., N. Doubrovine, C. Lafforgue and M. Lalande (1999). The effect of oscillatory flow on crossflow microfiltration of beer in a tubular mineral membrane system – membrane fouling resistance decreate and energetic considerations, *Journal of Membrane Science*, 152: 151–74.

Buijze, M. (1998). *Haalbaarheidsstudie naar Integratie van Twee Stuks Gasturbines (Feasibility Study for the Integration of Two Gas Turbines)*, Sittard, Netherlands: Netherlands Organization for Energy and the Environment.

CADDET (1996). *CADDET Register on Energy Efficiency Demonstration Projects*, Sittard, Netherlands: Centre for the Analysis and Dissemination of Demonstrated Energy Technologies.

(1998). *Concentration and Desalination of Whey in the Dairy Industry*, Sittard, Netherlands: Centre for the Analysis and Dissemination of Demonstrated Energy Technologies.

(1999). *Heat Recovery from Blowdown Steam in the Food Industry*, Sittard, Netherlands: Centre for the Analysis and Dissemination of Demonstrated Energy Technologies.

Chvála, W. D., D. W. Winiarski and M. C. Mulkerin (2002). *New Technology Demonstration Program: Technology Demonstration of Magnetically Coupled Adjustable-Speed Drive Systems*, Washington, DC: Office of Energy Efficiency and Renewable Energy, prepared for the Department of Energy.

Comb, L. (1995). Advances in membrane technology for beverage water treatment, *Fruit Processing*, September.

de Beer, J. G., D. Phylipsen and J. Bates (2001). *Economic Evaluation of Carbon Dioxide and Nitrous Oxide Emission Reductions in Industry in the EU*, Brussels: European Commission, Directorate-General Environment.

de Beer, J. G., E. Worrell and K. Blok (1998a). Future technologies for energy-efficient iron and steel making, in R. H. Socolow (ed.), *Annual Review of Energy and the Environment*, 23, Palo Alto, CA: Annual Reviews, 123–205.

(1998b). Long-term energy efficiency improvements in the paper and board industry, *Energy, The International Journal*, 23: 21–42.

De Keulenaer, H. (2004). Energy efficient motor driven systems, *Energy and Environment*, 15(5): 873–905.

DOE (1998). *United States Industrial Motor Systems Market Opportunities Assessment*, Washington, DC: Department of Energy.

Easton Consultants (1999). *Market Assessment of MagnaDrive ASD*, Portland, OR: Northwest Energy Efficiency Alliance.

ECCP (2001). *Long Report*, Brussels: European Commission, Directorate-General Environment, available from http://europa.eu.int/comm/environment/climat/pdf/eccp_longreport_0106.pdf.

EIA (2001). *Manufacturing Energy Consumption Survey*, Washington, DC: Department of Energy.

Eichhammer, W. (1995). Energy efficiency in industry: cross-cutting technologies, in K. Blok, W. C. Turkenburg, W. Eichhammer, F. Farinelli and T. B. Johansson (eds.), *Overview of Energy RD&D Options for a Sustainable Future*, Brussels: European Commission, Directorate-General XII, Science, Research and Development, 39–73.

Fok, S., and B. Moore (1999). Zero-discharge: an application of process water recovery technology in the food processing industry, in H. Chum (ed.), *Proceedings of the 1999 ACEEE Summer Study on Energy Efficiency in Industry*, Washington, DC: American Council for an Energy-Efficient Economy, 595–603.

Gach, G. J., D. J. Paulson and D. D. Spatz (2000). *Crossflow Membrane Filtration Applications in the Beverage Industry*, Minnetonka, MN: Osmonics, Inc.

Hoogers, G. (2003). Fuel cells for cogeneration, technology and markets worldwide, *Cogeneration and On-site Power*, 44: 80–91.

IPCC (2001). Technological and economic potential of greenhouse gas emissions reduction, in W. R. Moomaw, J. R. Moreira, K. Blok, D. Greene, K. Gregory, T. Jaszay, T. Kashiwagi, M. Levine, M. MacFarland, N. S. Prasad, L. Price, H. Rogner, R. Sims, F. Zhou, E. Alsema, H. Audus, R. K. Bose, G. M. Jannuzzi, A. Kollmuss, L. Changsheng, E. Mills, K. Minato, S. Plotkin, A. Shafer, A. C. Walter, R. Ybema, J. de Beer, D. Victor, D. Pichs-Madruga and H. Ishitani, *Climate Change 2001: Mitigation*, Geneva: United Nations and World Meteorological Organization, chap. 3.

Lehman, B., and E. Worrell (2001). Electricity production from natural gas pressure recovery using expansion turbines, in *Proceedings of the 2001 ACEEE Summer Study on Energy Efficiency in Industry*, Washington, DC: American Council for an Energy-Efficient Economy.

Lung, R. B., A. McKane, and M. Olzewski (2003). Industrial motor system optimization projects in the US: an impact study, in *Proceedings of the 2003 ACEEE Summer Study on Energy Efficiency in Industry*, Washington, DC: American Council for an Energy-Efficient Economy.

Mannapperuma, J. D., et al. (1995). *Membrane Applications in Food Processing*, Vol. I *Fruit and Vegetable Processing Industry*, Process Industries Offices Report no. CR-105377-V1, Palo Alto, CA: Electric Power Research Institute.

Martin, N., N. Anglani, D. Einstein, M. Khrushch, E. Worrell and L. Price (2000). *Opportunities to Improve Energy Efficiency and Reduce Greenhouse Gas Emissions in the US Pulp and Paper Industry*, Report no. LBNL-46141, Berkeley, CA: Lawrence Berkeley National Laboratory.

Martin, N., E. Worrell and L. Price (1999). *Energy Efficiency and Carbon Dioxide Emissions Reduction Opportunities in the US Cement Industry*, Report no. LBNL-44182, Berkeley, CA: Lawrence Berkeley National Laboratory.

Martin, N., E. Worrell, M. Ruth L. Price, R. N. Elliott, A. M. Shipley and J. Thorpe (2000). *Emerging Energy-Efficient Industrial Technologies*, Report no. LBNL-46990, Berkeley, CA: Lawrence Berkeley National Laboratory and Washington, DC: American Council for an Energy-Efficient Economy.

McKane, A., and B. Medaris (2003). *The Compressed Air Challenge: Making a Difference for US Industry*, Report no. LBNL-52771, Berkeley, CA: Lawrence Berkeley National Laboratory.

Nadel, S., R. N. Elliott, M. Shepard, S. Greenberg, G. Katz and A. T. de Almeida (2002). *Energy Efficient Motor Systems: A Handbook on Technology, Program, and Policy Opportunities*, 2nd edn., Washington, DC: American Council for an Energy-Efficient Economy.

Nakicenovic, N., J. Alcamo, G. Davis, B. de Vries, J. Fenhann, S. Gaffin, K. Gregory, A. Grubler, T. Y. Jung, T. Kram, E. L. La Rovere, L. Michaelis, S. Mori, T. Morita, W. Pepper, H. Pitcher, L. Price, K. Riahi, A. Roehrl, H.-H. Rogner, A. Sankovski, M. Schlesinger, P. Shukla, S. Smith, R. Swart, S. van Rooijen, N. Victor and D. Zhou (2000). *Special Report on Emissions Scenarios: Report of Working Group III of the Intergovernmental Panel on Climate Change*, Cambridge: Cambridge University Press.

Neff, J. (1999). The finer points of filtration: food and beverage companies find more reasons for range of membranes, *Food Processing*, 60(3): 96–100, available from http://www.foodprocessing.com/Web_First/fp.nsf/ArticleID/LKIE-4LYM98.

Nini, D., and P. Gimenez-Mitsotakis (1994). Creative solutions for bakery waste effluent, *American Institute of Chemical Engineers, Symposium Series*, 300: 95–105.

NOVEM (1995). *Benutting Turbine-afgassen voor het Drogen van Eiwit in de Zetmeelindustrie (Using Turbine Flue Gases for the drying of Protein in the Starch Industry)*, Sittard, Netherlands: Netherlands Organization for Energy and the Environment.

    (1997). *Membraanfilterinstallatie Bij de Bereiding van Alcoholvrij Bier (Membrane Filtration Installation for the Preparation of Alcohol-Free Beer)*, project factsheet, Sittard, Netherlands: Netherlands Organization for Energy and the Environment.

Office of Industrial Technologies (2000). *Energy and Environmental Profile of the US Chemical Industry*, Washington, DC: Office of Industrial Technologies, Department of Energy.

Onsite Sycom (2000). *The Market and Technical Potential for Combined Heat and Power in the Industrial Sector*, Washington, DC: Onsite Sycom Energy Corporation.

Paula, G. (1998). The rise of VSR motors, *Mechanical Engineering*, Febuary: 86–7.

Pollution Engineering (2002). *Casebook: National Raisin Cuts Wastewater Costs and Protects Environment*, available from http://www.pollutionengineering.com/CDA/ArticleInformation/features/BNP_Features_Item/0,6649,1114,41,00.html.

Price, L., S. de la Rue du Can, J. Sinton and E. Worrell (2005). *Sectoral Trends in Global Energy Use and Greenhouse Gas Emissions*, Report no. LBNL-56144, Berkeley, CA: Lawrence Berkeley National Laboratory.

Price, L., J. Sinton, E. Worrell, D. Phylipsen, X. Hu and J. Li (2002). Energy use and carbon dioxide emissions from steel production in China, *Energy, The International Journal*, 27: 429–46.

Price, L., E. Worrell and D. Phylipsen (1999). Energy use and carbon dioxide emissions in energy-intensive industries in key developing countries, in *Proceedings of the 1999 Earth Technologies Forum*, Washington, DC: Environmental Protection Agency, 83–95.

Schumacher, K., and J. Sathaye (1999). *India's Cement Industry: Productivity, Energy Efficiency and Carbon Emissions*, Report no. LBNL-41842, Berkeley, CA: Lawrence Berkeley National Laboratory.

SRI International (1998). *SRI International Forms Facilichem, Inc. To Develop And Market Novel Purification Technology*, News Release, Menlo Park, CA: SRI International, available from http://www.sri.com/news/releases/10-7-98. html.

Srikanth, G. (2004). *Membrane Separation Processes: Technology and Business Opportunities*, New Delhi: Technology Information, Forecasting and Assessment Council, available from http://chemistry.about.com/gi/dynamic/offsite. htm?site=http%3A%2F%2Fwww.tifac.org.in%2Fnews%2Fmemb.htm.

Steigel, G. J., M. Ramezan and J. Ratafia-Brown (2003). *Overview of Advanced Gas Separation Membrane Technology for Gasification Systems*, paper presented at 225th American Chemical Society National Meeting, New Orleans, 23–7 March.

Tham, M. T. (2003). *Distillation: An Introduction*, available from http://lorien. ncl.ac.uk/ming/dist/distilo.htm.

WEC (2004). *Energy Efficiency: A Worldwide Review – Indicators, Policies, Evaluation*, London: World Energy Council.

Wiesner, M. R., and S. Chellam (1999). The promise of membrane technology, *Environmental Science and Technology*, 33(17): 360–6A.

Worrell, E., N. Martin, N. Anglani, D. Einstein, M. Khrushch and L. Price (2001). *Opportunities to Improve Energy Efficiency in the US Pulp and Paper Industry*, Report no. LBNL-48354, Berkeley, CA: Lawrence Berkeley National Laboratory.

Worrell, E., N. Martin and L. Price (1999). *Energy Efficiency and Carbon Dioxide Emissions Reduction Opportunities in the US Iron and Steel Sector*, Report no. LBNL-41724, Berkeley, CA: Lawrence Berkeley National Laboratory.

(2000). Potentials for energy efficiency improvement in the US cement industry, *Energy, The International Journal*, 25: 1189–214.

(2001). Energy efficiency and carbon dioxide emissions reduction opportunities in the US iron and steel industry, *Energy, The International Journal*, 26: 513–36.

Worrell, E., L. Price and C. Galitsky (2004). *Emerging Energy-Efficient Technologies in Industry: Case Studies of Selected Technologies*, Report no. LBNL-54828 Berkeley, CA: Lawrence Berkeley National Laboratory, prepared for the National Commission on Energy Policy.

Zollar, J. (2002). *CHP Integration with Fluid Heating Processes in the Chemical and Refining Sectors*, presentation given to Distributed Power Program Quarterly Review, Medison, WI, July.

16 Transport

Pieter Vermeyen and Ronnie Belmans

16.1 Introduction

Two groups of electrically supplied transport modes exist: rail and road. Electric rail vehicles generally receive power from an external electricity supply, except for diesel-electric trains (and a very limited number of battery-supplied vehicles). Road vehicles have an internal electricity supply – e.g. a battery, a fuel cell or a combination of a combustion engine and a generator. An exception to this is the trolleybus, which receives electrical energy from an overhead power supply. All electric transport systems will be discussed in this chapter, but the emphasis will be on railway systems.

A very important component of any modern railway system and all electric and hybrid cars is the power electronic converter. Such a converter allows for the flexible operation of the vehicle and accurate and energy-efficient control of speed and torque. The power electronic converter will be referred to in several sections of this discussion, and is also discussed in chapter 11 in this volume.

Section 16.6 presents the results of a study by the IEA regarding the potential effect of policy in Western Europe on energy consumption and CO_2 emissions in the transport sector. The outcomes of two scenarios are compared: a scenario without policy measures and a scenario in which current and likely near-term measures are taken into account.

16.2 History of electrically driven transportation

Electric motors have been undergoing development since 1831, when Michael Faraday discovered electromagnetic induction. Very soon motors were being used to drive battery-powered road and rail vehicles. Later, supply systems with catenaries were developed for rail vehicles. In this historical overview electric cars will be discussed first, followed by railway systems.

16.2.1 Electric cars

At the end of the nineteenth century three road vehicle technologies coexisted: steam-powered cars (in use since the end of the eighteenth century), electric cars and petrol-powered cars (in use since the end of the nineteenth century). Around 1910 it was still the case that more electric cars than petrol-powered cars were in use. Because the development of petrol-powered cars made them more practical and less expensive than electric cars, and as access to electricity to charge batteries was limited, electric cars disappeared in the 1920s. In the 1970s, however, interest in electric cars reappeared, as a result of the oil crisis and environmental concerns (Husain, 2003, pp. 3–8). At present, hybrid electric vehicles represent the most promising technology, combining clean transportation, when required, high efficiency in general and long-distance capabilities.

16.2.2 Light rail systems

During the second half of the nineteenth century the first electric trams were developed. The vehicles were supplied with direct current, either provided by batteries or transmitted through the rails or overhead wires. The systematic electrification of the tramways started just before the end of the nineteenth century, as a parallel development in the United States and Europe.

After the Second World War two trends were observed. The first consisted of upgrading the tracks for higher speeds and segregating them from other traffic where possible. These measures not only increased speeds but also improved the economics of operation. The second trend was the removal of certain tramlines. Until the 1960s many European cities had tramway connections to the suburbs and villages further away. Because tramways were deemed to be old-fashioned, they were removed and replaced by bus lines. Buses were regarded as being more flexible and to have a lower exploitation cost. Since then the number of cars has exploded. As a result, buses are slowed down by congested roads and traffic jams as much as any car. Local authorities are now reconstructing tramlines in order to solve the traffic problems. In Germany, and to some extent in Belgium and the Netherlands, subways for tramlines in city centres have been built. This expensive solution could be financed in times of prosperity, but also meant that progress slowed dramatically when recession arrived.

The situation in the United Kingdom illustrates this evolution. Many cities in the United Kingdom used to have a tram system. These systems were all closed down, except in Blackpool, were trams have been operated since 1885. Currently eight cities have a modern tram system,[1] seven of which were put into service after 1980. In addition, a few lines with vintage trams exist, though more as museums and for entertainment or cultural purposes. New lines are now being developed (e.g. Leeds, London, south Hampshire, Edinburgh).

In France a similar development has occurred, with the reintroduction of trams in Bordeaux, Lille, Strasbourg, Paris, Toulon and Nantes. In Nantes, for example, trams driven by compressed air were used from 1879 to 1912 (see the Transports de l' Agglomération Nantaise website: http://www.tan.fr). In 1913 electrification of the tram system started. In 1958 the system was closed down and replaced by buses. In 1979 the decision was made to develop a new tram system, and the first trams were put into service in 1985.

16.2.3   Heavy rail systems

At the beginning of the twentieth century DC technology had evolved to a level that allowed the development of electric heavy-duty rapid transit lines. These rapid transit systems could replace steam traction in suburban areas, where high acceleration was needed. AC-powered railways were developed as well and the electrification of heavy rail tracks started. On non-electrified lines diesel-electric trains were used in order to retain the dynamic properties of electric traction. They also facilitated the transition to electric traction (Duffy, 2003).

Underground or metro systems were developed so as to provide high-speed transportation in large cities. Well-known examples in Europe are the metro systems of London, Berlin and Paris. Other heavy rail systems are above ground railways, ranging from local lines to intercity lines, used for the transportation of passengers and freight.

Multiple supply systems have been developed: single-phase and multiple-phase, different voltage levels, DC and AC. Today, different supply systems can be found around the world. The new European railways are evolving towards a uniform supply system, facilitating international transport. Power electronics is a key factor in this, as it enables the use of trains in different supply systems, as will be discussed later.

---

[1] Birmingham, Blackpool, Croydon, London, Manchester, Newcastle, Nottingham and Sheffield. (see the Light Rail Transit Association's Website: http://www.lrta.org).

16.3   General technology

The technology described in this section is used in railway applications as well as in electric road vehicles (see chapter 11 on power electronics). The subjects discussed here are frequency control and regenerative braking.

16.3.1   Frequency control

Traditionally, commutator motors are used. In these motors, current is injected into the rotor windings by means of sliding contacts. Commutator motors can be supplied with either direct current or low-frequency alternating current (50Hz for small applications, lower frequencies for larger power ratings, such as the 16 2/3Hz supply in central European railway systems). The characteristics of these motors are very well adapted to the requirements of traction. Speed control is simple, being carried out by adjusting the voltage magnitude, using variable resistances or tap-changing transformers. The disadvantage with this technique is that it is rather slow and inefficient. For DC motors, voltage can also be controlled by means of a chopper circuit. These classic drives require a lot of maintenance (both motor and control systems), because sliding contacts wear out quickly.

Modern trains are equipped with power electronic drives and induction motors. The motor speed is determined by frequency control. This technique is fast, requiring little or no maintenance (either to the control system or to the motor). It is also very energy-efficient: only the power necessary to drive the system is supplied to the motors, with the result that regenerative braking, as such, is possible.

Using converters with frequency control, train operation is independent of the supply voltage. Modern locomotives can be used in regions with different supply systems. No time is lost changing locomotives at border crossings, facilitating international transport. The application of frequency-controlled induction motors has led to a high degree of standardisation in drive design, reducing the cost of rolling stock.

Despite the flexibility of modern drives, the existence of different supply systems remains a problem for high-speed trains. On tracks with relatively low voltages (3,000V DC, 1,500V DC or 750V DC) trains can consume only a fraction of their nominal power, and therefore they cannot always travel at high speed. However, in Europe a tendency exists towards the use of a uniform supply system: 25kV, 50Hz. It has been adopted for all new, major infrastructure and electrification projects, apart from projects in Germany and Austria.

16.3.2   Regenerative braking

An important feature for all types of electric vehicles is regenerative braking. Electric motors are reversible devices. When the load torque, which is applied through the wheels, is higher than the motor torque, mechanical energy is converted to electrical energy: the motor becomes a generator. This can be achieved either by braking or by going downhill; in the former kinetic energy is converted, while in the latter potential energy is used.

In railway systems, this leads to bidirectional power flows. The vehicles inject the regenerated power into the supply grid. The amount of energy that can be saved depends on the way the regenerated energy is handled. This depends on the local storage capacity, the efficiency of the storage devices and the simultaneity of regeneration and demand. If the sub-station is also designed for bidirectional power flow, regenerated energy can be injected into the public electricity grid. If bidirectional power flow in sub-stations is not possible, regenerated energy can be consumed only by vehicles within the railway system. If devices for energy storage are connected to the supply system, regeneration and demand do not have to coincide. A useful storage device for railway systems is the flywheel; energy can be stored and returned very rapidly, and this cycle can be repeated many times. A battery is less suited, since its number of loading cycles is limited to less than about 1,000.

Whether or not regenerative braking is possible or allowed may also depend on the legal context. In a privatised rail sector, infrastructure and rail operations are separated, making it more complex to coordinate the use of storage elements and activities in the railway system. Energy exchange between vehicles of different companies would have to be tracked in order to allocate energy costs.

An example of flywheel storage can be found in the tram system of Hanover (Briest et al., 2000). Of the traction energy that is consumed by the tramcars, 29 per cent is the result of regenerative braking. The flywheel system can store up to 7.3 kWh, and the maximum rotation speed of the wheel is 3,600 rpm. The storage system supports the supply voltage by absorbing or releasing energy.

In electric road vehicles, recovered energy is stored in a battery, sometimes combined (certainly in the near future) with supercapacitors. Using this type of capacitor, large peak powers can be absorbed and released. These capacitors have a long lifetime. The combination with batteries provides a highly efficient, highly reliable storage system. Regenerative braking results in lower energy costs.

16.4 Railway technology

Two kinds of railway transport exist: light rail and heavy rail. Light rail systems provide fast and flexible passenger transport in urban areas, using trams and trolleybuses. Heavy rail transport is the medium- to long-distance transportation of passengers or freight. The vehicles can be metro trains, commuter trains or high-speed trains. Examples of high-speed trains are the TGV, ICE, Thalys and Eurostar in Europe and the Shinkansen in Japan. The maximum commercial speed of such trains is about 300 km/h.

In all sectors of transport by rail, the standardisation of equipment is very important, as it leads to large order quantities and reduced component costs. Downward pressure on prices seems to be the only driving force behind the competition between the remaining international market players, which are Alstom, Siemens and Bombardier.

The supply voltage of a railway system depends on the region. Differences exist between and within countries. In table 16.1 an overview of the main supply systems in thirteen European countries is shown. In the oldest systems the voltage is 1.5 kV DC or 15 kV AC (16 2/3 Hz). At present all newly constructed lines are supplied with 25 kV AC (50 Hz). All high-speed trains are equipped with power electronics. This allows for multi-voltage applications: trains can be operated using different supply systems. For extensions of autonomous urban systems (e.g. underground) the supply voltage of the existing system remains the logical choice. For light rail, DC is used almost everywhere, with voltage levels between 600 and 1,200 V.

For light rail, an overhead conductor (catenary supply) is used; for heavy rail, either an overhead conductor or a third rail is possible. A third rail is very common where sections of the line are underground, because of the small dimensions of tunnels.

Supplying electrical energy to railway vehicles has specific and difficult aspects. A first element is the fact that the vehicles are moving. Electrical loads are constantly changing as trains accelerate or slow down. Depending on the supply system, trains can be balanced or unbalanced loads. Energy savings can be obtained by regenerative braking, leading to a two-way power flow.

16.4.1 Light rail

According to the LRTA, light rail systems are characterised by a mix of features, including frequent services that rival the convenience of cars, easy interchange to and from other transport services, level boarding

Table 16.1 *Principal voltage supply systems for heavy rail*

	Voltage	
Country	DC	AC
United Kingdom	750V	25kV (50Hz)
Belgium, Luxembourg, Italy, Portugal, Spain	3kV	25kV
France	1.5kV	25kV
Netherlands	1.5kV	25kV (planned)
Germany, Switzerland, Austria, Norway, Sweden	–	15kV (16⅔ Hz)

with easy access for everyone, nearby parking facilities outside city centres and flexible ticket services. Light rail tracks are usually situated in or near streets.

Due to the developments in power electronics (robust solid-state components, digital control, high switching frequencies), drive systems can be independent of the supply voltage. Therefore, systems have emerged that perform part of their journey on heavy rail tracks and part as light rail, increasing the flexibility of light rail transport. Additional equipment is installed in these systems, making transitions between light and heavy rail tracks safe and flexible; in the light mode visual control is used, while in the heavy mode automatic signalling is customary.

More advanced, hybrid systems are found: part of the journey is diesel-engine-driven with rubber tyres (on the road), and part electrically on rails. In some cities trolleybuses are used for providing public transport without local pollution. They run on rubber tyres and are equipped with electric motors, energy being supplied via overhead conductors. This supply system is more complicated than supply to trams because the return path of the current is a second overhead conductor instead of a rail. Having a combustion engine as well, these buses have the capability to continue off-track.

In spite of the use of more efficient drives, the new rolling stock consumes more power than the replaced vehicles. This is due to the increased speed and new features for passenger comfort – e.g. air-conditioning and information systems.

The latest trend is to construct trams with low floors, in order to provide access for wheelchair users, parents with prams and people who have difficulty walking. In older vehicles, high floors were necessary to provide space for axles and motors. Nowadays powerful induction motors can be integrated into the wheel sets, eliminating the need for axles.

Table 16.2 *Average energy consumption by and cost of passenger transport in the Netherlands, 2000*

	Energy intensity (MJ/person km)	Cost (euro/person km)
Car		
Petrol	1.8	0.17
Diesel	1.4	0.11
LPG	1.4	0.11
Train	1	0.07
Bus, tram and metro	1.1	0.09
Bicycle	0.04	0.05
Walking	0.03	0

Source: Bouwman and Moll (2002).

Bouwman and Moll (2002) have calculated the energy intensity and cost of different modes of transportation, taking into account the life cycles of all systems. The results are shown in table 16.2. These figures show that travel by rail is cheaper and more energy-efficient than car travel. No distinction was made between buses on the one hand and trams and underground on the other.

16.4.2 High-speed heavy rail

After the realisation of national high-speed railway projects, such as the TGV in France and ICE in Germany, transnational initiatives were started. Well-known examples are:

- Thalys (Belgium, Germany, France, Netherlands); and
- Eurostar (Belgium, France, United Kingdom).

New links have been built or are planned between Germany and the Netherlands (ICE-based), Germany and France, Spain and France, and Italy and France. These high-speed links are reducing to a large extent the use of classical trains on international connections; many of them have disappeared during recent years.

16.4.2.1   Power quality aspects of AC supply   A number of measures have to be taken in order to minimise power quality problems in heavy-rail systems that are supplied with an alternating voltage – e.g. 25kV at 50Hz. Three important goals are balanced loading of the three-phase grid, the prevention of harmonic distortion and voltage stability.

Balanced loading. Trains are single-phase loads, yet power is supplied by a three-phase grid. In order to distribute power consumption over the

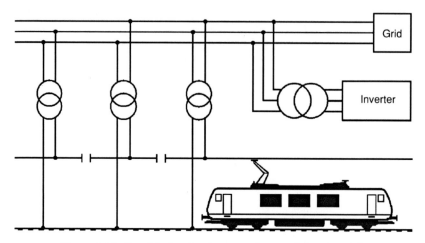

Figure 16.1. Load-balancing inverters in a traditional supply system.

three phases of the grid, line voltages of different phase combinations are applied to the power supply of subsequent track sections. Because of the phase difference between the line voltages, the supplies of subsequent sections are isolated from each other; this is shown in figure 16.1.

Another possibility for achieving balanced loading is using a power electronic converter to rectify the three-phase voltage of the grid, which results in a single direct voltage. This voltage is inverted, which results in a single-phase 50Hz voltage. At high powers, this technology is expensive; therefore, it is not used for railway. It is expected however, that it will become affordable in the future. An alternative is the use of a load-balancing inverter, which is also shown in figure 16.1. This device measures imbalance and injects compensating currents. As it has only to provide reactive power, all it requires is an energy buffer – i.e. a capacitor or a superconducting coil – at the DC side of the inverter.

The problem of creating balanced currents does not occur in the German railway system, which is supplied with 15kV at a frequency of 16 2/3Hz. The railway system receives power from a separate, single-phase, high-voltage grid (110kV), which is fed by single-phase generators. This grid is connected to the regular 50Hz grid by means of rotating and static converters, to permit energy exchange.

Harmonic distortion. Power electronic converters are non-linear loads. They generate nonsinusoidal currents, which, in turn, cause non-sinusoidal voltage drops. As a result, the supply voltage contains harmonic components, the presence of which can have negative consequences.

The following problems are possible: resonances in the supply system, the overloading of capacitive reactive-power compensators, increased transformer losses, unsuccessful current interruptions, the disturbance of electronic circuits due to interference and inaccurate energy measurements.

These problems can be tackled by using more advanced converters or by installing passive or active filters. Passive filters consist of a set of fixed inductor–capacitor combinations, tuned to certain frequencies. An active filter consists of a compensating converter, which injects current or voltage of a certain wave shape, eliminating the harmonic content. Active filters are more expensive than passive filters, but also more flexible.

Voltage stability. The impedance of the current path (from the supply to a moving train and back) determines the voltage drop. The simplest way to supply alternating current to a railway system is by connecting the single-phase source to the catenary and the rails. The drawback of this technique is the occurrence of stray currents. A portion of the current, about 30 per cent to 40 per cent (Boeck et al., 1996), leaves the rail and flows through the ground. A portion of the current may pass through metal structures in the vicinity of the track, which can lead to corrosion, certainly when DC is used.

As the distance between the catenary and the rails is large, the inductance of the current path is high. This results in large voltage drops; the voltage and thus the maximum power received by the train are both low. Another problem caused by the large distance between conductors is the electromagnetic field associated with these conductors. If the distance between the conductors is small, the fields of the conductors cancel each other out at close proximity. However, if the distance is large, strong electromagnetic fields arise close to the railway track. These fields can interfere with nearby communication infrastructure – e.g. the safety and control systems of the railway.

The solution to these problems is to install a return conductor close to the catenary. This conductor is connected to the rails at regular intervals. Due to the inductive coupling of the catenary and the return conductor, about 40 per cent of the current flows from the rails to the return conductor, attenuating the problems mentioned previously. The coupling of the catenary and the return conductor can be enhanced by installing single-phase transformers in series with both conductors. The catenary current flows through the primary winding of the transformer and the return current flows through the secondary. These transformers are called 'booster transformers'. They have a 1:1 transformation ratio and are installed about every five kilometres.

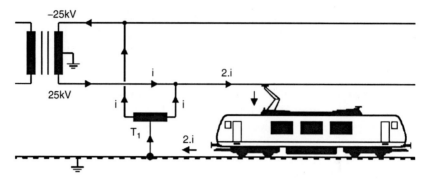

Figure 16.2. 50kV supply system.

A better technique is shown in figure 16.2. The catenary and the return conductor are connected to a 50kV supply. The rails and the central tap of the supply transformer are connected to earth potential. In this way the catenary voltage remains 25kV and the voltage of the return conductor becomes −25kV. Both conductors and the rails are connected through an autotransformer (T_1). The current in the rails flows through the autotransformer and is divided over the two overhead conductors. As a result, energy is transported at 50kV to the section in which the train is moving. Near the train, the power passes through the autotransformer and is delivered to the train at 25kV. Because the transport voltage is doubled, current is halved, resulting in lower losses.

16.4.2.2   Dedicated tracks and tilting mechanisms   Railway tracks contain bends. This is a problem for high-speed passenger transport. Following a bend at high speed gives rise to strong centrifugal forces, causing discomfort to passengers. Slowing down before and accelerating after a bend is time-consuming, jeopardising high-speed rail's greatest benefit. This problem can be solved in two ways. The first solution consists of building dedicated tracks: long, straight sections and slight bends. In places where a sharp bend is needed, a tilted track section is constructed, strongly reducing the lateral force on the passengers. A less expensive solution consists of using carriages equipped with tilting mechanisms. The carriages tilt on the bogies, using computer-controlled pistons that can adjust the tilt angle on bends, minimising passengers' discomfort. These trains can be operated on ordinary tracks (e.g. Pendolino trains). The introduction of such systems yields higher speeds, thus making energy demands higher as well. At the same time, however, it makes the railways more attractive due to the reduced travel time, again leading to more traffic.

16.4.2.3 Magnetic levitation vehicle A remarkable development in high-speed passenger transport is the magnetic levitation vehicle (Jacobs, 2002). It has an electromagnetic propulsion system that levitates and accelerates the vehicle (see also chapter 10 on superconductors in this volume). The drive for horizontal movement is a linear motor. This can be regarded as a rolled-out synchronous or asynchronous motor, where the vehicle is the rotor and the guideway is the stator. The guideway generates a magnetic field that travels along this guideway. This field interacts with the field generated by the vehicle's magnets or conductors. As a result, the vehicle is pulled forward. Because there is no contact between guideway and vehicle, only air resistance has to be overcome. This results in lower energy consumption than with high-speed trains. This is illustrated by table 16.3, in which the energy intensities of a high-speed train (ICE) and of a magnetic levitation vehicle (Transrapid) are shown. Because of the low consumption and little need for maintenance, operating costs are low. The investment cost, on the other hand, is very high.

Two main technologies have been developed. The German Transrapid system is based on electromagnetic suspension. Levitation is achieved by attractive forces between the guideway and electromagnets on the vehicle. The Japanese system is based on electrodynamic suspension, achieved by repulsive forces between the guideway and superconducting magnets on the vehicle. So far, only the Transrapid has been commercialised. It is the fastest land vehicle for transport, with a maximum speed of about 500 km/h. Commercial activities concerning this system are in an early phase. In Shanghai (China) a track thirty kilometers long connects the city centre and the new airport, the journey time between the two being just eight minutes. It has been transporting passengers since December 2003. In Munich a similar track thirty-eight kilometres long is planned. Other feasibility studies have been started in the United States and the Netherlands.

16.4.3 Freight transport

Freight trains provide a reliable and efficient alternative to road transport. It is safe, large amounts of cargo can be moved by one transport, no time is lost in traffic jams, and the well-developed European rail network facilitates environment-friendly and reliable international transport. Various types of cargo can be transported: containers, liquids, bulk goods, parcel goods, dangerous substances etc. During the day the capacity of the rail infrastructure is shared with passenger transport; at night railways are almost exclusively used by freight trains.

Table 16.3 *Specific energy consumption of ICE and Transrapid (Wh/seat km)*

	200 km/h	300 km/h	400 km/h
ICE	29	51	–
Transrapid	22	34	52

Source: Transrapid (see website: http://www.transrapid.de).

Intermodal (or combined) transport is defined as transport using at least two modes of transport for a specific journey. Rail is an essential mode in intermodal transport: it can be linked to both road transport and shipping, over sea or inland waterways. Used mainly for long distances, the combination of two or more transport modes is very interesting. The load can be a container or any other large unit. Since one train replaces dozens of trucks, intermodal transport holds a lot of potential for mitigating road congestion. A special kind of intermodal transport is the 'rolling highway', in which complete trucks are loaded onto the train and the truck driver also travels on the train (figure 16.3). This technique is used, for instance, in the Channel Tunnel between France and the United Kingdom, and also in the Alps.

Over a certain distance, the precise length of which depends on a number of factors, intermodal transport is faster, more economic, more energy-efficient and less polluting (in terms of greenhouse gas emissions) than pure road transport – as illustrated in a study report by the UIRR (2003). A comparison is made between the primary energy consumption and CO_2 emissions of pure road transport on the one hand and combined road–rail transport on the other, for eighteen combined transport routes, between cities scattered across Europe. The calculated average energy saving of using intermodal transport instead of pure road transport is 29 per cent. The average reduction in CO_2 emission is about 55 per cent.

Due to the advantages of intermodal transport, European policy-makers are interested in increasing its market share (European Commission, 2001, p. 18). A European intermodal transport network is in the process of being developed at present. The European Union aims to develop intermodal transport as a competitive alternative to pure road transport, the priorities being technical harmonisation and interoperability between systems.

In a study by the International Energy Agency (IEA, 2002; see table 16.8), forecasts were made regarding CO_2 emissions by truck transport in Western Europe in 2020. Taking into account current and probable

Figure 16.3. Example of intermodal transport: the rolling highway.

near-term policies to encourage intermodal transport, it is expected that activity (expressed in 'ton km') of transport by truck and by rail will increase by 70 per cent and 13 per cent, respectively, compared to 1997. CO_2 emissions by truck transport are forecast to increase by 50 per cent. Without government intervention, the activity increases are estimated at 74 per cent and 2 per cent, respectively, with an increase in emissions of 60 per cent. According to these predictions, the growth of truck transport is merely slowed down by government policy.

Terminals are the basis of intermodal networks. Here cargo is transferred from one mode to another. Designing terminals and choosing their locations are optimisation processes (Ballis and Golias, 2004). Terminals have to be built close to major traffic arteries (roads, railway lines, waterways) and centres of production and consumption, with environmental planning as a boundary condition. The capacity of a terminal is determined by the types of handling equipment (e.g. cranes) and the layout of the terminal. If a terminal has storage space, it is not necessary for two consecutive modes to be available at the same time, which creates a certain degree of flexibility. The possibility of storing depends on the cargo. The nature of the freight influences the need for space; containers, for example, can be stacked, while trailers cannot. Of course, space may be expensive and not always available. The nature of the cargo units depends on the market and the location; terminals near ports mainly process containers.

Different rail operating forms are used (Ballis and Golias, 2004). Direct trains travel back and forth between two terminals – e.g. shuttle trains, which are direct trains with a fixed composition. More complex systems involve multiple trains. On arrival at a terminal, these trains exchange cargo with trucks or other trains, after which they leave for the next terminal.

16.4.4 Liberalisation of the rail and energy sectors

Most railway systems in the European Union have been operated by state-controlled companies. As dictated by the European Directive

91/440, national governments are now opening their railway systems to third parties. Furthermore, this directive stipulates the unbundling of activities associated with infrastructure, traffic management and capacity allocation, on the one hand, and the commercial exploitation of rail services on the other. In the subsequent directives 95/18 and 95/19, the regulations for permit holders and capacity allowances are discussed.

The goal of these directives is to increase the efficiency of European railway organisations and to stop the decline of rail transport's market share (Crozet, 2004). The European Commission clearly acknowledges the importance of transport by rail (European Commission, 2001, pp. 16–18). It is expected that liberalisation and competition will increase the market share of railways and lower costs for customers. In freight transport, special attention is being paid to intermodality; for passenger transport, the situation has not been so clearly spelt out so far.

Currently, the European rail network contains many bottlenecks – for example, in the vicinity of urban areas. Trains of different types share the same tracks and priority is usually given to long-distance passenger trains. In order to eliminate these bottlenecks, investment must encourage the gradual development of trans-European lines. Freight and passenger transport should not interfere on these lines. Either time slots can be reserved for freight and passenger transport, or dedicated railway tracks can be used. To increase the capacity of existing rail infrastructure, low-traffic lines can be rehabilitated, new tracks can be constructed to bypass congested areas and completely new lines can be constructed.

Railway companies are important consumers of electrical energy. Until recently, electrical energy was bought from the local monopolist by means of long-term contracts. The advantages of this system were multiple: the supply company had to supply a guaranteed quantity of energy and the railway company had price stability. The new electricity market situation requires consumers to become far more involved in the process of buying energy. In order to make optimal use of the new market situation, the buying strategy has to match the railway's energy requirements. In order to cover the basic load and the daily, weekly and seasonal variations, railway companies have to make a balanced mixture of medium- and long-term contracts, on the one hand, and spot market purchases on the other.

16.4.5   *Research concerning rail transport*

An important subject in railway-related research is solving problems of electromagnetic compatibility (Busatto et al., 2004). Railway systems, including trains, contain electric and electronic equipment. Good EMC performance is obtained if all devices are immune to electromagnetic disturbances and if they do not emit noise in an unacceptable way. Recent developments in power electronics (e.g. the IGBT, high-frequency switching) have reduced power losses in power electronic systems. However, because of the higher frequencies, electromagnetic interference has increased, which means that EMC deteriorates.

Other research areas are management (Casson, 2004), logistic problems and railway planning (Arnold et al., 2004; Ballis and Golias, 2004; Bontekoning et al., 2004) – e.g. control of trans-European traffic. Reform of the sector is studied as well – for example how to charge transport companies for using infrastructure (Crozet, 2004; Link, 2004; Nash et al., 2004). Other topics are problems related to mechanical engineering (such as reducing acoustic noise and vibrations – e.g. Kalivoda et al., 2003) and materials engineering (such as material fatigue – e.g. Ringsberg et al., 2005).

16.5   Technology of electric road vehicles

Three types of electric road vehicles exist: battery-powered electric vehicles (BEV), hybrid electric vehicles (HEV) and fuel-cell electric vehicles (FCV). Electric vehicles (except for HEV) are silent and do not produce local emissions. Because of this they are ideal for city traffic, as the use of electric vehicles decreases emissions in urban areas. However, emissions increase at electrical power plants. Lindly and Haskew (2002) state that it is important to study the net effect on emissions. The emission change resulting from the shift of energy consumption from the roads to power plants depends on the sources of electric power (the generation mix).

Many car manufacturers have research programmes concerning battery, hybrid and fuel-cell vehicles. An important number of supply industries are involved as well. The component industry (e.g. batteries, electronics), universities and other R&D institutes play an important part. Electricity suppliers are also very interested, because battery-powered and hybrid electric vehicles constitute a large potential market for off-peak demand if batteries are charged at night.

Batteries are an essential component of all three types of electric vehicles. Demands on batteries are much higher in electric vehicles than in conventional vehicles. Energy is exchanged between the battery and the electric drive – constantly in BEVs, frequently in HEVs and FCVs. Besides propulsion, the batteries have to power peripherals – e.g. air-conditioning, on-board electronics and small servomotors. In short, batteries have to withstand heavy duty. Because present batteries do not yet meet requirements, research is aimed at extending the life of batteries, improving charge acceptance, increasing power (W/kg), improving reliability and efficiency and reducing cost (Anderman, 2004).

16.5.1 Battery-powered electric vehicles and fuel-cell vehicles

BEVs are efficient under low load conditions, but they have a limited range and recharging can take a few hours. Because of this, they are very suitable for niche markets in cities, such as delivery vans, small buses and car sharing schemes (Morita, 2003). In La Rochelle (France) a fleet of fifty self-service electric cars was introduced in 1999 (the Liselec project; see http://www.psa-peugeot-citroen.com/modules/liselec/en_intro.html   and http://www.keolis.com). The vehicles are parked at six recharging stations around the city. Scheme members use a card to access the cars and return them. The range of the vehicles is eighty kilometres. An electric car needs to be recharged every two to three days.

With prototype BEVs, ranges above 350 kilometres per charge have been reported (Hammerschlag and Mazza, 2005). This has not yet been achieved with FCVs; BEVs are far ahead of FCVs in delivering practical performance at a reasonable cost. Lithium ion batteries cost about $83 per MJ to manufacture. For BEVs to become marketable, this cost has to drop by a factor of three further. Fuel cells cost about $3,000 per kW to manufacture. For FCVs to become marketable, this cost has to drop by a factor of eighty-five further. Fuel-cell vehicles require fuel (e.g. hydrogen). To make this fuel available, new filling stations need to be constructed, adding further to the cost of fuel cell technology.

Eaves and Eaves (2004) compare the energy efficiency of BEVs and FCVs, taking into account the losses occurring between the power plant and the point where electrical power is supplied to the motor driving the wheels. They assumed that hydrogen gas is produced by means of electrolysis at filling stations. In a BEV about 77 per cent of the generated electrical energy is delivered to the motor, whereas for a FCV this efficiency is about 32 per cent.

16.5.2 Hybrid electric vehicles

Hybrid electric vehicles are equipped with an internal combustion engine, a storage system (e.g. a battery combined with a supercapacitor), a generator and an electric motor. The vehicle is powered by petrol. The engine's principal function is to drive the generator. The battery and/or the generator supply energy to the electric motor, which drives the wheels. In this system there is no strict relation between the operation of the combustion engine and the driving cycle. Generally, the combustion engine is operated in the most efficient region of its characteristic.

Hybrid electric vehicles appear to be the best medium-term solution for reducing the fuel consumption and CO_2 emissions of individual cars. HEVs have very interesting characteristics. They shut down automatically during short stops, they are powered electrically at low speed and regenerative braking is applied. These benefits are more noticeable in urban areas (Morita, 2003).

The first commercialised HEV is the Toyota Prius (see the website: http://www.toyota.com/prius). It is equipped with a planetary gear, used to manage the flow of mechanical power. At low speed the electric motor is powered by the battery, and if necessary, the battery is recharged at the same time. When high acceleration is required, the wheels are driven by both the engine and the electric motor. At high speed the wheels are driven by the engine. When the vehicle has to slow down, regenerative braking is applied. For short standstills the engine is switched off, and when the car starts again it is powered by the battery.

Lave and MacLean (2002) compare the emissions of a hybrid car (Toyota Prius, second-generation) and a similar, conventional car with an internal combustion engine (Toyota Corolla). The figures are shown in table 16.4. In the first column CO_2 emissions from the exhaust are shown. The second column shows CO_2 emissions during the fuel cycle (processing up to refuelling). In the third column the sum of the exhaust and fuel cycle emissions is shown. Total CO_2 emissions from the hybrid car are 71 per cent of those from the conventional, being reduced by the fact that the hybrid car consumes less fuel than the conventional.

16.5.3 Electric buses

Conventional buses have powerful diesel engines. In urban areas buses are frequently accelerating, decelerating and idling, resulting in high specific fuel consumption and much air pollution (particulate matter, CO, NOx, volatile organic compounds). Purely electric buses do not produce pollutants locally. Fuel-cell buses are clean as well, but since they are far too expensive they have been used solely in demonstration projects so far. Hybrid electric buses produce fewer pollutants than diesel ones.

Affordable electric buses are trolleybuses and battery-powered buses. These buses do not pollute the air in the streets, and they can be equipped with a regenerative braking system. Trolleybuses are electric buses receiving power from overhead wires. Since there are no rails and the buses are running on rubber tyres, two parallel overhead wires are

Table 16.4 *Emissions from a hybrid and a conventional car (Toyota Prius and Toyota Corolla)*

	Exhaust emissions (g/km)	Fuel cycle emissions (g/km)	Total CO_2 emissions (g/km)
Toyota Prius	112	43	155 (71%)
Toyota Corolla	157	60	217 (100%)

Source: Lave and MacLean (2002).

required. These buses can be equipped with batteries or a combustion engine to allow for short deviations from the electrified route.

The following is a comparison of hybrid and conventional buses (DOE, 2002). New York City Transit has been introducing hybrid electric buses in its fleet since 1998; by 2006 there should be 385. Ten such buses were in service in 2000. The performance of these buses was compared to fourteen conventional diesel buses (two types, seven of each), data being gathered for more than a year. During the evaluation period the hybrid buses had average fuel consumption about 8 per cent to 18 per cent lower than the diesel ones. Operating the hybrid buses with and without regenerative braking demonstrated the advantage of regenerative braking: an improvement of fuel economy of between 23 per cent to 64 per cent, depending on the drive cycle.

16.6   Potential effect of transport policy on energy consumption and CO_2 emissions

The IEA has evaluated the potential impact of policies regarding energy demand and CO_2 emission reduction in the transport sector (IEA, 2002, p. 12). These policies consist of a variety of measures, including encouragement of the development and use of fuel-efficient cars (e.g. hybrid vehicles), labelling and fiscal incentives, and shifting road and air transport to rail. The IEA considers three scenarios and forecasts energy consumption and CO_2 emissions for 2020. The regions considered are Western Europe,[2] North America and Japan. Here the discussion will be limited to Western Europe.

---

[2] In this discussion, the following European countries are collectively called 'Western Europe': Austria, Belgium, Denmark, Finland, France, Germany, Greece, Iceland, Ireland, Italy, Luxembourg, the Netherlands, Norway, Portugal, Spain, Sweden, Switzerland and the United Kingdom.

Table 16.5 *Estimated energy consumption in transport (Mtoe)*

		2020					
	1997	Scenario 1		Scenario 2		Scenario 3	
Western Europe, North America and Japan	1,000	1,424	+42%	1,384	+38%	1,211	+21%
Western Europe	300	451	+50%	422	+40%	380	+26%
Passenger transport	185	261	+41%	–	–	204	+10%
Freight transport	115	190	+65%	–	–	176	+53%

Source: IEA, (2002, pp. 13, 156).

In Scenario 1, used as a reference, no policy measures are taken. Scenario 2 implies current policies. This mainly consists of the 'Voluntary Agreement' as established by the European Union and three associations: the European Automobile Manufacturers Association (ACEA) and the Japanese and South Korean associations of car manufacturers (JAMA and KAMA). These manufacturers have agreed to reduce average CO_2 emissions from new passenger cars registered in the European Union by 25 per cent by 2008 with respect to 1995; this corresponds to a reduction from 186 g/km (1995) to 140 g/km (2008). This is pursued by developing and selling improved combustion engines and hybrid cars.

In Scenario 3, current policies are combined with likely near-term measures. The first of these measures is a continuation of the Voluntary Agreement after 2008, in order to reach an emission level of 100 g/km by 2020. Other measures consist of fiscal incentives, efficiency labels and higher fuel taxation. A certain modal shift from road to rail is predicted, achieved by means of kilometre charges for trucks and an improvement of the infrastructure for combined transport. Transport problems in urban regions are assumed to be tackled by means of parking and access restrictions and improvement and expansion of public transport (IEA, 2002, pp. 65, 67).

In table 16.5, energy consumption for the transport sector is shown: calculated values for 1997 and predicted values for 2020. Here energy is expressed in Mtoe (1 Mtoe = 11.6279 TWh). For western Europe, consumption for passenger and freight transport is shown separately as well. These figures indicate that, in spite of policy measures, energy consumption is expected to increase; the measures merely slow its growth. It can be expected that in western Europe the effect of policy will be greater for passenger transport (growth of 10 per cent instead of 41 per cent by 2020) than for freight (growth of 53 per cent instead of 65 per cent by 2020).

Table 16.6   *Greenhouse gas emissions in western Europe (Mt CO_2 equivalent)*

		1990	1997	2001	2012	2020
Total (GHG)	Kyoto Protocol	4,107	4,004	3,945	3,782	3,665
	UN, 2003	4,107	3,992	4,006	–	–
Transport (CO_2)	UN, 2003	723	808	863	–	–
	IEA, 2002, Scenario 1	–	884	–	–	1,338
	IEA, 2002, Scenario 3	–	884	–	–	1,129

Source: IEA, (2002, pp. 144–60); UN (1997, 2003).

In table 16.6, figures concerning greenhouse gas emissions in western Europe are shown. According to a report from the United Nations, total GHG emission in 1997 amounted to 3,992 Mt CO_2 equivalent (UN, 2003, table B.2). CO_2 emissions from transport for the same region amounted to 808 Mt (table B.6) (884 Mt according to the information in tables 16.7 and 16.8). If emission reductions are achieved by 2012 as outlined in the Kyoto Protocol (UN, 1997), emission will be 3,782 Mt per year (all western European countries on average have to achieve a reduction of 8 per cent compared to 1990, except for Iceland and Norway). If the same rate of decrease is maintained, emissions will decrease to 3,665 Mt per year by 2020. According to the IEA (2002), CO_2 emissions from transport will increase to 1,129 Mt per year in 2020 (Scenario 3).

In table 16.7, figures concerning passenger transport in western Europe are shown, once again estimates for 1997 and predictions for 2020 (Scenarios 1 and 3). Transport by air is not shown. For each mode of transportation the following quantities are given: activity, energy intensity ('intensity'), energy consumption ('energy') and CO_2 emissions ('CO_2'). Activity, energy consumption and CO_2 emissions are expressed both in absolute values and as a percentage of total activity, consumption or emission; these percentages indicate the share of each transportation mode. The final column gives the percentage difference between Scenarios 1 and 3.

The figures in the first row indicate there will be 5 per cent more passenger kilometres in 2020 with policy measures than in the case without measures. This is a rebound effect: vehicles that are more economical result in lower driving costs, encouraging their use. Higher fuel taxation could counter this effect. Despite the activity increase compared to Scenario 1, energy consumption (see table 16.5) and CO_2 emissions will be lower. In Scenario 3 the energy intensity of cars

Table 16.7 *Passenger transport in western Europe*

		1997		2020: Scenario 1		2020: Scenario 3		2020: difference
		Value	% share	Value	% share	Value	% share	%
Passenger transport (total)	Activity (10^9 pass.km)	5,263	100	7,670	100	8,035	100	+5
	Intensity (MJ/pass.km)	1.5	–	1.4	–	1.1	–	–21
	Energy (Mtoe)	185.1	100	261.4	100	204.2	100	–22
	CO_2 (Mt)	536	100	763	100	597	100	–22
Passenger transport by car	Activity (10^9 pass.km)	3,912	74	5,050	66	5,368	67	+6
	Intensity (MJ/pass.km)	1.5	–	1.6	–	1.1	–	–31
	Energy (Mtoe)	144	78	191.1	73	141.2	69	–26
	CO_2 (Mt)	421	79	561	74	417	70	–26
Passenger transport by bus	Activity (10^9 pass.km)	397	8	504	7	547	7	+9
	Intensity (MJ/pass.km)	1	–	1	–	1	–	0
	Energy (Mtoe)	9.1	5	12.2	5	13	6	+7
	CO_2 (Mt)	28	5	38	5	40	7	+5
Passenger transport by rail	Activity (10^9 pass.km)	297	6	358	5	400	5	+12
	Intensity (MJ/pass.km)	0.5	–	0.4	–	0.4	–	0
	Energy (Mtoe)	3.6	2	3.8	1	4.3	2	+12
	CO_2 (Mt)	2	<1	2	<1	3	<1	+50

Source: IEA (2002, pp. 144, 159).

decreases to about 1.1MJ/pass.km in 2020. This results in a status quo with regard to consumption and emissions from cars, in spite of an increase in activity between 1997 and 2020. Activity, consumption and emissions in bus and rail transport increase.

In table 16.8 similar figures concerning freight transport in western Europe are shown. Other modes of transportation (ship, aeroplane) are not shown here. The figures in the first row indicate that policy measures will bring about slightly less activity (−1 per cent) compared to the case without measures. In Scenario 3 the energy intensity of trucks decreases to about 2.9MJ/ton km in 2020. However, the increase in activity results in more consumption (141.9 Mtoe) and emissions. Consumption and emissions in rail transport increase.

With the figures for activity in tables 16.7 and 16.8, the evolution of the market share of the different modes can be calculated. The predicted figures for Scenario 3 in table 16.7 indicate that, in spite of absolute growth, the market share of passenger transport by car and rail will decrease. In 1997 the market share of cars was 74 per cent; it is expected to be 67 per cent in 2020. In 1997 the market share of the railways was 6 per cent it is expected to be 5 per cent in 2020. These decreases are caused by an expected large increase in air travel. In freight transport, the share of trucks is forecast to increase: from 75 per cent in 1997 to 80 per cent in 2020. Despite efforts to encourage intermodal freight transport, the market share of railways is projected to decrease from 15 per cent in 1997 to 11 per cent in 2020.

Assuming that rail transport is 100 per cent electric and that it is the only mode consuming electricity from the grid, the necessary electric power for transport (passengers and freight) in 1997 was 69.8TWh. In Scenario 1, the necessary electric power in 2020 would be 70.9TWh. In the probable case of Scenario 3, this will be 79.1TWh. Annual electricity consumption in western Europe was about 2,815TWh in 2004 (IEA, 2004). In Scenario 3, consumption by transportation will be 2.8 per cent of this amount of energy.

In table 16.9 the greenhouse gas emissions from transport according to the scenarios from the IEA study are compared to two possible emission levels in 2020 (see. table 16.6). If the objectives of the Kyoto Protocol are reached and then maintained until 2020 (i.e. no further improvement), emissions will amount to 3,782Mt per year. If emissions continue to decrease at the same rate after 2012, the level will be 3,665 Mt per year by 2020. The figures for Scenario 3 indicate that, in 2020, about 30 per cent of emissions will originate from transport. The savings of Scenario 3 (due to current policies and probable near-term policies)

Table 16.8 *Freight transport in western Europe*

			1997		2020: Scenario 1		2020: Scenario 3		2020: difference
			Value	% share	Value	% share	Value	% share	%
Freight transport (total)	Activity	(10^9 ton km)	1,633	100	2,608	100	2,588	100	−1
	Intensity	(MJ/ton km)	3	–	3.1	–	2.8	–	−10
	Energy	(Mtoe)	115.2	100	190	100	175.8	100	−7
	CO_2	(Mt)	348	100	575	100	532	100	−7
Freight transport by truck	Activity	(10^9 ton km)	1,224	75	2,124	81	2,083	80	−2
	Intensity	(MJ/ton km)	3.2	–	3	–	2.9	–	−3
	Energy	(Mtoe)	94.1	82	151.2	80	141.9	81	−6
	CO_2	(Mt)	287	82	461	80	433	81	−6
Freight transport by rail	Activity	(10^9 ton km)	248	15	252	10	280	11	+11
	Intensity	(MJ/ton km)	0.4	–	0.4	–	0.4	–	0
	Energy	(Mtoe)	2.4	2	2.3	1	2.5	1	+9
	CO_2	(Mt)	4	1	4	<1	4	<1	0

Source: IEA (2002, pp. 145, 160).

Table 16.9 *Emissions (CO$_2$ equivalent) from transport compared to the western Europe total, 2020*

		Transport		
		Scenario 1 1,338 Mt	Scenario 3 1,129 Mt	Savings 209 Mt
Kyoto 2012	3,782 Mt	35 %	30 %	5.5 %
2020	3,665 Mt	37 %	31 %	5.7 %

are 209 Mt, or about 5.5 per cent to 5.7 per cent of total emissions in 2020.

16.7   Conclusions

Electricity demand by transport, both for rail and road applications, will increase in the future. High-speed trains are finding their way as a major competitor to short-haul flights, having a much lower impact on the environment and improved energy consumption.

For light rail, electricity demand increases as new systems are introduced and existing ones are brought into action more frequently. Furthermore, as passengers' comfort is improved, for instance by means of air-conditioning, this leads to higher energy consumption.

Freight trains have to achieve a higher percentage of total transportation, in order to reduce traffic congestion on the roads and cut energy consumption. Intermodality is the key.

In the field of individual transport, the potential significance of the various developments is very considerable, but their actual impact on the transport market remains limited for the time being.

16.8   References

Anderman, M. (2004). The challenge to fulfill electrical power requirements of advanced vehicles, *Journal of Power Sources*, 127: 2–7.

Arnold, P., D. Peeters and I. Thomas (2004). Modelling a rail/road intermodal transportation system, *Transportation Research, Part E*, 40: 255–70.

Ballis, A., and J.Golias (2004). Towards the improvement of a combined transport chain performance, *European Journal of Operational Research*, 152: 420–36.

Boeck, R., O. Gaupp, P. Dähler, E. Bärlocher, J. Werninger and P. Zanini (1996). Vollstatische 100-MW-Frequenzkupplung Bremen, *ABB-Technik*, 9/10: 2–15.

Bontekoning, Y. M., C. Macharis and J. J.Trip (2004). Is a new applied transportation research field emerging? A review of intermodal rail-truck freight transport literature, *Transportation Research, Part A*, 38: 1–34.

Bouwman, M. E., and H. C. Moll (2002). Environmental analyses of land transportation systems in the Netherlands, *Transportation Research, Part D*, 7: 331–45.

Briest, R., S. Kähler and M. Victor (2000). Einsatz rotierender Energiespeicher im Fahrleitungsnetz der üstra Hannover, *Elektrische Bahnen*, 98(5–6): 214–21.

Busatto, G., L. Fratelli, C. Abbate, R. Manzo and F. Iannuzzo (2004). Analysis and optimisation through innovative driving strategy of high-power IGBT performances/EMI reduction trade-off for converter systems in railway applications, *Microelectronics Reliability*, 44: 1443–8.

Casson, M. (2004). The future of the UK railway system: Michael Brooke's vision, *International Business Review*, 13: 181–214.

Crozet, Y. (2004). European railway infrastructure: towards a convergence of infrastructure charging?, *International Journal of Transport Management*, 2: 5–15.

DOE (2002). *NYCT Diesel Hybrid-Electric Buses: Final Results*, Springfield, VA : National Technical Information Service.

Duffy, M. C. (2003). *Electric Railways 1880–1990*, IEE History of Technology Series no. 31, London: Institution of Electrical Engineers.

Eaves, S., and J. Eaves (2004). A cost comparison of fuel-cell and battery electric vehicles, *Journal of Power Sources*, 130: 208–12.

European Commission (2001). *European Transport Policy for 2010: Time to Decide*, White Paper Luxembourg: Office for Official Publications of the European Communities.

Hammerschlag, R., and P. Mazza (2005). Questioning hydrogen, *Energy Policy* 33(16): 2039– 43.

Husain, I. (2003). *Electric and Hybrid Vehicles: Design Fundamentals*, Boca Raton, FL: CRC Press.

IEA (2002). *Transportation Projections in OECD Regions: Detailed Report*. Paris: International Energy Agency.

(2004). *Monthly Electricity Survey: December 2004*, Paris: International Energy Agency.

Jacobs, J. (2002). Magnetic levitation: transportation for the 21st century?, *Harvard Science Review*, Spring: 52–6.

Kalivoda, M., U. Danneskiold-Samsoe, F. Krüger and B. Barsikow (2003). EURailNoise: a study of European priorities and strategies for railway noise abatement, *Journal of Sound and Vibration*, 267: 387–96.

Lave, L. B., and H. L. MacLean (2002). An environmental-economic evaluation of hybrid electric vehicles: Toyota's Prius vs. its conventional internal combustion engine Corolla, *Transportation Research, Part D*, 7: 155–62.

Lindly, J. K., and T. A. Haskew (2002). Impact of electric vehicles on electric power generation and global environmental change, *Advances in Environmental Research*, 6: 291–302.

Link, H. (2004). Rail infrastructure charging and on-track competition in Germany, *International Journal of Transport Management*, 2: 17–27.

Morita, K. (2003). Automotive power source in 21st century, *JSAE Review*, 24: 3–7.

Nash, C., S. Coulthard and B. Matthews (2004). Rail track charges in Great Britain: the issue of charging for capacity, *Transport Policy*, 11: 315–27.

Ringsberg, J. W., F. J. Franklin, B. L. Josefson, A. Kapoor and J. C. O. Nielsen (2005). Fatigue evaluation of surface-coated railway rails using shakedown theory, finite element calculations, and lab and field trials, *International Journal of Fatigue*, 27: 680–94.

UIRR (2003). *CO$_2$ Reduction Through Combined Transport*, Brussels: International Union of Combined Road–Rail Transport Companies available from http://www.uirr.com/document/news/ CO2_reduction_EN_def.pdf.

UN (1997). *Kyoto Protocol to the United Nations Framework Convention on Climate Change*, New York: United Nations.

(2003). *National Greenhouse Gas Inventory Data from Annex I Parties for 1990 to 2001*, Bonn: United Nations Framework Convertion on Climate Change Secretariat.

17 Prospects for smart metering in the United Kingdom

Hannah Devine-Wright and Patrick Devine-Wright

17.1 Introduction

I went to see [the leader of a UK parliamentary bill on metering] and he was 'disgusted with the state of metering in the UK'. And I said: 'I entirely agree with you'. (Representative of a UK metering organisation)

Reducing carbon emissions has become a major goal for the United Kingdom's energy policy (DTI, 2003) and 'smart metering' may have a significant role to play in achieving this goal. But, despite estimations that smart metering can reduce domestic UK gas and electricity consumption by 2 per cent and reduce annual CO_2 emissions by 2.25 million tonnes (SMWG, 2001), smart metering is not a priority issue on the UK government's energy agenda because of a lack of awareness of its 'costs and benefits' (NMTWG, 2002).

In Italy, one of the world's largest publicly traded utilities, Enel, expects to recoup the €4.5 billion it has invested in the installation of 30 million smart meters within four years (IEA, 2003). Enel benefited from economies of scale such that they paid the same for more technically sophisticated 'smart' electronic meters as they would have paid for traditional electromechanical meters. This smart metering investment represents approximately 70 per cent of all growth in the demand for electronic meters in Europe. Despite a high-profile launch in 2000 and Enel's significant level of financial investment, there have been no critical reports or press releases since the launch. As a result, it is difficult to evaluate how effective the extensive use of smart metering has been within Italy; it is also notable that the anticipated benefits of smart metering identified by Enel prior to its investment did not include significantly reducing carbon emissions.

This research was funded by the Engineering and Physical Sciences Research Council (GR/S28082/01) within the SuperGen Future Networks 'Technologies' consortium research project.

Approximately 50 per cent of electricity use within the United Kingdom is already metered by the half-hour.[1] However, these half-hourly meters account for less than 0.5 per cent of the total number of UK meters and are limited to use within the industrial/commercial sector. Whilst domestic consumers use approximately 35 per cent of UK electricity, this accounts for 91 per cent of the metering stock that does not consist of smart meters. Half-hourly metering per se benefits industrial/commercial customers only if they have the technical, economic and personnel resources to make good use of these data. Although the aggregation and analysis of half-hourly data can be conducted in-house by energy managers it can also be outsourced to energy service companies, some of which provide capital investment as well as energy efficiency advice. Half-hourly monitoring/metering enables companies to identify wastage, and by saving kWh they can also save money. Energy managers claim that monitoring/metering by itself will always lead to the identification of where energy savings are possible. The extent to which they are practical depends upon the specific company – for example, the willingness or ability to invest in new machinery to replace inefficient equipment, or the significance of the projected savings as a percentage of the total energy bill. It will also depend upon the regulatory environment – for example, as associated with article 8 of the UK building regulations.

Although the industrial/commercial sector consumes more energy than the domestic sector, this chapter focuses on the sub-100kW per annum domestic sector because of the greater volume of meters in that sector. The aim is to consider how 'smart' smart metering is compared to traditional and prepayment meters, with our focus on electricity rather than gas or water metering, and special consideration is given to the role of smart metering with embedded and renewable electricity generation. Both primary and secondary data sources have been combined, with quotations from primary data being used to illustrate and develop issues arising from secondary sources. The primary data consist of eighteen semi-structured interviews that were conducted in November–December 2004 with a cross-section of representatives of the UK electricity supply industry:

- distribution network operators;
- the industry regulator;
- supply companies;
- meter operators and metering experts; and
- consumer interest groups.

---

[1] Personal communication with P. Brain of the Carbon Trust, 13 March 2005.

In order to distinguish primary from secondary data, quotations from the interview transcripts have been italicised within the text.

17.2   What is 'traditional' electricity metering?

For most of us, the electric meter is a wholly innocuous – if utterly boring – household necessity with all the appeal and inner meaning of scrub brushes and scouring pads.

(See the Sustainer website: http://www.sustainer.org/community&culture/
Viridian/Wattbug_press.html, p. 1)

Electricity meters are a ubiquitous technology. At least, 99 per cent of UK households are connected to the electricity network through an electricity meter. The majority of these are 'humble' (NMTWG, 2002), single-rate 'traditional', Ferraris-type electromechanical meters that display only kWh usage. Across Europe traditional meter sales are declining, and they are forecast to fall from 43 per cent of total sales of meters to 25 per cent by 2010 (Frost and Sullivan, 2003).

In the United Kingdom, traditional meters are read manually by a data collector, who is contracted to provide readings to the energy supplier. The installation of the meters and the initial meter readings are the responsibility of the meter operator (MOP), who provides meters on behalf of the distribution network operator. At present, the meter remains the property of the DNO, but it is installed by a MOP and read by a data collector, and the energy use information is passed to the company that supplies electricity to the premises. When a UK customer changes supplier, the incoming supplier assumes that there is a meter in place that is owned by the 'regional' DNO and maintained and installed by the 'incumbent' meter operating company. The DNO is reluctant to develop new technologies that will make its existing meter assets redundant. If, on the other hand, the outgoing supplier owns the meter, then issues of asset transfer and asset ownership arise. In 2003 the meter asset base was estimated to be worth about £400 million (DGCG, 2003). Although 1.5 million meters are changed each year in the United Kingdom, many traditional meters are simply refurbished (NEA, 2002).

When an incoming supplier does not have the infrastructure to support smart metering, it uses the 'smarter' meters in a 'traditional kWh consumption only' way so as to meet the minimum regulatory requirements for billing and settlement. In this case, the incoming supplier will either offer only the price of a standard meter to the outgoing supplier or replace it with a standard meter, which means that the outgoing supplier cannot recover its costs (NMTWG, 2002). The complexity of the operational issues involved in metering is reflected in the following quotation from a representative of an electricity supply company.

The meter should be replaced every twenty years or thereabouts so...if a meter is...past its sell-by date then we will replace it [but] NOT [representative's emphasis] *with remote meters. There is a move within the company to say: 'Shall we start doing this?' [...] This is how the deregulation thing mucked things about. If we put a meter in we will pay for that meter and the customer can leave a month later or they can leave instantly. [...] We say, 'Do we go for a meter that costs five quid and someone to fit it or a meter that costs fifty quid and we set up all this remote metering software and whatever, and – oh! – they have left?' [...] If [supply companies] were FORCED* [representative's emphasis], *if there was enough of a carrot or stick, if the costs were 'neutralised', then – agreed – that would happen. But if you leave it to individuals, to the competitive market place, then it is always going to go for the lowest-cost option unless there is a guarantee of a payback.*

For settlement purposes, the electricity supplier estimates domestic customers' consumption rates based on standard consumption profiles that vary by day of the week, season and temperature. Consequently, despite reporting their meter readings or having their meter read, domestic electricity customers receive a retrospective and estimated cost of their consumption levels on their electricity bill. These estimates form the most frequent cause for complaint to the UK energy consumer group, Energywatch.

Compared to automated meter reading, manual meter reading is infrequent, inaccurate, unreliable and expensive, because of time pressures on meter reading visits, labour costs, a lack of incentives for accuracy and a lack of training in meter reading.

[Meter readers] have thirty seconds to find the building, get a reading and leave. I am not interested in who you are. Where is your meter cupboard? Where's the meter? I don't care what time of day it is!   (Local authority energy manager)

For embedded generation, although widespread in Europe and acknowledged as technologically feasible in the United Kingdom (Ofgem, 2003) the backward running of traditional meters is not an accepted practice in the United Kingdom. This is due to the economic disparity between the value of the energy generated and the value of the energy consumed, as well as concerns that running meters backwards would make it impossible to record the accurate flow of electricity to and from the grid, leading to distortion in billing and settlement procedures. This can be overcome by installing additional meters to measure export that can relate to different tariffs – for example, as offered to micro-CHP customers by Powergen. The use of additional meters for export as well as import is also being used to estimate the export capability of embedded generation technologies such as solar photovoltaic panels, such as within the DTI-funded Braunstone Solar Streets project in Leicester (Devine-Wright, 2005).

17.3   What is prepayment metering?

More 'smart' than the traditional meter, the prepayment meter is used by 3.8 million UK customers (Dick, 2003). It enables both one- and two-way communication: for credit to be transferred from the service infrastructure to the meter, or to link the customer and service provider using prepayment tokens. The principal reason for the use of prepayment meters is to ensure that the supply company gets paid both for the standing charge of the meter and for the electricity consumption. Prepayment meters usually incur premium-use rates to ensure that supply companies recoup their standing charges.

However, in 2000 Northern Ireland Electricity became the first UK supply company to charge the same rate for prepayment as traditional metered electricity, by installing Liberty keypads that do not incur premium rates. Their higher maintenance requirements and set-up charges can incur an additional social cost: electricity users crediting a prepayment meter after a period of absence can find that they have insufficient funds to cover both the standing charge and the cost of the electricity to run appliances or heating within their homes. However, this is not the case in Northern Ireland, where customers are able to see how many days' credit remain based on an estimation of their previous week's electricity consumption. The Liberty prepayment meters are programmed only to disconnect between 08:00 and 16:00 Monday to Friday, so avoiding disconnection at weekends or on public holidays, in order to minimise customer annoyance and frustration and the under-heating associated with fuel poverty. For the supply company, this socially aware arrangement has meant that it has been able to reduce its personnel costs, since it did not have to make manual reconnections outside normal working hours. Prepayment meters can clearly contribute some degree of control to consumers who wish to limit their potential debt – a fact that has led to increased demand for prepayment meters in Northern Ireland, since credit customers also prefer to be made more aware of the cost implications of their electricity consumption.

Modern prepayment meters are probably some of the smartest meters we have. They are designed and set up to get paid so historically all intelligence and all the system development is around [whispering] *getting them to pay their bills, not helping them to reduce. Now, they may as a side benefit help people to better budget, and that usually means use less.* (Representative of UK metering organisation)

Prepayment meters, unlike traditional credit meters, increase the salience or 'mindfulness' of energy consumption by bringing consumption and payment into the same time-frame, which can in turn increase the likelihood that people will consume energy more efficiently (Stern and Aronson, 1984; Wilhite, 1994). However, as the quotation above suggests, this mindfulness can have a social cost, where 'better budget' describes the process of self-disconnection from supply enabled by prepayment meters when the fuel-poor can no longer afford to buy credit. In this way, some prepayment technologies make the self-disconnection of marginal customers invisible (Marvin and Guy, 1997) and shift responsibility for electricity use (or non-use) further from the supplier onto the customer.

17.4   'Smart' metering

Although prepayment meters may be described as 'smart' because they convey cost as well as kWh data to the customer, smart meters may also be described as 'smarter' than traditional or prepayment meters because they require advanced communication technologies, have increased information provision capabilities, are automatically and remotely read and can provide additional functions and services to the customer.

Smart meters are 'advanced' (NMTWG, 2002), 'smart' (Porter, 2005) and 'intelligent' (DNO representative and local authority energy manager interviews, 2004). The main reason they are smart is their electronic communication capabilities, using power line signalling, fixed radio links, telephone lines, cabling, satellite links or fibre optics in the future. For some, the more advanced the technology the smarter the meter, and therefore the 'smartest meters' (DGCG, 2003) are internet meters using telephone lines or cables. And if smart meter internet connectivity can be extended to everyone with electricity (99.9 per cent of homes in the United Kingdom) then it may facilitate another government goal, namely that all citizens be connected to the internet. Such advanced information and communication technologies enable bidirectional information flow between the supplier and the end user: information that is multi-format, more frequent, accurate, real-time and high-quality.

If [the meter] is read properly and information fed back in a way that is friendly then [domestic customers] can cut demand quite easily.
(Representative of the industry regulator)

However, information provision is effective in terms of promoting sustained pro-environmental behaviour change only if it attracts attention and is perceived to be relevant, credible, reliable and trustworthy

(Gardner and Stern, 2002). Therefore, it is inappropriate to call half-hourly meters 'smart' if they just provide 'more' information – a point recognised in the following excerpt.

Actually, I was slightly embarrassed to be calling it smart metering because, really, we are just giving people half-hour profiles, which isn't really smart [laughing]. It is just a little bit more information. It is an awful lot more information than they have had previously but there are clearly lots of more clever things you could do with the information; I think it is not always obvious what do with it.

(Representative of UK metering organisation)

Consumption information such as kWh and cost (for example, linked to time-of-use tariffs) can address the 'invisibility' of electricity to the domestic customer (Hedges, 1991; Shove and Chappells, 2001). Timely delivery of consumption information can enable electricity users to associate specific behaviours with immediate financial or environmental consequences. In this sense, smart meters, along with redesigned billing (E4CEE, 2003), can contribute to the process of 'electricity disclosure' by enabling customers to make informed choices about the nature and timing of their energy consumption. Disclosure need not be limited to information about the financial cost of consumption. For example, by providing information about carbon emissions smart meters can serve to increase 'carbon consciousness', and assist customers to adopt the role of 'carbon managers' (E4CEE, 2003) with informed responsibility for the environmental consequences of their actions. Given that only 20 per cent of UK adults have indicated an awareness that domestic gas or electricity consumption is a cause of climate change (DEFRA, 2001), we would argue that smart metering could play an important role in closing this 'gap' in awareness and thus contribute to energy policy goals to reduce carbon emissions.

The 'Wattbug' is an interesting example of a 'smart' metering technology. Awaiting manufacture, in 2000 the Wattbug won the first Viridian International Design Competition (see the Sustainer website: http://www.sustainer.org/community&culture/viridian/wattbug-press.html). Designed to promote energy efficiency, the Wattbug is an internet-linked device that provides digital real-time energy use and kWh used information each month, to both the supplier (via the internet) and the customer (on an LED). It enables the customer to see and hear how much electricity she is using by 'purring' when demand for electricity is low and 'wilting' when demand is high. The Wattbug does not provide cost or CO_2 data nor does it specifically enable net metering, but it does have aesthetic and affective appeal – unlike 'ugly' (to quote the representative of a UK metering organisation) traditional meters.

Two alternative, but not mutually exclusive, customer–supplier relationships are envisaged with smart metering that closely parallel work on innovative billing procedures and network operation. In the first perspective, smart metering operates automatically and independently of customers in order to minimise supposed inconvenience – for example, through the automatic load management of appliances. In the second perspective, smart metering promotes the engagement of customers with their electricity consumption by enhancing its visibility, with goals such as optimising consumption choices, maximising financial returns and raising awareness of environmental consequences – for example, of carbon emissions. Both these approaches are 'technocentric' in the sense that they implicitly assume that harnessing new communication technologies in metering will lead to better outcomes for customers, the wider energy system and the environment. However, the second perspective differs from the first, as the metering technology is intended to foster the active participation of energy customers in the management of their energy demand, as well as the management of energy supply in the case of embedded generation, such as households with solar PV or micro-CHP.

Smart meters are characterised by their facility to be read both remotely and automatically, which reduces costs, increases accuracy and avoids customer complaints about incorrectly estimated bills. Being electronic, smart meters have the capacity to process significant amounts of data efficiently. Their automated meter reading enables remote disconnection and reconnection, and can increase suppliers' interest in 'difficult' customers who act fraudulently, don't pay or attempt to have a supply connected to 'vacant' properties.

A recent UK study has shown that providing energy consumption information to domestic electricity consumers using smart meters is estimated to result in energy savings of between 5 per cent and 10 per cent (Wright et al. 2000). The higher estimate of 10 per cent applies to consumers with electric heating in addition to electrical appliances. Reducing energy consumption by 10 per cent would have led to a reduction of approximately £24 per customer per year in 2001 on their annual electricity bill (SMWG, 2001). The effect of this overall reduction on carbon emissions will be influenced by the time of day, week or year in which the reduction occurs. Overall, shifting domestic electricity consumption from times of high to low peak load has been estimated to reduce carbon emissions by 2 per cent to 3 per cent.[2]

---

[2] Personal communication with Dr A. J. Wright, Senior Research Fellow, De Montfort University, Leicester, and EA Technology consultant, 13 March 2005.

In addition to energy efficiency and enabling net metering of real-time energy import and export with embedded generation, the NMTWG (2002) has identified benefits of smart metering that include: time-of-use pricing; reduced standing charge costs for prepayment customers; easier switching between prepayment and credit-type meters without changing the meter; better management of the overall power system, including automatic detection of inefficiencies or leakages in the energy supply system; a reduction in fraud and an increase in loss detection; and enabling new-entrant energy suppliers and/or companies that provide energy services. These benefits accrue to customers, DNOs, the National Grid Company, suppliers and the environment. Smart metering can also provide value-added customer services, such as:

- internet connectivity;
- the load management of appliances; and
- the provision of additional services such as home security, smoke detection, response to distress signals (already operating in Italy and Germany) and the remote monitoring of health or welfare payments (NMTWG, 2002).

These secondary benefits extend the influence of the supplier further into the home and 'beyond the meter' (Marvin and Guy, 1997), by enabling the utility company to control the communication of up-to-the-minute tariff information as well as energy efficiency advice, and to control demand remotely through the manipulation of the operation of appliances. Although ostensibly benefiting the customer, such enabled services are indicative of what has been called a 'producer-led' rather than 'user-led' technical development pathway (Marvin et al., 1999). The user-led TDP invokes more active participation by the user (customer) in energy consumption and/or production than the producer-led TDP – a distinction reflected in the difference between concepts of demand-side management and demand-side participation (Devine-Wright and Devine-Wright, 2004).

17.5   The potential for smart metering in the United Kingdom

Despite the relative absence of smart metering within the Energy White Paper (DTI, 2003) the Carbon Trust's Advanced Metering for Energy Savings project aims to cut costs for small and medium-sized enterprises by installing smart meters. In addition, load management enabled by smart metering will be covered in a near-future report (EA Technology, 2006) on 'time of use pricing' for small-scale electricity consumers that will assist demand-side management and reduce emissions of carbon dioxide across Europe. EA Technology will report upon the effectiveness of trials that have used financial, educational (consumption, cost and tariff information) and technological incentives (direct load control of appliances) to influence demand-side management.

According to the participants in our interview study, there was 'not much happening' with smart metering in the United Kingdom. This was attributed to a number of factors, including an industry culture that valued the 'tried and tested' rather than the innovative, was conservative and averse to risk taking. Suppliers were perceived to be 'resistant to innovative thinking' (Energy Metering Technology Ltd/ Leicester Energy Agency, 2004, p. 9) and willing to provide services only within the terms of their licence. Whilst the government sets targets to reduce carbon emissions and eradicate fuel poverty, these objectives, which can be enabled by smart metering, do not fit easily with the aim of suppliers to sell as many units of electricity as possible.

The 'traditional' Ferraris meter is very cheap, very reliable and durable, which leads to an evolutionary rather than revolutionary rate of change (NMTWG, 2002). An opportunity to 'revolutionise' metering occurred when the domestic electricity market in England and Wales became fully competitive in 1998. However, the industry regulator ruled that the market could develop without compulsory half-hourly meter installation when a domestic customer changed supplier. This has resulted in a transitional arrangement becoming an accepted custom and practice (DGCG, 2003) – a situation that only the regulator can redress.

I think [the opportunity] was there before and they need to put it back in and make the industry work to it. [. . .] I have heaped it on the regulator. Sorry.
                                                        (Local authority energy manager)

When asked as to where the responsibility for smart metering lies, a representative of the electricity industry regulator replied: '*Good question* [long pause].' There are currently no codes of practice concerning the installation and operation of smart meters in the United Kingdom, resulting in a fragmented, limited and reactive use of smart metering. Whilst a lack of standardised meter types may have exacerbated stranded assets, an absence of standards governing how data are obtained from the meter and processed means that, for example, a domestic customer with a smart meter for embedded generation may be unable to change his or her utility company as another company cannot process the information from the meter. However, since the UK electricity industry is already very heavily regulated, the introduction of more standards may actually depress innovation in metering even further (NMTWG, 2002).

With a twenty-year lifespan, many, including the following DNO representative, believe that the asset lifespan of the 'bog standard' traditional meter is a significant barrier to the use of smart metering.

The asset life [is] twenty years – what happens if someone after a month changes supplier? [...] Logically you would not [put another meter in] because it is more expensive. But in reality you get a big supplier saying: 'Well, I know it makes sense, but [because of the effect on] my systems and my mechanisms I might as well just because it is too hard.' There were instances of meters being put in plastic bags and brought back to us and saying: 'Well, here is your meter.' [...] If you have got a meter that is different to the bog standard then there is a chance it will stay there and still be used. (DNO representative)

Smart metering is perceived to be expensive, and yet with high-volume installation economies of scale can be achieved (e.g. by Enel in Italy, where smart meters cost the same as traditional electromechanical meters). However, these economies of scale will only bring the desired benefits if the 'right kind' of metering and communication technology is chosen and if standardised data protocols are developed. Since March 2004 Enel has teamed up with IBM to offer 'Enel Automated Metering System Solutions', which has attracted interest from utilities worldwide. This may help to offset some of the costs of trialling smart metering systems and speed the uptake of smart metering in other countries, including the United Kingdom.

The cost of meters differs from the cost of metering, with the latter varying as a function of the type and quantity of meters installed, the communication technologies that they employ and the type of data processing service that is required. The following estimates assume a single unit cost comparison and are based upon the installation and product supply costs for metering technologies from a range of UK sources (NMTWG, 2002; DGCG, 2003; SMWG, 2001): £50–70 for a standard credit meter, £80–100 for a prepayment meter and an additional £25–150 for a smart meter. The wider range of estimates for smart meters reflects a difference in communication technology, with internet-enabled smart meters currently estimated to be the most expensive. However, a large-scale uptake of internet-based metering could reverse this, with internet metering becoming the cheapest type of smart metering.

In the United Kingdom, the level of cooperation between regional utility companies can significantly affect the cost of enabling smart metering, which has been estimated to range from 12 per cent to 30 per cent of the total project cost (Metering Technology Ltd/Leicester

Energy Agency, 2004). The regional legacy, whereby meter operators and suppliers effectively 'own' the regions in which they are 'dominant', has led to a fragmentation and disparity in service costs and provision, which has been reinforced by regulations that require separate accounting for services even if the company is vertically integrated. This would reinforce pervasive 'fragmentary' as opposed to synergistic ways of thinking and operating within the electricity industry – a situation that can be challenged by customers, especially industrial or commercial customers or those with embedded generation technologies, demanding smart metering.

We are the first one to have...linked [2000 outlets] with smart metering; not trying to sound clever, it is just the FOG [interviewee's emphasis] and the MUD [interviewee's emphasis] that we tried to get through. The technology is one thing; the customer prepared to pay, they are almost easy. The industry hurdles are unbelievable. But now they are broken and now prices are coming down. The customer who was very big demanded the energy supplier to sort it out. [...] When the supplier said it cannot be done they said: 'No, I have got someone who can do it' – so 'boom, boom, boom', look, it can be done. And when one of the suppliers came good and had the desire to do it as well, it was two people hitting the supplier [with] the customer saying: 'I want this', and that broke it.   (Network operator)

17.6   Conclusions

A variety of often competing and conflicting factors shape the potential for smart metering (Guy and Marvin, 1995), including the availability of ICT, economic costs, asset lifespan, industry perceptions and practices, regulations and indecision about how best to prioritise the functional capacity of smart meters (e.g. for security of payment, asset durability, network reliability, carbon reduction or to enable embedded generation). The extent to which smart metering in the United Kingdom can increase energy efficiency and enable embedded generation (DGCG, 2002) as well as facilitate enhanced consumer choice and more sustainable electricity consumption is currently being investigated through trials such as the Carbon Trust's Advanced Metering for Energy Savings project and The Application Home Initiative (TAHI). Building on these initiatives, it is anticipated that smart metering could play a major role in achieving efficiencies in electricity supply and demand, leading to benefits for suppliers, customers and network operators alike. It could also serve to enhance policy goals for climate change, by disclosing more information about the environmental consequences of electricity consumption.

Although there has been little innovation in metering in the United Kingdom over the past few years, radical visions have been put forward that can be drawn upon in conceiving alternative energy futures in which metering may take a very prominent role. In particular, writers have pointed to the potential social, economic and environmental impacts of two sources of technical innovation: the embedding of novel information and communication technologies (e.g. Taylor, 2004) and the increased deployment of microgeneration (e.g. Dunn, 2000; Lovins and Lehmann, 2002). The resultant 'energy web' would be an electronic network similar to the World Wide Web, which would create communities of social actors who are empowered via greatly enhanced information provision concerning electricity demand and supply in real time (Rifkin, 2002). 'There will be billions of smart devices of all kinds connected wirelessly to each other and to the utility, enabling billions of people to be online all the time they want to be' (Taylor, 2004, p. 180).

The provision of information can include alternative energy products and services, including time-of-use tariffs within demand-side management programmes; information disclosing the types of fuel sources used to generate power; advice on energy conservation products and services; options for 'automatic' and 'voluntary' load management, including the economic and environmental benefits of each to the consumer; details of carbon emissions and additional services that utilities may wish to offer, including home security. Crucially, it is a two-way, responsive communication infrastructure, not a one-way, top-down pathway. Information is not provided; it is chosen by empowered actors (Grove-White et al., 2000).

There is a great distance between this type of networked future and traditional metering as currently practised in the United Kingdom. To effect change, there needs to be a greater realisation by government, as well as by industry stakeholders, of the role of smart electricity metering in meeting a range of policy goals, from fuel poverty to microgeneration, to active citizenship through internet connection. In our interviews, electricity industry stakeholders were clear that responsibility for effecting change in metering was insufficiently concentrated within any one stakeholder (e.g. supplier, DNO, meter operator) to make a viable economic case for innovation. This must change for the many benefits of smart metering to move from a possibility to a reality.

17.7   References

DGCG (2003). *Metering for Micro Generation*, Working Paper no. 1, London: Technical Steering Committee, Distributed Generation Coordinating Group.

DEFRA (2001). *Energy Efficiency Commitment 2001–2005: Consultation Proposals*, London: Department for Environment, Food and Rural Affairs.

Devine-Wright, P. (2005). *Braunstone Solar Streets Project*, available from http://www.iesd.dmu.ac.uk/contract_research/projects/page.php?format=web&project=braunstone_solar.htm.

Devine-Wright, H., and P. Devine-Wright (2004). From demand side management to demand side participation: tracing an environmental psychology of sustainable electricity system evolution, *Journal of Applied Psychology*, 6 (3–4): 167–77.

Dick, A. (2003). Electricity prepayment meters in the UK, *Metering International* 3: 1–51, available from http://www.metering.com/archive/032/22_1.htm.

DTI (2003). *Our Energy Future: Creating a Low-Carbon Economy*, Energy White Paper no. 68, Cm5761, London: Department of Trade and Industry, available from http://www.dti.gov.uk/energy/whitepaper/ourenergyfuture.pdf.

Dunn, S. (2000). *Micropower: The Next Electrical Era*, Washington, DC: Worldwatch Institute.

E4CEE (2003). *Consumer Choice and Carbon Consciousness for Electricity: Final Project Report*, Oxford: Environmental Change Institute, available from http://www.electricitylabels.com/downloads/4CE_exec_summ.pdf.

EA Technology (2006). *Time of Use Pricing for Demand Management Delivery*, report for International Energy Agency's Demand-Side Management Programme Task XI, Subtask 2, Chester: EA Technology.

Energy Metering Technology/Leicester Energy Agency (2004). *Quarterly Report for Advanced Metering for Energy Savings Project*, Slough: Energy Metering Technology, 3rd Quarter, 1–6.

Frost and Sullivan (2003). *Electronic Meters Set to Dominate Utilities*, New York: Frost and Sullivan, available from http://www.engineeringtalk.com/news/fro/fro199.html.

Gardner, G. T., and P. C. Stern (2002). *Environmental Problems and Human Behaviour*, Boston: Pearson Custom Publishing.

Guy, S., and S. Marvin (1995). *Pathways to 'Smarter' Utility Meters: The Socio-Technical Shaping of New Metering Technologies*, Global Urban Research Unit, University of Newcastle upon Tyne, GURU Electronic Working Paper no. 23, available from http://www.ncl.ac.uk/guru/publications.htm#gur.

Grove-White, R., P. MacNaghten and B. Wynne (2000). *Wising Up: The Public and New Technologies*, a research report, Centre for the Study of Environmental Change, Lancaster University.

Hedges, A. (1991). *Attitudes to Energy Conservation in the Home: Report on a Qualitative Study*, London: HMSO.

IEA (2003). *Energy Policies of IEA Countries: Italy 2003 Review*, Paris: International Energy Agency.

Lovins, A., and A. Lehmann (2002). *Small is Profitable: The Hidden Economic Benefits of Making Electrical Resources the Right Size*, Snowmass, CO: Rocky Mountain Institute.

Marvin, S., H. Chappells and S. Guy (1999). Pathways of smart metering development: shaping environmental innovation, *Computers, Environment and Urban Systems*, 23: 109–26.

Marvin, S., and S. Guy (1997). Smart metering technologies and privatised utilities, *Local Economy*, 12(2): 119–32.

NEA (2002). *Smart Metering*, Position Paper, Newcastle upon Tyne: National Energy Action.

NMTWG (2002). *Interim Report*, London: ELEXON.

Ofgem (2003). *Single-Phase Import Meters Operating under Export Conditions – Manufacturer Poll: Summary of Responses Received*, London: Office of Gas and Electricity Markets.

Porter, H. (2005). *The Potential for Smart Metering*, paper presented at Institution of Electrical Engineers conference The Energy White Paper – Will it Deliver?, Royal Society, London, 19 May.

Rifkin, J. (2002). *The Hydrogen Economy*, Oxford: Polity Press.

Shove, E., and H. Chappells (2001). Ordinary consumption and extraordinary relationships: utilities and their users, in J. Gronow and A. Warde (eds.), *Ordinary Consumption*, London: Routledge, 45–58.

Smart Metering Working Group (2001). *Report*, London: Department of Trade and Industry, available from http://www.dti.gov.uk/energy/environment/ energy_efficiency/smartmeter.pdf.

Stern, P. C., and E. Aronson (eds.) (1984). *Energy Use: The Human Dimension*, Washington, DC: National Academies Press.

Taylor, J. (2004). *The Information Utility*, London: Demos, available from http:// www.demos.co.uk.

Wilhite, H. (1994). Market signals fall short as policy instruments to encourage energy savings in the home, in *Proceedings of the ACEEE 1994 Summer Study on Energy Efficiency in Buildings*, Vol. I, Washington, DC: American Council for an Energy-Efficient Economy, 193–200.

Wright, A. J., J. Formby and S. Holmes (2000). *A Review of the Energy Efficiency and Other Benefits of Advanced Utility Metering*, Chester: EA Technology, confidential report for the British Electrotechnical and Allied Manufacturers' Association.

Index

Lightning Source UK Ltd.
Milton Keynes UK
13 October 2009

144886UK00001B/123/P